Racial and Ethnic Politics
in California

D0962440

CENTER FOR THE TEACHING AND
STUDY OF AMERICAN CULTURES
120 Wheeler Hall
U. C. Berkeley
Berkeley, CA 94720
(415) 642-2264

Racial and Ethnic Politics in California

Byran O. Jackson and
Michael B. Preston, *Editors*

IGS PRESS
Institute of Governmental Studies
University of California at Berkeley
1991

Library of Congress Cataloging-in-Publication Data

Racial and ethnic politics in California / Byran O. Jackson, Michael B. Preston, editors.
    p. cm.
  Includes bibliographical references.
  ISBN 0-87772-328-1
  1. Political participation—California. 2. Minorities—California—Political activity.
  3. California—Politics and government—1951-   I. Jackson, Byran O. II. Preston, Michael B.
JK8795.R33 1991
323'.042'09794—dc20   91-18676

CONTENTS

I. INTRODUCTION

Ethnic Politics in California: An Overview

California is one of the most ethnically diverse states in the United States. With a total population of slightly less than 30 million people, it is rapidly approaching a nonwhite majority. By the year 2000, approximately 29 percent of all Californians will be of Hispanic origin while 13 percent will be Asian, and 7 percent will be of African-American descent. Unlike the immigration occurring during the turn of this century, which was primarily European, 40 percent of new immigrants are coming from Asian countries with the Philippines having the highest percentage. Another 40 percent are coming from countries in Northern and Central America and the Caribbean. Immigrants from Mexico make up the bulk of this group.

As the demographics change, there is an expectation that the political environment and political institutions will do so as well. How realistic is this expectation? If political change does take place, what form will it take? Will the increasing number of minority groups eligible to vote translate into more political representation at the expense of whites? How likely are these groups to form coalitions to protect their interests? What strategies will individual candidates and political parties use to appeal to them over the next two decades? Since most minorities are located in metropolitan areas while the greatest growth is in the suburbs, will they be able to protect their interest *vis-à-vis* the growth of suburban power? Will reapportionment over the next two decades help or hurt these new groups? What role will redistricting play in the political development of these groups? This book will examine these and other problems related to the broad array of political changes likely to take place in the state, county, and municipal levels of government brought on by California's minority groups as they search for political empowerment.

While this book focuses on racial and ethnic minorities in California, these issues illustrate the experiences that other large states with large minority populations are likely to encounter—especially Texas, Florida, Illinois, and New York. We should also note that while a book of this nature emphasizes the political aspects of the changes these political institutions will encounter, we are aware that there are a number of other interrelated policy questions that also need to be addressed but cannot be in a volume of this nature. Among the policy-related questions likely to become significant issues in any future political equation: the aging and income of the population; changes in residential patterns; changes in labor needs; and the changing global demographic picture. While these are important questions, our attempt here is more modest—to draw out and examine some of the political implications of racial and ethnic change in a state that will be a barometer for the nation now and in the future.

The book opens with a critical assessment of the "concept of ethnic representation." In this chapter Bruce Cain explores the fragmentation of government brought on by the decline of political parties and the rise of interest groups. He also examines the political implications of the rise in ethnically related special interest groups and what this means for current and future political institutions.

The next four chapters are devoted to exploring both the historical and contemporary quest by Hispanic, Asian, black, and Jewish groups in their search for political equality in the golden state. Don Nakanishi's article attempts to explain why Asian political participation is different from other racial groups. Susan Anderson examines the history of African Americans (blacks) in California and looks at the attempts by blacks to seek inclusion into a political system that sought to exclude them from political involvement but could not preclude them from fighting back by establishing their own conventions and organizations. Harry Pachon's paper focuses on Latino participation in a state where Hispanics (or Latinos) have traditionally had limited political power. He explores what the growth of this population means for political empowerment in the future. Raphael Sonenshein does a superb job of showing how Jews gradually achieved political power and how their basically liberal stances on issues have led them into alliances with African-American politicians. He also discusses some of the current problems with old alliances and problems with emerging groups, such as Hispanics.

In section three, we examine the growth and development of minority political leadership. Fernando Guerra does an excellent job of describing chronologically how and when each racial group began to achieve elective office and what these changes may mean for the future. Larry Berg and C. B. Holman discuss the rise to power of Speaker Willie Brown and explain his changing constituency, shift on issues, and how he has survived in a diverse district in San Francisco and in the elite state legislature.

San Francisco and Los Angeles are the two largest and most ethnically diverse cities in the state of California. Richard DeLeon explores in detail how blacks, Asians, and Hispanics have contributed to political change in the city by contributing to a "Progressive Urban Regime," which has evolved in San Francisco over the past decade. Byran Jackson in turn assesses ethnic voting cleavages in Los Angeles and demonstrates that not only is ethnicity important in determining ethnic political behavior, but that social class must be taken into consideration as well.

One of the key questions pondered by observers of ethnic politics concerns the involvement of ethnic members in party politics. While political parties are not as strong in California as perhaps in other states, they indeed play a significant role in minority group politics. William Middleton provides an analysis of minority group participation in political parties in California. He argues that political parties should be strengthened in the state through reform and that a strong party system provides an opportunity for minority group empowerment. Dwaine Marvick gives an insightful longitudinal analysis of minority participation in party organizations in Los Angeles county. Richard Santillan and Subervi-Vélez show the importance of the Hispanic vote in Republican politics in California.

No volume on ethnic politics would be complete without a discussion of the conflict as well as the opportunities for interethnic cooperation brought on by each group's quest for political empowerment. Charles Henry and Carlos Muñoz then look at whether a rainbow coalition is possible in California. Carol Uhlaner provides an excellent discussion on the role that prejudice and racism plays in politics. James Regaldo concludes this section by looking at the conflict over redistricting, especially in Los Angeles County. He shows why and how Hispanics were finally able to get the court to throw out the 1981 County Board of Supervisors' districts in Los Angeles that fractured the Hispanic communities and rendered them powerless to elect an Hispanic to the board. He also shows how Hispanics were able to do this without alienating black interest.

There are few books that cover the broad array of issues covered here, and we hope this volume will begin a discussion of the critical issues that will face the state in the 21st century.

II. POLITICAL EMPOWERMENT IN ETHNIC COMMUNITIES

CHAPTER 1

BRUCE CAIN
University of California at Berkeley

The Contemporary Context of Ethnic and Racial Politics in California

Race and ethnicity in California have followed a cyclical pattern of electoral prominence. During the 19th century, party affiliations in the East and Midwest especially conformed to an "ethno-cultural" cleavage, aligning white protestant nativists against urban, European Catholics, and East European Jews. Some of the issues that were salient then are salient today such as bilingual education, tighter immigration restrictions, and the desired rate of cultural assimilation by new citizens. A somewhat different and even more bitter sort of racial division emerged in California and the West when large numbers of Asian and Mexican immigrants arrived to take railroad and agricultural jobs. Western state legislatures debated and then passed a series of measures restricting the property rights and educational freedom of these non-European immigrants, culminating in severe immigration quotas and, for certain groups, eventual exclusion from entry into the U.S.

The Great Depression of the 1930s brought a virtual halt to immigration and a lessening of related tensions. The problems of economic recovery dominated the political agenda in the years preceding World War II, but as the economy prospered in the postwar period, race became salient again. By the early 1960s, there was much public policy discussion about economic, political, and social discrimination against blacks and the elimination of inner-city ghetto poverty. The Vietnam War, Watergate, and the economic troubles of the late 1970s pushed racial issues into the background once again, although many of the same underlying tensions and problems persisted. By the early 1980s, the full implications of terminating racially based immigration quotas in 1965 and of fueling economic growth in the Southwest with undocumented labor had become very evident. Issues such as bilingual education and immigration reform had returned to the political agenda, and the rise of street violence and drug wars drew more attention to the situation of the black underclass. California politics, it can be said, entered the 1990s at or near the top of the race and ethnicity salience cycle.

While racial and ethnic interests have been continuous themes in American and Californian politics, the political context in which they have been played out has changed dramatically over time. The centrifugal nature of the contemporary political system has shaped racial and ethnic politics distinctively. In particular, a number of minority groups have adopted "special interest" tactics, learning from each other and the experiences of other interest groups. Unless future electoral reforms do more to strengthen the existing political parties or lower the threshold for new ones, this centrifugal trend in ethnic and racial politics will likely continue.

THE RENEWAL OF RACIAL AND ETHNIC POLITICS

Before the onset of recent events in Eastern Europe and the Soviet Union, Marxists debated whether and when racial/ethnic divisions would be subsumed by the class struggle. Although differing class interests often have a great deal to do with racial and ethnic political polarization, the former has not subsumed the latter in most polities, including the U.S. There have been historical periods when racial and ethnic divisions were sharper and more evident, but at the same time, there has always been a constant and measurable racial and ethnic component to political alignments in the U.S. and California since the 1840s. What does it mean to say that race and ethnicity are politically salient? It means that at least some of the distinct population groups in the U.S. have opposing interests and values and that they seek political control and influence in order to realize their goals. When this happens, the most salient political issues will involve racial and ethnic group interests, and the prevailing pattern of electoral alignment will manifest group polarization: i.e., members of a specific racial/ethnic group will tend to support and vote for candidates from their group over those from other racial/ethnic groups.

By this standard, the signs of racial and ethnic political division in the U.S. and California are well documented. First, there are interparty demographic differences. The Democrats and Republicans have been split along racial and ethnic lines since the New Deal, a trend that has accelerated since the late 1960s. Over 90 percent of America's black voters and nearly two-thirds of all Latinos consistently support the Democratic party versus only one-third of white voters. Leaders for both parties have sought to reverse this trend. As Professors Santillan and Subervi-Vélez point out in their contribution to this volume, the Republican party has made several attempts in the last two decades to woo the Mexican-American vote, but in their best year, the 1984 Reagan landslide, they managed to get only a third of the Latino voters' vote. By the next presidential election, the estimated Latino support for the Republican party's candidate had fallen to 25 percent.

If some Republicans would like to lessen the whiteness of their party, some Democrats concluded after Mondale's defeat in 1984 that their party had become too closely identified with special racial and ethnic interests and predicted that the Democrats would become a permanent minority party unless it recaptured the white vote. Paul Kirk, who subsequently became the leader of the national Democratic party, tried to abolish separate racial, ethnic, and gender caucuses, aspiring to weaken the party's image as the advocate of nonmainstream interests. Using the same logic to try to win back Reagan Democrats, Michael Dukakis kept a safe distance from Jesse Jackson during his 1988 presidential campaign.

The renewed salience of racial and ethnic cleavages in the 1980s was also evident in patterns of racially polarized voting during Democratic primaries and nonpartisan elections. At the national level, good examples of this are the 1984 and 1988 Jesse Jackson votes. In the 1988 Democratic primaries, Jesse Jackson won a fairly consistent 12 percent of the white vote as compared to over 90 percent of the black vote in almost all the states he contested. Race played a particularly important role in the critical New York and Pennsylvania primaries. Super Tuesday, as some had predicted, had propelled Jackson into the ranks of credible contenders, altering the calculus of white Democratic voters in subsequent primaries. The threat of Jackson winning the nomination helped to consolidate white, especially Jewish, support for Dukakis, because many of them felt that it was more important to support the candidate who would most likely stop Jackson (i.e., Dukakis) than the candidate who was most pro-Israeli (i.e., Gore). The lines of racial and ethnic division were particularly sharp between New York Jews and blacks due to a number of factors, including a history of Jewish-black tensions in New York dating back to controversies between Jewish teachers and black parents in the late 1960s, Jackson's remarks about New York being "Hymietown," his relationship with Rev. Farrakhan, differing positions on the Middle East, and to no small extent, the provocative remarks of Mayor Koch during the primary campaign.[1]

Electoral contests at the state and local level have also manifested racial and ethnic polarization. In Chicago, Mayor Daley's death split the city between nonwhite voters who favored Harold Washington and whites who supported Ed Vrodoliak. Washington won, but the city remained sharply divided along racial lines until Mayor Washington's death in 1986. In California, the 1982 gubernatorial race between Los Angeles City Mayor Tom Bradley, a black, and State Attorney General George Deukmejian, a white, ended in a narrow victory for the Republican caused by defections in key white rural and suburban areas of the state. Bradley supporters charged that the Republicans had used racist campaign ads evoking white voter fears of

---

[1]Bruce E. Cain, I. A. Lewis, and Douglas Rivers, "Strategy and Choice in the 1988 Presidential Primaries," *Electoral Studies*, vol. 8, no. 1 (1989): 23-48.

black crime to imply that Bradley, a former policeman, would be weaker on law and order issues than Deukmejian, the state's attorney general.

Racially polarized voting can also be found at the local level, as we have discovered from a number of Voting Rights Act cases involving California city and county governments in the last decade. One of the critical tests of a Section 5 violation is whether white voters, faced with a choice between white and nonwhite candidates, tend to vote overwhelmingly for the white candidates. Typically, this is proven by means of two types of tests. One examines the voting returns of white versus nonwhite primary and nonpartisan races in precincts that are overwhelmingly composed of voters from one racial or ethnic category (i.e., the "homogenous" precinct approach). The other examines the bivariate correlations between the racial/ethnic composition of census tracts and the percentage of votes cast for the different candidates.

A number of such tests have now been conducted in cities up and down the state (e.g., Watsonville, Los Angeles, Stockton, Pomona), and they have revealed numerous examples of statistically significant racially/ethnically polarized voting. In the Los Angeles city case, for instance, two separate analyses of voting in the Art Snyder recall elections of the early 1980s, both yielded correlation coefficients above .8 between the percent white in a census tract and the percent supporting Snyder against an Hispanic challenger. Although the 14th Council District had a 75 percent Latino population, it was only 50 percent Latino in voter registration. In essence, he could win by taking the vast majority of white voters located in the northern/Eagle Rock section of the 14 Council District and just enough of the Latinos from the southern portion to defeat Latino challengers. In another landmark case, *Gomez v. the City of Watsonville*, plaintiffs were able to demonstrate to the court's satisfaction racially polarized voting in the city council elections for 1973, 1979, 1981, and 1985, and the mayor's election in 1979.

This is not to say that all white voters in California vote along racial and ethnic lines, or that there are no countervailing examples of coalitional voting. Professor Sonnenshein's study clearly shows that Jewish liberal voters have been a critical component of Bradley's winning electoral coalitions since the early 1970s. Black support for Bradley in mayoral contests between 1973 and 1989 remained consistently above 90 percent until 1989 when he faced a black opponent, Nate Holden. White "Gentile" support hovered between 43 percent and 57 percent until 1989 and Jewish liberal support between 58 percent and 74 percent. Even in 1989, Bradley received a majority of the vote in the predominantly Jewish 5th Council District. Professor Byran Jackson's study for this volume shows that the strongest support for Bradley (aside from black voters) came from Latino areas but concluded that income and class were probably as important factors as race and ethnicity; that is to say, poorer Anglos and Latinos were more likely to vote for Bradley than wealthier, middle class ones. Browning, Marshall, and Tabb also found instances of successful multiracial electoral coalitions in their study of 10 California cities.[2] Finally, there have been some recent signs of racial depolarization at the national level. The elections of David Dinkins as mayor of New York and Douglas Wilder as governor of Virginia in 1989 depended upon their winning sufficient numbers of white voters in states with recent experiences of racial tension.

In California, as elsewhere, the white electorate is not monolithic in its behavior towards nonwhite candidates. Black candidates for statewide office in recent elections (e.g., Bradley in 1982) have run well below Democratic party registration in white, non-Jewish, suburban, and rural areas of the state such as the central valley, the northern San Fernando Valley, and the Inland Empire. But these are places in which liberal Democrats such as Jerry Brown and Walter Mondale have also done poorly. At least part of the reluctance some white voters have in voting for Latino and black candidates is ideological (moderate whites not wanting to support liberal white and nonwhite candidates), but many political observers suspect, although they find it hard to prove, that there is more than ideology behind this pattern; (i.e., that race played an independent role in the calculus of some white voters). The court has acknowledged the difficulty of disentangling the reasons for racially polarized voting and accepts the existence of a such a pattern per se as sufficient proof of a voting rights violation. From a political science point of view, however, it is important to know whether racially polarized voting is caused by racial attitudes per se or is a spurious manifestation of other cleavages. While there has been much work on this topic recently the answer remains controversial.[3]

All of this has occurred in spite of, or perhaps because of, substantial progress in the lessening of legal discrimination against racial and ethnic minorities in the U.S. A stream of landmark civil rights legislation in the 1960s aimed to eliminate bias in job hiring, school admissions, political representation, housing, and education, but it also provoked resentment in the white community towards the "opportunities" and "advantages" that government affirmative action programs conferred on inner-city minorities. Whether through its effect on conservative ideology or on racial tension per

---

[2]Rufus Browning, Dale Rogers, and David Tabb, *Protest is Not Enough: The Struggle of Blacks and Hispanics* (Berkeley: University of California Press, 1984).

[3]See Lawrence Bobo, "Group Conflict, Prejudice, and the Paradox of Contemporary Racial Attitudes," in *Eliminating Racism*, edited by Phyllis A. Katz and Dalmas A. Taylor (New York: Plenum Press, 1988); David Sears, "Symbolic Racism," in *Eliminating Racism, op. cit.*; and Jack Citrin, Donald Philip Green, and David O. Sears, "White Reactions to Black Candidates: When Does Race Matter?" *Public Opinion Quarterly* 54 (1990): 74-96.

se, this backlash seems to be part of what is motivating contemporary racial polarization.

Concurrently, California voters became less willing to spend money for inner-city programs. Rising property taxes led to the tax revolt of the late 1970s, highlighted by Proposition 13 in 1978 and Proposition 4 in 1979. This further tightened the resources available for social service and redistributive programs, at the county level especially. Even now, with the passage of Propositions 98, 99, and 111, the message politicians infer from these results is that voters will allow themselves to be taxed for explicitly defined, universalistic public goods (e.g., roads, prisons, mass transit) but not for discretionary or redistributive purposes. Due to the lower participation rates of Latinos and Asians especially, the California electorate is disproportionately white and middle class at all levels, but the potential beneficiaries of social service and redistributive programs are mostly nonwhite and low income. Thus, the clash over taxation and government services is at least implicitly about the white middle class sharing its resources with disadvantaged nonwhite populations. Class issues in this sense have also contributed to racial and ethnic tensions.

Another explanation for the renewed salience of race and ethnicity is demographic. As in the late 19th and early 20th centuries, the high volume and cultural diversity of the new immigrants has alarmed elements of the native-born population. Population forecasters predict that by the year 2010, California will be majority minority. The Latino community represented 19 percent of California's population in 1980 and about a quarter in 1990. As Professor Nakanishi points out, Asians alone are expected to make up 10 percent of the state's population by the year 2000, which, ironically, is the same share that they had before the imposition of restrictive immigration laws. The large number of immigrants from non-English speaking cultures have placed demands upon the school system, created greater competition for low-skilled jobs, and caused some concern among Anglos and blacks about how well the newcomers will integrate into American culture. At the same time immigration has provided much needed low-cost labor for agriculture and industry. Immigration reform has not succeeded in stemming the flow of undocumenteds in California, and unless the California economy takes a drastic turn for the worse, the immigrant share of the population will continue to rise throughout the 1990s. For this reason alone, it is safe to predict that race and ethnicity will remain salient in California for the foreseeable future.

CENTRIFUGAL FORCES AND RACIAL/ETHNIC POLITICS

The heightened salience of racial and ethnic issues does not necessarily increase electoral fracture. Immigrants in the 19th century voted according to ethnic and religious divisions and also along party lines, allowing the

Democratic party to forge electoral coalitions between urban ethnic groups and native working class voters. By comparison, contemporary minorities have uneasy relationships with the major political parties and are more likely to pursue special interest strategies. Black voters, for instance, have tended to vote overwhelmingly for the Democratic party in the postwar period, but in recent years, black leaders have expressed their concern that the Democratic party takes them for granted. Some of them have even suggested that blacks should act more like swing or volatile voters in order to maximize political influence. Or, to take another example, minority political activists frequently argue that it is more important for minority voters to elect representatives from their racial or ethnic group than to elect representatives of a given party, because incumbents who are racially or ethnically different from their constituents cannot serve them as well even when they share a common partisan affiliation.

A "special interest" strategy, as defined and as contrasted with a party strategy, is more independent, more focused on specific group concerns, more efficient in its expenditure of political resources, and more reliant upon "nonpolitical" strategies. A party structure links groups together in a relatively permanent alliance, bringing support to issues from coalition partners who might otherwise think it in their interest to be neutral toward or oppose those positions. Typically party allegiance fosters an ideology that gives logical coherence to or at least some reasoned connection between various issue positions held by its followers. By comparison, groups adopting a "special interest" orientation eschew permanent alliances for temporary partnerships of convenience and tend to prefer strategies that allow them to "go it alone" (such as forming PACs or resorting to litigation to change the political system).

A special interest approach is also more focused on specific group concerns rather than on sweeping political agendas—for instance, the empowerment of a particular community as opposed to altering the relations of production or effecting a general redistribution of economic wealth. Political resources are spent economically in order to advance immediate and direct political interests rather than to develop a coalition or party infrastructure or to assist coalition partners. Finally, a special interest orientation often means relying heavily on nonpolitical, especially legal, tactics to achieve political gains.

California's minorities, by this standard, tend to pursue a party strategy to a greater degree than other interest groups in the system (e.g., right to life groups, feminist organizations, environmentalists), but they also have been more disposed in recent years to employ special interest tactics. Also, there is considerable variation among California's various racial and ethnic minorities in the degree to which they pursue one or the other strategy. Blacks and Latinos, especially, have been the most "loyal" voters in the Democratic coalition, and a number of them have risen to positions of power in the Democratic party's hierarchy (especially in Southern California). Party has been an important coalitional glue for the Bradley coalition, and both San Francisco studies in this volume—one by Professors Berg and Holman on the basis of Willie Brown's political support and the other by Professor DeLeon on Mayor Agnos' progressive coalition—point to the importance of partisan ties in bringing blacks and Latinos into Mayor Agnos' progressive alliance. Asians, by comparison, are the least closely identified with the existing party structure, tending to act more as swing voters with weaker partisan attachments. In other words, on a spectrum aligning racial and ethnic groups from partisan to special interest orientation, California's Asians and whites are aligned further towards the latter direction than blacks and Latinos.

But in the area of representation especially, there are signs of an increasingly special interest orientation by all of California's minority communities. As mentioned earlier, electing more minorities to office has become a more salient goal in the last 15 years. To this end, Latino and black political groups have insisted that California's electoral rules be made more conducive to successful minority candidacies. As Professor Guerra shows, California minorities have made significant gains in officeholding over the last three decades at almost all levels. While not all black and Latino officeholders represent seats with majority minority populations, most do, which suggests that the nature of the electoral system and the composition of particular districts can be critical to future electoral success.

For this reason, minority attention will be closely focused on the 1991 redistrictings at both the state and local levels. Blacks and Anglos, faced with a decreasing share of the population, will try to resist any attempts to diminish their representation, and Latinos and Asians, faced with dramatically increasing populations, will seek to enhance their political power. All major racial and ethnic groups will closely monitor the specific effects that redistricting changes will have upon their political influence. All will spend resources economically in order to protect their specific redistricting interests. However, they will probably not form any united coalition to further the representational interests of all racial and ethnic minorities. Lastly, it is safe to predict that California's minorities will resort to legal action to secure whatever cannot be won by political influence and persuasion, relying especially on Section 2 of the 1982 Voting Rights Act. In short, the 1991 redistricting will manifest a great deal of special interest tactics.

DEMOGRAPHIC AND CONTEXTUAL INFLUENCES

What explains the strategies of contemporary racial and ethnic groups? Why has their political orientation evolved in a more "special interest" direction in recent years? Again, as with the issue of the renewed salience of race and ethnicity, the answer is partly (and only partly) demographic. California's racial and ethnic minorities are extremely diverse in race, language, culture, and ideology, and this demographic diversity forms the basis of political division. This is even true of the black and Latino communities. Despite important partisan and socio-economic similarities, there are significant differences between the interests and values of their populations. Blacks and Latinos have in common relatively low aggregate levels of education, income, and social status, and, as a consequence, on a number of standard welfare and social service issues, they share views that are statistically distinguishable from whites and Asians on average (even many Democratic whites and Asians). Also, because they often live in poor neighborhoods besieged by crime, drugs, and bad schools, they tend to share similar perceptions of problems at the local level.[4]

However, blacks and Latinos in California also have some divergent interests. During the debate over immigration reform, some black leaders in states such as Florida and California suggested that the flow of undocumented workers from Mexico and Central America took jobs away from blacks. On this issue, the position of the black community was closer to that of second- and third-generation Latinos (who shared the same fear) than to Latino immigrants. This is important, because, as Professor Uhlaner points out, blacks are the most sensitive of all groups to economic discrimination against them. In addition to the pressure of economic competition, the social service needs of the two communities are not identical. One study of social service usage in California found that Latinos were disproportionately less likely than blacks to make use of programs for children and the elderly, because, as compared with the black community, the Latino family structure has remained essentially intact.[5] In principle at least, this might cause blacks and Latinos to view decisions about budget cuts and essential services very differently.

One last and obviously relevant distinction between the two is that the vast majority of California's black population are native born whereas many Latinos are not. As a consequence, the Latino community has language and cultural concerns not shared by the black community. The Seaver report found that 60 percent of Latinos supported bilingual ballots and bilingual education as compared with only 49 percent of blacks. Moreover, bilingualism is not as high a priority for California's black community as it is for Latinos. Coalition building between their communities, such as was attempted by Jesse Jackson, will require that issues like these, which might

---

[4]Bruce Cain, Rod Kiewiet, and Carole Uhlaner, *Minorities in California*, Report to the Seaver Foundation, 1986.

[5]*Ibid.*

otherwise be ignored by black candidates, be put closer to the top of the black political agenda. As Henry and Muñoz point out, Jackson made more of an effort to reach out to Latinos in 1988 than he did in 1984 by vigorously opposing the Simpson-Rodino immigration bill and supporting bilingual education, and in return, he was able to double his Latino vote percentage. They speculate that Jackson might have done even better with Latinos had he made more of an effort to incorporate them into higher decision levels of his campaign organization.

Diversity within minority groupings can create potential coalitional problems as well. While it is common to refer to Latinos as a political group, it is important to realize that this term embraces a wide variety of nationalities. A majority of U.S. Latinos are Mexican in origin, but the Cubans in Florida, the Puerto Ricans in New York and other eastern cities, and the Central and South Americans in California are also growing in numbers and do not necessarily have the same perspective as Mexican Americans on policy issues. In particular, the Cubans and certain Central Americans, being virulently anti-Communist, are generally more conservative than the Mexican and Puerto Rican populations on foreign policy matters and hence more likely to vote for Republican party candidates.

The same can be said of Asians. There are a number of different Asian nationalities immigrating into the U.S. (e.g., Koreans, Chinese, Filipinos, Cambodians, Vietnamese), and they bring with them various languages, religions, and histories of mutual antagonism. In addition, some Asian groups are divided within their own ranks by political issues in the country of origin (e.g., the Filipinos). Overall, the Asian community tends to be fairly conservative, but there are discernible differences among the various Asian nationalities. For instance, newly arrived immigrant communities such as the Koreans tend to be more supportive of bilingual programs and liberalized immigration policies than the predominantly native-born Japanese-American community.

In sum, one reason that minorities have turned to special interest strategies may be the enormous diversity of interests and opinions within the minority communities themselves, which *ceterus paribus* makes broad-based coalition building more difficult. However, demographic diversity alone does not sufficiently explain recent strategic trends. A critical additional factor is structural change. Contemporary interest groups of all varieties must deal with a political environment that is not only vastly different from the 19th century, but one that has evolved rapidly over the last 25 years.

The contemporary electoral environment has become highly fractured in several ways. First, and most critically, parties are even more marginal now to American voters than they were in earlier periods. American voters (but especially whites and Asians) are generally less inclined to identify with either of the two major parties than in the past. The percentage of party identifiers in the U.S. has dropped from 80 percent in 1940 to 70 percent in

1980, there are fewer strong partisans, and the number of independents now stands at approximately one-third of the total electorate. During the same period in California, the combined percentages of registered Democrats and Republicans have dropped, and the decline to states has risen to between 10-15 percent. The decline of partisanship was strongest among younger, white, well-educated voters.

Related to this weakening partisanship is a decline in straight ticket voting. Nationally, the percent of those who voted for candidates from the same party at all levels of the ballot dropped from 66 percent in 1952 to 37 percent in 1980. Presidential coattails have declined, and split election results in congressional elections are on the rise. House and presidential outcomes differed in only 3.2 percent of the seats in 1920, but by as much as 44 percent in 1972 and 32 percent in 1980. As a result, the U.S. has had divided control at both the federal and state levels. Nationally, the Republican party has controlled the presidency for all but the Carter years since 1968, and at the state level, about one-half of all gubernatorial-state legislative elections have resulted in divided partisan control of the branches. In California, no Democratic presidential candidate has carried the state since 1964, and the governor has been a Republican since 1982 even though the legislature has been controlled continuously by the Democrats.

The absence of strong political parties is a critical factor in interest group strategies. In political systems with central party organizations that control nominations and critical political resources, it is rational for groups to channel their efforts towards influencing party leadership and working within a party structure. In systems with decentralized nominations, the responsibility for finding election resources lies with the individual candidate, and political parties matter less. In California, party organization is highly regulated, often lacking in resources, and generally irrelevant to the outcome of political races. Recent court decisions may liberate parties from legislative control and give them the right to endorse primary candidates, but few believe that this will do much to increase their political leverage.

It is important to bear in mind, however, that V. O. Key's distinction between the various senses of the term political party is nowhere more appropriate than in California. While the official state party organizations are weak, the "party in the legislature" has been quite powerful, acting as an important vehicle for the enhancement of minority power in California. As the essay by Berg and Holman shows, Willie Brown has used his position as speaker effectively to find the resources necessary to elect Democrats to the assembly. Beginning in 1982, he raised and spent over 2.5 million dollars on assembly races, most of it coming from businesses and other officeholders rather than individual contributors. The assembly Democratic caucus, under the leadership of such minority incumbents as Willie Brown, Maxine Waters, and Richard Allatore, actively intervened in a number of legislative races during the 1980s. The Assembly Democratic Caucus has acted like a true party in the sense of directing resources to where they are needed rather than to where powerful incumbents request, as is so often the case. This has meant that much more of the money has gone towards electing white Democrats in marginal districts (e.g., Clute, Peace, O'Connell) than towards electing more blacks and Latinos in safely Democratic seats, which is precisely what a party should do if it is using its resources efficiently. The problem that party renewalists have with this development is that the "party in the legislature" tends to act without consulting with the state party organization so that there is little of the healthy dialectic between activists and elected party officials that usually occurs in strong party systems such as the British.

California's minority candidates can expect little help from the state party organization and relatively high levels of voter disloyalty from white Democratic party identifiers, but once in power, they have used the legislative caucus party to advantage. Recent campaign finance reforms (Proposition 73 especially) have tried to weaken the power of the caucus parties by banning the transfer of money from one candidate to another and limiting the size of contributions that the speaker can give to any particular candidate. However, the central role of the speaker and the caucus in distributing electoral funds will not be seriously disrupted by this. In all likelihood, they will be able informally to direct independent and coordinated expenditures towards needy candidates.

All of this creates a curious mix of party and special interest electoral politics. Minority candidate recruitment is either the result of personal decisions (e.g., Molina) or of closed-door negotiations among minority officeholders and selected community leaders (e.g., Allard-Roybal, Polanco), but never the consequence of organized party input. Once elected, party-like caucuses create a network of alliances among minority incumbents. As a consequence, minority officeholders tend to pursue a more party-oriented strategy (especially once elected to office) while community activists and organizations (e.g., LULAC, NAACP, MALDEF) tend to adopt a more special interest approach.

A second trend in American electoral politics, which constrains minority political strategies, is the growing importance of the incumbency advantage and the so-called "personal vote." Incumbency is certainly not a new factor in American politics, and the "personal vote" has traditionally played a significant role at all levels of legislative elections. But in recent years, incumbent reelection rates have hovered over 90 percent for congressional and state legislative races, and between 64 percent (in 1976) and 93 percent (1982) in U.S. Senate elections. The ability of incumbents to get reelected is reflected in the decline of competitive seats: competitive congressional seats ranged between 33 percent and 59 percent from 1850 to 1898, between

10.6 percent and 36.5 percent from 1900 to 1948, but between 10.8 percent and 23.8 percent from 1950 to 1980.

The strength of the incumbency advantage has had several effects on contemporary ethnic and racial politics. First, it has placed the elected incumbent in a powerful position within minority political communities. Black and Latino incumbents have even more of an incumbency advantage than Anglo representatives, because their districts are usually overwhelmingly Democratic in registration, making serious challenge from the Republicans in the November election unlikely. Primary contests are also rarely close, as the minority incumbent is often much revered in the community and has access to more out-of-district resources than challengers. Since minority districts typically encompass economically disadvantaged areas of the state, challengers lack the base of in-district resources to mount serious opposition against an incumbent. In 1983-84, for instance, Latino assembly incumbents raised on average $169,209 for the primary as against $12,896 for Latino challengers. With the vacancy created in the 55th Assembly District by Alatorre's decision to move to the Los Angeles City Council, Richard Palanco, with considerable help from Democratic incumbents and the speaker of the assembly, ran a well-financed campaign for the open seat, which lessened the gap between average incumbent and challenger amounts in 1985-86 to $182,748 to $112,505. In 1987-88, the gap between Latino incumbents and challengers jumped back to $290,678 versus $46,498.

A second implication of the incumbency advantage for California's minorities is that it places an even greater focus on redistricting and litigation as a means of enhancing the prospect of minority representation. As Fernando Guerra demonstrates, many of the electoral opportunities that blacks and Latinos have had in Los Angeles County have come through newly reapportioned or recently vacated seats. Rarely do minorities take control by defeating a white incumbent. Indeed, the best conditions for electing additional minority representatives are advantageously reconfigured boundaries with no incumbent running for reelection—which is precisely how the Los Angeles city VRA suit was settled. Plaintiffs in VRA Section 2 cases are well aware that it is possible to create districts with majority minority populations that could nonetheless be won handily by entrenched white incumbents because of formidable advantages in name recognition, staff resources, and money. Art Snyder, for instance, was extremely skillful in cultivating a personal vote among both his white and Latino constituents through diligent casework and conspicuous community projects (many of them bearing his name). Incumbency in California initially serves as a barrier to enhancing racial and ethnic representation, but once elected to office, the incumbency advantage works to stabilize minority control over districts.

In addition to weak partisan ties and strong incumbency advantages, a third critical fact of contemporary political life for minorities is the central, unsuccessfully regulated role of money. Money is more critical than ever because elections have become more technology driven and media dominated. A credible candidate, even for state legislative and major city council races, relies on expensive new campaign technology: public opinion polls in order to assess the relative strengths and weaknesses of his or her candidacy, mailings targeted to specific types of voters, and diminished universe "get-out-the-vote" efforts concentrating on so-called "frequent voters." Statewide races require even more expensive campaign tools such as 30-second TV spots and radio advertisements to establish name recognition and positive images. Campaign organizations rely heavily on computer technology and professional expertise to assist them in fund-raising and get-out-the-vote logistics, and this, too, is costly. In short, those who can afford the means of reelection have an enormous advantage over those who cannot.

To operate effectively in the contemporary environment, candidates must raise lots of money. Until the passage of Proposition 73, campaign contributions were not regulated in legislative and statewide races except for disclosure requirements. Proposition 73 instituted in California what is essentially the congressional system of campaign finance regulations (i.e., limits on individual, party, and PAC contributions, but no public financing or expenditure limits). Based on the federal experience, it is possible to make several predictions about what will happen in California in the 1990s.

To begin with, since campaign costs cannot be controlled, election expenses will continue to rise, and raising money will remain critical for white and nonwhite candidates alike. Measures like Proposition 73 only constrain the forms of fund raising. By eliminating large donations, campaign contribution limits will encourage the formation of PACS to bundle small contributions together for maximum political impact. Among other effects, this may accelerate the trend towards an interest group orientation among California's minority communities. Because political parties and large PACs are put on equal footing, PACs may in the future play an even greater role in the election of minority candidates. Minority-run mailing operations such as Willard Murray's or computer-based campaign consulting operations such as George Pla's may assume a larger role in the future. The ban on caucus transfers would seem initially to be a severe blow to the "party-oriented" component of minority politics in California, but the law is so easily circumvented that this may never be realized.

In minority communities with a large potential base of middle class contributors (e.g., the Japanese and Chinese populations) but without a sizable voting population, fund raising in the 1990s could become the most critical means of political influence. In the more disadvantaged minority populations (e.g., black and Latino), the main sources of campaign funds will continue to be minority incumbents who chair so-called "juice committees," business PACS, and individual contributions from wealthy white liberal areas (e.g., the west side of Los Angeles). For no other reason than this, minority incumbents should continue to have a great advantage over minority challengers in the next decade.

A fourth development with significant implications for California's minorities is the trend away from representative government and towards direct democracy. The most important manifestation of this is the recent increase in the number of referendums and initiatives on state and local ballots. First introduced in South Dakota in 1898, 23 states now provide for some form of initiative, and all but four states provide for either the initiative, referendum, or recall of elected officials in at least some units of local government. The number of statewide initiatives placed on the ballot across the country has risen dramatically in recent years: there were only 85 in the 10-year period between 1960-1969, 120 between 1970-79, and 191 in the interval between 1980-87 alone.

The trend is most pronounced in California, as one might expect, where 181 measures began the petition gathering process in the 1970s (surpassing the total for the previous four decades combined). At any one time in California, it is possible to find constitutional amendments proposed by either the legislature or direct petition, bond referendums, statutes bypassing the legislature, referendums on legislative statutes, or amendments to laws originally adopted by initiative. These measures have served as vehicles for tax cuts, campaign finance reform, money for roads, hospitals, and prisons, and even insurance regulation, to mention just a few topics. Many of these matters are quite complex, and it is doubtful whether voters truly understood their contents. In addition, because the court has equated spending on initiative campaigns with the exercise of free speech, initiative costs cannot be regulated, which means that, contrary to their original purpose, ballot propositions have increasingly become vehicles for powerful economic interests in the state rather than mechanisms of populist control.

From the perspective of California's minority populations, the evolution towards greater direct democracy raises some critical questions. One is the irony of more decision making by direct democracy at a time when representative democracy is opening up to California's minorities. As Professor Guerra's essay shows, blacks and Latinos have made significant advances in representation at the state and local level since the early seventies. But many of these initiatives preempt the legislature's power by earmarking funds for specific expenditures (e.g., Propositions 98, 99, and 111), controlling the revenue base of the government (Proposition 13), or limiting state and local spending (Proposition 4). In a sense, initiatives and referendums are most analogous to at-large electoral mechanisms. Since they are decided at a city, county, or state level, using a majority or supermajority decision rule, they are explicitly majoritarian in bias. Many of the objections that minority groups have to at-large mechanisms apply to city and statewide initiatives as well—i.e., they do not adequately reflect minority opinion, they allow white majorities to dominate nonwhite populations, etc. In addition, as Mervin Field has argued, the problems of legitimacy are compounded when important initiatives win in special elections or low turnout primary elections.   Important legislation or amendments can be implemented when less than 15 percent of the eligible voters support it among an electorate that is skewed towards white, older homeowners and away from nonwhite, younger, renting, and disadvantaged populations.

Thus, the rise of direct democracy could present a serious challenge to minorities.   The initiatives that passed in the 1980s tended to reflect the concerns of California's white middle class: lower property taxes, English-only ballots, funding for prisons, roads, and schools but not, for instance, more money for welfare, rehabilitating the inner cities, or bilingual education. It is ironic that at a time when California's minorities have put much effort into capturing their fair share of legislative seats, the power of the legislature is being gradually eroded by the initiative process. Unless the initiative process is significantly reformed or curtailed by the court, California's minorities will have to find a way to counteract the strongly majoritarian bias of direct democracy mechanisms, or their hard earned voting rights victories will be negated.

CONCLUSION

Barring a major downturn in California's economic conditions, the flow of immigrants will continue to be significant, and racial/ethnic cleavages will remain salient.   Today's minority groups must compete in a political environment that is more fractured than ever before, and successful political tactics have to reflect that fact of political life.   The weakness of political parties, the central role of money-raising, the power of incumbency, and the increasing popularity of direct democracy mechanisms are important constraints for political groups that seek to be influential. California's racial and ethnic minorities, with the exception of the Asian Americans, tend to be more party oriented than most interest groups, but in various ways, they have had to adopt special interest tactics.   Even so, the power of the initiative and referendum process may greatly weaken the political power of minorities in the 1990s.

CHAPTER 2

DON T. NAKANISHI
University of California at Los Angeles

The Next Swing Vote? Asian Pacific Americans and California Politics

INTRODUCTION

Asians are once again a numerically significant population in California. This state has witnessed a phenomenal growth in the number of persons of Asian descent following the elimination of racially biased quotas in America's immigration laws in 1965. From 1960 to 1980, this population quadrupled, from less than a third of a million to 1.2 million. If current trends continue, Asians will number over 3 million by the end of the century, comprising about ten percent of the state's population, twice the percentage that existed in 1980 (Ong 1989, 1).

Projections of California's demographic future raise a number of significant and potentially controversial issues regarding the access, representation, and influence of Asian Pacific Americans and other racial minority populations in California's public and private institutions. Two major policy issue areas of recent concern to the state's rapidly growing and extremely diverse Asian Pacific American population—college admissions and electoral politics—offer provocative, and yet decisively different, scenarios of the problems and opportunities of again becoming 10 percent of California's populace.[1]

---

[1] As Ong (1989, 10) states, "If the projections hold, the Asian population would exhibit an interesting historical trend as a percentage of the state's [California's] total population. What we find is a U-shaped curve. . . . During the early part of California's history, Asians made up about one-tenth of the population. However, through the period of immigration restriction (1882-1965), its share declined dramatically, reaching a low of less than 2 percent in 1950. With the elimination of racially biased restrictions, the percentage has increased. If current trends continue, the Asian/Pacific Islander population will once again comprise about one-tenth of the population by the year

In the year 2000, on the one hand, if Asian Pacific American students represent 10 percent of the enrollment of California's public colleges and universities, especially those of the highly selective University of California system, it is very likely that the current fears and complaints over discriminatory freshman admissions quotas will have been realized (Bunzel and Au 1987; Hsia 1988; Nakanishi 1989; Tsuang 1989; Wang 1988). Indeed, unless the academic qualifications and aspirations of the ever-increasing Asian Pacific college-going sector were to dramatically and unexpectedly decline,[2] this future situation probably would indicate that new and different admissions policies and practices had been established in response to charges made by some current college officials that Asian Pacifics are overrepresented at their institutions. In 1990, for example, over a third of all applicants to the Berkeley and Los Angeles campuses of the University of California were Asian Pacific Americans. Based on current population projections for the future Asian Pacific college-age sector, it is highly likely that they will represent the same or higher proportion of those who apply in the year 2000.[3]

On the opposite extreme, if Asian Pacific Americans became 10 percent of California's electorate by the turn of the century, they would probably wield considerable political clout and would be wooed as much for their votes as they presently are for their campaign contributions (*Asianweek* 1984; Clifford 1985a, b; Tachibana 1986). Indeed, if Asian Pacifics simply represented a proportion of the electorate that was comparable to their numbers in the total population, they could become a highly influential "swing vote" in critical local, state, and presidential elections, in a manner

---

2000. It would have taken a century and two scores for Asians (and Pacific Islanders) to regain their position in California's population." For excellent historical treatments of the early history of Chinese, Japanese, and other Asian immigration and settlement in California, as well as the anti-Asian social movements and legislation that were initiated in response, see Daniels (1968), Saxton (1971), Chan (1986), Ichioka (1988), and Takaki (1989).

[2]Paralleling their growth in the general population, Asian Americans were the fastest-growing group in the American college-going population. In the fall of 1976, there were 150,000 Asian-American undergraduates in American higher education nationwide. A decade later, in fall of 1986, there were almost three times as many—448,000—Asian Americans in colleges and universities across the country. This student population is heavily concentrated in California. Over 40 percent of all Asian-American college students nationwide attend a public or private institution of higher education in California. See Nakanishi (1989), 42-45.

[3]Ong (1989, 25) estimates that the "Asian Youth" sector, ages 15-24 years old, will increase by 250,000 individuals from 1980-2000, for an increase of 113 percent, and the "Asian Children" sector, ages 0-14 years old, will increase by close to a half million for an increase of 165 percent.

akin to the role that American Jewish voters have traditionally played in several key electoral states like New York (Levy and Kramer 1973; Isaacs 1974). However, such a glowing political future could occur only if there were a series of profound reversals in the overall political participation of Asian Pacifics, especially in relation to their currently low overall rates of voter registration and the high levels of interest and concern which many of their immigrant and refugee sectors have towards controversial and significant international issues and events, most notably involving their countries of origin and ancestral homelands. This situation has led Asian Pacific Americans, in contrast to the allegations surrounding their enrollment in higher educational institutions, to be labeled as underrepresented among California's registered voters during the decade of the 1980s.

The dramatic demographic shifts that are occurring and are further anticipated in California have been the focus of extensive media and public policy attention in recent years. Although predictive analysis and forecasting are among the most difficult and complex forms of social scientific activity, there has been no paucity of both serious and fanciful commentaries devoted to speculating on the ramifications of changing population characteristics for the future California (Muller 1984; Bouvier and Martin 1985; Clifford 1990). Although it is always tempting to speculate about events and situations that could or should occur in years to come, this discussion will not offer a prediction of what the future holds for the state's Asian Pacific population. Instead, it has a far more modest, but hopefully more substantive, goal of offering a series of theoretical insights and empirical findings to capture the diversity of Asian American political involvement and mobilization in California, with special emphasis on their electoral participation. By doing so, it seeks to contribute to the public and academic discussions on the enormous political challenges and opportunties for Asian Pacific Americans and other groups in the context of the dynamic demographic shifts of the state's population. In this article, I have tried to provide an analogous analysis of the major structural and policy factors that have contributed to the unexpected escalation of the so-called Asian American admissions controversy to levels of national and statewide media and political focus (Nakanishi 1989).

This article has three major interrelated sections. It begins by offering an alternative conceptualization of minority politics, based on the Asian American political experience, which goes beyond the customary paradigmatic emphasis on electoral politics in the field of political science. It argues that Asian Americans, as well as other immigrant and minority groups, have traditionally pursued a range of political activities other than electoral politics in order to advance their group interests and to confront societal issues that are potentially damaging or harmful to their status and livelihood. Such a conceptualization will hopefully be helpful in understanding how the the diverse groups and sectors of the Asian Pacific population in

California and elsewhere weigh their present and future electoral representation and influence in the broader context of their participation in other highly valued forms of political action. This article will then examine several key characteristics of the dynamic growth and diversification of the state's Asian Pacific population during the past two decades and will illustrate how those demographic factors have an impact on their political participation. Next, this article will analyze major distinguishing features and trends in the current electoral participation of Asian Pacifics in California, which are based on an on-going research endeavor entitled, "The UCLA Asian Pacific American Voter Registration Project," a longitudinal study of voter registration and political party affiliations among Asian Pacific Americans (Nakanishi 1986b). This chapter concludes by assessing the various countervailing factors that will likely influence the ability of Asian Pacific Americans in reaching their full electoral potential and in becoming a critical swing voting bloc in California politics.

CONCEPTUALIZING ASIAN AMERICAN POLITICS

Asian American politics has received limited scholarly attention. Early works such as Grodzins' *Americans Betrayed* (1949) and Daniels' *Politics of Prejudice* (1968) focused on how American political institutions, especially the major political parties and West Coast state legislatures, had a decisive impact on creating and maintaining a system of exclusion and discrimination against Asian Pacific Americans. Until recently, there were few studies on the flip-side of that structural condition, namely how Asian Pacific Americans responded to such treatment and, more generally, how they pursued a variety of political activities in both the domestic and nondomestic arenas during the course of their historical experiences (Jo 1980; Nakanishi 1986). Indeed, Massey (1981) in his literature review of early and recent immigrants to the United States concluded, "There is no information on patterns of Asian political participation."

Although there has been an extreme paucity of serious academic work devoted to the political behavior and involvement of Asian Pacific Americans until recently, it should be apparent to most political commentators and practitioners that they are becoming increasingly visible and influential actors in American politics. At no other period in the over 150-year historical experience of Asian Pacifics in this society have so many individuals and organizations participated in such a wide array of political and civil rights activities, especially in relation to the American political system but also the recent tumultuous events in China, the Philippines, Korea, Pakistan, and other ancestral homelands in Asia. In traditional electoral politics, what has become a routine occurrence in Hawaii, namely the election of Asian Pacific Americans to public office (Coffman 1973), has become a less than surprising novelty in the so-called mainland states with the election and appointment of Asian Pacific Americans to federal, state, and local positions from Washington to Delaware. In California, Congressmen Norman Mineta and Robert Matsui, Secretary of State March Fong Eu, Los Angeles City Councilman Michael Woo, San Francisco Board of Supervisor Thomas Hsieh, Los Angeles Board of Education member Warren Furutani, and Monterey Park Mayor Judy Chu have become recognized players in the grand theater of politics in the Golden State. And perhaps most significantly, Asian Pacific Americans have demonstrated that they, too, have the organizational and leadership skills, the fiscal resources, the interethnic networks, and a growing sense of political efficacy to assert their policy positions and to effectively confront broader societal issues that are damaging to their group interests. Three widely reported grass-roots campaigns of recent years are illustrative of this new collective determination: the successful drive by Japanese Americans to gain redress and reparations for their World War II incarceration; the victorious mobilization of Asian Pacifics in coalition with other groups in defeating the nomination of Daniel Lundgren for California state treasurer; and the national movement to appeal and overturn the light sentences that were given to two unemployed Detroit auto workers who, in 1982, used a baseball bat to kill a Chinese American named Vincent Chin. (The two men mistook Chin for a Japanese, and therefore, as someone who was taking away their jobs.)[4] The emergence of Asian Pacific Americans in American politics probably could not have been foreseen. Early Chinese and Japanese immigrants, for example, were politically disenfranchised and excluded from fully participating in American life because of a plethora of discriminatory laws and policies, perhaps the most crucial being *Ozawa v. United States* (1922), which forbade Asian immigrants from becoming naturalized citizens.[5] This legal barrier prevented early Asian immigrants from being involved in electoral politics of any form—be it the type of ward politics practiced by European immigrants in the cities of the Atlantic states or to simply vote for their preferences in a presidential election—and substantially delayed the development of electoral participation and representation by Asian Americans in California and elsewhere until the second and subsequent generations during the post-World War II period; over 100 years after their initial period of immigration. Although the national news media has often touted them as America's "model minority"—a label that Asian Pacific

---

[4]For more detailed discussions of the recent rise in political activity among Asian Pacific Americans, see Nakanishi (1986a), Tachibana (1986), and Stokes (1988). An examination of the Japanese-American redress and reparations movement is provided in Chin (1981) and Nakanishi (1988).

[5]For an analysis of the Ozawa case and other major anti-Asian laws and legislative actions, see Chuman (1976) and Ichioka (1977).

leaders and scholars have vigorously criticized because of its simplistic implication that other minority groups can overcome racial and other discriminatory barriers by following the example of Asian Pacifics[6]—this reputed success has disguised their historical lack of access and influence in the nation's most significant political and social decision-making arenas and institutions.

Although electoral politics has become an increasingly significant focus of attention, it represents only one of several major forms of political participation that have been and continue to be pursued by Asian Pacific Americans in California and elsewhere. First, as the highly visible and determined responses in 1989 and thereafter by Chinese foreign students and Chinese Americans to the repression of the prodemocracy movement in the People's Republic of China demonstrates, Asian Pacific Americans have long been concerned about and affected by events, issues, and relationships that are nondomestic or international in nature, particularly as they relate to their ancestral homelands.[7] They have been active transnational participants in major revolutionary, nationalistic, and independence movements that have emerged in their respective homelands during the past century and have sought to contribute to subsequent national development efforts in those countries (Saxton 1966; Keohane 1971; Lyu 1977; Griffiths 1978; Jurergensmeyer 1978; Tsai 1981; Yu 1983; McKee 1986). They have also been affected to a greater extent than other American immigrant groups by the dramatic shifts in bilateral relations between the United States and their homelands like the World War II internment of Japanese Americans or the thwarting of Asian American leftist activities during the McCarthy era and other "cold war" periods in American diplomatic history.[8]   At present, interest among different sectors of the Asian American population in Asian-oriented issues ranges from restoring democratic rule to both right-wing and Communist political systems in Asian countries to playing a greater role in United States-Pacific Rim relationships in trade, cultural exchanges, and economic development activities. In the past, Asian Americans have not been as successful as other American immigrant groups in being an influential lobbying force in American foreign policy decision making. However, this should not minimize the significance that Asian-oriented

---

[6]For critical assessments of the model minority thesis, see Suzuki (1977) and Chun (1980).

[7]A fuller treatment of the international dimensions of the Asian-American political experience is provided in Nakanishi (1986a).

[8]This, of course, does not imply that the war was the sole, or even the most decisive, factor leading to the decision to incarcerate Japanese Americans during World War II. Two excellent treatments of this event are provided in Irons (1983) and Weglyn (1976).

political involvement has had and will continue to have for Asian Americans and, more specifically, in competing with domestic-oriented political issues in mobilizing Asian American communities.

At the same time, Asian Pacific Americans, like other American racial minorities that have been historically disenfranchised from the American electoral system, have engaged in an array of nonelectoral political activities to advance or protect their group interests. As recent scholarship has documented, Asian Americans have been active participants in labor-organizing efforts in the Far West, Hawaii, New York, and the Rocky Mountain states, and indeed were at the forefront of creating labor unions for agricultural workers in California and Hawaii (DeWitt 1980; Kwong 1981; Daniel 1981; Yoneda 1983). Like other racial minorities, Asian Pacific Americans also have a long history of seeking social justice and equal treatment by continuously engaging in legal challenges against discriminatory laws and practices in education, employment, housing, land ownership, immigration, and other significant public policy issue areas, and many of their legal cases (e.g., *Korematsu v. United States* (1943) or *Lau v. Nichols* (1974), have become landmark civil rights decisions (Chuman 1976; Wang 1976; United States Commission on Civil Rights 1979; Los 1982; Irons 1983). Although electoral participation is increasing among Asian Americans, it is clear that nonelectoral forms of political participation are still vigorously pursued by the Asian American community. In recent years Asian Americans have formed a number of their own parallel organizations in conjunction with broader social movements in American society dealing with civil rights, women's issues, and nuclear proliferation and have established an assortment of leftist organizations, which continue a long-standing Marxist-oriented sector in Asian American communities. They have also launched major nationwide campaigns seeking justice for individuals like Chol Soo Lee and Iva Ikuko Toguri D'Aquino, commonly known as Tokyo Rose, who were viewed as victims of discriminatory legal treatment, and protested the Soviet downing of Korean Air Lines flight 007, and the assassinations of Benigno Aquino, Henry Liu, and Indira Gandhi (Uyeda, 1978; Kim and Lai, 1982; Chin, 1981; Lim, 1985).

Conceptualizing Asian American politics in this multifaceted manner involving domestic and nondomestic orientations, as well as electoral and nonelectoral types, goes beyond what is customarily considered under the general rubic of minority politics (Nakanishi 1986a). However, such an expanded conceptual framework is necessary to highlight the fact that electoral politics is only one of several major competing forms of political activity that the diverse ethnic subgroups and sectors of the Asian Pacific American population have pursued and will likely continue to pursue in the years to come. A broader view that recognizes their extensive historical record, as well as their abundant contemporary examples, of both nondomestic and nonelectoral political activities should guard us against making unwarranted generalizations about their overall political behavior based solely on their relatively low rates of electoral participation in the past as well as present. Instead, taking these nonelectoral and nondomestic activities into account should serve to focus our attention on the structural and legal barriers that led to their historical condition of being disenfranchised from the American electoral system, and that continues to have lasting consequences.

BECOMING TEN PERCENT OF CALIFORNIA'S POPULATION AGAIN

The Asian Pacific American population in California and nationwide has undergone a series of dramatic demographic transformations during the past two decades that have greatly augmented their numbers and led to their increased internal heterogeneity. These demographic trends have had and will continue to have a significant impact on their electoral participation and more generally with issues dealing with their access, representation, and influence in both public and private institutions. To begin with, Asian Pacific Americans, according to the U.S. Bureau of the Census (1983), are the nation's fastest growing group, having increased by 128 percent during the past decade, from 1.5 million in 1970 to 3.5 million in 1980. This substantial increase can be attributed in large measure to the Immigration Act of 1965, which eliminated the discriminatory quota provisions of the Immigration Act of 1924 regarding the numbers of immigrants from specific sending countries, and the Indochinese Refugee Resettlement Program Act of 1975 and the Refugee Act of 1980, which permitted the migration and entry of close to 1 million refugees from Southeast Asia.[9]

In reversing a four-decade longitudinal trend, Asian Pacifics now represent the largest group of legal immigrants to the United States. Between 1931 and 1960, when the provisions of the 1924 National Origins Act were in effect, 58 percent of the immigrants were from Europe, 21 percent from North America, 15 percent from Latin America, and the smallest portion, 5 percent, were from Asia. However, this situation had nearly flip-flopped by the reporting period, 1980-1984. Legal immigration from Europe had decreased to 12 percent of the overall total, North

---

[9]The Immigration Act of 1965 repealed the national origins provisions, which were legislated through the Immigration Act of 1924. The 1965 law created an annual Eastern Hemisphere ceiling of 170,000 with an annual per-country limit of 20,000, and an annual Western Hemisphere ceiling of 120,00 with no country limitations. On the other hand, over 200,000 Southeast-Asian refugees entered the United States under the Indochinese Refugee Resettlement Program Act of 1975. See, for example, Fawcett and Carino (1987).

America to 2 percent, while Latin America had increased to 35 percent and Asian immigration had substantially increased to 48 percent of the United States' total (United Way 1985, 11-15).

During the decade from 1970-1980, the Asian Pacific population also dramatically shifted from being largely American-born to predominantly foreign-born, as a result of this upsurge in international migration. According to the 1980 census, 63.1 percent of all Asian Pacifics in Los Angeles County were foreign-born; with 92.9 percent of the Vietnamese, 85.9 percent of the Koreans, 72.8 percent of the Filipinos, and 70.3 percent of the Chinese having been born abroad. In marked contrast, 10.4 percent of the county's white residents, 2.4 percent of the blacks, and 45.5 percent of the "Spanish-Origin" population were foreign-born (UCLA Ethnic Studies Centers 1987).

By the beginning of the decade of the 1990s, it is estimated that the Asian Pacific population nationally will have doubled again, and number close to 7 million (Muller 1984; Bouvier and Martin 1985). California, with a projected 2.5 million Asian Pacifics in 1990, continues to be the largest population center with over 35 percent of the nation's Asian Pacific total, but there continues to be large concentrations in Hawaii, New York, Washington, Illinois, and Texas (Gardner, Robey, and Smith 1985). Indeed, the greater New York City area, which is estimated to have nearly one million Asian Pacifics in 1990, comes close to rivaling both the greater San Francisco Bay Area and southern California as the largest Asian Pacific community. In 1990, the Asian Pacific population in California is projected to eclipse the state's black population and become second to the rapidly growing Latino populace, which will continue to be California's single largest minority group (Bouvier and Martin 1985; California Department of Finance 1985).

The Asian Pacific population, as many previous scholarly and public policy studies have demonstrated, should not be conceptualized as a single, monolithic entity (Kim, Bok-Lim 1978; United States Commission on Civil Rights 1979; Chun 1980; Endo 1980; Endo, Sue, and Wagner 1980; Nakanishi and Hirano-Nakanishi 1983; Gardner, Robey, and Smith 1985; United Way 1985; Fawcett and Carino 1987). It is a highly heterogeneous population, with respect to ethnic and national origins, cultural values, generation, social class, religion, political ideologies, and other socially differentiating characteristics. For example, as Fawcett and Arnold (1987, 453) describe recent Asian and Pacific immigrants:

> The most evident fact about Asian and Pacific immigration
> is its diversity. Whether one looks at the political and
> economic status of the countries of origin, the characteris-
> tics of the immigrants themselves, or their modes of
> adaptation in the host society, differences are more striking
> than similarities. Sending countries include socialist

Vietnam, capitalist South Korea, and colonial American Samoa—each having quite different economic resources and strategies for development. Significant groups of immigrants include Hmong hill farmers, Indian scientists and engineers, Chinese businessmen, and Filipino service workers—as well as Thai, Filipino, and Korean women immigrating as marriage partners.

Even within any particular Asian Pacific American subgroup like Chinese Americans, the within-group differences can be quite pronounced, reflecting different historical waves of immigration and different segments of a class hierarchical structure. Brett and Victor Nee, in their rich ethnographic study of San Francisco Chinatown, *Longtime Californ'* (1974), provide a revealing socio-historical analysis of such within-group diversity for Chinese Americans. On the other hand, Hirschman and Wong (1981) use census data to illustrate significant within-group differences in socio-economic achievement among Chinese, Japanese, and Filipinos, who are immigrants versus those who are American-born.

In contrast to the study of other, larger minority populations, a common technical, methodological problem facing researchers is that empirical data are not routinely collected or reported on Asian Pacifics *in toto,* or more importantly with respect to the different ethnic subgroups of the population. Census data tapes, for example, represent one of the few quantitative data sources that provides such ethnic breakdowns with respect to nine different Asian Pacific groups—Asian Indians, Chinese, Guamanians, Hawaiians, Japanese, Koreans, Filipinos, Samoans, and Vietnamese.[10] Census data, however, have assorted technical and substantive limitations, especially in terms of the restricted set of individual-level characteristics that are surveyed, the long periods of delay between the collection and public dissemination of data, and the special sampling problems resulting in substantial undercounting that persistently have hampered the gathering of data from Asian Pacifics and other minority populations (United States Commission on Civil Rights 1979; Yu 1982).

---

[10]Most publications of the U.S. Bureau of the Census, however, report data on the larger population category of Asian and Pacific Islanders and do not provide detailed information on these nine different ethnic subgroups. For the 1970 census, the Bureau issued PC(2)-1G, "Subject Reports: Japanese, Chinese, and Filipinos in the United States," which provided data at the national, state, and major SMSA levels for these three Asian-Pacific groups. However, the bureau has decided not to issue a comparable report based on the 1980 census. The category, "Other Asians," includes groups such as Thais, Cambodians, Burmese, Lao, Hmong, and others.

As a result, those who are engaged in research on the Asian Pacific population must often initiate and undertake specially tailored data-collection activities, which are based on familiarity with or expertise about Asian Pacifics, in order to gain sufficient empirical information to investigate topics such as the extent of interracial marriages, utilization rates of mental health facilties, or levels of political involvement for specific Asian Pacific subgroups prior to the application of rigorous data analysis tools (Kikumura and Kitano 1973; Sue and Kirk 1973; Yu 1982; Chan 1986; Nakanishi 1986b). Public records on marriages or voter registration do not contain specific information on the ethnicity, national origins, generation, or racial background of the individuals who are recorded. Nor does there presently exist a computer-based dictionary of Asian Pacific surnames for the different ethnic subgroups; although this writer is currently developing the first software package for that purpose.[11] Therefore, it is often necessary to devise special data collection strategies that are specifically geared towards identifying and analyzing those of different Asian Pacific backgrounds from all the others who are listed in these public records. For instance, in undertaking research to determine interracial marriage rates or voter registration trends among Asian Pacifics, scholars have had to carefully assemble and train panels of bilingual and bicultural researchers to identify and locate Asian Pacific surnamed individuals from others who obtained marriage licenses or registered to vote. Undertaking what some may believe to be a simple data collection exercise for Asian Pacifics in a municipality like Los Angeles County involves the analysis of literally tens of thousands of marriage licenses or the listing of millions of registered votes. The reliability of the overall identification processes is controlled through the multiple verification of names in which two, and usually three, professionally trained and linguistically or culturally knowledgeable readers examine and verify the same records. Other equally important methodological issues in undertaking research on Asian Pacifics should also be addressed (Kikumura and Kitano 1973; Nakanishi 1986a, b). Such added methodological attention

---

[11]This software package is being developed in order to conduct further research on voter registration trends among different Asian Pacific American groups—the Japanese, Chinese, Korean, Filipinos, Samoans, Vietnamese, and Asian Indians. The software consists of an extensive listing or dictionary of surnames for each of the groups, which was compiled from previous data collection activities for the UCLA Asian Pacific American Voter Registration Study. See Nakanishi (1986a). The software program will allow us to mechanically identify Asian Pacifics from voter registration rolls and to analyze longitudinal trends. The program should be transferrable for other research purposes, in which it is necessary to identify and differentiate individuals of Asian Pacific backgrounds from others who are part of a general listing of names.

during the initial research stage of gathering reliable and valid data is highly crucial in the examination of research topics dealing with the diverse Asian Pacific subgroups and in the analysis of their within-group differences and similarities. Future academic and policy inquiries on the political participation and behavior of different groups and sectors of the Asian Pacific population should be guided by similar methodological considerations and should avoid some common pitfalls that result from not being fully informed or appreciative of the complexities of this growing sector of the state's population. Grant Din (1984) provides a revealing example:

> A *San Francisco Examiner* analysis of the 1984 California presidential primary discussed the results of the ABC News exit polling in California and New Jersey. According to these results, in California, "Mondale carried the Asian vote with 40%, Hart trailed with 33% (and Jackson had 20%)." A closer examination, however, reveals that only 2% of the 1,125 voters surveyed, or 23, were Asian American. This translates into 9 votes for Mondale, 8 for Hart, and 5 for Jackson! The poll claimed an overall margin of error of 3%, but it must have been higher for such a small population.

Differences in educational attainment levels provide a glimpse of this internal diversity. Census data from a collaborative research project on changes in quality of life indicators between 1970 and 1980 for Los Angeles County's major racial minority groups, which are now the numerical majority of the county's populace, underscore the necessity for analyzing within-group differences among Asian Pacifics in applied and basic research.[12] For example, Table 1 provides 1980 STF4 sample census data on educational attainment levels for adult males and females, 25-44 years of age, one of the sectors most likely to be targeted for voter registration campaigns, for six

---

[12]The census data presented here are part of a collaborative research endeavor entitled the UCLA Ethnic Studies Census Project, which is sponsored by the four ethnic studies organized research units at the University of California at Los Angeles and funded by the Institute of American Cultures and the California Community Foundation. See UCLA Ethnic Studies Centers (1987). The specific data presented here are from the 1980 STF4 Sample and 1970 Public Use Sample for the Los Angeles-Long Beach SMSA. The tables on sex by age by years of schooling completed for persons 25 years and older of the different ethnic populations were derived from 1980 Table P-B48. Although educational attainment data were available on other age categories, information on individuals 25-44 years of age were selected because they would be the age group that would most likely fit the designation of adult learner presented in footnote 2.

Table 1:   *Educational Attainment Levels for Males and Females, 25-44 Years of Age in Los Angeles County, 1980*

	% Eight Years or Less of Schooling	% Non-High School Graduate	% College Graduate
Asian Pacifics			
Males	2.9%	6.4%	54.7%
Females	5.1%	9.7%	44.5%
Blacks			
Males	2.5%	13.7%	16.6%
Females	2.0%	13.3%	14.7%
American Indians			
Males	5.8%	21.1%	17.7%
Females	6.6%	25.3%	10.3%
Spanish Origin			
Males	41.7%	57.2%	6.6%
Females	42.0%	59.2%	4.5%
Whites			
Males	8.5%	16.6%	22.5%
Females	8.5%	17.5%	22.3%
Others			
Males	31.1%	45.1%	14.7%
Females	30.1%	49.0%	9.8%
Total Population			
Males	11.3%	20.0%	29.4%
Females	11.0%	21.1%	20.9%

Source: UCLA Ethnic Studies Census Project.

mutually exclusive[13] ethnic categories of Asian Pacifics, blacks, American Indians, Spanish-origin, whites, and others. Asian Pacifics and individuals of "Spanish-origin" appear to be at polar extremes of the educational continuum, with the former having a seemingly unrivaled percentage of college graduates and the latter exhibiting a disturbingly unmatched percentage of individuals with less than eight years of formal schooling. Indeed, on practically all educational attainment indicators, Asian Pacifics far

---

[13]These mutually exclusive categories were created through statistical manipulations of 1980 STF4 sample data. Summary data tables provided in publications by the U.S. Bureau are not mutually exclusive with respect to the Spanish-origin population.

outdistance every other population group.[14]   Other studies have made similar observations (Brown, et al. 1980; Duran 1983; Davis, Haub, and Willette 1985; Sue and Padilla 1986).

Table 2, which differentiates the monolithic Asian Pacific category among nine different ethnic subgroups, illustrates the necessity for recognizing and analyzing the internal heterogeneity of this population. Several Asian Pacific groups such as the Vietnamese, Hawaiians, Guamanians, Samoans, and other Asians clearly do not reflect high educational attainment levels and generally have far fewer college graduates and proportionately more nonhigh school graduates than Asian Pacifics as a whole, as well as blacks and whites in the county. At the same time, other groups, which appear to have stronger group-level academic profiles like the Chinese, Koreans, and Asian Indians, still had large numbers of individuals who were not high educational attainers. Close to one in five women of these three groups, 25-44 years of age, had not completed high school, and one in 10 Chinese women had less than eight years of schooling. Such between and within-group differences in educational attainment levels, as well as other quality of life indicators, are expected to be further pronounced in the 1990 census.

The combination of unprecedented demographic growth, along with extraordinary internal diversification, has a number of implications for Asian Pacific American electoral participation. On the one hand, there is no question that as Asian Pacifics have come to represent an increasingly sizeable proportion of the population in certain states, most notably California, and in specific urban areas like the greater San Francisco Bay Area, the West San Gabriel Valley and South Bay regions of Los Angeles County, and portions of Orange County, that heretofore rarely considered topics like reapportionment, redistricting, and fair political representation have become critical policy issue-areas for Asian Pacific Americans. In contrast to the 1960s and 1970s, when their population size and density might not have been substantial enough for Asian Pacifics to place special emphasis on these issues or to seek participation in the rough-and-tumble political decision-making process that is associated with creating political districts, the demographic patterns that currently exist and are forecast for the decade of the 1990s will justify and necessitate enhanced involvement and monitoring of these processes. Indeed, a number of Asian Pacific communities across the nation from the Silicon Valley in northern California to the Queens and Chinatown areas of New York have expressed deep concern about potential gerrymandering practices and the possible dilution of Asian Pacific electoral strength. Unlike previous years, Asian

---

[14]The only exception appears to be in the percentage of males and females with less than eight years of schooling for Asian Pacifics and blacks.

Table 2: *Educational Attainment Levels for Asian Pacific American Males and Females, 25-44 Years of Age, 1980*

	% Eight Years or Less of Schooling	% Non-High School Graduate	% College Graduate
Japanese Americans			
Males	1.9%	5.1%	47.4%
Females	1.4%	4.2%	35.4%
Chinese Americans			
Males	6.8%	11.3%	54.7%
Females	10.3%	16.0%	40.5%
Filipino Amerians			
Males	2.4%	6.8%	51.1%
Females	2.7%	6.5%	61.6%
Korean Americans			
Males	3.6%	6.8%	54.2%
Females	6.3%	13.4%	32.6%
Vietnamese Americans			
Males	12.2%	23.1%	20.2%
Females	23.8%	37.4%	10.6%
Hawaiian Americans			
Males	3.0%	16.2%	18.6%
Females	1.4%	14.5%	9.0%
Asian Indians			
Males	2.1%	5.0%	69.6%
Females	10.2%	17.6%	39.7%
Guamanians			
Males	17.2%	32.6%	8.3%
Females	22.2%	40.0%	5.9%
Samoans			
Males	6.4%	26.7%	10.4%
Females	8.0%	29.6%	5.8%
Other Asians			
Males	7.3%	13.4%	38.8%
Females	11.6%	22.4%	26.3%

Source: UCLA Ethnic Studies Census Project.

Pacific leaders have begun to organize for the next round of reapportionment and redistricting efforts in 1991, particularly in California.

On the other hand, their unusual internal heterogeneity will challenge leaders and organizers of different Asian Pacific sectors and communities—who are often separated by both real and symbolic boundaries of national origins, language, culture, social class, religion, and other character-istics—to find common ground on key policy issues to cope with the uneven political development and maturation of different ethnic subgroups, and to seek effective mechanisms for pursuing their shared interests in a unified manner on both a continuous and *ad hoc* manner. Although this may appear to be visionary, there are enough examples from the past two decades, be it in terms of their concerted lobbying activities against university admissions quotas, anti-Asian violence, or unfair immigration policy legislation, to illustrate the potentiality and necessity of such collective endeavors. And finally, it is highly likely that the terms "Asian American" or "Asian Pacific American," which have been imbued with constantly changing strategic, ideological, and tactical connotations since they were first articulated in the 1960s, will undergo further reconsideration in response to the conditions of the decade of the 1990s.

BECOMING TEN PERCENT OF CALIFORNIA'S ELECTORATE

The future size, characteristics, and impact of the Asian Pacific American electorate in Los Angeles County remains to be shaped. Hopefully, this study has served to move us a step beyond our previous uncertainty and speculation about Asian Pacific American voters, and has provided some insights into a variety of factors which appear to influence their present reality, along with their future potential. The study clearly underscores the need for further voter registration efforts by Asian Pacific American organizations, the two major political parties, and others who believe that the right of political franchise must not be taken for granted. . . . And although Asian Pacific Americans as a whole currently reflect a majority preference for the Democratic party, it should be obvious that the large and growing pool of non-registered voters could have a profound impact on the overall partisan identification of Asian Pacific Americans, and especially among groups like Koreans and Vietnamese, which are overwhelmingly composed of recent immigrants. Therefore, the extent to which the two major parties further cultivate their relations with, and address the specific concerns of, the Asian Pacific American community will greatly determine the future partisan direction of the Asian Pacific American elector-ate.[15]

---

[15]See Nakanishi (1986b), 16.

In recent years, a body of scholarly knowledge has gradually emerged on Asian Pacific electoral political involvement. Two consistent findings from all empirical studies suggest that the glowing predictions of enhanced future electoral clout by Asian Pacifics might not be realized unless there are several major reversals of current voting trends among Asian Pacifics. One common finding is that Asian Pacific Americans, even after statistical manipulations have been performed to control for the high proportion of age-eligible individuals who cannot vote because they are not United States citizens, still have lower voter registration rates than whites, blacks, and Latinos.[16] The UCLA Asian Pacific American Voter Registration Study estimated that Japanese Americans who have the largest number and the highest proportion of citizens of all the Asian Pacific groups in Los Angeles County, had a voter registration rate in 1984 of 43.0 percent for those who were 18 years and older. At the same time, 35.5 percent Chinese Americans, 27.0 percent Filipino Americans, 16.7 percent Asian Indians, 13.0 percent Korean Americans, 28.5 percent Samoan Americans, and an extremely low 4.1 percent Vietnamese were estimated to be registered voters in the region. These registration rates were well below the average for Los Angeles County of close to 60 percent for all individuals 18 years and older. As a result of these low rates of voter registration, Asian Pacific voters represented less than 3 percent of all voters in the county in 1984, despite the fact that they were over 6 percent of the county's population. Similiar findings of low registration rates have been found for Asian Pacifics in other areas of California and New York.[17]

The other consistent and yet puzzling finding about Asian Pacific American voters deals with the pattern of their partisan affiliations and specifically the extremely high proportion of them who designate themselves as independents or "no party" registrants. When the UCLA Asian Pacific American Voter Registration Study conducted its initial empirical analysis of registered voters in 1984,[18] it identified large numbers of "independent" Chinese, Vietnamese, Korean, and Asian Indians, in which one in five declined to state a party preference at the time of registering to vote. Although recent polls and studies of the American electorate report that a growing number of voters now consider themselves to be independents,[19] the official registration indexes for Los Angeles County indicated that only 10 percent of all voters—like the Japanese, Filipinos, and Samoans who were also identified in the study—decline to specify a party affiliation. In

---

[16]See Din (1984), Nakanishi (1986b), and Uhlaner, Cain, and Kiewiet (1987).

[17]See Chen, New, Tsutakawa (1989), Din (1984), and Uhlaner, Cain, and Kiewiet (1987).

[18]See *ibid.*, for details on the special methodology employed by the project.

[19]See, among others, Finkel and Sarrow (1985).

subsequent, annual follow-up studies for the UCLA project, certain Asian Pacific groups like the Chinese Americans have been found to continue to register in large numbers as independents.

The Asian Pacific American voters in the city of Monterey Park in Los Angeles County are illustrative.[20]   Table 3 compares and contrasts different groups of ethnically identified registered voters in Monterey Park—Chinese Americans, Japanese Americans, Asian Pacifics as a whole, non-Asian Pacific Americans, and the overall citywide electorate—in 1984 and 1989. In 1984, for example, there was a plurality of Democrats (43.1 percent) over Republicans (30.8 percent) among Chinese American voters, but also a relatively high proportion of individuals (25.3 percent) who specified no party affiliations. By 1989, Chinese American voters, who accounted for the vast majority of new registered voters in the city since 1984, were nearly evenly divided among Democrats (34.9 percent), Republicans (37.1 percent), and independents (26.1 percent). The "practical" or "political" implication of this observation is that a Chinese American candidate, who seeks the nomination of a specific political party in a primary election, will be faced with a situation in which practically two-thirds of all Chinese American registered voters, who would likely represent a sympathetic bloc of voters for the candidate, will be unable to cast ballots during the initial, "party members only" primary election. This is what occurred in the November 1987 primary election when Lily Chen, a Chinese American and a former mayor of the city of Monterey Park, sought the Democratic party nomination for the United States Congress. Although her campaign staff tried to persuade Chinese Americans who were registered as independents or Republicans to switch their party affiliations for the Democratic primary election, very few actually did. Although she raised substantial campaign contributions from Chinese and other Asian Americans, she was soundly defeated by her incumbent opponent. In contrast, Japanese Americans in Monterey Park, who have experienced far less population growth especially as a result of immigration, continue to reflect a different electoral profile than Chinese American voters. Similiar to Japanese Americans in other cities and neighborhoods of Los Angeles County, those in Monterey Park

---

[20]Monterey Park has attracted substantial media and scholarly attention because of its growing Asian Pacific population, as well as its extreme racial tensions. According to the U.S. census, 33.7 percent of the city of Monterey Park's population in 1980 consisted of Asian Pacifics (18,312 of 54,338). By 1986, when the Bureau of the Census conducted its "test census" of cities in central and eastern Los Angeles County, Asian Pacifics accounted for 51.4 percent of the city's total population (31,467 of 61,246). Between 1980 and 1986, the city's Asian Pacific population increased by 71.8 percent, whereas the city's white and Latino populations declined by 16.7 percent and 11.2 percent, respectively.

Table 3: *Asian Pacific American Registered Voters, Monterey Park, 1984 and 1989*

	Registered	Democrats	Republicans	Other Parties	No Party
'84 Citywide	22,021	13,657	5,564	368	2,290
	(100.0%)	(62.0%)	(25.0%)	(1.7%)	(10.4%)
'89 Citywide	23,184	13,243	6,684	369	2,888
	(100.0%)	(57.1%)	(28.8%)	(1.6%)	(12.5%)
'84-'89 Net Gain/Loss	+1,163	-414	+1,120	+1	+598
'84 Chinese Americans	3,152	1,360	972	23	797
	(100.0%)	(43.1%)	(30.8%)	(0.7%)	(25.3%)
'89 Chinese Americans	5,356	1,868	1,989	100	1,399
	(100.0%)	(34.9%)	(37.1%)	(1.9%)	(26.1%)
'84-'89 Net Gain/Loss	+2,204	+508	+1,017	+77	+602
'84 Japanese Americans	2,586	1,429	838	21	298
	(100.0%)	(55.3%)	(32.4%)	(0.8%)	(11.5%)
'89 Japanese Americans	2,919	1,516	991	42	370
	(100.0%)	(51.9%)	(33.9%)	(1.4%)	(12.7%)
'84-'89 Net Gain/Loss	+343	+87	+153	+21	+72
'84 Asian Pacific Total	6,441	3,265	1,944	54	1,178
	(100.0%)	(50.7%)	(30.2%)	(0.8%)	(18.3%)
'89 Asian Pacific Total	8,988	3,754	3,198	168	1,868
	(100.0%)	(41.8%)	(35.6%)	(1.9%)	(20.8%)
'84-'89 Net Gain/Loss	+2,547	+489	+1,254	+114	+690

Source: UCLA Asian Pacific American Voter Registration Project.

show a majority preference for the Democratic party (55.3 percent in 1984 and 51.9 percent in 1989). They are also far more likely than Chinese American voters to register for one of the two major parties rather than declaring themselves to be independents. And finally, Asian Pacific Americans as a whole, who increased their representation among the city's total registered voters from 29.2 percent in 1984 to 38.8 percent in 1989, have come to reflect overall party and nonparty identification patterns that are even more distinctive than those of non-Asian Pacific American voters in Monterey Park. Indeed, as the above passage from the initial report of the

UCLA study anticipated, the ever-increasing pool of potential Asian Pacific registered voters, especially those who have recently acquired the right of franchise through naturalization, "could have a profound impact on the overall partisan identification of Asian Pacific Americans" in Monterey Park, in Los Angeles County, and elsewhere. In 1984, Asian Pacific American registered voters as a whole in Monterey Park showed a slight majority preference for the Democrats. By 1989, with an increase of over 2,500 new registered Asian Pacific voters, it was no longer possible to characterize the Asian Pacific electorate in the city in this manner.

When political organizers and community leaders confront these two puzzling aspects of the electoral participation of Asian Pacific Americans, their remedies tend to be short-term, action-oriented outreach efforts like initiating a major voter registration campaign or organizing forums for partisan officials to speak to ethnic organizations (Arax 1986). This is generally what has occurred in the southern California area in response to the findings and analyses of the UCLA Asian Pacific American Voter Registration Project. These and other voter outreach activities are undoubtedly important and there is no reason why they should not be vigorously pursued. However, such immediate and action-oriented solutions may be masking far more fundamental and unique issues of political participation that must be addressed, especially for the large numbers of Asian Pacifics who are recent immigrants and refugees. It has been hypothesized that the low rates of voter registration and the unexpectedly high proportion of independent voters among certain Asian Pacific groups has far more to do with their political experiences in nation-states like Taiwan and the People's Republic of China, which have different voting procedures, and where the connotation of a "political party" as being the Communists or Kuomintang is far different than what is normally associated with the Democratic and Republican parties. At the same time, traditional adult education classes in American civics and government that are required for naturalization applications may expose newcomers to the most rudimentary facts of American government but have little or no impact on their pre-existing political belief systems, their general sense of political efficacy towards government and other public institutions like schools, or their knowledge of the inner workings of American politics. And finally, the continued interest in homeland issues, the lack of vigorous recruitment and educational outreach efforts by the two major political parties towards these potential new voters, and the sizeable numbers of poor and disadvantaged Asian Pacifics, particularly among Southeast Asian refugees, may also be important contributing factors.

Although low rates of electoral participation appear to be evident for both American-born and foreign-born Asian Pacifics, there also may be unique political, psychological, and cultural barriers that immigrants and refugees must overcome in order to participate fully in the American political system. Zvi Gittleman's pioneering study (1982), *Becoming Israelis,* which examines the process of "political resocialization" that American and Soviet adult immigrants to Israel undergo in adapting to the Israeli political system, offers highly suggestive insights on the potential underlying causes of this situation. According to Gittleman, "political resocialization" can be seen as a process by which adult immigrants and refugees, who have largely acquired their fundamental political values, attitudes, and behavioral orientations in one socio-political system undergo "adult political socialization, or *re*socialization" in migrating to and making the transition to a newly adopted society that has its own, and usually different, political traditions, procedures, and philosophical or legal principles. He writes (Gittleman 1982, 343):

> Are immigrants, in fact, resocialized politically, or do they
> remain outside the political arena? If they are resocialized,
> is it only on the level of outward behavior, while the
> fundamental political *weltanschauung* remains unchanged,
> a product of the political culture of the "old country?"
> What remains, if anything, of their former political cultures
> if they are resocialized into a new one? If there is, indeed,
> a process of resocialization going on, who are its "agents"?

The concept of political resocialization might well serve to direct policy and scholarly attention to the largely neglected process by which Asian Pacific and other immigrants and refugees to the United States come to participate in the nation's political system. Most policy reports and needs asssessments of these recent international migrants focus on a wide range of issues dealing with their transition and adaptation to American life and society—be it cultural, linguistic, or occupational—but avoid so-called "political" aspects, and largely treat them as socially taboo. Indeed, Tomas Hammar (1978, 16), after reviewing works on international migration and political socialization, wrote that, "In the latter we find very little about migration, in the former not much about politics." However, by not seriously and rigorously considering these potentially signifiniciant political learning and adaptation issues, we may be overlooking one of the most critical and fundamental aspects of their immediate and long-range adjustment to and full participation in this society. As Philip Coombs writes (1985, 48):

> In the United States it is difficult enough for a small-town
> New England family, for example, to adapt to its new home
> in Houston, Texas. But it is obviously far more difficult for
> a Latin American or Vietnamese or Korean family of rural
> origin to adjust to whatever U.S. city or town it happens to
> end up in. Other matters may further complicate the
> situation. Those who began their lives under dictatorial
> regimes may, within a democratic haven, have learning
> needs that are as much political as cultural and occupation-

al. Moreover, as a result of the chaotic national situations that uprooted them and subsequent years spent in refugee camps, some may have psychological problems in dealing with their new environments that are incorrectly diagnosed as learning disabilities. At stake here is the education of parents as well as children, as in the case of parents who fear that if they sign documents to allow their children to go on a school-sponsored trip they may never see them again.

CONCLUSION

In recent years, many outside political observers and media commentators have optimistically predicted that Asian Pacifics will soon become a major new force in American politics, perhaps akin to American Jews, especially because of their extraordinary demographic growth and concentration during the past two decades in certain key electoral states like California, Texas, and New York.[21] Like American Jewish voters, many believe that if Asian Pacifics come to represent a proportion of the electorate that is comparable to their numbers in the total population that they could become a highly influential "swing vote" in critical local, state, and presidential elections. In California, for example, if Asian Pacifics come to represent not only one of 10 residents, but also one of 10 California voters—who will continue to control the nation's largest number of congressional seats and presidential electoral college votes—then they would be a strategically important constituency for national, as well as state, political elections.

Although the future course of Asian American political involvement cannot be easily forecast, it does appear that the ability of this population to realize its full electoral potential will be influenced by an array of currently visible trends. To begin with, for many Asian Pacific immigrant and refugee groups, homeland issues continue to dominate their ethnic political leadership agendas and the front pages of their vernacular media, and compete with, if not at times overwhelm, efforts to steer the ever-growing numbers of naturalized citizens towards greater involvement in the American electoral system. In this respect, these groups are involved in a very familiar and yet normally conflict-filled process, which other earlier American immigrant populations have undergone, of coming to grips with and seeking a balance between their domestic and nondomestic political orientations. At the beginning of the decade of the 1990s, groups like the Korean American Coalition and the Taiwanese American Citizens League, both of Los

---

[21]See, for example, Tachibana (1986) and Stokes (1988).

Angeles, have been founded to enhance the participation of members of their largely immigrant communities in American electoral politics and to address major domestic civil rights issues facing their ethnic groups. Both have gained footholds in their respective ethnic community power structures, which are dominated by elderly leaders whose attention is geared far more towards resolving highly volatile situations in their countries of origin. The decade of the 1990s will probably provide us with important answers about how the leaders of these and other Asian Pacific immigrant and refugee communities reach a meaningful accommodation between their domestic issues and their homeland concerns.

Conventional wisdom assumes that interest towards nondomestic or homeland politics is limited to the initial immigrant generation, and that involvement declines with succeeding, acculturated generations. However, there is much to suggest that such a linear conceptualization fails to consider changing conditions in California and elsewhere for Asian Pacific Americans and other groups in society. For example, large numbers of second- and third-generation Asian Pacific Americans, particularly those in business, law, and academics, are visibly involved in emerging Pacific Rim affairs, and more generally in the structural transformations that are occurring as a result of the internationalization of California's political economy. In the decade of the 1990s, some Asian Pacific leaders may use their real and symbolic linkages with Pacific Rim issues to define a unique and highly significant niche in American domestic politics and business affairs. At the same time, the continued interest and involvement of groups as diverse as American Jews, Poles and other Eastern Europeans, Ukranians, Cubans, Greeks, Armenians, Chicanos, and African Americans with their "homeland" issues demonstrate that acculturation does not automatically signal the end of involvement.

Second, the ability of Asian Pacific Americans to reach their full electoral potential also will be determined by the extent to which they politically develop beyond their most visible, and what some might argue is their most rewarding, manner in which they currently participate in recent American electoral politics, namely by giving money. During the past decade, Asian Pacific Americans have become increasingly recognized as a major new source of campaign funds, a veritable mountain of gold for Democratic and Republican prospectors in California and across the nation. Indeed, during election periods, there are a staggering number of fund-raising activities in Asian Pacific communities. In the 1988 presidential election, it is estimated that Asian Pacifics contributed over $10 million, divided almost equally between George Bush and Michael Dukakis, and were second only to the American Jewish population in the amount of campaign money raised by an ethnic or minority group. For longtime political allies and friends like Los Angeles Mayor Thomas Bradley, contributions from Asian Pacifics usually amount to over 10 percent of the total campaign war chest.

This emerging view of Asian Pacific Americans as the new political moneybags of American politics has had a mixed reaction. For some Asian Pacific leaders, the wooing of Asian Pacifics by the two major political parties is viewed positively, especially in light of the decades-long history of political disenfranchisement and the general lack of outreach and recruitment activities by party officials in the past, particularly in California. Other Asian Pacific community leaders, however, argue that Asian Pacifics may be the victims of something akin to political consumer fraud. They claim that Asian Pacifics have not received the types of political benefits and goods—be it greater access or more high-level decision-making appointments—that they sought or were promised when they contributed to party coffers. Some point an accusing finger at politicians for such "deceptive" practices, although it is hardly newsworthy to find elected officials promising one thing, and doing something else. Others blame inexperienced Asian Pacific political fund-raisers, who are accused of behaving more like philanthropists than the shrewd entrepreneurs that many of them happen to be. Instead of cutting deals and seeking maximum returns for their investments, it is alleged that Asian Pacific political money usually takes the form of charity, since few strings are ever attached to it.

Although political contributions will undoubtedly continue to play an inordinate role in American politics, it probably would be unfortunate and misguided if Asian Pacific Americans, by their own volition or at the encouragement of politicians and party officials, largely restricted their participation in American electoral politics to giving money. In recent years, many Asian Pacific American organizations in California like the Asian Pacific Legal Center of Southern California and Leadership Education for Asian Pacifics (LEAP) have undertaken innovative projects and activities like leadership training symposia and voter education drives that go beyond the limited and narrow development of Asian Pacific Americans as political donors. Many of these efforts fall under the general rubic of political education and are variously directed at uplifting the political awareness, efficacy, and participation of the diverse sectors of the Asian Pacific population in different political activities, be they as seemingly simple and fundamental as registering to vote, or as complex and involved as running for public office. These activities are far removed from the glamorous and flashy side of politics that is usually associated with political fund raising. Instead, they are geared towards the long-range political development of the Asian Pacific population rather than immediate political payoffs. Indeed, as Asian Pacifics attempt to enhance their representation and influence in electoral politics in California and nationally during the decade of the 1990s and beyond, it will probably be necessary for them to engage in these and other innovative political education endeavors.

Although there has been a visible increase in political involvement and representation by Asian Pacific Americans in all forms of political activity during the past two decades, it would be highly remiss to conclude that they have now become a powerful and unified political entity, or that they are now capable of competing equally with other political actors, be they other immigrant and minority groups or special interests, in achieving their specific political goals. In comparison with other more established political actors like American Jews and African Americans, they still have not fully developed and used the wide array of real and symbolic resources that are needed to compete on an equal basis with other groups, and their various levels of internal diversity (of ethnic origins, generations, social classes, political perspectives, and other characteristics) have ofttimes prevented them from being the type of unified political actor that is suggested by their overarching umbrella label of Asian Pacific Americans. In some of the smaller California suburban cities like Gardena and Monterey Park and to a much lesser extent the big cities of San Francisco, San Jose, Los Angeles, San Diego, and Sacramento, Asian Pacific Americans have become increasingly viable and recognized political participants. However, in most areas aside from Hawaii and at higher levels of state and federal decision making they remain largely ignored and underrepresented. No Asian Pacific American, for example, currently serves in either the assembly or the senate of the California state legislature. Indeed, as a result of both structural and group-specific constraints, they have not been able to sufficiently cultivate either a statewide or national political presence, or an explicit set of statewide or national priorities, which is at least recognized when major public policy issues dealing with education, the poor, the elderly, or even United States relations with Asia are legislated and implemented. At best, their present impact on American politics has been regional and sporadic rather than national and continuous, and their reputed success as a model minority continues to disguise their overall lack of influence and representation in many of the most significant political arenas and social institutions of American society.

The decade of the 1990s, which is widely viewed in glowing and optimistic terms because of seemingly positive demographic trends, will be a provocative and significant one to witness and analyze because of the extraordinary challenges and opportunities that it will undoubtedly present for Asian Pacific Americans in realizing their full electoral potential. Whether or not they will become California's next swing vote by the year 2000 is nearly impossible to predict. However, our ability to raise and seriously entertain such a question in the context of the historical conditions of disenfranchisement and exclusion that Asian Pacific Americans faced in California and elsewhere is quite revealing in itself.

REFERENCES

Arax, Mark. "Group Seeks to Reverse Voter Apathy by Asians." *Los Angeles Times,* March 3, 1986, 1, 3.

Asianweek. "Asians Called a 'Major National Force' in Political Fundraising." Asianweek, June 1, 1984, 5.

Bouvier, Leon, and Philip Martin. *Population Change and California's Future.* Washington, D.C.: Population Reference Bureau, 1985.

Brown, George, et al. *The Condition of Education for Hispanic Americans.* Washington, D.C.: National Center for Educational Statistics, 1980.

Bunzel, John H., and Jeffrey K. D. Au. "Diversity or Discrimination? Asian Americans in College." *Public Interest,* no. 87, 49-62.

California Department of Finance. *Projected Total Population of California Counties.* Sacramento: Department of Finance, 1985.

Chan, Sucheng. *The Bittersweet Soil.* Berkeley: University of California Press, 1988.

Chen, Marion, Woei-Ming New, and John Tsutakawa. "Empowerment in New York Chinatown: Our Work as Student Interns." *Amerasia Journal* 15 (1989): 299-306.

Chin, Rocky. "The Long Road-Japanese Americans Move on Redress." *Bridge* (1981): 11-29.

Chuman, Frank. *The Bamboo People: Japanese Americans and the Law.* Del Mar, California: Publisher's, Inc., 1976.

Chun, Ki-Taek. "The Myth of Asian American Success and Its Educational Ramifications." *IRCD Bulletin* 15 (1980): 1-12.

Clifford, Frank. "Contributors to Mayoral Race Seek A Friendly Ear." *Los Angeles Times,* March 11, 1985a, 1, 3, 14.

_____. "Election Money—The New, the Old, the Bid to Limit It." *Los Angeles Times,* March 27, 1985b, 1, 3.

_____. "Barriers to Power for Minorities." *Los Angeles Times,* May 7, 1990, 1, 24, 25.

Coffman, Tom. *Catch A Wave: A Case Study of Hawaii's New Politics.* Honolulu: University of Hawaii Press, 1973.

Coombs, Philip H. *The World Crisis in Education: The View From the Eighties.* New York: Oxford University Press, 1985.

Daniel, Cletus. *Bitter Harvest: A History of California Farmworkers, 1870-1941.* Ithaca, New York: Cornell University Press, 1981.

Daniels, Roger. *The Politics of Prejudice.* New York: Atheneum, 1968.

Davis, Cary, Carl Haub, and JoAnne Willette. "U.S. Hispanics: Chaning the Face of America." In *Majority and Minority,* edited by Norman Yetman, 464-89. Boston: Allyn and Bacon, Inc., 1985.

DeWitt, Howard. *Violence in the Fields: California Filipino Farm Labor Organizing During the Great Depression.* Saratoga, California: Century Twenty-One Publishing, 1980.

Din, Grant. "An Analysis of Asian/Pacific American Registration and Voting Patterns in San Francisco." Master's thesis, Claremont Graduate School, 1984.

Duran, Richard. *Hispanics' Education and Background: Predictors of College Achievement.* New York: College Entrance Examination Board, 1983.

Endo, Russell, Stanley Sue, and Nathaniel Wagner, eds. *Asian Americans: Social and Psychological Perspectives, Vol. 2.* Palo Alto: Science and Behavior, 1980.

Fawcett, James T., and Fred Arnold. "Explaining Diversity: Asian and Pacific Immigration Systems." In *Pacific Bridges,* edited by James T. Fawcett and Benjamin Carino, 453-73. Staten Island, New York: Center for Migration Studies, 1987.

Fawcett, James T., and Benjamin Carino, eds. *Pacific Bridges.* Staten Island, New York: Center for Migration Studies, 1987.

Finkel, Steve E., and Howard Sarrow. "Party Identification and Party Enrollment: The Differences and the Consequences." *Journal of Politics* 47 (1985): 620-42.

Gardner, Robert, Bryant Robey, and Peter Smith. "Asian Americans: Growth, Change, Diversity." *Population Bulletin,* vol. 4, no. 4 (1985).

Gittleman, Zvi. *Becoming Israelis: Political Resocialization of Soviet and American Immigrants.* New York: Praeger, 1982.

Griffiths, Stephen. "Emigrant and Returned Migrant Investment in a Philippine Village." *Amerasia Journal* 5 (1976): 45-67.

Grodzins, Morton. *Americans Betrayed.* Chicago: University of Chicago Press, 1949.

Hammer, Tomas. "Migration and Politics: Delimitation and Organization of a Research Field." Paper presented to the Workshop on International Migration and Politics, European Consortium on Political Research, Grenoble, France, 1978.

Higham, John, ed. *Ethnic Leadership in America.* Baltimore: The Johns Hopkins University Press, 1979.

Hsia, Jayjia. "Limits of Affirmative Action: Asian American Access to Higher Education." *Educational Policy* 2 (1988): 117-36.

Ichioka, Yuji. "Early Japanese Quest for Citizenship: The Background of the 1922 Ozawa Case." *Amerasia Journal* 4 (1977): 1-22.

_____. *The Issei.* New York: Free Press, 1988.

Irons, Peter. *Justice At War.* New York: Oxford University Press, 1983.

Isaacs, Stephen D. *Jews and American Politics.* Garden City: Doubleday and Company, 1974.

Jo, Yung-Hwan, ed. *Political Participation of Asian Americans: Problems and Strategies.* Chicago: Pacific/Asian American Mental Health Research Center, 1980.

Jurergensmeyer, Mark. "The Ghadar Syndrome: Nationalism in an Immigrant Community." *Center for South and Southeast Asian Studies Review* 1 (1978): 9-13.

Keohane, Robert. "The Big Influence of Small Allies." *Foreign Policy* 2 (1971): 161-82.

Kikumura, Akemi, and Harry Kitano. "Interracial Marriages." *Journal of Social Issues* (1973): 570-82.

Kim, Bok-Lim. "Problems and Service Needs of Asian Americans in Chicago: An Empirical Study." *Amerasia Journal* 5 (1978): 23-44.

Kim, Hyung-Chan, and Nicholas Lai. "Chinese Community Resistance to Urban Renewal." *Journal of Ethnic Studies* 10 (1982): 67-81.

Kwong, Peter. *Chinatown, New York: Labor and Politics, 1930-1950.* New York: Monthly Review Press, 1981.

Lai, Him Mark. "China Politics and United States Chinese Communities." In *Counterpoint: Perspectives on Asian America,* edited by Emma Gee, et al., 152-59. Los Angeles: UCLA Asian American Studies Center, 1976.

Levy, Mark, and Michael Kramer. *The Ethnic Factor: How America's Minorities Decide Elections.* New York: Touchstone Books, 1973.

Lim, Derrick. *Learning From the Past: A Retrospective Look at the Chol Soo Lee Movement.* Master's thesis, University of California, Los Angeles, 1985.

Low, Victor. *The Unimpressible Race: A Century of Educational Struggle by Chinese in San Francisco.* San Francisco: East-West Publishers, 1982.

Lyu, Kingsley. "Korean Nationalist Activities in Hawaii and the Continental United States, 1900-1945, Part I and II." *Amerasia Journal* 4 (1977): 23-90.

Massey, Douglas S. "Dimensions of the New Immigration to the United States and the Prospects for Assimilation." *Annual Review of Sociology* 7 (1981): 57-85.

McKee, Delber. "The Chinese Boycott of 1905-1906 Reconsidered, The Role of Chinese Americans." *Pacific Historical Review* 55 (1986): 165-91.

Muller, Thomas. *The Fourth Wave: California's Newest Immigrants.* Washington, D.C. : The Urban Institute, 1984.

Nakanishi, Don T. "Asian American Politics: An Agenda for Research." *Amerasia Journal* 12 (1986a): 1-27.

_____. *The UCLA Asian Pacific American Voter Registration Study.* Los Angeles: Asian Pacific American Legal Center, 1986b.

_____. "Seeking Convergence in Race Relations Research: Japanese Americans and the Resurrection of the Internment." In *Eliminating*

Racism, edited by Phyllis A. Katz and Dalmas A. Taylor, 159-80. New York: Plenum Publishing Corporation, 1988.

————. "A Quota on Excellence? The Debate on Asian American Admissions." *Change* (November/December 1989): 38-47.

Nakanishi, Don, and Marsha Hirano-Nakanishi, eds. *The Education of Asian and Pacific Americans.* Phoenix, Arizona: Oryx Press, 1983.

Nee, Brett, and Victor Nee. *Longtime Californ': A Documentary Study of an American Chinatown.* Boston: Houghton Mifflin, 1974.

Ong, Paul. "California's Asian Population: Past Trends and Projections for the Year 2000." Los Angeles: Graduate School of Architecture and Urban Planning and the Asian American Studies Center, University of California, Los Angeles, 1989.

Saxton, Alexander. "The Army of Canton in the High Sierra." *Pacific Historical Review* 35 (1966): 141-52.

————. *The Indispensable Enemy.* Berkeley: University of California Press, 1971.

Sengstock, Mary C. "Social Change in the Country of Origin As A Factor in Immigrant Conceptions of Nationality." *Ethnicity* 4 (1977): 54-70.

Stokes, Bruce. "Learning the Game." *National Journal,* no. 43 (October 22, 1988): 2649-54.

Sue, Derek, and B. Kirk. "Differential Characteristics of Japanese and Chinese American College Students." *Journal of Counseling Psychology* 20 (1973): 142-48.

Sue, Stanley, and Amado Padilla. "Ethnic Minority Issues in the United States: Challenges for the Educational System." In *Beyond Language.* Bilingual Education Office, 35-72. Sacramento, California: California Department of Education, 1986.

Suzuki, Bob. "Education and Socialization of Asian Americans," *Amerasia Journal* 4 (1977): 23-51.

Tachibana, Judy. "California's Asians: Power from a Growing Population." *California Journal* 17 (1986): 534-43.

Takaki, Ronald. *Strangers From A Different Shore.* Boston: Little, Brown, and Company, 1989.

Tsai, Shih-Shan Henry. "The Emergence of Early Chinese Nationalist Organizations in America." *Amerasia Journal* 8 (1981): 121-44.

Tsuang, Grace. "Assuring Equal Access of Asian Americans to Highly Selective Universities." *Yale Law Journal* 98 (1989): 659-78.

Uhlaner, Carole, Bruce E. Cain, and D. Roderick Kiewiet. "Political Participation of Ethnic Minorities in the 1980s." *Social Sciences Working Paper,* no. 647, Division of Humanities and Social Sciences, California Institute of Technology, 1987.

UCLA Ethnic Studies Centers. *Ethnic Groups in Los Angeles: Quality of Life Indicators.* Los Angeles: UCLA Ethnic Studies Centers, 1987.

United States Commission on Civil Rights. *Civil Rights Issues of Asian and Pacific Americans: Myths and Realities.* Washington, D.C.: United States Commission on Civil Rights, 1979.

United Way, Asian Pacific Research and Development Council. *Pacific Profiles: A Demographic Study of the Asian Pacific Population in Los Angeles County.* Los Angeles: United Way, 1985.

Uyeda, Clifford. "The Pardoning of 'Tokyo Rose': A Report on the Restoration of American Citizenship to Iva Ikuko Toguri," *Amerasia Journal* 5 (1978): 69-94.

Wang, Ling-Chi. "*Lau v. Nichols:* History of a Struggle for Equal and Quality Education. In *Counterpoint,* edited by Emma Gee et al., 240-63. Los Angeles: UCLA Asian American Studies Center, 1976.

_____. "Meritocracy and Diversity in Higher Education: Discrimination Against Asian Americans in the Post-Bakke Era." *Urban Review* 20 (1988): 189-209.

Weglyn, Michi. *Years of Infamy.* New York: William Morrow, 1976.

Yoneda, Karl. *Ganbatte.* Los Angeles: UCLA Asian American Studies Center, 1983.

Yu, Eui-Yang. "Koreans in Los Angeles: Size, Distribution, and Composition." In *Koreans in Los Angeles,* edited by Eui-Young et al., 23-48. Los Angeles: Korean and Korean American Studies Program, California State University, Los Angeles, 1982.

Yu, Renqiu. "Chinese American Contributions to the Educational Development of Toisan, 1910-1940." *Amerasia Journal* 10 (1983): 47-72.

CHAPTER 3

SUSAN ANDERSON
Journalist

Rivers of Water in a Dry Place—Early Black Participation in California Politics

The statute books and the common law, the great bulwark of society, which should be to us as the rivers of water in a dry place, like the shadow of a great rock in a weary land, where wretched should find sympathy and the weak protection, spurn us with contempt and rule us from their very threshold and deny us our common humanity.

—Proceedings of the State Convention of the Colored Citizens of California, Sacramento, 1855.

INTRODUCTION

Black politics in California are as old as the state itself. Indeed, if one examines the history of the state prior to admission to the Union, it could be argued that black political participation began with the Mexican era. Not only were many citizens of Mexico of mixed and African descent, but historians have shown that the state's first governor, Pio Pico, was of mixed Spanish and African descent, a mulatto who rose to power in Alta California. During the gold rush era and following the entry of California into the U.S., black political expression began to be articulated on a wide range of issues that were to affect large numbers of residents for many decades to come.

During the first 50 years of California statehood, black political activity was conducted outside the official structures of electoral power, for obvious reasons: blacks had been excluded from such participation by law as well as custom, violence, and threats. Black political history in the state, however, is not so much a story of white repression of black civic involvement. Rather, it is a revealing drama of black California's increasing political sophistication and concomitant power and presence on the state's political stage.

Although the black population in California remained small, hovering between 4,000 and 6,000 by the end of the 19th century, its impact on state politics and its ability to pursue its own political ends had preternatural power. The black population constituted about 1 percent of the total residents in the state in the 19th century. Those numbers would grow dramatically in the 1920s and 1930s; however, one thing remained constant. Blacks in California have always been a smaller proportion of the state's population than other people of color. At various times in the state's history the Chinese, Indian, Japanese and, later, once immigration expanded, Mexican populations outweighed blacks in California. Compared with the other groups, however, blacks historically have been perhaps the most unified, aggressive, and successful in their various campaigns.

There are several reasons why this may be true. One, the freed black population that immigrated to the state in the first place was often educated and materially well off. Many were veterans of the abolitionist movement and brought with them sophisticated political skills. In addition, the frontier provided opportunities for some blacks to gain wealth, opportunities not available elsewhere. Two, since California entered the Union as a free state, the structure of laws, codes, and restrictions against blacks elsewhere in the country were not as intense in the Golden State. Blacks found discrimination in the West to have its own peculiarities. However, they also found avenues of redress, such as the courts and sympathetic white legislators, particular to the region as well. Third, the black movement itself had been active in the U.S. since the 18th century. Blacks in California had the benefit of more than 100 years of collective experience in the fight against slavery. The black church, mutual aid societies, political networks, and a tradition of oratory and organizing antedated the black experience in California and, perhaps, provided 19th century blacks in the state with an advanced place along the political learning curve.

Blacks in California in this period also exhibited certain political traits that would be evident in the 20th century. Black politics was an exclusive and pragmatic affair, rarely addressing the, at times, more repressive conditions for other people of color. Black political leadership in the 19th century was unable or unwilling to build coalitions with such groups. Also, the character of California's black political concerns was distinctly middle class. Although wealthier blacks were engaged in charitable giving and aid for the poor within the black community, the poor themselves were nearly absent as the subject of black politics. Advocates for black farmers, workers, and the poor were rarely among the most outspoken of black political leaders. Finally, black leaders in 19th century California seemed less inclined toward the insurrectionary fervor that was a distinct part of black political discourse in the rest of the country. This may have been due partly to California sitting out the Civil War—the state was not required to send troops to the Union and one year was even exempt from the draft—and escaping its bloodiest consequences. Also, black Californians perhaps resembled their counterparts in the state who, according to one writer, "never thought of themselves as being part of the Union. Nothing expresses this relationship quite so clearly as the then popular phrase, 'back in the states.'"[1]

Black politics in California in the 19th century rested on a dichotomy, perhaps still in evidence. On the one hand, there was the abiding vision expressed by one migrant to the state, " . . . we always had the impression that going to California was like going to heaven, there is no racism—you do what you want."[2] On the other hand, as the state's political leadership discovered through experience, W. E. B. DuBois was accurate when he wrote that California "is not Paradise, much as the sight of its lilies and roses might lead one at first to believe. The color line is there sharply drawn."[3]

SLAVERY

A German visitor during the Gold Rush noted that wealthy black Californians "exhibit a great deal of energy and intelligence in saving their brothers" and were "especially talented" in aiding runaway slaves.

—William Loren Katz, *The Black West*

From its inception as a state, California politics were centered on the status of blacks within its borders. The debate over statehood for California occurred during the extraordinary political events leading up to the Civil War. California became "an apple of contention" between free and slave states represented in the U.S. Congress.[4] Leaders in the state "settled the question for themselves . . . by adopting a state constitution and applying for admission to the Union" in 1850.[5] That constitution contained an amendment stating that "neither slavery nor involuntary servitude, unless for punishment of crimes, shall ever be tolerated in this state."

Despite the illegality of slave-holding in California, early black inhabitants of the state found that they still had to combat its practice. California had its own Fugitive Slave Law and complied with such national laws as well. California's law, however, granted slaveowners only the most

---

[1]Carey McWilliams, *California: The Great Exception* (Current Books, 1949), 60.

[2]Black Angelenos, "The Afro-American in Los Angeles, 1850-1950" (California Afro-American Museum exhibit book, June 11, 1988-March 6, 1989), 10.

[3]Quoted in Rudolph M. Lapp, *Afro-Americans in California* (San Francisco: Boyd and Fraser Publishing Co., 1987), 39.

[4]McWilliams, *op. cit.*, 42.

[5]*Ibid.*, 43, 44.

limited rights of property. Only "visitors" to the state were allowed to hold slaves. Once ownership of a slave was established, the slaveowner was "required to remove the slave from the state." Indeed, if slaves were kept in the state beyond a minimum of established time, they were considered free by law.

Robert Owens was one of the black pioneers in the state who participated in antislavery activities under the new state's constitution. Owens, one of the largest property owners in downtown Los Angeles, was instrumental in bringing a court case against a slave owner in 1856. The owner illegally kept 14 slaves in bondage in the Santa Monica Canyon. When the slaves were brought to court under a writ of *habeas corpus*, the court decided that the entire group should have their freedom.[6] One of those freed by the court's action was Biddy Mason, who was to become one of the most prominent, wealthy, and active members of the Los Angeles black community before she died in 1891.

By far the most notorious case regarding the legal status of a slave in California was the Archy Lee case of 1858. It was said to rival the Dred Scott decision "in significance and interest."[7] After much legal and public circumlocution, the state supreme court heard and decided the case. Justice Burnett, especially, made known his antiliberty views in the court's decision to return Archy to his owner. As a consequence, newspapers in Sacramento and San Francisco asserted their harsh criticisms of the decision, going as far as calling Burnett "a jackass." Editors, along with California's black and white abolitionists, were dismayed at the decision, which the *San Francisco Chronicle* claimed seemed to "abrogate the Constitution, annul the law, and defeat the will of the people of the state" by demonstrating that California was a slave state.[8]

Eventually, Archy Lee was set at liberty by U.S. Commissioner Johnson. His case highlights California's ambivalence toward slavery in the years before the Civil War settled the issue by drastic means. And it shows the early political environment with which California blacks had to contend. Indeed, California's black political organizations, including the Colored Convention, were thoroughly occupied with the Archy Lee case, which occurred during the midst of the campaign to gain the right to testify in California's courts. But the black movement in the 19th century was required to maintain a wide scope in its response to unexpected crises.

---

[6]W. Sherman Savage, *Blacks in the West* (Westport, Connecticut: Greenwood Press, 1976), 40.

[7]William E. Franklin, "The Archy Case," *Pacific Historical Review* 22 (February 1963).

[8]Savage, *op. cit.*, 153.

IMMIGRATION

We desire only a white population in California.
—Californian Newspaper, March 5, 1849

The first battle over immigration to California had blacks as its main source of contention. Nineteenth-century inhabitants of the state had little idea that immigration would become one of the recurring themes of California politics, through the twentieth century and current times. Nevertheless, California's initial political debates over black immigration set the tone for the state's ongoing controversies regarding immigration.

According to one of California's most astute analysts, Cary McWilliams, "If the future can be seen in a crystal ball, the past can be discerned in a mirror. The face of California is the face of the immigrant nation, but it is California that has been the preeminent destination of immigrants since the 19th century."[9]

The gold rush drew unprecedented numbers of seekers of wealth to California. The pattern of immigration to the state shows whites from Ireland and Germany, as well as from the East coast and slave-holding southern states of the U.S., with the largest numbers. By the 1800s, Chinese immigrants were about 10 percent of the state's population and "constituted the state's largest foreign-born group and the largest nonwhite minority."[10] Also, during the last decades of the 19th century, Japanese immigration increased severalfold, going from 2,000 in the entire U.S. in 1890 to 41,000 in 1910 in California alone.[11]

Among the newcomers to the state were groups of freed blacks and black slaves, some of whom gained their liberty through wage earnings in the mines. Blacks were able to establish themselves in the mines with individual claims and in black-owned mining companies, such as "Negro Bar with 700 people in 1851" and "Negro Hill . . . named after subsequent Negro miners in 1849, had in 1853 over 1,000 inhabitants."[12] However, the number of blacks in California from the 1840s gold rush era until the late 19th century was only around 1 percent of the total state population.

However, these small numbers did not prevent blacks from being the focus of anti-immigrant agitation in the earliest days of California's self-government. Nativist sentiments, though incongruously expressed by

---

[9]McWilliams, *op. cit.*, 21.

[10]Charles Wollenberg, *All Deliberate Speed* (Berkeley: University of California Press, 1976), 30.

[11]*Ibid.*, 49.

[12]Odell A. Thurman, *The Negro in California Before 1890* (Rail Research Associates, reprinted 1973), 29-30.

immigrants themselves in and out of government, characterized the state's politics. And they were first and most powerfully articulated against black immigrants to California.

This was reflected in the meeting of the first Constitutional Convention of the state of California in Monterey in 1849, which was marked by a vociferous debate regarding the exclusion of free Negroes from the state. It is said that convention delegates "spent more time debating whether to exclude black migrants from the state than on any other topic."[13] Pro-exclusion delegates argued in favor of a resolution to inhibit black settlement in California, saying, "You will find the country flooded with a population of free Negroes—the greatest calamity that could befall California."[14] This exclusion resolution was defeated in that session. In 1857 a bill was introduced into the state legislature that was "designed to regulate the immigration of free blacks who might come to the state after October 1, 1858."[15] Among its opponents were the California Colored Convention and leaders such as black clergyman and equal rights activist, Reverend J. J. Moore, who spoke against it during the legislative session in Sacramento.[16] The bill was defeated by the legislature.

During the public furor over blacks' right to immigrate to California, a group of black residents estimated at 65 met in San Francisco in 1858 to discuss emigrating to Vancouver, British Columbia. It is not known exactly how many made the journey and took up citizenship, but it is believed that Archy Lee, the former slave of legal fame, was among them. The group decided to leave because they "were fully convinced that the aim, spirit, and policy of the mother country was to oppress, degrade, and outrage them."[17] Although this was a singular event in California, it was an expression of the pre-Civil War times that found many free blacks throughout the United States despairing of their political fate.

As one writer discussing the state's anti-immigration law put it, "The opposition to foreigners was not one of nationality then; it was one of race. Nowhere have I found evidence of open hostility to foreign whites. Rather, the opposition was directed toward those people of color who were easily distinguished—the Chinese, the Indian, the Negro, and even the Mexicans, whether from Mexico or natives of the soil. . . ."[18] Although black exclusion was never made law, the state's political battle over this issue

---

[13]William Loren Katz, *The Black West* (New York: Anchor Press/Doubleday, 1973), 124.

[14]*Ibid.*, 124.

[15]Savage, *op. cit.*, 15.

[16]*Ibid.*, 16.

[17]*Ibid.*, 143.

[18]Thurman, *op. cit.*, 40.

paved the way for restrictive laws concerning black participation in California's civic life. And the state's opposition to immigrants of color was consolidated in preparation for the coming periods of legal exclusions of Chinese, Japanese, and Mexican newcomers.

THE RIGHT OF TESTIMONY

You have enacted a law, excluding our testimony in the courts of justice in this State, in cases of proceedings wherein white persons are parties; thus openly encouraging and countenancing the vicious and dishonest to take advantage of us; a law which while it does not advantage you, is a great wrong to us . . . People of California! We entreat you to repeal that unjust law.

—Proceedings of the First State Convention of the Colored Citizens of the State of California, Sacramento, 1855

In 1850 the California legislature passed a law (extended later to include Chinese residents) prohibiting blacks and native Americans from testifying in court. The law itself stated, "No black or mulatto person or Indian shall be permitted to give evidence in favor of or against any white person. Every person who shall have one-eighth part or more of Negro blood shall be deemed a mulatto, and every person who shall have one-half Indian blood shall be deemed an Indian." This move on the part of the California legislature sparked a political fight lasting more than a decade that united the state's blacks against the antitestimony law and provided a focus for the black community's earliest push for civil rights.

Several dramatic cases demonstrated the shackling effect the law had for blacks. One case involved the murder of a black barber in his own shop by a white man. In this case, a fair-skinned witness to the crime was disqualified as a witness because "he had one-sixteenth part of a drop of Negro blood."[19] The other eyewitness was white and identified the attacker. Well-known black businessman, Mifflin Wistar Gibbs, was robbed "in broad daylight" when a pair of whites took off with stolen boots "and walked off laughing."[20] Later, a judge threw out the testimony of a black sailor who had witnessed the murder of his white fellow shipmate.[21] In addition, as one protester argued, the law against black testimony was

---

[19]*Ibid.*, 41-42.

[20]Lapp, *op. cit.*, 8.

[21]James A. Fisher, "The Struggle for Negro Testimony in California, 1851-1863" (Historical Society of Southern California, December 1969), 317.

dangerous to the whites of the state as well in cases where the only witness to a crime was a black person. "Murderers and arsonists . . . may go unpunished because only a colored man saw the act or heard the plot . . . is it not evident that the white citizen is an equal sufferer with us? When will the people of this state learn that justice to the colored man is justice to themselves."[22]

Several petitions were brought before the state legislature asking for changes in California's testimony laws. Indeed, a petition movement was begun, lasting several years and including blacks from many legislative districts in the state. However, according to the San Francisco black newspaper, *Pacific Appeal*, they were "met with adverse fate; they were either indignantly thrown out the window, or laid on the table. . . ."[23] But the petition movement was superseded by the formation of the State Convention of the Colored Citizens of California, first convened in 1855.

The Colored Convention, a series of statewide meetings in Sacramento between 1855 and 1882, was the premiere political organization of California's black population in the 19th century. Formed originally to protest and remove the state's prejudicial testimony laws, the convention developed into a force for the redress of black inequality in public life in California.[24]

Two of the leaders of the California Colored Convention, William H. Yates and Reverend Jeremiah B. Sanderson, were veterans of the 19th century black protest movement. Yates, from Philadelphia, was an ex-slave, abolitionist pamphleteer, and conveyor of slaves along the Underground Railroad. Sanderson was a colleague of Frederick Douglass. However, according to Fisher, the character of the California Colored Convention, even under the leadership of these two, exhibited "a certain restraint and sobriety often absent in those of abolitionist persuasion."[25] This may have been for several reasons. One, because California had outlawed slavery in its constitution, that fight was less consuming than in other states. Two,

---

[22]Proceedings of the First State Colored Convention of California, Sacramento, 1855.

[23]Fisher, *op. cit.,* 314.

[24]The State Convention of the Colored Citizens of California was an outgrowth of the National Negro Convention, formed in 1830 in Philadelphia and periodically active through 1864. The National Negro Convention and the various state black conventions were one of the primary vehicles for free blacks' sustained efforts to win abolition for southern slaves and equality and economic elevation for the black population in northern states. The proceedings and effects of the negro conventions have been well documented by historians; however, it should be stated that they, along with their California counterpart, played a powerful, if relatively unknown role in establishing the black movement not only in the 19th century, but in the 20th as well.

[25]Fisher, *op. cit.,* 316.

California's black population during this period tended, on an average, to be fairly wealthy. In 1857 the *San Francisco Daily Evening Bulletin* estimated black property in that city to total $5 million for a population of fewer than 4,000. And one writer asserts that 19th century "Afro-Americans in California were . . . matching, if not exceeding, the wealth of their counterparts in the eastern states."[26] Finally, like other races, the blacks who had emigrated to the state had come far in order to settle what was still the frontier. The awareness of being "at the end of line" may have influenced a certain willingness to engender levels of cooperation with other Californians.

At any rate, the first Colored Convention session in 1855 "had no effect on the state legislation" barring blacks and others of color from court testimony.[27] But the convention movement grew. Between 1855 and 1865, the scope of the Colored Convention included the fight against the state's immigration and fugitive slave laws dramatized in the case of Archy Lee. It took the outbreak of the Civil War, increased agitation, and three conventions to win the California legislature's repeal of the prohibitions against blacks' court testimony in 1893.

This repeal, however, did not extend to Indians and Chinese in the state who were also singled out by the testimony law. Not only did the black leadership of the convention movement limit its advocacy to the black right to testimony, there was a calculated effort to exclude the others. The black newspaper, the *Pacific Appeal*, for instance, reminded its readers that "a more plausible excuse might be offered for depriving the Indian and Chinese of their oaths than the colored Americans: they being heathens and not comprehending the nature and obligation of our oath or obligations which would be binding on their consciences."[28]

The struggle for testimony highlighted an important dilemma for black political leadership in the state: the desirability and possibility of coalition with other people of color who suffered, sometimes more severely than financially comfortable blacks, from legal restrictions based upon race prejudice. In the last years of the century, such coalitions were strenuously avoided by the state's experienced black leadership. Blacks themselves seemed to share some of the bigotry of whites, and "Negroes . . . ignored the idea that justice for all should be equal for all—for Chinese as well as Negroes."[29] Among others, pragmatism was raised as an argument against coalitions. Some at the first Colored Convention argued that the white supporters of blacks would not support equal testimony for Chinese and

---

[26]Lapp, *op. cit.,* 7.
[27]Fisher, *op. cit.,* 317.
[28]*Ibid.,* 320.
[29]*Ibid.,* 320.

Indians. "So they agitated only for their own group. The expression 'third world solidarity' would not be heard until over a hundred years later."[30]

SUFFRAGE

We still believe this to be a white man's government, and the extension of the natural rights to the Negro is degrading, impolitic, and unnatural.

—Union Party Statement, Yuba County, 1865

The vote in California prior to 1870 was explicitly denied to blacks as well as to Indians, Chinese, and nonwhite Mexicans. However, it was the combination of experienced black political leadership and post-Civil War political compulsions that extended the franchise "regardless of race, color, or previous condition of servitude."

W. Sherman Savage tells of the isolated attempts by blacks to register to vote in California prior to the Civil War. "The experience of a black man known as 'Old Gabe' was shared by many others," Savage says. "He applied to Harry Dixon, Clerk of the Fresno County Court, for registration to vote. Dixon refused him. . . ."[31] And the incident of Joseph Francis of Rattlesnake, California, was also indicative of blacks' inability to participate in electoral politics. Francis "was known only as a name when he went to the Republican Convention at Auburn. Without debate, he was selected as delegate to the State Convention, but because the California Constitution denied citizenship to Negroes, Francis was removed when his race was discovered."[32] There were other cases of blacks who threatened to sue in the highest courts for the right to vote.

Once the testimony struggle was won, black leadership in the state focused on winning the vote. At the 1865 Colored Convention, "this demand had become a burning issue for blacks and many whites as well."[33] The Colored Convention was joined in this effort by a new organization—the Franchise League—and they "bombarded the legislature with petitions recommending an amendment to the state constitution."[34] At its 1865 convention in Sacramento, the League's Committee on Elective Franchise presented an appeal that was sent to Sacramento. The document asked for

---

[30]Lapp, *op. cit.*, 9.

[31]Savage, *op. cit.*, 157.

[32]Kenneth G. Goode, *California's Black Pioneers* (Santa Barbara: McNally and Loftin, 1973), 80.

[33]Royce D. Delmatier, Clarence F. McIntosh, and Earl G. Waters, editors, *The Rumble of California Politics, 1848-1970* (New York: John Wiley and Sons).

[34]Lapp, *op. cit.*, 17.

"an amendment to the Constitution of California . . . so that the same may read as hereinafter set forth, to the end that American citizens of African descent . . . may be admitted to the rights of suffrage and citizenship to the State of California."[35]

Whites such as State Senator Thomas Hart Benton sponsored measures to extend the franchise.[36] However, the attempts to encourage passage of a state law extending the franchise to California blacks failed. They did not receive the vote until 1870, with the passage of the Fifteenth Amendment to the U.S. Constitution.

Even though blacks did begin to vote in greater numbers after 1870, their constitutional right to do so existed in a peculiar legal limbo. Republican-turned-Democratic Governor Haight had made known his opposition to extending the franchise in California beyond whites, and he had referred several times to his repugnance toward the black vote. When he submitted the constitutional amendment to the legislature for ratification, he successfully agitated against it referring to California's largest populations of color.

"If this Amendment is adopted, the most degraded Digger Indian . . . becomes at once an elector . . . also, by a slight amendment to the naturalization laws, the Chinese population could be made electors."[37]

The Fifteenth Amendment was not ratified by the state legislature until 1962, 92 years after it had become part of the U.S. Constitution. This was not corrected until State Senator Albert S. Rodda sponsored a measure that finally achieved ratification.[38]

The failure of the state to ratify the Fifteenth Amendment did not prevent black Californians' involvement in electoral politics, although there was resistance to black registration, voting, and party involvement. However, black leadership in the state organized political participation in the era following the Civil War with an energy similar to prewar struggles. At the same time, historian Rudolph Lapp notes that the state government's failure to extend the franchise contributed to California blacks' enduring belief that the national government was the more likely source of their redress.

EDUCATION

The necessity of establishing schools for the education of our youth would seem too evident to need urging. And yet, there

---

[35]Thurman, *op. cit.*, 54.

[36]Brainerd Dyer, "One Hundred Years of Negro Sufferage," *Pacific Historical Review* (February 1968), 9.

[37]Rumble, *op. cit.*, 34.

[38]Katz, *op. cit.*, 134.

*is scarcely a village or town in California that possesses a
common school for the education of colored children . . . we
are compelled to pay taxes for the support of those already
established, and from which our children are excluded. . . .
Without schools for the education of . . . the next generation
of actors on this great stage, we cannot expect our condition
to be permanently improved. . . ."*
—*Letter to the Editor, Mirror of the Times, December 1857*

From the passage of its first public school laws in 1851, California
exhibited an unwillingness to provide public education for its children of
color. Under the administration of the state's first two superintendents of
public instruction, laws were consolidated that established the public support
of California's burgeoning school system. Blacks, too, paid taxes, which
supported these early schools. However, in 1855 California school laws were
amended to state that public funds would be distributed to schools based
upon the count of white students only. At the same time, Paul K. Hubbs,
the second school chief in the state, made clear California's intention to
maintain segregation based upon race. "Our public school system permits
no mixture of the races," he was reported as having said in the *Sacramento
Daily Union* in 1855. "Whilst I will foster by all proper means the education
of the races, I should deem it a death blow to our system to permit the
mixture of the races in the same school."[39]
It was during the administration of California's third state
superintendent of public instruction, A. J. Moulder, that "whites only"
privileges became entrenched in state school law. Moulder pronounced that
"the schools of California were intended for whites alone."[40] And he
added, "to force African, Chinese, and Diggers into one school . . . must
result in the ruin of the schools. The great mass of our citizens will not
associate in terms of equality with these inferior races; nor will they consent
that their children do so."[41] At the same time, local communities resisted
maintaining educational facilities for pupils of color because of the lack of
available state funding. In 1860 Moulder successfully argued to the state
legislature to withhold funds from school districts "that permit the admission
of the inferior races—African, Mongolian, or Indian—into the Common
Schools."[42]

---

[39]Savage, *op. cit.*, 170.

[40]Wollenberg, *op. cit.*, 13.

[41]Irving Hendricks, *California Education: A Brief History* (San Francisco: Boyd
and Fraser Publishing Co., 1980), 10.

[42]Goode, *op. cit.*, 82.

Because of such racism, black students did not attend public schools and only began to receive education when private black schools were established in the 1850s in Sacramento and San Francisco. Following that, private black schools were set up "in San Jose, Stockton, Marysville, Chico, Grass Valley, Red Bluff, Oakland, and other cities with sizeable black populations."[43]

By 1870 the public education laws were rewritten to read that "the education of Indian children and children of African descent should be provided for in separate schools," although the state was yet reticent in claiming its responsibility, even for such segregated schooling.[44] Local communities retained the power to assign students, and it required the diligent agitation of black parents to ensure they had even segregated facilities.

Black leadership in California became dissatisfied with the limitations of private and public schools for blacks. They felt a political solution to the situation was required. The Education Committee of the Franchise League reported in 1865 that funds were needed to support a black school in San Jose. But the emphasis of that gathering was on fighting for "more educational advantages" from state-run schools, which their taxes supported.[45] By the 1870s, the status of black education was "distressing," consisting of "second-rate school facilities funded by local government and paid in part by taxes levied on black parents." The black weekly, the *Pacific Appeal*, described conditions for black school children in San Francisco: "The main school on Russian Hill . . . resembles a picture of Noah's Ark landed on Mount Ararat, and the other, a small room rented by the Board of Education, is a dwelling house in the neighborhood of Fifth and Folsom Streets. There are 43 or more splendidly built school houses in the city . . . while colored children have to travel the two extremes of the city to gratify the prejudices of proscription."[46]

Black leadership in the state convened an Education Convention in Stockton in 1871. Their first action, led, among others, by the most distinguished black pedagogue in California, the Reverend Jeremiah B. Sanderson, was to ask the legislature to amend public school codes to end segregation of black students. The meeting demanded an end to "caste schools."[47] Again, black leaders followed what they believed to be the road of political pragmatism and focused on their own—"children of African descent"—in their advocacy.

---

[43]*Ibid.*, 83.
[44]Thurman, *op. cit.*, 47.
[45]Lapp, *op. cit.*, 21-23.
[46]Wollenberg, *op. cit.*, 19.
[47]*Ibid.*, 23.

In 1872 two bills were introduced into the legislature that would require the removal of all mention of race in school laws as well as open admission to all children. When the legislation was defeated, black parents and activists launched a campaign that culminated in a decision by the California Supreme Court in 1874. After a group of black parents were kept from enrolling their children in all-white schools in San Francisco, they retained an attorney to represent the grievance of Mary Ward, a black pupil.

The State Supreme Court decision disappointed black leaders. It upheld maintaining separate schools based upon race in an opinion that anticipated the famous *Plessy v. Ferguson* case by 22 years. "We regard it as a compromise . . . to satiate the prejudice of color phobists . . . and the growing sentiment, even among liberal-minded Democrats," declared the *Pacific Appeal.*[48] But historians have noted that the decision at least had the effect of altering state laws to guarantee black children access to public education. And by 1890, as the outcome of another case of litigation on behalf of a black high school plaintiff, the state supreme court pronounced that "separate schools cannot be established for colored children."[49] The same was not true for other children of color.

THE END OF A POLITICAL ERA

In view of our peculiar situation here (in California), we must oppose all forms of separation.
                                        —*Oakland Sunshine*, March 20, 1915

By the end of the 19th century, black Californians could draw upon a half-century of increasingly sophisticated and effective political action. At the same time, with the attainment of the vote, especially, black politics grew increasingly preoccupied with official party matters. However, blacks were less interested in regular party issues than they were in how those parties stood on issues concerning the welfare of blacks. This duality of emphasis, with the most prominent being on black rights and status, would become an enduring feature of black politics in California.

Black political leadership remained vigorous in the state and found its expression in both the Republican party as well as new formations based on black concerns for equal rights, such as the Afro-American Leagues. In 1891 the Afro-American Leagues replaced the Colored Convention as the main vehicle for organized black political expression and the pressure for civil rights. The small black population formed Republican clubs, fought

---

[48]*Ibid.*, 23.
[49]*Wysinger v. Crookshank*, 82 CAL. 588 720 (1890).

and won a public accommodations act, pushed and achieved the right to sit on juries, and formed other organizations to carry out their civic programs.

By the start of the modern era in California politics, California blacks had grown in numbers and had established branches of national organizations such as the NAACP and Urban League in cities around the state. In 1919 black Republican Frederick M. Roberts was elected to the state assembly from a district in Los Angeles. Roberts had prevailed over a white opponent who, believing that an outburst of race hatred would be enough to defeat the black candidate, distributed buttons to voters declaring, "My Opponent is a Nigger." Roberts' most noted political achievement was the success of legislation to prevent the use of antiblack materials in public school texts. When Roberts was defeated by 27-year-old New Deal Democrat, Augustus Hawkins, in 1934, the previous era of black politics had come to a definite close.

CHAPTER 4

HARRY PACHON
Pitzer College

U.S. Citizenship and Latino Participation in California Politics

Congress shall have the power to . . . establish a uniform Rule of Naturalization.
—Article One, Section 8 of the U.S. Constitution

Naturalization is the process by which legal immigrants acquire citizenship in this country. Despite the fact that the naturalization process confers on the successful applicant a status virtually equivalent to the U.S. citizenship of native-born Americans, little attention has been placed on the process by which immigrants become citizens.[1]

A reason for this may be that, on the surface, the basic requirements for immigrants who wish to pursue U.S. citizenship are straightforward. These requirements are as follows:

• legal residence for five or more years (three years if married to a U.S. citizen);

• demonstration of good moral character and not being a public charge;

• the successful completion of an exam on spoken and written English and U.S. history and government administered by an Immigration and Naturalization Service (INS) examiner (applicants 50 years of age and older who have lived in the U.S. for more than 20 years are exempt from this requirement).

As a nation, the naturalization process will become increasingly important. If current trends continue, by the turn of the century naturaliza-

---

[1]For a historical view of how the concept of naturalization developed in the U.S., see James H. Kettner, *The Development of American Citizenship, 1608-1870* (Chapel Hill: University of North Carolina Press, 1978). For an early 20th century perspective see John Gavitt, *Americans by Choice* (New York: Harper and Brothers Publishers, 1922).

tion will add 500,000 or more new U.S. citizens each year.[2] With steadily declining birth rates, naturalization, even at current rates, could account for 7.4 percent of new citizens each year by the year 2000. Moreover, under the newly enacted amnesty program, approximately 3 million undocumented immigrants, 90 percent of whom are Latino, may be eligible for U.S. citizenship through the naturalization process beginning in 1993.

Although naturalization may be one of the most basic behavioral political acts an immigrant can undertake, most literature on immigration assumes that naturalization is the automatic final step in the immigration process.[3] A quick look at the facts indicates otherwise. Some immigrants never politically integrate into American society despite their permanent resident status. Little data are collected on these individuals. However, some estimates can be made. The 1980 census shows that only half of 14 million foreign-born residents are naturalized. Among the nonnaturalized are 1.3 million Europeans, 1.6 million Asians, and 3.4 million Latin Americans. In each of the last three decades, immigration has exceeded naturalization by a factor of 3 or 4. In this century, only two decades (the 1930s an the 1940s) saw naturalization exceed immigration (see Table 1). Currently, no other immigrant community has an incidence of nonnaturalization higher than Latino immigrants.[4]

NONCITIZENSHIP IN THE LATINO COMMUNITY

Nationwide, the census has found that one out of every three Latino adults in this country is not a U.S. citizen. In the 1988 presidential elections, there were more Latinos ineligible to vote due to noncitizenship than there were Latino registered voters (see Figure 1).

---

[2]U.S. Bureau of the Census, *Population Projections of the Hispanic Population 1983 to 2080* (Current Population Reports, Series No. 995), 25, (U.S. Government Printing Office: Washington, D.C. November 1986).

[3]Louis DeSipio, "Social Science Literature and the Naturalization Process," *International Migration Review*, vol. 21, no. 2 (Summer 1987): 390-405. For an overview of social science and research on citizenship in the Hispanic community see the naturalization symposium published in the *International Migration Review*, Summer 1987.

[4]Harry P. Pachon, "An Overview of Citizenship in the Hispanic Community," *International Migration Review* 21 (Summer 1987). The incidence of noncitizenship among Mexican immigrants has been observed since the early decades of this century. For an overview of the importance of citizenship in the Hispanic community see *First National Conference on Citizenship and the Hispanic Community: Proceedings* (Washington, D.C.: NALEO Educational Fund, 1985).

Table 1: *Immigration and Naturalization: 1907-1986*

	Immigrants Admitted	Naturalizations Awarded
1907-1910	3,861,575	111,738
1911-1920	5,735,811	1,128,972
1921-1930	4,107,209	1,173,185
1931-1940	528,431	1,518,464
1941-1950	1,035,039	1,987,028
1951-1960	2,515,479	1,189,946
1961-1970	3,321,677	1,120,263
1971-1980	4,493,314	1,464,772
1981-1986	3,466,114	1,241,316

Note: Data on naturalization was not collected by the federal government prior to 1907.
Source: U.S. Department of Justice, U.S. Immigration and Naturalization Service, *1986 Statistical Yearbook of the Immigration and Naturalization Service*, Washington, D.C.: Government Printing Office, 1987.

Not only is the incidence of noncitizenship high among Latino immigrants, but the rates of naturalization among Hispanic immigrants is among the lowest of all immigrant groups. For example, the average European, and Asian immigrant waits about seven to eight years before naturalizing. In contrast Hispanic immigrants wait about 14 to 15 years.

U.S. citizenship, however, has been traditionally overlooked as a significant factor in the Hispanic community's empowerment. The reasons for this are many. Foremost among these reasons is that many categorize the legal status of Latinos in the U.S. into two simple groups:
• Latino immigrants, who they perceive are all illegal aliens; and
• all other Latinos—the native-born.

The reality of the legal status of Latinos in this country is considerably more complex. Significant segments of the adult Latino population include:
• native-born Latino U.S. citizens;
• foreign-born Latino naturalized U.S. citizens;
• foreign-born Latino legal resident immigrants;
• foreign-born undocumented Latino immigrants eligible for legalization under the Immigration Reform and Control Act of 1986 (IRCA);
• foreign-born Latinos awarded temporary legal status in the U.S. as refugees or asylees; and
• foreign-born Latino undocumented immigrants who are not eligible or who did not apply for amnesty under IRCA.

While considerable attention has been placed on the growing political potential of native-born Hispanics as well as on the problems of Latino

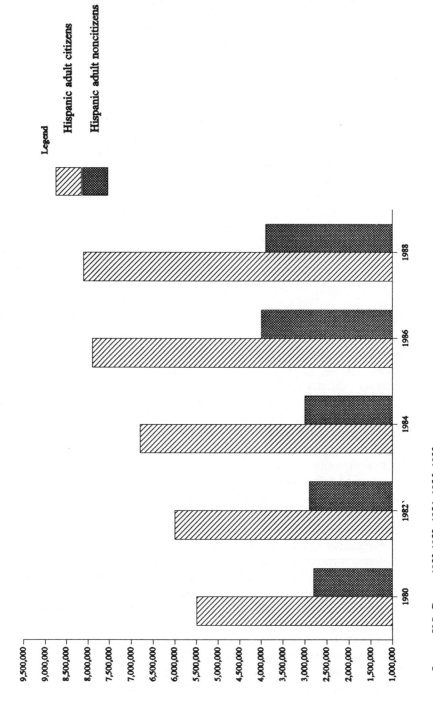

Figure 1: *Hispanic Adults Ineligible to Vote Because of Noncitizenship, 1980–1988*

Legend

Hispanic adult citizens

Hispanic adult noncitizens

Source: U.S. Census, 1980–1982, 1984, 1986, 1988.

undocumented immigrants, the staggeringly high number of Latino legal immigrants has been consistently overlooked by the media, political analysts, and even the scholarly community. Yet Latino legal immigration to this country has constituted a significant segment of all legal immigration for the past five decades.

As Tables 2 and 3 indicate, Latino *legal* immigration continued to be high. During this past decade more than 1.5 million legal Latino immigrants have entered this country from different Latin American countries.

The cumulative impact of this immigration is most pronounced in those states with large Hispanic populations. Figure 2 indicates the percentage of adult foreign-born Hispanics who were not U.S. citizens in selected states in 1980.

CONSEQUENCES OF NONCITIZENSHIP

The large numbers of legal Latino noncitizens permanently residing in this country have consequences for American society at large and the greater Hispanic community. The foundations of our democratic government are built on individual and community-based representation in the political system. Having large segments of what is soon-to-be the largest ethnic minority in this country ineligible to participate in the political system because of noncitizenship thus affects the basic principles of American democratic government. The powerlessness and political alienation that have been attributed to the Hispanic community may result in part from the presence of large numbers of legal resident aliens who are excluded from participation in many aspects of the political process, and in many cases, are recent immigrants who have not had the time to develop an understanding of the U.S. political process.

Another and less well-noted consequence of having large numbers of individuals ineligible to participate in the political process is the potential effect on accountability of publicly elected officials, who may believe that they can ignore those constituents who cannot participate.

Other civic consequences of noncitizenship include restrictions on holding elected office and serving on juries. The latter is relevant to the underrepresentation of Hispanics on juries in most urban areas. This underrepresentation may be attributable not only to institutional discrimination, (e.g., exclusion of Hispanics from jury selection panels), but also to the existence of a pool of eligible jurors that is considerably smaller than the Hispanic population from which the jurors are selected.

There are a host of other rights and benefits that are not available to Hispanic legal residents because of noncitizenship. These include:

•Exclusion from most federal government positions, state and local public safety positions, and in some states, public school teaching positions;

Table 2:   *Legal Immigration Rates From Selected Latin American Nations and Regions*

	Mexican	Dominican Republic	Central America	South America
1977	44,079	11,655	16,485	32,965
1978	92,367	19,458	20,153	41,764
1979	52,096	17,519	17,547	35,344
1980	56,680	17,245	20,968	39,717
1981	101,268	18,220	24,509	35,913
1982	56,106	17,451	23,626	35,448
1983	59,076	22,058	24,601	36,087
1984	57,557	23,147	24,088	37,460
1985	61,077	23,787	26,302	39,058
1986	66,533	26,175	38,380	41,874
1987	72,351	24,858	29,296	44,385
Total	719,190	221,573	255,955	420,015

Source: U.S. Department of Justice, U.S. Immigration and Naturalization Service, *Statistical Yearbook of the Immigration and Naturalization Service: 1987*, Washington D.C.: Goverment Printing Office, 1988, Table 3, pp. 6-7.

Table 3:   *Latino Legal Immigrants From Selected Latin American Countries into Selected States in 1988*

	Columbia	Cuba	Dominican Republic	El Salvador	Mexico	Total Latino
California	771	645	55	6,829	53,622	61,922
Illinois	231	200	57	151	5,904	6,543
New York	3,021	1,096	17,570	1,367	557	23,611
Florida	2,193	13,444	878	320	751	17,585
Texas	332	193	320	751	22,739	24,079
Total	6,548	15,578	18,605	9,437	83,573	133,470

Source: U.S. Department of Justice, U.S. Immigration and Naturalization Service, *1988 Statistical Yearbook of the Immigration and Naturalization Service*, Washington, D.C.: Government Printing Office, 1988, Table 16, pp. 33-34.

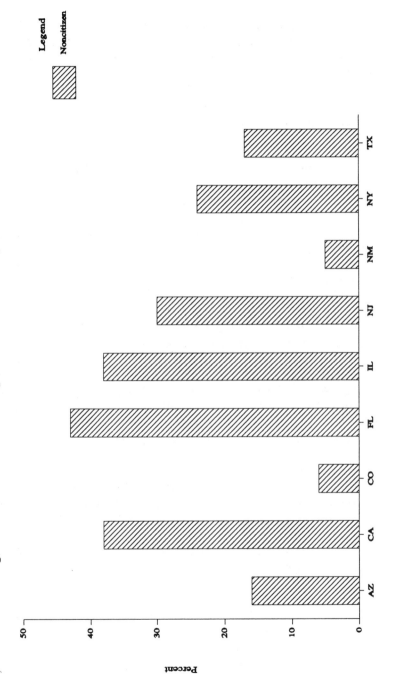

Figure 2: % Noncitizen Adult Hispanics in Selected States, 1980

Source: U.S. Census, 1980

•Exclusion from certain positions in the defense industries, which require security clearances;

•Exclusion from full Social Security benefits if retired and living abroad;

•The right to travel abroad for unrestricted periods of time; and•The right to immigrate immediate relatives outside the current immigration preference system.

U.S. citizenship is thus, not merely a symbolic act for the immigrant. U.S. citizenship confers on the naturalized citizen the full set of rights and responsibilities of native-born American citizens.

LATINO IMMIGRANT ATTITUDES TOWARD CITIZENSHIP: THE NATIONAL LATINO IMMIGRANT SURVEY

The recently completed National Latino Immigrant Survey[5] (NLIS), undertaken by the National Association of Latino Elected and Appointed Officials Educational Fund, of which this author was the principal Investigator, casts some light on how Latino immigrants perceive U.S. citizenship. Although final analysis of survey findings has not been completed, summary findings are available.

Generally, Latino immigrants believe that becoming a U.S. citizen is important. As shown in Table 4, when respondents were asked to assess the importance of various reasons for becoming a U.S. citizen, the reason considered important by the highest proportion of respondents (95 percent) is that U.S. citizenship allows you to vote. Family considerations also play a key role in the assessment of the importance of U.S. citizenship. Ninety percent of the respondents consider "U.S. citizenship provides greater opportunities for your children's future" as an important reason for becoming a citizen, and 88 percent similarly assess "U.S. citizenship helps your relatives to immigrate to the U.S. more quickly."

When asked about the importance of various disadvantages of or obstacles to becoming a citizen (Table 5), the reason cited as important by the highest proportion of immigrant noncitizens (46 percent) was that there are no real perceived benefits to becoming a U.S. citizen. Fears about the difficulty of the INS citizenship examination is the obstacle considered important by the next highest percentage of noncitizens (39 percent); however, fears about INS mistreatment is cited as important by only a relatively small proportion of noncitizens.

---

[5]NALEO Educational Fund, *The National Latino Immigrant Survey* (Los Angeles: NALEO Educational Fund, 1989). See also, the U.S. General Accounting Office (GAO), *Immigration: The Future Flow of Legal Immigration to the United States* (Washington, D.C.: U.S. Government Printing Office, 1988).

Table 4:   *Respondents' Assessment of Reasons for Becoming a U.S. Citizen*

	Percentage of respondents who assessed reason as important
U.S. citizenship allows you to vote in U.S. elections	95%
U.S. citizenship provides greater opportunities for your children's future	90%
U.S. citizenship helps your relatives to immigrate to the U.S. more quickly	88%
U.S. citizenship offers you more protection under the law	87%
U.S. citizenship enables your children to become U.S. citizens	85%
U.S. citizenship makes you eligible for U.S. government programs	84%
U.S. citizenship helps you get a better job	84%
U.S. citizenship allows you to participate more equally in American life	83%
U.S. citizenship makes your life better overall	82%
U.S. citizenship helps you earn more money	69%

(n=1,636)

Source: National Latino Immigrant Survey, 1989

LATINO IMMIGRANT EXPERIENCES WITH THE NATURALIZATION PROCESS

The NLIS also reveals that the process of obtaining U.S. citizenship involves a series of steps, and Latino immigrants may be winnowed out at several points along the way. There are three ways to acquire U.S. citizenship: by birth, by derivation, or by naturalization. All children born in the United States are automatically U.S. citizens regardless of the citizenship of their parents, unless they are born to foreign diplomats. Derivation is far rarer and usually occurs by birth abroad to U.S. parent(s); it is not automatic but must be processed through either the INS or the State Department. If one does not obtain U.S. citizenship through birth or derivation, he or she can obtain it only through naturalization. For further information about the naturalization process, see Table 6 below and *The Long Gray Welcome: A Study of the American Naturalization Program.*

Table 5:   *Respondents' Assessment of Reasons for Not Becoming a U.S. Citizen*

	Percentage of noncitizen respondents who assessed reason as important
There are no real benefits to becoming a U.S. citizen	46%
The INS exam will be too difficult	39%
There is discrimination against Latinos in the U.S.	35%
You would lose property rights in your home country	25%
You would feel disloyal to your home country	24%
You want to maintain your political ties with your home country	23%
You are afraid of losing the culture of your home country	18%
You plan to return to your home country someday to live there permanently	17%
You feel you would be mistreated by the INS	15%

(n=1,085)

Source: National Latino Immigrant Survey, 1989

To initiate the bureaucratic component of the naturalization process, immigrants must obtain a naturalization application. The average length of time between the year respondents received their permanent resident visas and the year they first attempted to obtain the naturalization application was seven years. About one-half of Latino immigrants (47 percent) in the NLIS have attempted (on their own, or with the help of others) to obtain a naturalization application, but 6 percent of those who tried did not actually obtain one. Some of the reasons why 6 percent of these Latino immigrants are not able to obtain forms include:
   •a lack of time (22 percent);
   •a lack of knowledge about where to get one (6 percent);
   •trying to obtain forms at the INS, were unable to get them (10 percent).
   More than 30 percent of the Latino immigrants in the NLIS who attempted to obtain the naturalization application sought assistance from another person or organization, and a surprisingly high 30 percent of those

Table 6: *Administrative Steps in the Naturalization Process*

Step	Administrative or Judicial Process
1.	File the application with the INS
2.	Review of application by INS (Failure to complete the satisfaction of INS results in application becoming administratively denied.)
3.	Examination by an INS adjudicator which tests: • U.S. history and government • Spoken English • Accuracy and completeness of the application • Written English (Failure to satisfy the examiner on each of these components results in a recommendation that the applicant withdraw the application. The applicant may, but rarely does, request that the court review the application.)

4.	Final hearing by court on application and judicial swearing-in ceremony.
	    INS must formally petition the courts to approve all applications deemed to have passed its administrative review. The courts virtually always follow the INS recommendation for approvals.
	    The courts have final jurisdiction over all applications that have passed through INS review, including those administratively denied.

Source: National Latino Immigrant Survey, 1989.

who sought assistance paid for it. Although the average amount paid ($28) was relatively small—any immigrant can obtain the application from the INS for free—this finding may indicate that some confusion exists about the naturalization process.

The bureaucratic part of the naturalization process begins when the immigrant files the application with the INS. Of those respondents who initially tried to obtain an application form, 71 percent have actually filed a form with the INS. When asked to identify the reasons why they didn't file, the immigrants respond that they do not understand or speak English well enough, that they are still studying or preparing for the examination, or that they do not know how to file. Other reasons given by Latino immigrants include that they lack sufficient understanding of the U.S. government, that they are waiting to live long enough in the country to qualify for the 50/20 exemption from taking the examination in English, that the form is too difficult, that they fear contacting the INS, or that they do not have time to prepare for the examination or file the form.

After review of the application by the INS, the next step in the process for applicants is the INS citizenship interview/examination, which tests the applicants' English proficiency and U.S. government and history knowledge. Ninety-two percent of the applicants who took the examination passed it, and they generally did not find it to be difficult (77 percent). When asked what parts of the exam they found to be the hardest, 30 percent cited the U.S. history and government portion, 11 percent named the knowledge of English, and 6 percent named the written English portion.

Given the history of the often controversial relationship between the INS and the Latino community, particularly in the Southwest, one surprising finding of the NLIS study is that Latino immigrants do not generally believe that the INS mistreats naturalization applicants. More than two-thirds (69 percent) believe the INS is helpful when people apply for U.S. citizenship. Latino immigrants who are citizens more frequently report satisfaction with INS treatment than noncitizens. Seventy-five percent of the naturalized citizens believe the INS is helpful when people apply for citizenship, compared to 66 percent of noncitizens. The fact that contact with the citizenship process may influence Latino immigrants' perception of the INS is also reflected in the citizens' assessment of the helpfulness of the INS examiner during their naturalization interview. Eighty percent of the citizens believe the INS examiner was helpful, and 9 percent believe the examiner was rude.

The National Latino Immigrant Survey shows, however, that much confusion exists on the real benefits of U.S. citizenship and the process by which to attain it. This basic fact may become a cornerstone for developing a political strategy involving mobilization for citizenship in the Hispanic community. For the Latino community the stakes are high and the political implications evident.

POLITICAL EMPOWERMENT THROUGH U.S. CITIZENSHIP: SOME STRATEGIC CONSIDERATIONS

Any look at the voting statistics of Latinos highlights the significance of U.S. citizenship. Over 80 percent of the difference in voting between Latinos and black Americans can be explained by noncitizenship among Latino adults.[6] In certain states, California and Florida, for example, the

---

[6]Harry Pachon and Louis Desipio, *The Latino Vote in 1988* (Washington, D.C.: NALEO Educational Fund, 1988). Specifically, the U.S. census found that in 1988 black Americans voted at a rate of 51.5 percent. Hispanic/Latino voters participated at an apparent rate of 28.8 percent. If one factors in voter ineligibility due to noncitizenship, Hispanic voting rates increase to 46 percent and black voting rates increase to 53 percent. The difference in voting rates is reduced from a 22.7 percent

lack of U.S. citizenship may be the single, largest obstacle to political empowerment in the Hispanic community. Consider southern California. Table 7 indicates the percent of noncitizens that were present in selected southern California cities in 1990.[7] These percentages in all likelihood have increased since the last census.

Yet the National Latino Immigrant Survey indicates that many of these legal residents wish to undertake the steps necessary to become citizens. (And, according to the NLIS, once they become U.S. citizens their political participation is higher than native-born Americans.)[8]

What are the implications of U.S. citizenship for Latino political empowerment strategies? The answer to this question is complex and has several dimensions. These are as follows:

Policy Implication #1: *A realistic assessment for Latino electoral strength in any community requires knowledge of the number of Latino legal residents living in that community who have not yet become U.S. citizens.*

Subsidiary points of analysis might include:

• How recently arrived are the legal residents in the community? Is the community a port of entry community, or are the legal residents long-term homeowners?

• Are there significant numbers of legal residents who have obtained their residency through the amnesty and therefore are not eligible for U.S. citizenship until 1993?

Policy Implication #2: *Legal Latino immigrants are not, as they are often portrayed, sojourners who are planning to return to their homeland.*

Legal Latino immigrants are permanent residents who are establishing roots in their communities and who are interested but confused about the benefits of U.S. citizenship. Political empowerment strategies aimed at the Latino population need to include components of educating the Latino immigrants on the opportunities and responsibilities of U.S. citizenship.

Policy Implication #3: *Given the relatively low average levels of income and education among Latino immigrants, the naturalization process is not an easy process for Latino immigrants to negotiate.*

The National Latino Immigrant Survey reveals that one-third of all applicants who begin the naturalization process fail to complete the process. Citizenship promotion campaigns by themselves may not be sufficient. Direct assistance to Latino immigrants in the form of "demystifying" the

---

difference to one of 7 percent.

[7]NALEO Educational Fund, *National Roster of Hispanic Elected Officials* (Washington, D.C.: NALEO Educational Fund, 1989).

[8]The NLIS found that voter registration among naturalized Latino immigrants was 10 percentage points higher than native white non-Hispanics and over 20 points higher than native-born Hispanics.

Table 7:   *Hispanic Foreign-Born and Non-Naturalized Populations for Selected Cities in Los Angeles County, 1980*

	Spanish Origin Population	Total Foreign Born	Not Naturalized	Percentage Not Naturalized of Total Spanish Origin
Alhambra	24,294	8,048	5,699	23%
Arcadia	3,157	991	645	20%
Azusa	12,443	3,997	3,301	27%
Baldwin Park	29,336	10,276	8,579	29%
Bell	16,058	8,973	7,803	49%
Bellflower	7,943	2,196	1,635	21%
Bell Gardens	21,956	11,232	10,106	46%
Claremont	2,316	386	283	12%
Commerce	8,937	3,471	2,839	32%
Compton	17,162	9,505	7,401	43%
Covina	4,278	665	404	9%
Downey	13,926	4,248	2,991	21%
Duarte	5,044	2,047	1,665	33%
El Monte	48,704	21,546	18,628	38%
Glendora	3,483	540	302	9%
Hawaiian Gardens	5,540	2,434	2,085	38%
Huntington Park	37,320	22,702	20,051	54%
La Mirada	7,729	1,423	934	12%
La Puente	19,288	5,103	3,964	21%
Los Angeles	815,305	446,842	375,030	46%
Monrovia	5,599	2,140	1,699	30%
Montebello	31,296	8,545	6,282	20%

naturalization process, bureaucratic form assistance, and preparation for the citizenship examination will be required.

Policy Implication #4: *The adult education system in local educational agencies offers a standing educational delivery system that can address the citizenship education needs of the Latino immigrant population.*

While most school systems offer citizenship adult education classes, these are usually limited in number. Urging that adult education departments expand their class offerings and revise curricula, if necessary, to prepare Latino immigrants for the citizenship examination is a strategy that allows Latino advocacy and community-based organizations to maximize the use of their resources in a cost effective way. For example, having one school district add just one course per semester to service the citizenship needs of Latino immigrants saves Latino organizations from having to

Table 7:   *(continued)*

	Spanish Origin Population	Total Foreign Born	Not Naturalized	Percentage Not Naturalized of Total Spanish Origin
Monterey Park	20,969	4,778	3,116	15%
Norwalk	34,214	9,766	7,540	22%
Paramount	16,807	7,978	7,047	42%
Pasadena	21,784	11,740	9,604	44%
Pico Rivera	40,705	9,837	7,614	19%
Pomona	28,302	9,207	6,963	25%
Redondo Beach	6,549	2,060	1,434	22%
Rosemead	24,404	8,721	7,383	30%
San Dimas	3,136	639	373	12%
San Fernando	12,219	5,883	4,962	41%
San Gabriel	11,491	3,827	2,901	25%
San Marino	620	195	115	19%
Santa Fe Springs	8,746	1,948	1,564	18%
Sierra Madre	768	204	177	23%
South El Monte	12,927	5,833	4,935	38%
South Gate	38,951	19,743	16,916	43%
Temple City	3,734	738	529	14%
West Covina	16,964	3,197	3,064	12%
Whittier	16,266	4,029	3,221	20%
LA/Long Beach SMSA	2,066,103	913,591	759,879	37%

Source: U.S. Census Bureau, 1980 Census, Summary Tape File 4B

expend resources to provide such services. Certain school districts' adult education programs can already serve as potential models. For example, the Evan Adult School in Los Angeles offers a full range of citizenship classes at night as well as on weekends.

Policy Implication #5: *Mass mobilization techniques can be utilized to facilitate naturalization drives among Latino legal residents.*

Here some valuable lessons can be learned from the research and demonstration project that the NALEO Educational Fund has been undertaking in Latino communities in the southern California area for the past three years. NALEO's research has shown that most approaches to promoting and facilitating naturalization among Latino legal residents have been modeled on the "casework" approach. In other words, a trained professional, or para-professional, assists legal residents on a case-by-case basis. While this assures a high degree of quality control for the individual being served, the numbers of legal residents served is minuscule in proportion to the number of eligible legal residents (southern California alone had over 800,000 Latino legal residents in 1980). Instead, mass mobilization campaigns charged with facilitating the application process (filling out naturalization forms, fingerprints, official photographs) can effectively assist large numbers of Latino immigrants in the first step of the naturalization process.

Policy Implication #6: *The contemporary naturalization process is essentially a bureaucratic process.*

The agency in charge of this activity, the Immigration and Naturalization Service (INS) is a bureaucracy that needs to be monitored and overseen like any other public agency. Traditionally, the INS has responded to its more glamorous role of a law enforcement agency dealing with immigration law enforcement.[9] Its service component, and naturalization in particular, has been a stepchild of INS activities. For example, naturalization activities account for only 10 percent of the INS budget.[10] Latino interest and advocacy groups need to consider building coalitions with each other for the purpose of serving as a constituency pressuring INS to enhance and expand its naturalization activities. Interestingly, this type of advocacy is not necessarily confrontational with the INS. INS personnel are witnessing an ever increasing naturalization case load[11] and would not automatically oppose groups trying to add fiscal/personnel resources to the agency. Moreover, developing coalitions with other immigrant groups such as Asians, who also may be supportive of improving INS activities in this area, is feasible and possible.

---

[9]Milton Morris, *Immigration: The Beleaguered Bureaucracy* (Washington, D.C.: The Brookings Institution, 1985), 127.

[10]In 1987, the INS Authorization and Budget Request submitted to Congress allocated 7,287 work years to enforcement, e.g., Border Patrol, 2,303 positions to immigration support, e.g., visa processing, and 1,306 work years to citizenship processing. U.S. Immigration and Naturalization Service, *FY1987 Authorization and Budget Request for the Congress* (Washington, D.C.: Government Printing Office, 1986), 10; NALEO Educational Fund, *The Long Grey Welcome* (Washington, D.C.: NALEO Educational Fund, 1985).

[11]INS Management information system data documents that examiners clocked 254,389 productive hours to process 406,445 naturalization applications. This average of .63 hours per case includes the exam itself, processing the paperwork for the court ceremony, and applicant contact at the ceremony. INS also records 374,496 clerical hours (or .92 hours per naturalization applicant). U.S. Immigration and Naturalization Service, *G22.3 Reports*, Washington, D.C. (Unpublished Data). See also, U.S. General Accounting Office, *op. cit.*, 1988.

Policy Implications #7: *Latino advocacy groups, civil libertarian organizations, and others need to maintain pressures on the INS to prepare to provide naturalization services to the approximately three million immigrants who are in the process of obtaining legal status under IRCA.*

These potential U.S. citizenship applicants will begin to become eligible to apply in 1993. In order to obtain permanent residency, legalization applicants generally must either demonstrate their English and civic proficiency by passing an examination, or they must take classes to obtain this proficiency. Those who choose to meet the requirement by passing an examination may take a test that will also satisfy the U.S. citizenship examination requirement. Consequently, immigrants who obtain permanent residency through legalization may have an easier time meeting the U.S. citizenship examination requirement than other permanent residents; the newly legalized residents may have already satisfied the requirement by passing the examination taken to obtain permanent residency, or they may be better prepared for the examination because they have already received some English and civic instruction. While those who are completing the legalization requirements through classroom instruction may not yet have sufficient knowledge to pass the U.S. citizenship examination, they are likely to be more aware of the U.S. citizenship requirements than other legal immigrants. As the National Latino Immigrant Survey suggests, the U.S. citizenship examination and the preparation it requires is perceived by Latino immigrants as an obstacle to naturalization; the newly legalized may have already surmounted this obstacle or may be better prepared to face it.

Additionally, many of the newly legalized may also be particularly motivated to become U.S. citizens in order to obtain legal status for their immigrant relatives who did not qualify for Legalization (for reasons such as residence in the United States for an insufficient period of time or inability to document their residence). The survey found that the desire to immigrate relatives quickly was considered an important reason to become a U.S. citizen by 88 percent of Latino immigrants, and many of the newly legalized will have this strong inducement to complete the naturalization process as soon as they can.

Not only are these applicants potentially more prepared and motivated than the traditional legal immigrant pool, but the INS will also be able to process their naturalization applications more easily. (The INS will have relatively current addresses for these applicants.) Some (26 percent) of these applicants will have already met the English and civic proficiency requirement for naturalization, and the processing of their applications will be more straightforward.

Consequently, the INS should be made to consider undertaking a concentrated effort to inform legalization applicants of their eligibility for naturalization and to facilitate their U.S. citizenship application. Because of its knowledge of applicants' addresses, the INS is in a position to inform each legalization applicant of his or her eligibility when the applicant first becomes eligible.

CONCLUSION

The over 4 million Latino legal residents who are not yet U.S. citizens present a hidden potential of Latino political empowerment. For example, if only 10 percent of Los Angeles County's Latino legal resident adults became U.S. citizens, this would add close to 100,000 new Latino voters. Efforts, most notably those of NALEO's, to promote naturalization are showing the dramatic results that can be possible in a relatively short period of time. Since NALEO began U.S. citizenship promotion in 1984, the Mexican immigrant naturalization rate has gone up annually, from 14,000 to 28,000 and now hovers around 21,000 per year. In four years, the rate at which Mexican immigrants naturalize when they first become eligible—after five years of residency—has increased by a factor of six, from .2 of 1 percent to 1.2 percent.

If citizenship promotion and education become widespread, equally significant results can be expected among not only Mexican immigrants, but Central/South American and Caribbean immigrants.

Latino political empowerment strategies have to confront the reality of Latino immigrants constituting a large segment of the U.S. Latino population. Ignoring the Latino immigrant means ignoring one out of three Latino adults. Incorporating the Latino immigrant into Latino empowerment strategies presents the possibility of the Latino community fully realizing the political potential commensurate with its numbers.

CHAPTER 5

RAPHAEL J. SONENSHEIN
California State University—Fullerton

Jewish Participation in California Politics

Jewish political behavior has long fascinated those who study ethnic politics. As Jews moved from working-class status into the middle- and upper-middle classes after World War II, they maintained a remarkably hardy brand of liberalism (Fuchs 1956; Fisher 1979). Of all major religious groups, only Jews held liberal attitudes at variance with their increasing economic status. This behavior contrasted sharply with other white groups, whose conservative or liberal views could easily be predicted from their socio-economic position (Allinsmith and Allinsmith 1948). More than one observer has noted that "Jews live like WASPs, and vote like Puerto Ricans." The impact of Jewish liberalism has been augmented by high levels of political mobilization and activism.

Much of the literature on Jewish political life tests the proposition that new social pressures have eroded Jewish liberalism. Academic and journalistic studies appear with every state and national election. The question has been especially lively after periods of confrontation between blacks and Jews. But the bulk of research indicates that nationally Jews continue to support the Democratic party and its candidates and to disproportionately favor liberal social and economic positions (Fisher 1979). Jews still differ significantly from all but the more liberal whites in their political orientation.

This chapter explores Jewish political behavior in California, the most rapidly growing center of American Jewish life. To what extent do western Jews retain the special characteristics of Jewish politics associated with its base in the northeastern states? After all, the Sun Belt migration has made more than one group conservative. Over the years, there has been increased conflict between blacks and Jews, and there has been tension within the

---

The author gratefully acknowledges that this study was completed with the assistance of a grant from the John Randolph Haynes and Dora Haynes Foundation.

Democratic party over the state of Israel. When combined with the Sun Belt's conservatism, have these developments changed California's Jews?

The inclusion of this chapter in a book on California ethnic politics suggests that an examination of Jewish political behavior could offer more than another test of the persistence of Jewish liberalism. Generally, Jews are not included as a separate group in ethnic studies. Whites are usually treated as monolithic. The U. S. census does not measure the Jewish population, greatly increasing the costs of examining Jews as another minority.

This chapter argues that Jews represent a particularly important ethnic group in California politics because of their political mobilization and their political relationship to other minorities. The study of Jewish political participation can therefore be a stepping-stone to a broader exploration of *the role and function of the Jewish community in California's ethnic politics.*

The California Jewish community has received far less study than it deserves. The specific political behavior of California Jews has not been studied in nearly two decades (Maller 1971). A growing number of Jewish community studies have examined Jewish social and political life in individual cities. San Francisco (Narell 1981) and Los Angeles (Vorspan and Gartner 1970; Sandberg 1986) have both been the subjects of extensive community analyses. But the state as a whole needs further attention.

THE CALIFORNIA JEWISH COMMUNITY

The American Jewish community has historically had its base in the Northeast, particularly New York City. When other Americans began to migrate in large numbers to California around the turn of the century, Jews were represented in a smaller than average proportion. By 1930, however, Jews began coming out West in larger numbers than non-Jews (Goldstein 1981). The steady migration of Jews to California has continued unabated ever since (Kosmin, Ritterband, and Scheckner 1987).

Table 1 indicates the proportion of Jews living in the four regions of the United States. In 1930, the vast majority of Jews lived in the "frostbelt" regions, the Northeast and North Central. By 1988, the "sunbelt" regions, the South and West, had become far more significant areas of Jewish population than they had been previously.

As Table 2 indicates, California is now much closer to New York State as a center of Jewish population. The ratio of Jews in New York to Jews in California went from 15.5 to 1 in 1930 to 2 to 1 in 1988. By 1988, 15.3 percent of all American Jews lived in California compared with only 2.9 percent in 1930. Jews now represent 3.4 percent of California's population (Kosmin et al. 1989, 235).

Table 1: *Regional Patterns of Jewish Population*

	1930[a]	1988[b]
Northeast	68.3	51.0
North Central	19.6	11.0
South	7.6	19.5
West	4.6	18.5

[a]Goldstein 1981, Table 5, p. 31.
[b]Kosmin, Ritterband, and Scheckner 1989, Table 2, p. 237.

Table 2: *Jews in California and New York State*

	1930[a]	1988[b]	Change
California	123,000	905,500	+636.2%
New York	1,904,000	1,844,000	-3.2%

[a]Kosmin et al., 1987, Table 1, p. 168.
[b]Kosmin et al., 1989, Table 1, p. 235.

California has "been extraordinarily hospitable to Jewish life. . . . In the last decade or so, the focus of American Jewish life has come to center more and more on California" (Zipperstein 1982). It has been suggested that "California may one day become one of history's great Jewish communities" (*Jewish Living* 1980).

California's Jewish community has already become distinct from the Jewish world on the East Coast. A recent study of California Jews found strong advances in education, occupation, and income. California Jews are younger and better educated than Jews nationwide and more affluent than non-Jewish Californians. The authors concluded:

> New York is losing Jewish population, while California is gaining; New York Jews are becoming older and many of them poorer, while California Jews, on the whole, are maintaining their relative youthfulness and becoming wealthier (Fisher and Tanaka 1986, 216).

This demographic profile suggests that California Jews might be even more liberal than Jews on the East Coast. While Jews in all strata are more liberal than white non-Jews, there are significant differences among Jews. In the specific area of racial attitudes, Harris and Swanson (1970) found that among New York City Jews, the young, the college-educated, and the least religious were by far the most liberal. In general, even less affluent, older, and more traditional Jews remain more liberal and Democratic than other whites of similar socio-economic status. It is surely ironic, however, that while being Jewish has a deep impact on building and sustaining political liberalism in the United States, being working class and *religiously* Jewish may tend to reduce that effect to some degree.

Regional Differences: Northern vs. Southern California

The large influx of Jews to California significantly altered the existing patterns of Jewish settlement. Until 1930, the center of Jewish population had been the San Francisco Bay Area. After 1930, most Jewish migrants flooded into Los Angeles. During World War II, the Jewish population of Los Angeles grew by leaps and bounds (Kohs 1944). By 1970 there were more than 500,000 Jews in Greater Los Angeles. The Los Angeles Jewish community was the nation's second largest, behind only New York City (Vorspan and Gartner 1970).

The Jewish community of Los Angeles moved from downtown and the eastside to the western sections of the city and then expanded to the San Fernando Valley. Looked at today, the Jewish community runs from mid-city through the west side and into the nearside of the valley. By 1980, about 210,000 Jews lived within the Los Angeles city limits, representing about 7 percent of the city's population.

The pattern of Jewish life was considerably different up north. The German Jews who migrated to the Bay Area tended to be assimilationist, and the liberal San Francisco community incorporated them as founding members. "Jews assimilated more easily here than in other cities . . . because they were part of the pioneer settlement from its beginnings during the Gold Rush in the late 1840s" (Dr. Monroe Rischin, quoted in the *San Francisco Chronicle*, April 15, 1976). Jews became central figures in the commercial development of the city and were numbered among the most prominent and successful business leaders.

The Jewish community of the Bay Area today is not unusually affluent, but it is very well educated and secular, according to a study conducted by the Jewish Community Federation (*San Francisco Chronicle*, May 10, 1988). An extraordinarily high number of Bay Area Jews are "unaffiliated," which is less religiously-identified than Reform, the most liberal branch of Judaism. Such Jews could be expected to be among the most liberal Jews anywhere in the nation.

There are few identifiable Jewish neighborhoods, and no state assembly district has more than about 15 percent Jewish population (Winslow 1989). One Jewish reporter who migrated from New York City complained:

> For me, being a Jew in the Bay Area has been an eerie
> experience. After having lived in several Eastern cities, it

was a shock for me to encounter a metropolis with almost no Jewish ethos (Mandel 1981).

Yet with more than 100,000 Jews, the Bay Area represents one of the largest Jewish communities in North America, ranking eighth after New York, Los Angeles, Miami, Philadelphia, Chicago, Boston, and Montreal (*San Francisco Chronicle*, May 10, 1988). Perhaps 10 percent of San Francisco is Jewish (*Ibid.*).

By contrast, Los Angeles has a fully defined Jewish community. Los Angeles Jews may be unobservant and untethered by group loyalty compared with Jews in eastern cities. But compared with Jews in the Bay Area, Los Angeles Jews are practically New Yorkers. The same reporter who complained about the attenuated Jewishness of the Bay Area added, "I've met plenty of Jews who were born in Los Angeles, and they are as ethnic as any New Yorker" (Mandel 1981), With the greater socio-economic diversity of Jews in Los Angeles, one might imagine that they would be somewhat less liberal than Jews in the Bay Area.

Los Angeles Jewry grew much later than San Francisco's, and the Jewish migrants were slower to assimilate. In addition, the dominant Los Angeles culture in the 1930s and 1940s was highly conservative, dominated by white Protestants from the Midwest (Singleton 1979; Gelfand 1981). While Jews were able to secure a solid economic niche, they found fewer openings in political and social life (Vorspan and Gartner 1970; Gelfand 1981). Stable Jewish neighborhoods developed, and even today a number of state assembly districts have significant Jewish populations (Siwulec 1989). Thus in the state that increasingly influences national Jewish life, two different models have emerged: assimilation in the Bay Area, and a more visible, feisty community life in the Los Angeles region.

The Jewish migration from the crowded, grimy cities of the Northeast to the balmy climate and easier lifestyle of California might suggest a lessening of political patterns shaped in the Northeast—particularly, high levels of mobilized liberalism. Has the movement of Jews to California changed the nature of Jewish political behavior?

JEWISH POLITICAL BEHAVIOR IN CALIFORNIA

Various studies have indicated that California's Jews display the liberalism normally associated with the Jewish community nationwide. As far back as 1964, a statewide ballot initiative designed to repeal fair housing legislation (Proposition 14) received a heavy "no" vote in communities with large Jewish populations. Statewide, two-thirds of Jews rejected it (Wolfinger and Greenstein 1968). Of the 25 cities that opposed the proposition, only three were in southern California—"the largely Jewish communities of Beverly Hills and Lake Elsinore, and Compton, which were 40 percent Negro in 1960" (*Ibid.*). While southern California was far more conservative than northern California on Proposition 14, the Jewish areas in the southland were comparable in their vote to liberal Berkeley in the north. Among 10 northern California cities, Berkeley registered by far the highest share of whites opposed to the proposition (Browning, Marshall, and Tabb 1984, Table 10, 105).

Maller (1971) analyzed a Jewish subsample of a statewide poll conducted in 1968. At the height of a period of racial tensions, Maller found that Jews registered virtually no support for George Wallace and overwhelmingly backed Democrat Hubert Humphrey. Jews differed significantly from other whites on these measures. In their views on civil rights, Jews were substantially more liberal than the white community as a whole. Maller concluded that "the Jewish community still remains the strongest supporter of civil rights within the white community" (164).

In a study of Jewish voting nationwide, Fisher (1979) included some California state and local elections. Gubernatorial races and statewide propositions revealed a high level of liberalism among Jews, far beyond whites in general. Fisher concluded that "in Los Angeles, as in New York, within similar income areas, the more Jewish the precinct the higher the Democratic vote for Congress as well as president" (111).

Unfortunately, such polls generally must rely on a small subsample of Jews. More importantly, polls cannot communicate the flavor of Jewish participation at the constituency level. For those in politics, the impact of Jewish participation is often felt in communities with a major Jewish presence.

In this section several political jurisdictions with large Jewish populations are examined. For reasons already outlined, these identifiable Jewish areas will be found in Los Angeles, not in San Francisco. However, socio-economic differences among Jews in the two areas suggest that Bay Area Jews will, if anything, be more liberal than Jews in southern California.

I will compare these Jewish communities with constituencies dominated by two different types of white non-Jews: affluent and middle/working-class. Comparisons will also be drawn to a white liberal community without a dominant Jewish population. The targeting of Jews will not be exact, but where possible will follow Fisher's prescription that "the district contain a very high proportion of Jews [and that] the non-Jews in each district be politically similar to the Jews" (1979, 103).

Two political jurisdictions with significant Jewish populations will be examined: the 5th City Council District in Los Angeles and the city of Beverly Hills.

The 5th Council District is 30 to 40 percent Jewish, more than 10 times the Jewish concentration in the state as a whole. The 5th contains a wide variety of wealthy, middle-class, and working-class Jewish neighborhoods, from Bel Air to Fairfax. Beverly Hills, a wealthy community within Los Angeles but separately incorporated, has a Jewish population conservatively estimated at 27 percent, eight times the state level (Siwulec 1989). It physically borders the 5th Council District.

For the Bay Area, I will examine Berkeley, one of the most liberal communities in the state. The Jewish population of Berkeley has been estimated at 7,500 (Scheckner 1990). The Jewish proportion of the total population is 7.3 percent, and 11.4 percent of the white population. Berkeley therefore provides a useful comparison to the far more Jewish 5th Council District and Beverly Hills.

Unlike the other white-majority jurisdictions studied, Berkeley has a large black population (about 20 percent). The Berkeley figures can be seen as overestimates of white liberalism, as the black vote is likely to be consistently liberal and Democratic. (If we presume black voters to be at least 85 percent Democratic and liberal, then we can deduct perhaps 15-18 percent from the vote total to assess the white liberal vote.)

Two white Los Angeles city council districts with relatively small Jewish populations are also examined. The 12th Council District in the northwest San Fernando Valley is one of Los Angeles' most affluent areas and is overwhelmingly white. Jews have been moving into the 12th District in recent years, but the district remains dominated by white Gentiles. Until the 1986 city council redistricting, the 7th Council District in the north-central valley was dominated by white middle-class and working-class homeowners. (In 1986, the city placed a large Latino population into the 7th, making it less appropriate as a measure of white middle-class voting. For elections after 1985, the 7th District is excluded.)

Finally, the largely black and working-class 8th City Council District in Los Angeles has been examined in order to explore the relative distances of all the white districts from the black political position.

Demographics

A demographic comparison among the communities reveals some important differences.

As seen in Table 3, all five white districts had clear white majorities. Minorities were a clear presence only in Berkeley and in the 7th Council District.

Tables 4 and 5 explore the socio-economic status of the districts and cities. Beverly Hills and the 5th and 12th Council Districts are the most affluent while the 7th District is comprised of working-class and middle-class people, many of them homeowners. The 12th District is a bedrock area of homeownership at a rate of over 70 percent. Beverly Hills is the wealthiest, while Berkeley is middle class. The black district is the least affluent.

The 5th and 12th Districts provide a good test of the notion that racial liberalism is a luxury of wealthy whites who do not live in close proximity to minorities. The 12th is much farther away from areas of black concentration

Table 3:   *Population of Districts, 1980*

	White	Black	Hispanic
Jewish			
5th CD	77.8	7.7	9.5
Beverly Hills	94.1	1.5	4.2
White Liberal			
Berkeley	63.8	20.1	5.1
White Gentile			
7th CD	63.5	3.1	28.4
12th CD	83.1	1.7	10.0
Black			
8th CD	5.8	73.0	18.7

Source: United States census and city of Los Angeles figures.

Table 4:   *Economic Data, 1980*

	Mean Household Income	Homeownership	Home Value
Jewish			
5th CD	$29,098	36.2%	$179,010
Beverly Hills	52,815	42.2	200,000+
White Liberal			
Berkeley	18,940	37.8	96,400
White Gentile			
7th CD	19,937	39.9	94,072
12th CD	31,308	70.8	136,669
Black			
8th CD	13,062	40.6	48,229

Source: United States census and city of Los Angeles figures.

Table 5: *Education as Percent of Adult Population, 1980*

	% High School	% Undergrad	% Graduate
Jewish			
5th CD	83.5	58.4	31.6
Beverly Hills	86.6	61.2 (1-3 yrs)	35.2 (4+)
White Liberal			
Berkeley	86.4	52.3	35.6
White Gentile			
7th CD	80.5	36.3	13.4
12th CD	85.0	51.3	23.1
Black			
8th CD	58.6	28.1	6.0

Source: United States census and city of Los Angeles figures.

Note: Los Angeles districts are from city figures, calculated as percentage of population 18 and over; Beverly Hills and Berkeley are from census figures as share of population 25 and over.

Table 6: *Voter Registration, 1984 and 1988*

	1984		1988	
	Voters	Percentage of Adults	Voters	Percentage of Adults
Jewish				
5th CD	111,976	67.3	123,186	74.0
Beverly Hills	19,925	75.2	19,386	73.2
White Liberal				
Berkeley	83,291	95.3	79,341	77.0
White Gentile				
7th CD	76,558	50.9	—	—
12th CD	106,719	72.2	113,088	76.5
Black				
8th CD	87,870	66.2	84,241	63.7

than the west side 5th District. In Berkeley, there is a greater racial mix than in the other five white districts, which could theoretically make racial liberalism harder to sustain.

Levels of education differ significantly among the communities (Table 5). Berkeley is not a wealthy community compared with Beverly Hills, but it has a very well-educated population.

Differences in income among the communities are more than counter-balanced by education. The Jewish districts most resemble the white liberal community of Berkeley in educational profile. The 5th District is the best educated of the three council districts, with nearly one-third of the adult population holding graduate degrees. Despite its greater socio-economic variety than Beverly Hills, the 5th District is comparable in education.

Politics

With its large Jewish and educated constituency, the 5th District generates a high level of registration (Table 6). The number of registered voters is, however, matched by the affluent valley 12th District. In each of the years listed, the 5th and the 12th were among the city's highest in registration. Beverly Hills and Berkeley have even higher shares of eligible voters registered.   Registration was considerably lower in the white middle-class 7th.   Despite its low socio-economic status, the black 8th generated a significant level of political mobilization. Overall, the well-educated, affluent white districts, whether or not Jewish, had by far the highest level of registration.

Substantial differences emerge among the high-status white areas in the matter of party and voting preferences. The Democratic percentage in the Jewish areas greatly exceeds the party's base in the affluent white Gentile community (Table 7) and is most similar to white liberal Berkeley. (And Berkeley's Democratic share is augmented by a large black population.) The less affluent white Gentile area has a Democratic percentage comparable to the Jewish areas. But there are many thousands more Democrats in the Jewish liberal 5th. The 5th District has both high Democratic registration and high overall registration. In fact, there are about as many Democrats in the 5th District as there are in the black 8th and as there were registered voters in the 7th.

Table 7 most likely understates the difference between Los Angeles Jewish and non-Jewish whites in party registration. An analysis of Jewish surnames by a Los Angeles political consultant revealed that in 1988 76.5 percent of the city's Jews were Democrats (Siwulec 1989). In 1988, 61.9 percent of the city's voters were Democrats. Subtracting black Democrats, Latino Democrats, and Jews, we can estimate that less than half of Los Angeles' non-Jewish whites were registered Democrats. When the black

Table 7: *Democratic Party Registration, 1984 and 1988*

	1984			1988		
	Voters	Dems.	D %	Voters	Dems.	D %
Jewish						
5th CD	111,976	74,785	66.8	123,186	76,681	62.2
Beverly Hills	19,925	12,388	62.2	19,386	11,552	59.6
White Liberal						
Berkeley	83,291	59,353	71.3	79,341	57,597	72.6
White Gentile						
7th CD	76,558	44,978	58.5	—	—	—
12th CD	106,719	50,660	47.5	113,088	49,637	43.9
Black						
8th CD	87,510	77,879	89.0	84,241	73,734	87.5

vote is removed in Berkeley, the powerful Democratic identification of Jews in Los Angeles and Beverly Hills is magnified.

In statewide elections, the Democratic/liberal preferences of the Jewish districts emerge clearly. Table 8 includes the most hotly contested issues on the 1982 and 1986 statewide ballots: black Democrat Tom Bradley for governor in 1982 and 1986; Proposition 15 (handgun control) in 1982; and the retention of liberal Chief Justice of the Supreme Court Rose Bird in 1986. As in most indicators thus far, the Jewish areas in Los Angeles County most resemble the white liberal community of Berkeley and least resemble the affluent conservative 12th Council District.

In these two statewide elections, ideological differences among the white districts were significant. In Bradley's two gubernatorial races, for instance, the liberal 5th and the conservative 12th were about 25 points apart each time. They were nearly 30 points apart on Rose Bird and 27 points apart on gun control. The high level of political mobilization in the Jewish districts helps counterbalance the high political involvement of the white conservative area.

The Jewish district was also significantly distant from the white Democratic 7th District. The 5th was more pro-Bradley than the 7th in 1982 and 1986 by more than 15 points and nearly 12 points, respectively.

The liberal Jewish districts and Berkeley were significantly closer to the black district in three of the four elections than were either of the white Gentile areas. The one exception was gun control, in which only the Jewish and white liberal areas backed the unpopular measure.

In Bradley's four winning mayoral races before the 1986 city redistricting, the Jewish 5th was by far Bradley's strongest white district, and the conser-

Table 8:   *Statewide Voting*

	Tom Bradley 1982	Prop. 15 1982	Tom Bradley 1986	Rose Bird 1986 (yes)
Jewish				
5th CD	66.9	64.7	56.5	52.4
Beverly Hills	62.9	72.2	50.9	50.0
White Liberal				
Berkeley	77.6	69.2	71.5	74.9
White Gentle				
7th CD	50.6	39.5	—	—
12th CD	39.9	37.2	31.5	25.8
Black				
8th CD	93.1	32.5	90.1	68.1

vative 12th was generally his worst.   In fact, year by year the Bradley percentage in the 5th drew closer to the black 8th (Table 9).   The 7th fell in the middle among white districts.

Notably, in Bradley's narrow 1989 reelection, his margin of victory came from an unusually high turnout in the Jewish liberal 5th District. This was the only nonminority council district in which Bradley won a majority (Sonenshein 1989a; 1990b). See Table 10.

The assertions that white liberalism is a function of distance from black communities or that liberalism is a luxury of those of high status are challenged by this evidence. The most liberal areas were not always the wealthiest nor the farthest from minority communities. Areas with large Jewish populations, regardless of demographics, were the most reliably liberal in southern California.

The analysis of voting by constituency reveals that the pattern of high mobilization and consistent liberal and Democratic preferences characterizes Jews in the Los Angeles area where they are most clearly seen as a community. Jewish voting provides an important counterbalance to the traditional conservatism of southern California whites and most resembles the liberalism of Berkeley in northern California. The socio-economic profile of Bay Area Jews suggests that the same pattern is likely to be true up north. The combination of high educational levels and Jewish political traditions seems to have been upheld even 3,000 miles from the East Coast.

A Note on Jewish Conservatism

This study indicates the persistence of Jewish liberalism in California politics. The socio-economic status and lifestyle of California's Jews indeed

Table 9: *Bradley Mayoral Vote, 1973-1985*

	1973	1977	1981	1985
5th Jewish Liberal	57.7	61.7	68.7	73.7
7th White Gentile Dem.	46.4	43.2	49.8	56.7
8th Black	91.1	90.2	91.5	92.4
12th White Gentile Rep.	44.0	40.3	44.3	50.3

Table 10: *Voting in the 1989 Los Angeles Mayoral Election*

	Bradley Percentage	Bradley Margin
5th Jewish Liberal	51.8	4,949
8th Black	73.2	10,407
12th White Gentile Repub.	39.1	-3,930

make it possible that they are even more liberal than Jews on the East Coast. However, the Jewish community is not monolithic, and there is some evidence of Jewish conservatism.

There is, however, little basis in California politics for the long-predicted realignment of Jews toward the Republican party. More common is Jewish ambivalence toward liberalism on certain issues that either threaten personal interests or the interests of Jews as a group. This phenomenon may best be seen as "selective conservatism" in the midst of broad liberalism.

I have already noted that less affluent, educated, and mobile Jews may feel more personally threatened by social change. Another possible source of Jewish ambivalence is suburbanization, and a place to look is the San Fernando Valley in Los Angeles. Have Jews made the valley more liberal or has the valley made Jews more conservative?

In the 1970s, the busing issue generated a strong degree of selective conservatism among valley Jews. As parents with children in city schools, they were an important element of the antibusing movement. (Other Jews played critical roles in the probusing effort.) A key test occurred in the 1980 congressional election in which liberal valley Democratic Congressman Jim Corman was upset by Jewish Republican antibusing activist Bobbi Fiedler.

A Jewish activist who played a key role in aiding Corman's losing fight recalled that "while 100 percent of the official Jewish organizations backed Corman, Fiedler had the Jewish grass roots" (Plotkin 1980). For suburban Los Angeles Jews, the busing issue certainly pulled them away from liberalism (Caditz 1976). But as busing as city policy faded, valley Jews once again displayed liberal Democratic patterns. Fiedler is no longer in office, and her district is represented by a Jewish liberal Democrat. The 3d Council District in the valley, formerly represented by an archconservative, now has a Jewish liberal councilwoman (Joy Picus). While surely divisive, the busing issue does not seem to have had the same fracturing effect on black-Jewish relations in Los Angeles as the New York City school strike had in that city.

On this issue, then, Jewish liberalism was tempered by severe conflicts with self-interest, as Jewish parents did not want their children bused to inner-city schools. Some saw in this evidence of a growing Jewish conservatism, but this analysis indicates that it is an important exception to an overall rule. Below we will see another example of selective conservatism in Jewish opposition to Jesse Jackson, not due to personal self-interest but from the standpoint of group protection.

Jewish Officeholding

Jews have lived in California since the middle of the last century, when a contingent of Jews entered California as pioneers and traders. The original base of the Jewish community was the Bay Area, and Jewish officeholding began early. The first state legislator from the gold Rush region was Jewish. Joseph Shannon was San Francisco city treasurer in 1851, and there were two Jewish justices in the first state supreme court in 1852. The governor elected in 1886 was half-Jewish, and San Francisco's Mayor Adolph Sutro (1894) was Jewish. Republican Julius Kahn was elected to the U.S. Congress in 1899 and served until 1924 (Narell 1982).

Although the early Jewish community in Los Angeles was much smaller, it fully participated in community life. Until the turn of the century, Jews served in public offices, and Jewish voters were eagerly courted by both parties in the 1876 presidential election (Stern 1981). Jews served on the city council and appeared as mayoral candidates (Stern 1980; Caper and Stern 1984). However, the influx of midwestern white Protestants led to the growth of a conservative ideology that was hostile to Jewish involvement. From 1900 until the early 1950s, Jews found themselves shut out of elective offices in Los Angeles (Vorspan and Gartner 1970). Ironically, Jews were on the way to becoming a Los Angeles-based community in those years.

This political exclusion in southern California is certainly no longer the pattern. In recent decades, an important shift has occurred in the nature of Jewish political participation. Jewish activists have moved from behind the scenes (as voters, organizers, and campaign donors) and have run for office in increasing numbers. The trend is not limited to California; in New York City today, a large number of elected officials are Jewish.

The rise of Jewish officeholding is an indication both of self-confidence and the need to protect group interests. There is less fear that the larger public will attack Jews for seeking an open role in the civic culture. Direct participation also reflects the concern of Jews for the protection of the group and of the state of Israel. This new political assertiveness dates approximately from the 1967 Six-Day War in the Middle East (Sandberg 1986).

The rise of Jewish politicians has been an important recent phenomenon (Guerra 1987; Willens 1980). Jewish candidates have been highly successful in Jewish constituencies but have also won offices in districts with small Jewish populations. Virtually the entire west side of Los Angeles (with the exception of Tom Hayden's 44th Assembly District) is represented by Jewish politicians in the city council, the state assembly, the state senate, and the United States Congress. Jews also constitute an important element of Democratic party fund raising at national, state, and local levels. Some Jewish conservatives have also been successful. Even the 12th Council District in the San Fernando Valley has a Republican Jewish council representative.

Jews have won significant offices in the Bay Area, including Dianne Feinstein's term as mayor of San Francisco. Along with the rise of Jewish candidates (including 1990 Democratic gubernatorial candidate Feinstein) has come a "combine" of Jewish elected officials led by Congressmen Henry Waxman and Howard Berman of Los Angeles. The liberal Waxman-Berman group unites west side candidates and also reaches outside the Jewish community to assist black and Latino candidates. By their ability to raise money and run direct-mail legislative campaigns, Waxman and Berman have been able to place favored liberal allies into numerous offices (Littwin 1976).

In recent years, Jewish candidates have been quite successful in California politics. They seem to be able to win elections even in constituencies with smaller Jewish populations. In the next section, the impact this continuing political success may have in developing multi-ethnic coalitions will be explored.

COALITIONS

This chapter has indicated the persistence of Jewish liberalism and political mobilization in the "New World" of California. Consistent with the bulk of research, there has not been a general desertion of liberalism by Jews in the face of racial conflict and threats to Israel. Jews in California play a major role in liberal Democratic politics as voters, activists, and politicians. Few national Democratic politicians miss the opportunity to take a fund-raising tour through the west side of Los Angeles, one of the cornerstones of state and national liberalism.

In this section the role and function of the Jewish community in California ethnic politics will be considered. What is the impact of a highly mobilized, activist, liberal, ethnic group with relatively high socio-economic status in a state where other minority groups are seeking power, recognition, and equality?

Earlier conceptions of the Jewish role in ethnic politics are becoming outdated. For instance, the view of the Jewish community as only a benevolent facilitator/philanthropist in ethnic politics—such as during the civil rights movement—must be expanded and revised. Since the 1967 Middle East War, and the rise of black anti-Semitism, Jews have clearly defined one goal of Jewish politics to be the protection of group interests. The coalition environment has therefore become much more complex and now resembles what coalition theorists refer to as a "mixed-motive" situation (Hinckley 1981).

Coalitions are formed between groups with different resources and goals. But the game within which coalitions form has a mixture of motives—cooperation and competition. Any group has interests to protect, but it may also be drawn into alliance with another group based on shared ideology or mutual interest. Ambivalence arises when shared ideology conflicts with group interests. Extremely strong coalitions can arise when shared ideology is merged with common interests.

The continued liberalism of the California Jewish community has made it a potential partner in the minority search for equality. In fact, persistent, mobilized liberalism makes the Jewish community a "blue chip" ally much sought after in private. At the same time, the increased political success of Jews makes them a potential competitor for other minority groups, and there is concern about how to form an equal relationship with a group that has significant political resources.

White liberalism, in which Jews have played a major role, has been an integral part of the rise of black and Latino representation in California cities. The chances for minority incorporation have been much better in cities with large white liberal communities. Browning, Marshall, and Tabb found that in the Bay Area (where Jews are less visible in a separate manner from the white liberal community) the strongest biracial coalition with the greatest degree of minority incorporation occurred in Berkeley.

"Berkeley established a model for the peaceful and strong incorporation of blacks into city government—a model that was not to be followed in other cities" (Browning et al., 48). A strong black political movement joined with the white liberal reform wing of the Democratic party. This city with only a 20 percent black population elected a black mayor and a biracial liberal city council and developed strong and innovative policies for minorities (Browning et al., 48-52).

The other extraordinary case of minority political incorporation followed a remarkably similar pattern in Los Angeles, far to the south. There, too, a highly effective black political movement had organized earlier and won a beachhead in city government. Then a powerful alliance was formed with

Jewish liberals active in the reform wing of the Democratic party (Sonenshein 1986; 1989b).

In Los Angeles, a large and active Jewish population acted as the functional equivalent of the white liberal base in Berkeley. More than in Berkeley, with its black-liberal alliance, the Los Angeles coalition explicitly featured a black-Jewish coalition. The Jewish vote was the core of a white liberal electoral base crucial to Bradley's success. Specifically, Jewish activists provided the bulk of Bradley's campaign treasury in his winning 1973 campaign (Sonenshein 1984). Time and again, Bradley and his white liberal and black allies rode this coalition to reelection. Once in power, the coalition was able to distribute substantial benefits to minority communities.

Thus the two most outstanding cases of biracial coalitions winning a surprising degree of minority power in cities with small black populations occurred in cities with large and powerful white liberal or Jewish communities.

Naturally such full-fledged coalitions are rare, but these California cases demonstrate that the role and function of the Jewish community go beyond liberal voting to include the art of interracial alliance. During the same era that despair has gripped those on the East Coast interested in building black-Jewish coalitions, they have been a prominent element of minority success in California.

One possible explanation of the difference is that in California, Jews are younger, better educated, and more mobile. These are the types of whites who are most likely to be allied with minority movements for incorporation. There have been fewer interest conflicts and more interest alliances between Jews and blacks in Los Angeles than in New York City (Sonenshein 1990a).

Biracial alliances advanced the political interests of the white liberal community (Sonenshein 1986). As Browning et al., note, "It may also have been fortunate for the cause of a biracial coalition that the Democratic edge in voter registration was very small in Berkeley. To achieve victory, a Democratic challenge absolutely had to have the enthusiastic participation of blacks" (50).

This was not just a reprise of the civil rights movement. Rather it was the application of ideological affinity in a setting of concrete, careful political action. This perspective helps mightily to avoid the notion that liberal politics is philanthropy; rather it is a pragmatic liberalism.

Since the Los Angeles coalition involved a black-Jewish alliance, these political gains could be accrued within the Jewish community. In Los Angeles, Jews had been generally excluded from the civic culture in a conservative community. Challenges to city hall from liberal reformers in the California Democratic Clubs (CDC) had been rebuffed. Alliance with the black community, already highly sophisticated and mobilized, created an awesome force bringing joint incorporation to blacks and liberal Jews. This coalition led to commission appointments and to the further development of Jewish political life, while at the same time solidifying the political gains of minorities (Sonenshein 1989b).

There has generally been concern among nonblack minorities that Jewish involvement in the minority struggle has been focused on blacks. Latinos in Los Angeles have often made this complaint.

Ironically, given the concern that blacks and Jews are closely tied at the expense of other minorities, the greatest challenge to biracial coalitions comes from the relationship between blacks and Jews. While other minorities resent the close relationship, the view from within the coalition is less sanguine. The rise of Jewish political candidacies has created the possibility of black-Jewish conflict over public offices. The Los Angeles biracial coalition barely dodged a bullet in 1989 when 5th District Councilman Zev Yaroslavsky, backed by the Waxman-Berman group, decided not to oppose Bradley for the mayoralty.

Many blacks resent and fear Jewish involvement in their search for equality while black politicians continue to cultivate Jewish support. Black leaders have arisen who say and do things that strike at the heart of Jewish interests. Other black leaders are torn between the desire not to appear "controlled by the Jews" and their realization that Jews are the most reliable white coalition partners available.

The symbol of the conflict is Rev. Jesse Jackson. Enormously popular among blacks, Jackson is seen by many Jews as hostile to their most vital group interests: support for Israel and opposition to anti-Semitism. Jackson's views on Israel alarm Jews, and his close association with Louis Farrakhan adds to the problem.

Fundamentally, Jackson presents an alternative plan for minority coalitions that excludes Jewish *interests* while hoping to retain non-Jewish white progressives and those ideologically liberal Jews who do not focus on the defense of Jewish interests.

Many Jews have reacted to Jackson by adopting the posture of broad liberalism and selective conservatism. In other words, Jews are by far the most likely white group to support a black or white liberal candidate, unless that candidate violates core Jewish interests. Thus, Jackson received little Jewish support in the Democratic primaries.

Analysis of the Democratic primary vote in 1984 and 1988 indicates that the Jackson candidacy stands virtually alone in its ability to close the gap between Jewish and non-Jewish whites. The Jackson phenomenon also separated Jews from other white liberals to an unusual degree. Berkeley Democrats were significantly more likely to support Jackson than Jewish Democrats in Los Angeles, even taking into account the impact of the black vote in Berkeley. This is consistent with the evidence that Jackson's main base of white support came from educated non-Jewish white liberals (Plissner and Mitofsky 1988). It is also possible that Bay Area Jews, with their high proportion of educated and unaffiliated Jews, may be somewhat less opposed to Jackson than southland Jews. See Table 11.

In the 1984 primary, a nationwide study of Jewish voting found that Jews rejected Jackson and supported mainstream Democratic liberals. California Jewish voters were found to be distinctive in that they supported Mondale; other white Democrats backed Hart. The suggested reason was that Hart had been hinting that he would not foreclose the possibility of placing Jackson on his ticket (American Jewish Committee 1984).

A California Poll (Field 1988) conducted just before the 1988 state primary discovered that an admittedly small subsample of Jewish voters favored Dukakis over Jackson by 62 percent to 16 percent. Among whites as a whole, the edge was 64-20.

But the Republicans were unhappy to discover that Jews remained Democratic and liberal in the general election. As Jews had provided heavy support for Bradley's two gubernatorial races, they also supported the national Democratic ticket in 1984 and 1988 (Table 12).

This pattern persisted despite numerous attempts by Republicans and Jewish conservatives to force the contradiction posed by Jackson to a head. One disappointed conservative, upon noting that Jews had stayed with the Democratic ticket in 1984, commented somewhat bitterly that during the campaign,

> Jews began with ever greater intensity to lecture other Jews to the effect that by turning Republican the Jews would be voting according to their base self-interest, as opposed to their traditionally noble concern for social justice (Dannhauser 1984, 4).

The future of minority coalitions involving Jews is likely to center around the dynamic movement for Latino representation, and to a lesser degree, the struggle of Asian Americans. Jews tend to be oriented toward minority coalition politics and to be strongly concerned with intergroup relations. (Each annual issue of the *American Jewish Yearbook* has an article on intergroup relations, and both the conservative *Commentary* and the liberal *Tikkun* magazines treat black-Jewish relations as prime subjects of Jewish interest.)

While relationships with the black community have dominated Jewish involvement in minority politics, there is reason to believe that alliances with Latinos and Asian Americans are practical and could be mutually beneficial. Although Jews do not have the same history of involvement with Latinos and Asian Americans, there is also less history of conflict.

Key tests will arise in the area of redistricting. The Latino community both in Los Angeles and statewide will be advancing strong claims to fair representation. These assertions have important coalition implications. For instance, can the interests of the liberal west-siders represented by Los Angeles County Supervisor Ed Edelman be reconciled with the need for

Table 11: *Vote for Jesse Jackson in the California Democratic Primary*

	1984[a]	1988
Jewish		
5th CD	12.5	17.8
Beverly Hills	4.4	9.8
White Liberal		
Berkeley	36.7	60.4
White Gentile		
7th CD	9.4	—
12th CD	8.1	19.2
Black		
8th CD	51.6	88.6

[a]In the 1984 presidential primary in California, delegates were selected on a slate basis. I averaged the vote for delegates pledged to particular candidates in order to estimate the vote for the presidential candidates.

Table 12: *Vote for President, 1984, 1988*

	Mondale 1984	Dukakis 1988
Jewish		
5th CD	59.2	64.6
Beverly Hills	50.8	58.7
White Liberal		
Berkeley	80.4	83.5
White Gentile		
7th CD	43.8	—
12th CD	31.1	40.5
Black		
8th CD	85.2	84.9

a Latino seat on the county board? [As this book goes to press, Latina Gloria Molina has won the seat without jeopardizing the existing black and white liberal seats. A new liberal majority now controls the county board.]

A very promising outcome of the recent federal court decision declaring Los Angeles County supervisorial lines void is that it sets up a potential three-way alliance among Jews, blacks, and Latinos. Liberals need one more seat to control the board, and both ideology and interest suggest that each group will control one of the three seats needed to take power for an insurgent coalition. The same efforts that were placed into black-Jewish coalitions will need to be implemented at the elite level to turn potential conflict into alliance.

IMPLICATIONS

It is ironic that Jewish political interests are most under attack from the Left these days, whether the white Left or the minority Left. Given the role Jews have played in progressive California politics, they ought to be the target of the Right. The function of Jews in California politics, as in many communities, has been to promote progressive social change within moderate bounds. This has meant support for progressive causes, whether through the vote, finance, or direct activism.

Among many Jews these attacks are taken with bafflement and anger. Why should a progressive group be the target of attacks from the Left? But this chapter has shown that Jewish progressivism has thus far continued in California despite such attacks. The persistence of Jewish liberalism suggests that the basis of Jewish progressive beliefs and participation is deeply rooted.

In the study of minority politics, analysts have tended to underestimate the scope and importance of Jewish liberalism. Jewish political behavior presents a baffling dilemma for scholars who see economic interest as the only explanation of progressive voting. Jewish political behavior is often evaluated incorrectly. It is often compared with the voting preferences of blacks, and issue disagreements between the two groups are highlighted. Alternatively, it is compared to former attitudes held by Jews.

The most illuminating comparison is between Jews and non-Jewish whites on the same issue at the same time. It will then be seen that Jewish liberalism is a highly distinctive and persistent phenomenon. Only the most direct attacks on Jewish survival interests are likely to place Jews on the other side from the most liberal whites. At the same time, as active participants in California politics, Jews will inevitably face the slings and arrows of political conflict among minorities.

Progressives need to find a balance between competition within a coalition, and the need to consider Jews as alliance partners worthy of being treated well. It is worth remembering that Jews are another minority group with hopes and fears of their own. Groups who wish them to be allies need to expend some energy cultivating them and reducing their fears.

At the same time, Jews will need to understand the political needs and expectations of other minorities. As a group with important political and economic resources, Jews may find other minorities fearful of losing their own autonomy through too-close alliance. Further, the prevalence of broad liberalism and selective conservatism can be confusing to non-Jews who may be seeking a single description of Jewish political behavior.

The future of coalition behavior by Jews depends on the willingness of all parties to see liberalism among Jews as a constant balancing of survival interests and commitment to social justice. The Jewish philosopher Hillel's questions apply: "If I am not for myself, who will be for me? If I am only for myself, what am I? And if not now, when?"

Finally, theories of ethnic politics that treat "whites" as a single ethnic entity without regard to severe ideological differences among whites will fail to provide an accurate picture of the setting for minority politics. The distinctive political behavior of Jews is a dramatic illustration of how white liberals differ from white conservatives. As Browning et al., (248) have noted, "Liberals on race issues are very different from conservatives, and ideology has an important influence on the nature and outcome of the minority struggle. . . ." How Jews are treated in such analysis is a metaphor for whether researchers are willing to acknowledge the importance of ideological division among whites in the struggle for minority equality.

REFERENCES

Allinsmith, Wesley, and Beverly Allinsmith. "Religious Affiliation and Politico-Economic Attitudes: A Study of Eight Major U.S. Religious Groups." *Public Opinion Quarterly* 12 (Fall 1948): 377-89.

American Jewish Committee. *Jewish Voting in the 1984 Democratic Primaries.* A research note published by the Institute of Human Relations, New York, New York, 1984.

Browning, Rufus, Dale Rogers Marshall, and David H. Tabb. *Protest is Not Enough: The Struggle of Blacks and Hispanics for Equality in City Politics.* Berkeley: University of California Press, 1984.

Caditz, Judith. *White Liberals In Transition: Current Dilemmas of Ethnic Integration.* Holliswood, NY: Spectrum Publications, 1976.

Caper, Gene, and Norton B. Stern. "First Jewish President of the Los Angeles City Council." *Western States Jewish History* 17 (October 1984): 63-76.

Dannhauser, Werner J. "Election '84: The Constancy of the Jewish Vote." *Congress Monthly* 3-5 (December 1984).

The Field Organization. *The California Poll, Release #1441,* The Field Organization, May 25, 1988.

Fisher, Alan M. "Realignment of the Jewish Vote?" *Political Science Quarterly* 94 (1979): 97-116.

Fisher, Alan M., and Curtis K. Tanaka. "California Jews: Data from the Field Polls." *American Jewish Yearbook* 86 (1986): 196-218.

Fuchs, Lawrence H. *The Political Behavior of American Jews.* Glencoe, Ill: Free Press, 1956.

Gelfand, Mitchell B. "Chutzpah in El Dorado: Social Mobility of Jews in Los Angeles, 1900-1920." Ph.D. thesis, Carnegie-Mellon University, 1981.

Goldstein, Sidney. "Jews in the United States: Perspectives on Demography." *American Jewish Yearbook* 81 (1981): 3-60. Published by the American Jewish Committee.

Guerra, Fernando J. "Ethnic Officeholders in Los Angeles County." *Sociology and Social Research* 71 (1987): 89-94.

Harris, Louis and Bert E. Swanson. *Black-Jewish Relations in New York City.* New York: Praeger, 1970.

Hinckley, Barbara. *Coalitions and Politics.* New York: Harcourt Brace Jovanovich, 1981.

Jewish Living. "Jewish California: An Insider's Guide." *Jewish Living* (March/April 1980): 50-51.

Kohs, Samuel C. "The Jewish Community of Los Angeles." *The Jewish Review* (July-November 1944): 87-126.

Kosmin, Barry A., Paul Ritterband, and Jeffrey Scheckner. "Jewish Population in the United States, 1986." *American Jewish Yearbook* 87 (1987): 164-94. Published by the American Jewish Committee.

Kosmin, Barry A., Paul Ritterband, and Jeffrey Scheckner. "Jewish Population in the United States - 1988." *American Jewish Yearbook* 89 (1989): 233-45. Published by the American Jewish Committee.

Littwin, Susan. "How Waxman and Berman Run the Bagel Boroughs." *California Journal* 7 (1976): 299-302.

Maller, Allen S. "Notes on California Jews' Political Attitudes - 1968." *Jewish Social Studies* 33 (1971): 160-64.

Mandel, Bill. "The Bay Area's Closet Jews." *San Francisco Chronicle*, September 27, 1981.

Narell, Irena. *Our City: The Jews of San Francisco.* San Diego, CA: Howell North Publishers, 1981.

_____. "Northern California." *Present Tense* (Spring 1982).

Plissner, Martin, and Warren Mitofsky. "The Changing Jackson Voter." *Public Opinion* (July/August 1988): 56-57.

Plotkin, Carol. Associate Director, American Jewish Congress, Los Angeles. Telephone interview with the author, June 12, 1990.

Sandberg, Neil C. *Jewish Life In Los Angeles: Window to Tomorrow.* Lanham, MD: University Press of America, 1986.

Scheckner, Jeffrey. Research consultant, Council of Jewish Federations. Telephone interview with the author, May 3, 1990.

Singleton, Gregory H. *Religion in the City of the Angels: American Protestant Culture and Urbanization, Los Angeles, 1850-1930.* UMI Research Press, 1979.

Siwulec, Dan. Researcher for political consulting firm Below, Tobe, and Company. Telephone interview with the author, 1989.

Sonenshein, Raphael J. "Bradley's People: Functions of the Candidate Organization." Ph.D. thesis, Yale University, 1984.

_____. "Biracial Coalition Politics in Los Angeles." *PS* 19 (Summer 1986): 582-90.

_____. "The Los Angeles Brand of Biracial Coalition Politics." *Los Angeles Times*, April 16, 1989a.

_____. "The Dynamics of Biracial Coalitions: Crossover Politics in Los Angeles." *Western Political Quarterly* 42 (June 1989b): 333-53.

_____. "Biracial Coalitions in Big Cities: Why They Succeed, Why They Fail." In *Racial Politics in American Cities*, edited by Rufus Browning, Dale Rogers Marshall, and David Tabb, 193-211. New York: Longman Press, 1990a.

_____. "Continuity and Change in a Biracial Coalition: The 1989 Los Angeles Mayoral Election." Paper presented at the annual meeting of the Western Political Science Association, 1990b.

Stern, Norton B. 1980. "The First Jew to Run for Mayor of Los Angeles." *Western States Jewish Historical Quarterly* 12 (April 1980): 246-59.

_____. "Los Angeles Jewish Voters During Grant's First Presidential Race." *Western States Jewish Historical Quarterly* 13 (January 1981): 179-85.

Vorspan, Max, and Lloyd P. Gartner. *History of the Jews of Los Angeles.* San Marino, CA: The Huntington Library, 1970.

Willens, Michele. "The Sudden Rise of the Jewish Politician." *California Journal* 11 (April 1980): 146-48.

Winslow, Doug. American Data Corporation. Telephone interview with the author, 1989.

Wolfinger, Raymond E., and Fred I. Greenstein. "The Repeal of Fair Housing in California: An Analysis of Referendum Voting." *American Political Science Review* 62 (1968): 753-69.

Zipperstein, Steve. "The Golden State: An Introduction." *Present Tense* (Spring 1982): 28-29.

III. ETHNIC POLITICAL LEADERSHIP IN CALIFORNIA

CHAPTER 6

FERNANDO J. GUERRA
Loyola Marymount University

The Emergence of Ethnic Officeholders in California

With its diverse population and numerous political offices, California provides the ideal location to examine the increase in minority officeholding. Minorities holding public office in California are a recent phenomenon. With the exception of a few rare and limited cases, blacks, Latinos, and Asians were excluded from holding political office in the first six decades of this century. Of the 300 most significant elective positions in California, there were two blacks, one Latino, and no Asians holding such a position in 1960. By 1989, there were 31 blacks, 17 Latinos, and six Asians holding significant positions in California. In terms of officeholding, minorities have made gains in the last three decades. These previously excluded groups have become significant contributors to the pool of public officeholders. This study documents this increase by laying out the electoral opportunities in California and examining the extent to which minorities have capitalized on these opportunities. This study will also focus on patterns that appear as minorities gain elective office in California.

The nomination of Tom Bradley in 1982 as the Democratic candidate for governor was the high point of contemporary minority politics in the state of California. Had he won he would have been the first elected black governor of the state of California and in the United States. However, he would not have been the first black elected statewide in California. Wilson Riles had been elected superintendent of public instruction in 1970, and Mervyn Dymally was elected lieutenant governor in 1974. Further, Bradley would not have been the first minority governor in California. A Latino, Romualdo Pacheco, was governor in 1875. Also, Bradley would not have been the only minority to win statewide office in 1982. March Fong Eu was reelected secretary of state, which she had first won in 1974. Another Asian, S. I. Hayakawa, served as U.S. senator from 1976 to 1982. These individuals have won some of the most visible positions in California. However, the electoral opportunity structure of California extends beyond statewide offices.

With 47 members, two in the Senate and 45 in the House, California has the largest congressional delegation in the United States. This delegation is expected to grow by five or as many as eight in the '90s. At the state level, there are seven, soon to be eight, constitutional (statewide) offices, 120 legislators, and four members of the Board of Equalization. In addition there are 58 counties, over 400 cities, and over 1,000 school districts, all of which elect officeholders. In total, including special district, judicial, and political party positions, there are over 10,000 electoral opportunities available in California.

Not all 10,000 positions can be considered of equal significance. While it is important for minorities to gain elective office at every level, it is especially important for them to gain the more significant positions in California. Significant positions control more resources, affect more people, and, due to their strategic location, provide more visibility for the elected public official. Holding a significant elective position would increase the ability of minorities to articulate, pursue, and protect their interests.

There are many measures that can be used to stratify the 10,000 positions to arrive at the most significant. Among these measures are budget size, constituent size, salary of the position, media exposure, full-time status of the position, and staff assistance. To simplify the process and because it complements the other measures, constituent size will be utilized. Stratifying the 10,000 elective positions is an attempt to reduce the number of positions being examined to a manageable size. A minimum threshold of 300,000 constituents as of 1988 was utilized. This permitted all federal and state positions to be included. It also included positions in the seven most populous cities and the seven most populous counties. Table 1 lists the positions that will be examined. None of the positions has less than 300,000 constituents, but some positions with as many constituents are excluded. Those excluded with over 300,000 constituents are mostly positions in mid-size counties.

The focus on minority representation further justifies the examination of these specific 300 positions. While minorities are not yet the majority of California's population, the pattern over the last several decades, as seen in Table 2, suggests that they will be within the next two decades, if not sooner. Further, the populations of selected counties in California, Table 3, indicate that minorities are concentrated in the very counties whose elected positions are being examined.

How have minorities done in winning some of the 300 most significant elective positions in California? Before the decade of the sixties very few minorities held one of the positions being examined. Between 1900 and 1960, no Asian held any of the 300 positions. A Latino, Miguel Estudillo from Riverside County, served in the state assembly from 1905 to 1908 and

Table 1:   *Elective Positions Being Examined, 1988*

	Total
Constitutional Offices: Governor; Lt. Governor, Attorney General; Secretary of State; Controller; Treasurer; and Superintendent of Public Instruction	7
Board of Equalization	4
Congressional: U.S. Senator (2); U.S. House of Representatives, 1958-61 (30); 1962-71 (38); 1972-81 (43); and 1982-89 (45)	47
California State Legislature: Senate (40); Assembly (80)	120
Counties:[1] Alameda (5); Los Angeles (5); Orange (5); Sacramento (5); San Bernardino (5); San Diego (5); and Santa Clara (5)	35
Cities:[2] Long Beach (9); Los Angeles (16); Oakland (9); Sacramento (9); San Diego, 1958-64 (7), 1965-89 (9); San Francisco (12); and San Jose, 1958-80 (7), 1981-89 (11)	75
Congressional, State and Local	288

[1]These are the seven most populous counties of California's 58 counties. Only the board of supervisors are being examined. Positions such as district attorney, assessor, and sheriff are exluded from analysis.

[2]These are the seven most populous cities in California. San Francisco is a consolidated city and county and has an 11-member board of supervisors and a mayor. Los Angeles has an elected mayor and a 15-member council. In all other cities being examined the mayor is part of the council, though it may be elected separately. Positions such as city attorney, city clerk, and city treasurer are excluded from analysis.

in the state senate from 1909 to 1912.[1] The only other Latino to hold a significant elective position was Ed Roybal, who was elected to the Los Angeles City Council in 1949 after having failed in 1947. Roybal also won the Democratic nomination for lieutenant governor in 1954, losing in the general election. In 1958, Roybal ran for the Los Angeles County Board of Supervisors and lost. That same year Hank Lopez won the Democratic nomination for secretary of state. He was the only Democrat that lost a statewide election in the Democratic landslide.[2] Blacks have been represented in the assembly since the second decade of the century. In 1918, Fred

[1]Fernando Padilla, "Roster of Chicano Legislators in the Five Southwestern States," unpublished manuscript.

[2]For coverage of this period see Rodolfo F. Acuna, *A Community Under Siege: A Chronicle of Chicanos East of the Los Angeles River, 1945-1975* (Los Angeles: UCLA Chicano Studies Research Center Publications, 1984).

Emergence of Ethnic Officeholders

Table 2:   *California Population by Race and Ethnicity, 1960-1990*

	1960		1970	
Asian[1]	378,100	2.4%	648,000	3.2%
Black	883,900	5.6%	1,378,000	6.9%
Latino[2]	1,426,500	9.0%	2,377,100	11.9%
Minority	2,688,500	17.0%	4,403,100	22.0%
Jewish[3]	530,300	3.4%	721,000	3.6%
Ethnic	3,218,800	20.4%	5,124,100	25.6%
White[4]	12,581,200	79.6%	14,915,100	74.4%
Total	15,800,000	100%	20,039,200	100%

	1980		1990	
Asian	1,582,900	6.7%	2,799,200	9.7%
Black	1,791,900	7.6%	2.157,000	7.5%
Latino	4,565,100	19.2%	7,099,100	24.7%
Minority	7,939,900	33.4%	12,055,300	41.9%
Jewish	753,900	3.2%	868,200	3.0%
Ethnic	8,693,800	36.6%	12,923,500	44.9%
White	15,081,600	63.4%	15,910,900	55.3%
Total	23,775,400	100%	28,771,200	100%

[1] Asian category includes Asian and Pacific Islander, American Indian, Eskimo and Aleut, and others.

[2] Latino category includes Hispanic (1980), Spanish Origins (1970), and Spanish Surname (1960).

[3] Figures for Jewish category are from the *American Jewish Yearbook* 1960, 1970, 1980, and 1988.

[4] White category excludes Latinos and Jews.

[5] Estimate from "Projected Total Population for California By Race and Ethnicity," Report 88, p-4, Population Research Unit, Department of Finance, State of California.

Table 3: *Population of Selected Counties in California by Race and Ethnicity, 1980*

	Total	Asian	Black	Latino	Minority
California	23,667,900	1,582,900	1,791,900	4,565,100	7,939,900
Alameda	1,105,379	97,199	203,698	129,665	430,562
Los Angeles	7,477,503	511,262	943,124	2,065,503	3,519,889
Orange	1,932,709	110,077	24,560	285,722	420,359
Sacramento	783,381	50,879	58,596	73,918	183,393
San Bernardino	895,016	28,816	47,964	165,837	242,617
San Diego	1,861,846	111,542	104,407	274,530	490,479
San Francisco	678,974	152,835	86,190	84,194	323,219
Santa Clara	1,295,071	111,933	42,835	226,388	381,156
Total	16,029,879	1,174,543	1,511,374	3,305,757	5,991,674
Percent of State Total	67.7%	74.2%	84.3%	72.4%	75.5%

Source: U.S. Bureau of Census.

Roberts, a Republican from Los Angeles, was elected. He was defeated by a black Democrat, Augustus Hawkins, in 1934. In 1948, William B. Rumford was elected to the assembly from Alameda County. Thus, in 1960 there were no Asians, one Latino, Roybal, and two blacks, Hawkins and Rumford, holding one of the 300 significant elective positions in California.

There was no change in the level of minority representation throughout the '50s. The decade began with three minorities holding significant positions and ended with the same number. The '60s would be another story. As Table 4 reveals, by the end of the '60s, minorities had increased their representation to 23. By the end of the '70s, they had more than doubled their representation to 47. Finally, by the end of the '80s, Asians, blacks, and Latinos held 54 or 19 percent of the elective offices being examined.[3]

---

[3]The sources used for the identification of ethnic officeholders are as follows: Asian American Studies Center, *The National Asian American Roster* (Los Angeles: UCLA Asian American Studies Center, 1979, 1982, 1984); Joint Center for Political Studies, *The National Roster of Black Elected Officials* (Washington, D.C.: Joint Center for Political Studies, 1970-1989); National Association of Latino Elected and Appointed Officials, *The National Roster of Hispanic Elected Officials* (Washington, D.C.: NALEO 1984-1989); Sethard Fisher, *Black Elected Officials in California* (San Francisco: R & E Research Associates, 1978); *Los Angeles Herald Examiner*, several issues; *Los*

Table 4:   *Asian, Black, and Latino Officeholders in 288 Selected Elective Offices in California, 1958-1989*

Year	No. of Pos.	Asian No.	%	Black No.	%
1958	267	0	0	2	.8
1959	267	0	0	2	.8
1960	267	0	0	2	.8
1961	267	0	0	2	.8
1962	275	1	.4	4	1.5
1963	275	2	.7	7	2.6
1964	275	2	.7	8	2.9
1965	277	2	.7	10	3.6
1966	277	5	1.8	12	4.3
1967	277	5	1.8	12	4.3
1968	277	6	2.2	13	4.7
1969	277	6	2.2	14	5.1
1970	277	7	2.5	17	6.1
1971	277	7	2.5	17	6.1
1972	282	7	2.5	17	6.0
1973	282	8	2.8	18	6.4
1974	292	9	3.2	21	7.5
1975	282	9	3.2	22	7.8
1976	282	10	3.6	23	8.2
1977	282	10	3.6	25	8.7
1978	282	10	3.6	23	8.2
1979	282	11	3.9	26	9.2
1980	282	8	2.8	28	9.9
1981	286	7	2.5	28	9.8
1982	288	6	2.1	27	9.4
1983	288	6	2.1	29	10.1
1984	288	5	1.7	29	10.1
1985	288	7	2.4	29	10.1
1986	288	5	1.7	30	10.4
1987	288	5	1.7	29	10.1
1988	288	6	2.1	30	10.4
1989	288	6	2.1	31	10.8

Angeles Times, several issues. Office of the Secretary of State, *Statement of Vote*, Sacramento, 1960-1988. Secretary of the Senate, *California Legislature at Sacramento: Biographies and Photographs of Senate and Assembly Members and Officers*, Sacramento, 1960-1988; California Journal *Almanac of California Government and Politics*, 7 volumes, (Sacramento: California Journal Press, 1989).

Table 4:   *1958-1989 (continued)*

| Latino | | Minority | | % Min. | Ratio |
No.	%	No.	%	Pop.	Quotient
1	.4	3	1.1	15.3	.07
1	.4	3	1.1	16.2	.07
1	.4	3	1.1	17.0	.06
1	.4	3	1.1	17.9	.06
3	1.1	8	2.9	18.7	.16
3	1.1	12	4.4	19.6	.22
2	.7	12	4.4	20.4	.22
2	.7	14	5.1	21.3	.24
2	.7	19	6.9	22.1	.31
2	.7	19	6.9	23.0	.30
3	1.1	22	7.9	23.8	.33
3	1.1	23	8.3	24.7	.34
6	2.2	30	10.8	25.6	.42
6	2.2	30	10.8	26.4	.41
10	3.6	35	12.4	27.2	.46
10	3.6	37	13.1	28.0	.47
11	3.9	41	14.5	28.8	.50
12	4.3	43	15.3	29.5	.52
12	4.3	45	16.0	30.3	.53
12	4.3	47	16.7	31.0	.54
11	3.9	44	15.6	31.8	.49
10	3.6	47	16.7	32.6	.51
10	3.6	46	16.3	33.4	.49
10	3.5	45	15.7	34.2	.46
13	4.5	46	16.0	35.1	.46
13	4.5	48	16.7	35.9	.47
14	4.9	48	16.7	36.8	.45
15	5.2	51	17.7	37.6	.47
15	5.2	50	17.4	38.5	.45
16	5.6	50	17.4	39.3	.44
17	5.9	53	18.4	40.2	.46
17	5.9	54	18.8	41.0	.46

Several patterns emerge from Table 4. First, at any one point, blacks have more than half of the minority gains. This is so even though the Latino population is a larger proportion in the state, and it is estimated that Asians have surpassed the black population total in 1990 (see Table 2).

Second, while the black gains compared with Latino and Asian gains in the '60s and '70s are impressive, they slowed considerably in the '80s. In fact, Latinos surpassed blacks in winning significant positions seven to three in the '80s. Third, Latino gains are slow but continuous, especially after the late '60s. Finally, Asian gains are erratic. They actually equal Latino gains by 1964, surpass Latinos from 1966 to 1971, maintain about the same level of representation in the '70s and then decline throughout the '80s.

A focus on the congressional delegation and the Los Angeles City Council where all three groups have achieved representation illuminates further patterns that should be pursued in explaining the emergence of minority officeholders. Nine congressional positions have been held by minorities since 1962—four by blacks, three by Latinos, and two by Asians. In 1962, Augustus Hawkins left the assembly and won the 21st Congressional District. In the reapportionment of 1974 the district number was changed to the 29th. He held the seat for 28 years until his retirement in 1990. It seems likely that Maxine Waters from the assembly and the Democratic primary winner will replace him. In 1970, Ron Dellums, then a Berkeley City Councilman, defeated the incumbent in the Democratic primary for the 7th District. He has held what is now the 8th District into the '90s. In 1972, Assemblywoman Yvonne Brathwaite-Burke won the newly established and vacant 37th District. In 1978, she ran for attorney general and was replaced, in what was by then the 28th District, by Assemblyman Julian Dixon. In 1980, Mervyn Dymally, former assemblyman, state senator and lieutenant governor, defeated the incumbent in the Democratic primary for the 31st District, which he has held into the '90s.

Latinos first won representation in 1962 when Los Angeles City Councilman Ed Roybal defeated Republican incumbent Gordon McDonough in the 30th District, which was drastically altered by the Democratic reapportionment. He has held onto what is now the 25th District into the '90s. In 1982, Assemblyman Marty Martinez won the 30th District in a special election in July and then defeated Republican Congressman John Rousselot, who had lost his seat in the 1981 redistricting. Also, in 1982, Estaban Torres won the newly created and vacant 34th District. In 1974, San Jose Mayor Norman Mineta became the first Asian congressman from California when he won the newly created and vacant 13th District. In 1978, Sacramento City Councilman Robert Matsui won the vacant 3d District.

Several patterns become apparent in reviewing the ascension of minorities to the U.S. House of Representatives. First, of the 11 minorities to have held a congressional seat from California, 10 held a previous elective office.[4] Six had previously served in the state legislature and four at the

---

[4]The total includes Maxine Waters.

local level. The lone exception was Estaban Torres who had been a White House aide and ambassador to UNESCO in the Carter administration. It would be interesting to compare this prior experience with the nonminorities. Statewide data have not been examined. However, a prior examination of the Los Angeles County delegation, which is a third of the state total, revealed that of the 32 whites (non-Latino and non-Jewish) who held a congressional seat since 1960, only 17, or 53 percent, had prior elective service.[5]

Second, of the nine congressional seats that have been won by minorities, six were vacant when they were first captured. One of those that was not vacant had been so changed by redistricting that 70 percent of the district was new to the incumbent. The role of redistricting is the third pattern that appears. Of the nine seats, six had been won in the election immediately after a reapportionment. Combining the second and third pattern, of the nine seats, seven were initially won when they were vacant or in the election immediately after a reapportionment or both. The two exceptions are the primary victories over incumbents by Dellums and Dymally.

Fourth, none of the incumbent minorities has been defeated for reelection. It can be further said that none has been seriously challenged by either minority or nonminority candidates. While all nine seats have been safe Democratic districts, not all have a minority population that is over 50 percent. Further, half of the districts do not include 50 percent registered voters who are of the same ethnic background as the incumbent, let alone 50 percent of the voters who turn out. Incumbency provides protection beyond ethnicity once a position is captured. It will be interesting to see if the seats remain in minority hands after the retirement of the incumbent. This is especially the case with the two Asian seats and the one held by Dellums. Two black seats have changed hands, from Burke to Dixon and from Hawkins to Waters. However, of the four black seats, these two were the safest.

All three minority groups have won representation on the Los Angeles City Council. In 1949, Latino Ed Roybal captured the 9th District. He resigned his seat in late 1962 to assume his congressional position. In 1963, the council appointed Gilbert Lindsay, a black aide to County Supervisor Hahn, to fill the Roybal vacancy. Later in the same year, Tom Bradley and Billy Mills both won seats as well. Bradley would become mayor in 1973 and be replaced in the 10th District by David Cunningham. Cunningham would resign in late 1986 and be replaced by Nate Holden in 1987. Billy

---

[5]Fernando J. Guerra, "Ethnic Politics in Los Angeles: The Emergence of Black, Jewish, Latino and Asian Officeholders, 1960-1989." Ph.D. dissertation, University of Michigan, 1990.

Mills held on to the 8th District until 1974 when he was appointed to the Superior Court. He was replaced by Bob Farrell later that year.

Latinos did not regain representation on the Los Angeles City Council until December 1985 when Assemblyman Alatorre was elected to the 14th District. In February 1987, Assemblywoman Gloria Molina was elected to the 1st District, which was newly created to settle a Voting Rights Suit by the U.S. Justice Department. In 1985, the only Asian to ever be elected to the council, Michael Woo, defeated the incumbent in the 13th District. Thus, from 1963 to 1990, blacks have held three of the 15 or 20 percent of the seats. In contrast, Latinos had no representation from the time of Roybal's resignation to Alatorre's election, a span of 23 years.

Many of the same patterns that emerged for minorities at the congressional level also emerge at the council level. While the extent of prior elective service is not as great, Alatorre and Molina did move directly from the state assembly, and Holden had previously served in the state senate, most did have prior public sector service. For instance, of the current six minorities on the council, all began their public service as legislative aides. Alatorre for Assemblyman Karabian; Molina for Assemblyman Torres; Woo for State Senator Roberti; Ferrell for Councilman Mills and Mayor Bradley; and Lindsay and Holden for County Supervisor Hahn. The rise of staff at the federal level has been noted[6] as has the movement from staff to elective position.[7] However, that all current minority councilmembers were former legislative aides is a strong indication that increasingly such positions are channels to elective office, especially for minorities.

As with winning congressional office, vacancies and reapportionment played a role in minority victories for Los Angeles City Council positions. Of the six council positions held by minorities, four were vacant when first captured. Also, four were captured in the election immediately after a reapportionment. In total, five of the six positions were initially captured when they were either vacant, immediately after a reapportionment, or both. The lone exception was Michael Woo's victory. Finally, as was the case at the congressional level, none of the minorities has been defeated for reelection or seriously challenged.

---

[6]Norman Ornstein, Thomas E. Mann, Michael J. Malbin, and John F. Bibby, "The Growth of Staff," in *Congress and Public Policy: A Source Book of Documents and Readings*, 2d ed., edited by David C. Kozak and John D. Macartney (Chicago: Dorsey Press, 1987), 94-100. On the staff of Los Angeles elected officials see, John D. Macartney, "Congressional Staff: The View from the District," same volume, 100-16.

[7]Charles Price and Charles Bell, "Lawyer-Legislators: The Capitol's Endangered Species," *California Journal* 20 (April 1989): 181-83.

While the focus was only on the congressional delegation and the Los Angeles City Council, these patterns are also evident at the state senate, state assembly and most of the county and city positions being examined.

These patterns of prior public service, vacancies, reapportionment, and incumbency strength are not new in American politics. What is new is the extent to which they structure the emergence of minority officeholders. In California, these patterns apply to minorities to a greater extent than they do to nonminorities.

The emergence of minority officeholders coincides with the emergence of the Democrats as the dominant party in California. The Democratic party of California prior to the late 1950s was weak and disorganized. It won few elections at the statewide level and was underrepresented in the state assembly, state senate and the congressional delegation as compared with its percentage of registered voters. In the election of 1958, the Democrats were finally able to capitalize on their registration edge. They won five of the six statewide partisan offices, the U.S. Senate seat, and majorities in the state assembly, state senate, and congressional delegation.

Democrats soon began formulating strategies to maintain their new won majorities. At the center of this was Jesse Unruh. Unruh was elected speaker of the assembly in 1961 and was looking to strengthen his hold on the party and the party's hold on power. Unruh's vision of the party was the 41 Democratic assemblymembers required to elect the speaker. He therefore looked to strengthen the party by strengthening the elected officeholders. This he did by professionalizing the legislature. Among the reforms instituted by Unruh were higher pay, longer sessions, and an increase in staff. Minority inclusion was a by-product of the broader strategy to maintain and expand the dominance of the Democrats in part by professionalizing the legislature. As Bell and Price comment,

> When the legislature was part-time and legislative salaries were minimal, California legislators were mostly middle-aged, white, male, Anglo-Saxon Protestants. Many of the legislators who served were the well-to-do who could afford to be away from their jobs for a few months each year, and who did not have to live off their meager legislative salaries. Professionalization of the legislature has helped broaden opportunities and has encouraged heretofore un- or under-represented groups within society to seek a legislative position. Obviously, a host of reasons helps account for the increasing numbers of minority members and women getting elected to the California legislature—reapportionment, growing political awareness in minority communities, and more minorities going to law school or working on legislative staff—but the increased pay, status, and career potentials in the legislature have

helped break down the formerly white, "Gentlemen's Club" atmosphere.[8]

Unruh and the Democrats were transforming California politics for partisan gain. The more they could change the nature of officeholding from when the Republicans dominated, the greater the likelihood that they could continue to increase their control. However, increasing the salary, staff, and status of elected officials did not prevent Republicans from effectively competing. The one possible exception would be to change or include a new social category (ethnicity) of elected official. While there are black, Latino, and Asian Republicans, there are not enough to create majority districts of such individuals who would elect ethnic Republicans. On the other hand, there were areas where the creation of black districts would lead to the election of black Democrats. Therefore, it is no surprise that the Democrats actively assisted in the transformation of the ethnic background of the elected officeholders of California.

From the examination of the congressional delegation and the Los Angeles City Council, it appears that this was done by structuring electoral opportunities for minorities through newly created or reapportioned and vacant seats. Also, through the recruitment of well-known and loyal candidates who served in prior elective office or as legislative aides.

This structuring of opportunities and recruitment of minorities needs to be systematically studied. Central to the focus has to be the new form of politics that has emerged with the increase of paid political staff.

The emergence of minority officeholders in California has coincided with a shift in the recruitment of candidates from political parties, local government, and the bureaucracy to the political staff of the incumbent officeholders themselves. Each officeholder with associated staff can be seen as constituting an organization from which potential candidates for elective office may emerge. Each of the significant positions, with the exception of some of the councils, have at least four and sometimes as many as 20 staff positions that are filled at the discretion of the officeholder. Thus, there are hundreds of legislative aides in the pool of eligibles in California. Over a thousand individuals are in the pool of eligibles if former staffers who have moved on to other public sector positions, usually with the support of the officeholder, and maintain an interest in running for office are considered.

With the available resources, each officeholder is a potential sponsor. However, not all officeholders have a significant interest in sponsoring a candidate for a particular vacancy. The interest increases the more the vacant position is of geographic, ethnic, and partisan concern. This list of interest is not exhaustive. Other possible concerns such as policy pref-

---

[8]Charles G. Bell and Charles M. Price, *California Government Today: Politics of Reform?* 3d edition (Chicago: Dorsey Press, 1988), 179.

erences can come into play.   These concerns usually originate from secondary recruitment groups such as labor, the business community, environmentalists, community organizations, and other groups from specific issue areas. Invariably, these groups will be frustrated at certain points and field their own candidates. Most of the time, however, they work through existing officeholders in recruiting candidates.

With most minority officeholders being geographically concentrated and of the same party, there is a convergence of the above interests. This convergence has created identifiable regions within the state that determine the general makeup of the sponsors and candidates that will emerge. For instance, there exists the black Democratic recruitment network in South Central Los Angeles and another in Alameda County and the Latino Democratic recruitment network in East Los Angeles and the Southwestern San Gabriel Valley. Recruitment networks are coalitions of incumbent organizations. In each network there are established sponsors to whom officeholders from other networks usually defer in recruiting candidates in their region. Competition from other networks or regions occurs as one network expands into the territory of another because of demographic shifts. Competition within networks also occurs when consensus is not reached on the network's candidate.

The emergence of political recruitment networks in California's minority communities can be seen in a case study of Latinos in Los Angeles. The major recruitment camp revolved around Richard Alatorre, an assemblyman and later city councilman, and Art Torres, also an assemblyman and later a state senator. Alatorre had been a legislative aide to Assemblyman Walter Karabian who was the majority leader in the assembly and represented an increasingly Latino district. Alatorre had first run for the College Board in 1969 and was not competitive. In 1971 he ran in a special election to fill a vacancy for an assembly seat and again lost. In 1972 he ran again for the same assembly seat in the regularly scheduled election and won. One of his first legislative aides, Art Torres, would win a vacant assembly position in 1974. What was key to both of their victories was not only the support they received from officeholders to whom they were aides, but to the expansion of the Latino political region. Both of the positions they captured were in part opened up by the retirement or movement to higher office of white incumbents who understood the changing ethnic nature of their districts, reapportionment, or both. This lesson was not lost on both Alatorre and Torres who were poised for the next opportunity to expand the Latino region.

A key year for the development of the Latino recruitment network was 1982. The 1982 election would be the first after a major reapportionment orchestrated by Alatorre himself. Because of Alatorre' and Torres' support in the speakership battle of 1980, the new Speaker Willie Brown gave Alatorre the chairmanship of the assembly committee in charge of reapportionment. With this position, Alatorre ensured that two new Latino congressional districts were drawn and that the three state senate and four assembly positions that were held by Latinos were secure.

A meeting, attended by most of the Latinos holding significant positions, was held to discuss candidates for these new congressional districts and other possible vacancies. It was decided that Assemblyman Marty Martinez would run for the more secure of the new congressional seats. The second seat would go to Esteban Torres, a former White House aide and UNESCO ambassador. Charles Calderon, a former Alatorre aide and Montebello School Board member, was chosen to replace Martinez in the assembly. Further, Art Torres, a former Alatorre aide and an incumbent assembly member, had decided to challenge Alex Garcia, a former aide to Congressman Roybal and the incumbent state senator, who had not been invited to the meeting. A decision could not be reached on the assembly replacement for Art Torres. Two legislative aides were seeking the support of the group. Neither Richard Polanco, an aide to Alatorre, nor Gloria Molina, an aide to Torres, would concede. Thus, both ran in the Democratic primary with Molina winning.

The inability to resolve which aide would replace Torres within the group led to the emergence of a rival recruitment camp within the Latino network. While Molina had the official support of some of the Latino officeholders, as did Polanco, much more pressure had been exerted on her to withdraw. After her victory, Molina felt independent of the recruitment group and chose to endorse a rival candidate in the next election for a vacant assembly position. This vacancy occurred when Alatorre gave up his assembly seat after his election to the city council in late 1985. Richard Polanco was endorsed by Alatorre and Torres, but Molina endorsed Mike Hernandez. Also endorsing Hernandez was Congressman Roybal who had felt uncomfortable with the emergence of the recruitment network. Roybal along with other Latinos elected before 1980 were not strong members of the recruitment network. In order to foster competition, Roybal was willing to support rival candidates with Molina.

While Mike Hernandez, the first Roybal-Molina candidate, lost, the second, Molina herself, was successful. Just as Alatorre had done, Molina sought election to the city council from the assembly in 1987. Opposing her was Larry Gonzalez, a Los Angeles School Board member and legislative aide to Senator Torres, who had defeated a white incumbent for the school board in 1983. Molina easily won the city council seat and was replaced in the assembly by Roybal's daughter Lucille Roybal-Allard. Roybal-Molina also endorsed the candidacy of David Lopez-Lee for college board in 1987. Lopez-Lee won a position left vacant by Leticia Quesada, an Alatorre sponsored candidate for school board, the position that had been vacated by Gonzalez when he ran against Molina. Thus, in the '80s, all of the new

Latino officeholders for significant positions in Los Angeles were recruited by the two rival camps.

How important are the recruitment networks to the emergence of ethnic officeholders? Some Latinos in Los Angeles had won before the establishment of such networks or coalitions of candidate organizations. However, no Latino or black officeholder was elected in the '80s without support from a network. What made election almost automatic was the sponsorship of a recruitment network. These networks provided the necessary resources required to run an effective modern campaign. Money, professional campaign expertise, and campaign workers who had previously been mobilized in other campaigns were shifted to the network's sponsored candidate. Only a rival network could compete with such resources.

These recruitment networks went beyond electing ethnics to districts whose ethnic makeup predetermined the ethnicity of the officeholder. They made ethnic candidates competitive in districts that were becoming ethnic but had not yet completed the transition. There are numerous examples of candidates sponsored by secondary recruitment groups, such as community organizations, who were unable to defeat the white incumbent. These campaigns had banked on the shifting demographics alone and failed. These efforts were usually followed by a recruitment network candidate with the necessary resources winning the next time around.

Officeholders who emerged from these networks were also protected from any effective challenges to their newly acquired position. No incumbent Latino, or black officeholder in Los Angeles who emerged from one of these networks was ever defeated for reelection. On the other hand, of the six Latinos who were elected to significant positions in Los Angeles County before the establishment of the Latino recruitment network, four were eventually defeated. These networks not only endorsed candidates and protected incumbents, but also disciplined members and punished challengers.

The impact of reapportionment, vacancies, the rise of the Democratic party, and the establishment of recruitment networks on minority officeholding in California needs further study. Further, these are not the only trends that should be examined when studying minority politics. Specifically, the growth of minority communities and the increasing organization and mobilization of these communities need to be more carefully addressed. The growth and organization of minority communities provide the rationale or necessity for their inclusion into politics. However, reapportionment, vacancies, Democratic support, and recruitment networks to a great extent can provide the means to political inclusion.

CHAPTER 7

LARRY L. BERG AND C. B. HOLMAN
University of Southern California

Ethnic Voting Patterns and Elite Behavior: California's Speaker of the Assembly

Ethnic group politics first emerged as a major focus of scholarly attention in the 1960s with the increased visibility of minorities in the political process. The turbulence of the civil rights movement coincided with a dramatic rise in the number of minority candidates for public office, especially among black Americans. The growth of minority representation was most obvious at the local level. The number of black mayors in the United States increased from 29 in 1969 to 107 by 1974. But minority representation has also made significant strides at the state and national levels. Today in California the second most powerful state officeholder, Speaker of the Assembly Willie L. Brown, Jr., is African American.

Research on ethnic group politics as it pertains to blacks has focused largely on electoral patterns and elite behaviors in local politics. This study attempts to provide some insights to racial politics by analyzing the elections of Willie Brown among a predominantly white constituency and his ascension to power in a predominantly white state legislature. Although distinct racial voting patterns among Brown's constituency are apparent, the authors document a growing acceptance of the incumbent candidate across all ethnic groups and social classes under study. Legislative histories and campaign financial records also demonstrate a dramatic enhancement of the speaker's clout in state government.

CALIFORNIA'S ETHNIC BACKGROUND

California's Ethnic Politics

California is a multiracial society whose minority groups are expected to comprise a majority of the state's population by the year 2000. Blacks, Hispanics, and Asians currently make up about one-third of California's residents. According to 1990 census figures, there are about 2.1 million blacks in the state, or 7 percent of the population. Nevertheless, blacks constitute only 3 percent of all elected officials in the state.

The largest minority group in California is the Hispanic community. There are 7.7 million Hispanics in the state amounting to 26 percent of the total population. Despite their greater numbers, Hispanics hold only 7.6 percent of the 2,861 elected offices in the state of California (Bizjak 1991, 1).

Black representation in California government was very rare prior to the 1960s. Frederick Roberts became the first black member of the assembly in 1934 followed by W. Byron Rumford in 1948. Reverend F. Douglas Ferrell and Mervyn Dymally both moved into the assembly in 1962. By 1967, there were six black representatives in the state legislature, with Dymally moving into the state senate and the additions of Willie Brown, Yvonne Burke, Bill Greene, Leon Ralph, and John Miller to the assembly. Julian Dixon and Frank Holloman won assembly seats in 1972. Teresa Hughes and Curtis Tucker were elected in 1974, Maxine Waters in 1976, and Gwen Moore in 1978. The growth in black representation in the California legislature in the 1980s has slowed somewhat compared to the previous decade.

This pattern of substantial growth in black representation in the 1970s, only to wane somewhat in the next decade, similarly occurred nationwide. When the Voting Rights Act was approved in 1965, there were less than 500 elected black officials in the nation. By January 1985, blacks held 6,065 elected positions in the United States, although blacks still comprise less than 1.5 percent of the total number of elected officials. Most of this jump in black representation took place between 1970 and 1975. The rate of increase in elected black officials was 138.5 percent in the first half of the 1970s, 40.2 percent from 1975 to 1980, and 23.3 percent from 1980 to 1985 (Williams 1987, 111, 124). Nevertheless, important strides in black representation are continuing to date, as evidenced by the 1990 election of the nation's first black governor, Douglas Wilder of Virginia.

Willie L. Brown, Jr.

It is widely recognized that Speaker of the Assembly Willie L. Brown, Jr. has emerged as the second-most powerful current officeholder in California politics—a remarkable accomplishment given his background. Brown came from an impoverished family from Mineola, Texas. His father abandoned the family; his mother worked as a domestic servant. Brown performed a number of odd jobs, including migrant work, as he excelled through the all-black Mineola Colored High School. In 1951, he moved to San Francisco with a relative and eventually worked his way through law school. Brown's early years of law practice primarily involved the defense of prostitutes and drug users.

Brown lost his first bid to the assembly in 1962 but was able to recoup and win the seat in 1964. He became part of San Francisco's "left-leaning" Burton machine in the 1970s and, partly due to that greater respectability and influence, refocused his continuing law practice to represent various developer interests.

In the assembly, Willie Brown earned a reputation as somewhat of a maverick. Then-Speaker Jesse M. Unruh appointed Brown chair of the unimportant Legislative Representation Committee in 1967 to punish him for his independence. But seen more favorably in the 1970s by Speaker Bob Moretti, Brown was appointed chair of the powerful Ways and Means Committee where he developed an acumen for political maneuvering. He became known as the "consummate compromiser," a reputation that provided both advantages and disadvantages. For example, in 1974 Brown lost his first bid for the speakership to Leo McCarthy because several assembly blacks abandoned their support. Ironically, he finally captured assembly leadership in 1980 with support from many of the body's Republican members. He had not intended to run for the speakership, but a Democratic deadlock between McCarthy and Howard Berman enabled Brown to forge a winning Democratic-Republican coalition.

To the admiration of some and the scorn of others, Willie Brown solidified his authority over the assembly. As will be shown, he has nurtured a strong constituency base and devised funding and legislative techniques to maintain firmly the long-sought reigns of leadership.

THEORIES OF ETHNIC POLITICS

Much of the research on ethnic voting patterns in elections in which a minority candidate is involved has looked at mayoral and other local contests. Several early studies found substantial racial distinctions in voting patterns. In each case, a successful black mayoral candidacy was attributed more to the growth of black populations in cities than to the receptivity by white voters of a black candidate. A 1969 mayoral bid in Detroit by black candidate Richard Austin garnered only 19 percent of the white vote (Lewis 1971, 67). Austin's black successor in 1973, Coleman Young, fared no better among white voters. Similar patterns of black mayoral candidates receiving very small margins of white votes have been documented in 1967 in Gary, Cleveland, in 1974 in a host of smaller cities, and in 1983 in Chicago."[1]

---

[1]See, for example, Jeffrey Hadden, Louis Masotti, and Victor Thiessen, "The Making of the Negro Mayors, 1974," *Trans-Action* (January 1968): 21-30; Thomas Pettigrew, "When a Black Candidate Runs for Mayor: Race and Voting Behavior," in *People and Politics in Urban Society,* edited by Harlan Hahn (Beverly Hills: Sage Publishers, 1972); Michael Preston, Lenneal Henderson, Jr., and Paul Puryear, *The*

A study on the Los Angeles mayoral elections in 1969 and 1973 provided some new insights (Hahn et al. 1976). Unlike other cities studied, blacks comprised no more than 18 percent of Los Angeles' population. Yet, black candidate Thomas Bradley ran competitively in the first election and won in the second. In both elections, large margins of white voters cast ballots for Bradley. Certainly, distinctive ethnic voting patterns were observed—most notably the cohesiveness of the black electorate—but the elections also revealed the potential for black-white electoral coalitions. In the Los Angeles study, the authors identified lower socio-economic whites as voters most likely to join such a coalition.

These findings of a potential black-white electoral coalition have significant implications for minority candidacies at the state or national level where the electorate is overwhelmingly white. Harry Holloway (1968) proposes three general types of coalitions between black and white voters that could avail black interests in a predominantly white district. One is "independent power politics" in which white candidates offer concessions in exchange for the black vote. A second strategy is called the "conservative coalition" in which mutual interests are emphasized between the black community and the predominantly white business and financial sectors. Finally, a "liberal coalition" best describes the successful black mayoral candidacies in Houston and Los Angeles where black voters are enjoined with lower-income whites, Hispanics, and white liberals.

A study of black electoral mobilization in 10 California cities by Browning et al. (1984) gave further definition to strategies for maximizing minority representation in government. Political representation was divided into two types: demand-protest versus electoral mobilization. It was found that high levels of protest outside the system are closely related to the absolute number of minority persons who feel estranged, while high levels of electoral mobilization are related to the relative size of the minority population rather than the absolute number. The demand-protest and electoral mobilization strategies were often used effectively in tandem in achieving strong minority representation. Best results for minority representation came from a "biracial electoral alliance"—in effect, a liberal coalition—in which blacks and whites jointly formed a liberal electoral alliance prior to the peak of demand-protest activities. As opposed to blacks being co-opted into a pre-existing white-dominated liberal coalition or remaining outside any systemic coalition at all, the biracial alliance most effectively incorporated minority interests into the policymaking apparatus.

It is within this framework that the authors will analyze the successful candidacies of Speaker Willie L. Brown, Jr. But instead of analyzing only individual elections, this research charts ethnic voting patterns in Brown's

New Black Politics: The Search for Political Power (New York: Longman, 1987).

assembly district over a 24-year period in an effort to discern stability or flux in electoral coalitions.

METHOD

The purpose of this research is twofold. First, ethnic voting patterns in Brown's assembly district will be examined from 1964 through 1988 for compatibility with the black-white coalition framework discussed above. Second, Brown's legislative history over the same 24-year period and campaign financial activity since 1976 will be examined in order to better understand elite coalition building within the assembly itself.

The first issue of ethnic voting patterns is approached using precinct general election results every four years from 1964 through 1988. U.S. census data at the neighborhood block level are employed to identify predominant ethnic compositions of the precincts. Block-level census data allow three ethnic groupings: white, black, and Pacific Asian. Dramatic shifts in district boundaries over the 24-year period limit the number of precincts applicable to this longitudinal analysis. Thus, seven precincts within each ethnic group have been selected for study according to degree of ethnic "purity" and geographic location guaranteeing their inclusion in Willie Brown's district throughout the reapportionment plans of three decades. Precincts within each ethnic group are ranked by socio-economic status on a relative four-point scale of lowest to highest. Income levels used for the ranking are derived from census data at the tract level. Ethnic voting patterns are then discerned by aggregate race and by economic ranking relative to the same race.

The second issue of elite coalition building through which Willie Brown has attained leadership authority within the assembly is approached by analyzing legislative histories and campaign finance data. All legislation sponsored or cosponsored by Brown since 1964 have been categorized according to issue and traced for their eventual rejection or approval by the legislature. This tactic provides some indication of changes in Willie Brown's policy interests over time as well as a "legislative effectiveness" index measuring Brown's ability to secure legislation. Campaign finance data since 1976 (the earliest year available) are examined for relevance to elite coalition building.

RESULTS

Voting Patterns in the Electorate

Our analysis of ethnic voting patterns reveals that Willie Brown has enjoyed immense popularity among all groups of his constituency beginning in 1968. Only in his first election victory of 1964 was Brown unable to win majority support within each of the three ethnic groups. Pacific Asian voters were nearly split between Brown and his opponent, while a small majority of white voters favored the opponent. Apparently, the overwhelming support for Brown among black precincts (89 percent) was instrumental in the 1964 victory (see Appendices A, B, and C).

Despite Brown's popularity, Figure 1 shows distinctive ethnic voting patterns among his constituency that have generally persisted over time. Black precincts have consistently and strongly favored Brown, usually casting in excess of 90 percent of their ballots for the black candidate. Voters in the selected white and Asian precincts have favored Brown with much less intensity, falling within or below a 70 percent support rating. Somewhat surprisingly, voting behavior in the white and Asian precincts have followed very similar patterns. There is very little evidence to distinguish the electoral choices of these Asian and white voters. Finally, it is interesting to note the stability of ethnic voting patterns, at least since 1972. Black precincts have consistently supported Brown in excess of 90 percent of ballots cast; white and Asian precincts have generally supported Brown within a range of 60 to 70 percent of votes cast.

Voting turnout between ethnic groups appears to follow expected trends. As shown in Table 1, the overall turnout in black precincts in 1984 and 1988 lags significantly behind turnout in Asian and white precincts. It would have been interesting to see whether this pattern of low black voter turnout remained the same in Brown's earlier elections. Unfortunately, voter registration data at the precinct level have not been preserved by the County of San Francisco for those years.

There is no clear sign that Willie Brown's candidacy directly affects turnout along ethnic group lines. In 1984, of those blacks who voted, blacks were slightly more inclined than Asian and white voters to cast ballots in the assembly race as well as in races for higher offices. But in 1988, actual voters in white precincts were more inclined to participate in the assembly contest than blacks or Asians. Perhaps the most intriguing observation in voting turnout is the sharp drop in voter participation from 1984 to 1988 among all groups. Although the data here provide no explanations for the declining vote, one possibility is that a less exciting presidential race accounted for the change.

Table 2 shows some interesting trends in voting behavior according to economic rank. Regardless of the economic ranking of black voters, they consistently favor Brown's candidacy. There appear to be no significant differences in black voting behavior based on income.

However, there are significant class-based voting patterns among Asian and white voters. Upper-income Asian voters have regularly shown less propensity to vote for Brown than lower-income Asians. This is not the trend among white voters. The third highest income ranking among white precincts (with a median household income level of $18,782 in 1980) has

Figure 1: *Percentage of Ethnic Precinct Vote For Willie Brown, 1964-1988*

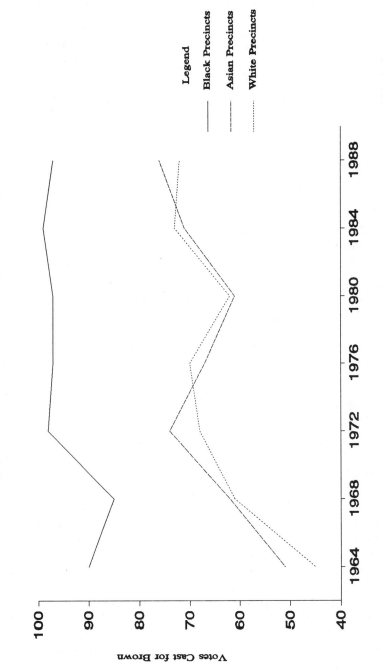

Note: Source precinct election results available from the Registrar's office of the County of San Francisco and at the California State Archives, Sacramento.

Table 1:   *Voter Turnout by Ethnic Precinct, and Percentage of Turnout Votes Cast for Assembly Race in Willie Brown's District, 1984 and 1988*

	1984			1988		
	Overall Turnout	Cast Votes for Assem.	DF*	Overall Turnout	Cast Votes for Assem.	DF*
Black Precincts	52%	48%	4%	40%	32%	8%
Asian Precincts	59%	53%	6%	49%	39%	10%
White Precincts	60%	54%	6%	51%	49%	2%

Note: Data derived from precinct election results available from the Voter Registrar's Office of the County of San Francisco.

*DF designates the percentage difference between overall turnout and the turnout for the assembly race.

backed Brown with far greater enthusiasm than any other economic rank. The least support comes from the second lowest income level ($11,432), while the upper-income group has historically favored Brown by greater margins than the lowest-income group. It is interesting to note, however, that many of these distinctive economic voting patterns among white precincts appear to be dissolving in the most recent elections. By 1988, there is very little difference in the voting patterns between income groups of white precincts, with the exception of the second-lowest income group, which continues to be less supportive of Brown's candidacy.

The data provide several suggestions for constituent coalition building by a black candidate in the San Francisco area. Willie Brown's initial campaign victory in 1964 appears to have been the result of a coalition between black voters and upper middle-income white voters. Brown did not fare nearly as well among the Asian precincts nor the lowest and highest-income whites. Judging from census tract information, the white precincts that joined blacks in voting for Brown also tended to have populations that are younger than the lower- and upper-income precincts and better educated than the lower-income precincts. Evidently, Brown was carried into office by a "liberal" coalition of blacks and younger, well-educated whites.

By 1972, Brown became more or less the favored candidate by most groups. And by 1988, he received strong approval ratings by all ethnic groups and by all economic ranks in the precincts under study. His base of constituent support is no longer just a liberal coalition but now encompasses the wealthiest voters as well as the poorest, regardless of race.

Table 2:   *Distribution of Ethnic Ballots Cast in Favor of Willie Brown by Intraracial Economic Rank, 1964-1988*

Economic Ranking	1964	1968	1972	1976	1980	1984	1988
Lowest							
Black	86%	82%	95%	94%	94%	98%	97%
Asian	45	62	70	72	64	73	73
White	40	56	63	62	49	67	74
2							
Black	92%	86%	97%	94%	94%	97%	92%
Asian	—	—	—	—	—	—	—
White	30	43	54	53	48	58	63
3							
Black	88%	87%	96%	95%	95%	97%	96%
Asian	—	—	—	—	—	—	—
White	70	78	85	76	73	81	76
Highest							
Black	80%	88%	91%	92%	87%	94%	87%
Asian	—	—	63	67	59	70	68
White	42	59	73	70	63	68	75

Note: The economic rank of each ethnic group is calculated as the lowest-to-highest quartiles of median household income as provided by 1980 U.S. census tract data. Specifically, the income levels for each group is as follows. Blacks: Lowest= $6,109; 2=$8,179; 3=$10,207; Highest= $10,575. Asians: Lowest= $14,009; Highest= $19,428. Whites: Lowest= $6,981; 2= $11,432; 3= $18,782; Highest= $21,096.

Asian precincts can be separated only into lowest and highest quartiles because of the limited number of precincts containing predominant Asian populations. Asian persons are defined according to U.S. census bureau standards.

In terms of constituent coalition building, Willie Brown forged a biracial electoral coalition of blacks and liberal whites that presented black leadership with the opportunity to have a significant impact on state public policy. This is a critical and, perhaps, primary step in affecting policy, but making full use of the opportunity for influence does not end here. As we have seen in the struggles of major black leaders from Tom Bradley to Harold Washington, the effectiveness of a leadership depends largely on the formation of supportive coalitions among the policymaking elite as well. Voting blocs within the policymaking elite dramatically impact whether or not a minority leader can accomplish his or her agenda.

Elite Behavior

Over the years from Willie Brown's first legislative session in 1965 through 1987-1988, the legislator's ability to make law has indeed undergone a metamorphosis. As shown in Table 3, Brown entered the assembly in 1965 with a flurry and sponsored or cosponsored 149 bills. Only 36 of these bills ever became chaptered, leaving a "legislative effectiveness" rate of 24 percent. Each session thereafter, his legislative effectiveness steadily improved, reaching 51 percent in 1979-1980. Brown's ability to secure legislation soared to 71 percent in the first session following his election as speaker of the assembly and remains high (59 percent) today.

There has been a notable shift in which issues are most prominent in Brown's legislative history. In 1965, the largest single share of bills concerned matters of social welfare and civil rights. Such concerns occupied 32 percent of Brown's legislative efforts. Environmental issues were not a major concern, while the remainder of the bills were nearly evenly distributed among education (14 percent), crime (9 percent), business (15 percent), consumer affairs (11 percent), and governmental organization (17 percent).

Although there is considerable fluctuation from session to session, business matters clearly emerged as a leading concern between 1979-1980 and 1983-1984. This is the period in which Willie Brown dramatically ascended into leadership stature. After his leadership position was firmly entrenched, his preoccupation with business matters began to fade. In the last session under study, only 15 percent of Brown's legislative agenda addressed business matters, the same percentage as in 1965. Importantly, the issue concern that has now emerged as dominant is the environment (20 percent). Bills sponsored or cosponsored in the area of social welfare and civil rights remain a major emphasis of Brown's efforts (17 percent), but much less so than in earlier years. More attention is now directed to crime than in 1965 (17 percent), while less attention is given to education (8 percent) and consumer affairs (5 percent).

The picture that emerges from this review of legislative history is one of legislative prowess on the part of Willie Brown while still not abandoning a commitment to liberal issue concerns. As a newly elected member of the assembly by a liberal coalition constituency, Brown focused his legislative efforts on social welfare and civil rights—an emphasis that persisted strongly until 1979-1980. In that year, the largest share of his attention turned toward business matters—the same year in which Brown maneuvered a Republican-Democratic coalition to win the speakership. By the last legislative session business matters still received considerable attention by the speaker, but more of his efforts have been directed to the environment, social welfare and civil rights, crime, and governmental reorganization.

Campaign finance records provide some insights on how Willie Brown has managed to solidify his leadership authority over the assembly and enhance his legislative effectiveness. For most of the years under study, California has had virtually no campaign finance restrictions other than a reporting requirement.[2] During this time, campaign contributions and expenditures were not limited nor were the sources of contributions restricted. Corporations, for instance, could make direct and unlimited contributions to state-level candidates.

As speaker of the assembly, Willie Brown has made extensive use of campaign finance strategies to help secure his leadership position and strengthen his legislative effectiveness. As shown in Table 4, Brown's level of contributions and expenditures rose dramatically after ascending to the speakership. More importantly, much of that money is not used for his own campaigns; Willie Brown has long held a "safe" legislative seat not requiring any concerted campaign to get reelected. Rather, Brown's funds frequently are redirected to assist other legislative candidates. For example, in 1982, Brown was responsible for allocating at least $1,181,685 in campaign funds to other candidates. In 1986, he distributed at least $824,661 in candidate support.[3] It is noteworthy that a great deal of this money allocated by

---

[2]California voters approved one of the nation's strongest campaign finance laws in 1974, California's Political Reform Act. The law relied heavily on restrictions on candidate and independent *expenditures* rather than restrictions on campaign *contributions*. Most of the law, except its reporting requirements, was struck down as unconstitutional in the wake of the U.S. Supreme Court ruling, *Buckley v. Valeo* (1976) 424 U.S. 1. The federal ruling generally prohibits restrictions on campaign expenditures except when public funds are involved. While candidates for federal office face the campaign contribution limits and public funding restrictions of the Federal Elections Campaign Act, the federal law does not pertain to state and local races, leaving no contribution limits in California.

In June 1988, California voters again approved two campaign finance laws, one strict measure calling for public financing of campaigns and a second far weaker measure prohibiting public funding but imposing some contribution limits and restrictions on the transfer of funds between candidates. The weaker initiative (Proposition 73) received more votes and thereby canceled out the public funding initiative. However, implementation of the campaign finance law has been slow pending agency interpretations and legal challenges. It is not yet clear what impact this law may have on California politics, but thus far it appears to be of negligible importance. The prohibition against transfers of funds between candidates, for instance, is being bypassed by candidates requesting potential donors to send their contributions directly to third parties. Tupper Hull and Steven Capps, "Tougher Rules Mean Less Power for Willie Brown," *San Francisco Examiner*, February 9, 1990.

[3]These figures on campaign dollars transferred directly by Willie Brown to other candidates tells only part of the story of Brown's financial clout over other candidates. The speaker often exerts his influence over corporations and other special interest groups to give—or *not* give—campaign contributions to selected candidates. A recent example of this practice occurred during the 1990 Democratic primary contest for

Table 3:   *Legislative History of Assembly Member Willie Brown, 1964-1988, Bills Sponsored or Cosponsored, by Issue Category, and Percentage of Emphasis of Legislative Efforts, by Issue Category*

	1965		1968		1972	
	Cases	%	Cases	%	Cases	%
Social Welfare and Civil Rights	47	32%	23	24%	37	28%
Education	21	14%	14	15%	16	12%
Environment	3	2%	9	9%	8	6%
Crime	14	9%	22	23%	12	9%
Business	23	25%	13	14%	22	17%
Consumer Affairs	16	11%	5	5%	19	15%
Government	25	17%	10	10%	17	13%
Total Cases	149	100%	96	100%	131	100%
Chaptered Cases	36		34		49	
Legislative Effectiveness	24%		35%		37%	

Note: Assembly Legislative Histories, Bill Room, Capitol Building, Sacramento.

Brown to other candidates was originally donated to him by other well-endowed legislative officeholders—presumably with the intent to enrich the speaker's authority. For example, in 1982, officeholders and party organizations contributed $801,446 to Brown even though he had already amassed an unnecessarily exorbitant campaign warchest of $1,311,572.

Partly through this strategy of providing substantial financial support to other candidates, Willie Brown has been able to forge sufficient allegiance to maintain legislative leadership. And, with his authority bolstered, Brown appears reasonably able to pursue a legislative policy agenda that may at times offend corporate and other lobbying interest groups that can be so powerful in the unregulated atmosphere of California politics.

---

governor. Gubernatorial hopeful John Van de Kamp encountered tremendous difficulty raising campaign funds after sponsoring an initiative to limit the terms of legislators, which angered the speaker and many legislators.

Table 3:   *(continued)*

1975-76		1979-80		1983-84		1987-88	
Cases	%	Cases	%	Cases	%	Cases	%
40	25%	7	11%	19	22%	10	17%
21	13%	5	8%	2	2%	5	8%
6	4%	3	5%	7	8%	12	20%
29	18%	11	17%	18	21%	10	17%
30	19%	27	42%	20	23%	9	15%
12	8%	4	6%	6	7%	3	5%
20	13%	8	12%	15	17%	10	17%
150	100%	65	100%	87	100%	59	100%
73		33		36		35	
46%		51%		71%		59%	

POLITICAL IMPLICATIONS AND CONCLUSION

This study provides a longitudinal analysis of the emergence and establishment of the black speaker of the assembly, Willie L. Brown, Jr., in California state politics. The authors attempt to identify the coalition-building process that has taken place both at the constituent level and at the elite legislative level that has affected Brown's elections and leadership. Ethnic voting patterns and legislative histories are traced for a 24-year period for indications of change in electoral coalitions as well as changes in elite behavior.

The longitudinal approach offers several unique insights to our perspectives on ethnic politics. Willie Brown's initial electoral success depended largely on a coalition of blacks and upper-middle class, educated whites—known as a "liberal coalition." Strengthened with the advantages of incumbency, Brown eventually became the favored candidate of all ethnic groups and most socio-economic ranks within these groups. Nevertheless, clear differences in ethnic voting patterns have persisted to date, with blacks supporting Brown overwhelmingly ahead of Asians and whites. By the 1984 and 1988 elections, socio-economic differences in voting patterns among Asians and whites have all but disappeared. Willie Brown now has a con-

Table 4:   *Campaign Expenditures and Contributions on Behalf of Assembly Member Willie Brown*

Campaign Expenditures by Willie Brown, Calendar Years 1974-1986

	1974	1978	1982	1986
Total Brown Expenditures	$48,206	$47,720	$2,554,944	$2,913,980
Brown Transfers of Funds to Other Candidates	$35,719	$20,517	$1,181,685	$824,661
Median Campaign Expenditure for All Assembly Candidates	—	$42,861	$78,766	84,656

Campaign Contributions for Willie Brown, Broken Down by Source, General Elections 1976-1986

	1976	1978	1980	1982	1984	1986
Total Contributions	$20,325	$32,561	$45,675	$2,113,018	$1,641,508	$1,441,960
Sources of Brown Contributions						
Individuals	$500	$900	$10,075	$125,369	$100,651	$145,162
Officeholders	$0	$0	$200	$801,446	$713,159	$44,150
Business	$13,175	$20,811	$19,750	$685,545	$544,298	$736,923
Financial Entities	$1,850	$1,700	$9,050	$89,720	$110,300	$193,950
Labor	$4,700	$650	$4,700	$323,407	$87,925	$197,900
Law Firms	$0	$1,750	$1,700	$76,651	$60,700	$84,550
Other	$100	$6,750	$200	$8,880	$24,475	$39,325

Source: California Secretary of State's Office and California State Archives, Sacramento.

stituency base that includes more or less all income levels of each racial group.

Willie Brown's early legislative performance strongly reflected the constituent concerns of a "liberal coalition." Over time, his legislative efforts drifted toward moderation and even toward a major focus on business issues between 1979-1980 and 1983-1984. This moderation may have played a critical role in expanding his appeal to legislative colleagues as well as upper-income constituencies back home. From this solid base of constituent and elite support, Willie Brown has ascended to leadership of the assembly and has achieved a high rate of legislative effectiveness. Reasonably entrenched as assembly speaker, Brown's legislative agenda has undergone further changes in issue emphasis, drifting somewhat away from business matters and refocusing on environmental issues and other social concerns.

Ethnic electoral patterns and coalition building at both the constituent and elite levels are dynamic processes. In state politics or in any predominantly white district, the case of Willie Brown serves as a brilliant example of a black candidate who forged a broad base of support among voters and colleagues without necessarily losing the allegiance of the original supportive electoral coalitions. The mobilization of a biracial liberal electoral coalition gave Willie Brown the opportunity to advance minority interests; an acumen for compromise and mastering the rules of the game provided the means.

REFERENCES

Bizjak, Tony. "Majority Rules State's Politics: 43% of Residents are Minorities, But 88% of Office Holders are White." *Sacramento Bee*, March 31, 1991, 1.

Browning, Rufus, Dale Rogers Marshall, and David Tabb. *Protest Is Not Enough.* Berkeley: University of California Press, 1984.

Buckley v. Valeo, (1976) 424 U.S. 1.

Hadden, Jeffrey, Louis Masotti, and Victor Thiessen. "The Making of the Negro Mayors, 1974." *Trans-Action* (January 1968): 21-30.

Hahn, Harlan, David Klingman, and Harry Pachon. "Cleavages, Coalitions, and the Black Candidate: the Los Angeles Mayoralty Elections of 1969 and 1973." *Western Political Quarterly* (December 1976): 507-20.

Harvey, Richard. *The Dynamics of California Government and Politics.* Monterey: Brooks Cole Publishers, 1985.

Holloway, Harry. "Negro Political Strategy: Coalition or Independent Power Politics?" *Social Science Quarterly* (December 1968): 534-47.

Lewis, Denise. "Victory and Defeat for Black Candidates." *Black Politician* (April 1971).

Pettigrew, Thomas. "When a Black Candidate Runs for Mayor: Race and Voting Behavior." In *People and Politics in Urban Society*, edited by Harlan Hahn. Beverly Hills: Sage Publishers, 1972.

Williams, Linda. "Black Political Progress in the 1980s: The Electoral Arena." In *The New Black Politics: The Search for Political Power*, edited by Michael Preston, Lenneal Henderson, Jr., and Paul Puryear. New York: Longman, 1987.

Appendix A: *Percentile Party Vote of Seven Selected Black Precincts, in Assembly Elections of Willie Brown, 1964-1988*

Precinct	Dem.	Rep.	Other
		1964	
6132	88%	12%	0%
6143	83%	17%	0%
6128	88%	13%	0%
6118	93%	7%	0%
6120	89%	12%	0%
6142	88%	12%	0%
6138	80%	20%	0%
		1968	
6132	83%	13%	4%
6143	80%	13%	7%
6128	84%	9%	7%
6118	88%	2%	10%
6120	84%	8%	9%
6142	87%	9%	4%
6138	88%	8%	4%
		1972	
6132	97%	3%	0%
6143	97%	3%	0%
6128	90%	10%	0%
6118	99%	1%	0%
6120	93%	7%	0%
6142	96%	4%	0%
6138	91%	9%	0%
		1976	
6132	96%	4%	0%
6143	92%	5%	3%
6128	92%	6%	2%
6118	93%	5%	2%
6120	95%	2%	2%
6142	95%	3%	2%
6138	92%	3%	5%

Appendix A: *(continued)*

Precinct	Dem.	Rep.	Other
		1980	
6132	93%	3%	4%
6143	97%	2%	1%
6128	91%	6%	3%
6118	99%	1%	0%
6120	88%	9%	3%
6142	95%	1%	4%
6138	87%	4%	9%
		1984	
6132	98%	2%	0%
6143	98%	2%	0%
6128	97%	3%	0%
6118	97%	3%	0%
6120	97%	3%	0%
6142	97%	3%	0%
6138	94%	6%	0%
		1988	
6132	97%	2%	1%
6143	97%	2%	1%
6128	94%	4%	2%
6118	95%	2%	3%
6120	91%	6%	3%
6142	96%	1%	3%
6138	87%	9%	4%

Note: The percentage of black population in each precinct is as follows: Precinct 6132-92%; Precinct 6143-87%; Precinct 6128-78%; Precinct 6118-85%; Precinct 6120-83%; Precinct 6142-79%; Precinct 6138-78%.

Appendix B: *Percentile Party Vote of Seven Selected Asian Precincts, in Assembly Elections of Willie Brown, 1964-1988*

Precinct	Dem.	Rep.	Other
		1964	
4853	48%	52%	0%
4855	48%	52%	0%
4854	41%	59%	0%
4850	39%	61%	0%
4737	—	—	—
4738	—	—	—
4739	—	—	—
		1968	
4853	64%	32%	5%
4855	65%	34%	1%
4854	65%	29%	6%
4850	50%	47%	3%
4737	—	—	—
4738	—	—	—
4739	—	—	—
		1972	
4853	70%	30%	0%
4855	71%	29%	0%
4854	73%	27%	0%
4850	65%	35%	0%
4737*	65%	35%	0%
4738*	59%	41%	0%
4739*	66%	34%	0%
		1976	
4853	73%	24%	3%
4855	75%	22%	3%
4854	74%	24%	2%
4850	59%	38%	3%
4737*	71%	26%	3%
4738*	66%	32%	3%
4739*	65%	32%	3%

Appendix B: *(continued)*

Precinct	Dem.	Rep.	Other
		1980	
4853	66%	27%	8% ·
4855	67%	24%	9%
4854	—	—	—
4850	55%	35%	10%
4737	58%	34%	8%
4638	59%	33%	8%
4730	61%	32%	7%
		1984	
4853	72%	28%	0%
4855	75%	25%	0%
4854	73%	27%	0%
4850	73%	27%	0%
4737	71%	29%	0%
4738	73%	27%	0%
4739	65%	36%	0%
		1988	
4853	73%	19%	8%
4855	73%	19%	8%
4854	74%	19%	7%
4850	73%	25%	2%
4737	—	—	—
4738	67%	27%	6%
4739	69%	26%	4%

Note: The percentage of Asian population in each of the precincts are as follows: Precinct 4853-64%; Precinct 4855-64%; Precinct 4854-72%; Precinct 4850-60%; Precinct 4737-51%; Precinct 4738-51%; Precinct 4739-58%. Election data of 4854 in 1980 and 4737 in 1988 are missing. Precincts 4737, 4738, and 4739 were not within assembly boundaries in the 1960s.

  *Figures for the 1972 general election are actually derived from the 1974 general election for these precincts.

Appendix C: *Percentile Party Vote of Seven Selected White Precincts, in Assembly Elections of Willie Brown, 1964-1988*

Precinct	Dem.	Rep.	Other
		1964	
4877	42%	58%	0%
4867	40%	60%	0%
4871	30%	70%	0%
5903	70%	30%	0%
5901	69%	31%	0%
4611	37%	63%	0%
4614	44%	56%	0%
		1968	
4877	54%	43%	4%
4867	59%	40%	1%
4871	43%	54%	4%
5903	78%	14%	8%
5901	78%	16%	6%
4611	57%	33%	10%
4614	60%	33%	7%
		1972	
4877	66%	34%	0%
4867	60%	40%	0%
4871	54%	46%	0%
5903	87%	13%	0%
5901	85%	15%	0%
4611	75%	25%	0%
4614	73%	27%	0%
		1976	
4877	63%	33%	4%
4867	59%	40%	1%
4871	53%	43%	4%
5903	81%	14%	4%
5901	69%	27%	4%
4611	59%	39%	2%
4614	75%	23%	2%

Appendix C: *(continued)*

Precinct	Dem.	Rep.	Other
		1980	
4877	57%	33%	10%
4867	62%	27%	11%
4871	48%	46%	7%
5903	73%	13%	14%
5901	—	—	—
4611	56%	42%	2%
4614	66%	27%	7%
		1984	
4877	65%	35%	0%
4867	68%	32%	0%
4871	58%	42%	0%
5903	86%	14%	0%
5901	76%	24%	0%
4611	68%	32%	0%
4614	69%	31%	0%
		1988	
4877	76%	17%	7%
4867	73%	21%	6%
4871	63%	30%	7%
5903	80%	12%	8%
5901	72%	20%	8%
4611	75%	21%	4%
4614	75%	23%	2%

Note: The percentage of white population in the precincts are as follows: Precinct 4877-87%; Precinct 4867-83%; Precinct 4871-82%; Precinct 5903-85%; Precinct 5901-83%; Precinct 4611-93%; Precinct 4614-93%. Data for Precinct 5901 in 1980 are missing.

IV. POLITICAL MOBILIZATION AND ELECTORAL POLITICS

CHAPTER 8

RICHARD DELEON
San Francisco State University

The Progressive Urban Regime: Ethnic Coalitions in San Francisco

INTRODUCTION

Just days after his inauguration, San Francisco's new progressive mayor, Art Agnos, was besieged at city hall by community activists demanding affordable housing and neighborhood preservation. "They'd become so accustomed to fighting city hall, I think they forgot who they were talking to," recalled Agnos. "I told them, 'Hey, you don't have to convince me, we own this place now'" (quoted in Garcia 1988, 1). By "we," Agnos meant the broad coalition of neighborhood advocates, tenant groups, ethnic minorities, liberal gays, slow-growth activists, and small business owners who had languished as political outsiders during the decade of Mayor Dianne Feinstein's administration and who participated in the grass-roots mobilization that swept Agnos to victory in December 1987. (See Witteman 1987; Jacobs 1987; Stein 1988.) Some analysts argue that the progressive victory was long overdue. According to Calvin Welch, a long-time community organizer and slow-growth activist: "In historic terms, this election represents San Francisco finally righting itself politically after the assassination of [liberal Mayor George] Moscone [in 1978]. The Feinstein interregnum was an historic anomaly" (quoted in Roberts 1987b). Nearly all observers agree that the Agnos victory placed San Francisco once again in the national political spotlight. Local Congresswoman Nancy Pelosi, for example, claims that San Francisco "has become the capital of the progressive political movement in this country" (quoted in Starr 1988, 157). Even conservative historian Kevin Starr concedes that Agnos "capture[d] San Francisco with an openly liberal campaign" and that the Agnos victory is now part of a political pattern revealing San Francisco to be "the temporary capital of the liberal wing of the Democratic party in the United States" (Starr 1988, 44).

The transfer of political ownership of city hall to the progressives in 1987 clearly was not the result of a one-man electoral *coup d'etat*. A year

before, San Franciscans passed Proposition M, the most ambitious growth
control measure ever enacted in the United States (DeLeon and Powell
1989). A year after, voters elected two new progressives to the board of
supervisors, Angela Aliota and Terrence Hallinan, producing a progressive
majority for the first time in memory. Supervisor Harry Britt, avowed
socialist and gay-activist, was the top vote-getter in that same election,
making him president of the 11-member board, which now contains five
women, two blacks, one Hispanic, one Asian, and one gay. Further, during
his first six months in office, Mayor Agnos "accomplished the first wholesale
change of people around city hall in almost a decade," appointing ethnic
minorities, small-business people, slow-growth activists, and neighborhood
advocates to key city commission posts and administrative positions (Garcia
1988). The "political incorporation" of ethnic minorities (Browning,
Marshall, and Tabb 1984), in particular, accelerated quickly. Mayoral
appointments included Chinese Pius Lee (Police Commission), Wayne Hu
(Planning Commission), and James Ho (Deputy Mayor for Business and
Economic Development); Hispanics Jose Medina (Police Commission) and
James Morales (Planning Commission); and blacks James Jefferson (Fire
Commission), Helen Mason (Housing Authority), and Rev. James Goode
(Housing Authority).

While it is true that San Francisco is a long way from becoming another
Paris Commune or Red Vienna, the Agnos victory may well prove to be a
significant milestone in the history of American urban politics. What
happened was not merely a changing of the guard or a shift in policy but a
transformation of regime, i.e., a fundamental reconstitution of relationships
between community and capital through a reassertion of local popular
control over private decision making. (On the concept of "urban regime," see
Elkin 1987.) The progressive movement that brought Agnos to power was
motivated by an ideology that encourages an expanded role for local
government in promoting distributive justice, limits on growth, neighborhood preservation, and ethnic-cultural diversity under conditions of public
accountability and grass-roots citizen participation. Progressive ideology is
an amalgam of traditional liberal and populist thinking about urban political
life. It imposes terms on business elites for access to the city's land and
resources (Daykin 1988, 383), gives priority to community-use values over
capital-exchange values as guides to policy, and seeks to empower neighborhoods and groups historically excluded from public leadership roles.

In many ways, this conception of San Francisco's progressivism is
ideologically consistent with Castells' theory of urban social movements
(Castells 1983). Outside the local urban context, however, it dissolves into
variants of "liberalism," particularly in the state and national political arenas
where the critical links to land-use issues and city life are more remote and
abstract. Although mislabeled by some detractors as socialist or radical in
the Marxist tradition, progressive ideology is concerned with consumption

more than production, meaning more than materialism, residence more than workplace, community empowerment more than class struggle (Castells 1983; Clavel 1986; Lowe 1986). Within the framework of this ideology, the Agnos victory meant something more than merely the arrival of yet another political broker accommodating interests and reconciling conflicts among the city's various parts. It meant there was now a coherent political vision radiating from the top of San Francisco's government, one formative of new aspirations and relationships among citizens, leaders, groups, and coalitions.

Although regime transformations of this sort have occurred in smaller U.S. cities, such as Berkeley and Santa Monica (Clavel 1986; Daykin 1988), similar progressive efforts in larger cities, such as Cleveland and Atlanta, have been aborted, co-opted, or contained by the progrowth hegemony and "preemptive power" of local business elites (Stone 1988; also see Swanstrom 1985; Molotch 1988; Reed 1988). While electoral mobilization and political incorporation of ethnic minorities occurred in some of these cities (Browning, Marshall, and Tabb 1984; Stone 1986; Mollenkopf 1986), such gains often came, as Reed points out, "at the price of making peace with the regressive policy framework that stimulates protest and mobilization in the first place" (Reed 1988, 172). Stone writes: "Incorporation is a complex phenomenon, shaped by the political character of both the group achieving incorporation and the coalition it is being incorporated into" (Stone 1988, 618). This line of argument stresses the importance of the local political economic context (urban regime) in which incorporation of ethnic minorities takes place. It implies that political incorporation without regime transformation tends to decapitate protest leadership through co-optation, convert "constituencies into clients" (Mollenkopf 1983, 292), and narrow the political vision guiding social change. Under these conditions, political incorporation can actually disempower ethnic minorities rather than empower them. What seems distinctive about the political incorporation process under the Agnos regime is that it is coordinated with counter-ideologies and policy initiatives aimed at altering the progrowth framework used for years by the Feinstein administration to accommodate downtown business elites. It is in this sense that the Agnos victory in 1987 was a progressive victory, not merely a victory of progressives.

Ethnic minorities, particularly Hispanics and blacks, played a key role in achieving the Agnos victory and preparing the political ground for regime transformation. This paper will examine that role through an analysis of the demographic bases, political organization, and electoral alliances of the groups involved. Particular attention will be given to the types of issues within the progressive agenda that activate and sometimes polarize ethnic cleavages. The thesis will be advanced that San Francisco's progressivism has at least three dimensions—liberalism, populism, and quality of life—and that coalition formation supporting a progressive urban regime is complicated by competing group priorities assigned to each of these broad goals. The argument will also be made that ethnicity was an important factor in the Agnos victory, but not more important than social class or housing tenure. The success of Mayor Agnos' progressive regime will depend on his ability to respond in a politically coherent way to constituency demands arising simultaneously from these three cross-cutting cleavages. The paper will conclude with speculations about the future of San Francisco politics under conditions that both help and hinder Mayor Agnos' efforts to build an effective governing coalition without compromising his progressive vision.

THE DEMOGRAPHICS OF ETHNIC DIVERSITY IN SAN FRANCISCO

San Francisco is the most ethnically diverse county in the United States, according to a recent study by geographers James Allen and Eugene Turner (cited in McLeod 1988). Based on their rating system (using 1980 census data), there is an 83 percent probability that two randomly selected residents will belong to different ethnic or racial groups (from a list of 14). Considering the very strong immigration flows to San Francisco, particularly from Southeast Asia and Central America (Viviano 1988a; Cordova 1987), the city's ethnic diversity rating in 1990 should be even higher.

Patterns of foreign immigration (legal and undocumented), combined with demographic trends within the city's Anglo and black communities (McCarthy 1984), have completely transformed the ethnic-racial composition of San Francisco's population since 1970. In that year, there were an estimated 409,365 Anglo residents, 108,782 Asian Pacific Islanders, 101,626 Hispanics, and 95,900 blacks (calculated from figures in Godfrey 1982, 125). Anglos were then a solid majority of the city's population (57 percent). Blacks, Asians, and Spanish-speaking minorities were described by Wirt as "arriving ethnic groups" who were just then starting to establish their communities in a small number of neighborhoods (Wirt 1974, 240-71). He mentioned that Asians, in particular, were finding political mobilization difficult because they "find their limited numbers a handicap" (Wirt 1974, 245). Even as he wrote those words, San Francisco's ethnic makeup was changing dramatically.

In 1980, the estimated figures were 360,535 (Anglos), 149,374 (Asian Pacific Islanders), 84,102 (Hispanics), and 84,192 (blacks) (U.S. Bureau of the Census 1983). Projections for the Asian Pacific Islander and black populations in 1990 are 300,000 (including 150,000 Chinese) and 80,000, respectively (Viviano 1988a). Assuming the same rate of attrition for the Anglo population as occurred between 1970 and 1980, the projected number of Anglos is 317,000. The projected size of the Hispanic population is much more difficult to estimate because of the large influx of undocumented Central Americans during the 1980s. Focusing just on El Salvadoreans alone, estimates range from 50,000 to 90,000, most living in San Francisco's

Mission District (Cordova 1987, 11). With these uncertainties duly noted, a plausible projection of the 1990 Hispanic population is 110,000.

Based on these projected 1990 figures, a reasonable estimate of the city's current ethnic-racial mix is 39 percent Anglo, 37 percent Asian Pacific Islander, 14 percent Hispanic, and 10 percent black. This means that Anglo residents are now merely one racial minority among other minorities. The Asian population is exploding, and clearly their numbers are now a political asset, not a handicap. The Hispanic population is growing but includes many undocumented immigrants. The black population is declining in size and is now, demographically, the minority of minorities.

A useful starting point for studying the politics of ethnic coalition formation in San Francisco is an examination of interracial and intraracial differences in socio-economic circumstances and family life-style characteristics. The primary data source used for comparing San Francisco's major ethnic-racial subpopulations is the Public-Use Microdata Sample (PUMS) for San Francisco. This is a 5 percent sample of individual records randomly drawn from the 1980 Census of Population and Housing (U.S. Bureau of the Census 1983). The PUMS sample for San Francisco is large enough (N = 33,982) to permit very detailed breakdowns and comparisons of census information by racial groups. Although 1980 census information is now dated, it is assumed that the overall pattern of group comparisons has remained fairly stable.

Table 1 compares Anglos, Asians, Hispanics, and blacks on selected socio-demographic indicators. Six general patterns can be seen in the comparative statistics. First, Anglos occupy a much higher socio-economic status (SES) than the other three groups. Proportionally more of them are in the upper-income strata, own income-producing assets (wealth), have formal schooling at the college level, and work in professional-managerial careers. Second, Anglos are also distinguished from the other three racial groups in terms of family life-style characteristics. As a group they are older, have fewer children, and are much more likely to live in nonfamily households. Third, Asians as a group are more socio-economically advanced than Hispanics and blacks (especially in terms of wealth and education) but similar to them in terms of family life-style characteristics. Fourth, blacks as a group are significantly poorer and more reliant on public assistance and local government employment than Asians and Hispanics. Fifth, the recent growth of the Asian and Hispanic populations is fueled by high levels of immigration, Asians much more than Hispanics (at least in terms of official census statistics). Sixth, variation in the rate of homeownership across the major racial groups is surprisingly small considering the large interracial differences in SES. This implies significant levels of *low-income* homeownership in all racial groups, a prediction confirmed by breakdowns of the PUMS data showing homeownership rates for those earning less than $10,000: Anglos, 38.2 percent; Asians, 44.2 percent; Hispanics, 36.0 percent; blacks,

Table 1: *Comparisons of Anglos, Asians, Hispanics, and Blacks on Selected Socio-Demographic Indicators: San Francisco, 1980 (5% Public-Use Microdata Sample)*

Indicators	Anglos	Asians	Hispanics	Blacks	Total
1 % Managerial-professional	34.5	18.4	14.1	14.9	26.7
2 % Low-wage service occup.	6.3	14.3	15.4	10.4	9.4
3 % Government workers	17.5	16.6	15.8	33.4	18.8
4 % Some college +	59.3	47.7	34.1	35.7	51.5
5 Per/capita income ($)	13,408	9,902	9,256	9,288	11,837
6 % Earning > $14,999	30.3	19.2	15.9	17.3	24.7
7 % Earners with income from interest, dividends, rent, or royalties	42.0	37.1	16.6	10.1	34.9
8 % Individuals with income below 125% of poverty line	15.3	17.1	22.1	27.8	18.0
9 % Earners receiving public assistance	5.7	8.0	10.0	16.7	7.8
10 % Homeowners	39.7	49.6	38.2	39.1	41.4
11 % Homeowners with first mortgage	52.1	77.4	67.5	80.1	62.5
12 % Lived in same house in 1975	48.5	47.5	45.1	53.4	48.3
13 % Lived in a foreign country in 1975	3.2	23.4	10.8	0.7	7.8
14 % Total population 15 years or younger	8.4	20.9	24.4	23.7	15.0
15 % Total population 60 years or older	26.5	14.4	11.8	13.7	20.3
16 % Individuals living in nonfamily households	49.0	14.4	21.9	27.2	36.4

Source: Census of Population and Housing, 1980: Public-Use Microdata Sample: San Francisco, 5% Sample. (Machine-readable data file available through Computing and Communications Resources, California State University.) Bureau of the Census. (Washington, D.C., 1983). All indicators except 14, 15 are for individuals 16 years or older.

34.8 percent. (See Jackson 1988, for a very similar profile of ethnic group differences in Los Angeles.)

Additional patterns are revealed in the socio-demographic characteristics of major subgroups within the Asian (Japanese, Chinese, Filipino, Other Asian) and Hispanic (Mexican, Other Hispanic) populations. First, the socio-economic and family life-style profile of San Francisco's more assimilated Japanese Americans is quite similar to that of Anglos and markedly different from that of the other Asian-American groups. Second, the Chinese and Filipino populations share a similar socio-demographic profile, except that the Chinese as a group display greater income inequality, own more income-producing assets, and are residentially more well established. Third, those classified as Other Asians (along with Filipinos and Other Hispanics) can lay claim to the title of San Francisco's *new* "arriving ethnic groups." In the 1980 census, 46.9 percent of Other Asians 16 years or older said that they lived in a foreign country in 1975 (28.4 percent of Filipinos and 12.7 percent of Other Hispanics reported the same). Of all racial subpopulations, those classified as Other Asians are the most impoverished, least settled, and youngest in terms of average age. Fourth, within the Hispanic category, Mexican Americans and those classified as Other Hispanics have virtually identical socio-demographic profiles. On most socio-economic and family life-style indicators, these subpopulations are similar to blacks and Other Asians.

The population flows that created San Francisco's unrivaled ethnic diversity were pushed and pulled there by a number of forces. Wars in Southeast Asia and Central America are an obvious push factor. An important pull factor is the existence of well-established Asian and Latin-American neighborhood enclaves, which provide security, social services, and cultural identity to arriving immigrants and refugees (Cordova 1987; Viviano 1988a). Another pull factor is the consequence of economic restructuring on a global scale. Recent studies of urban economic growth by Saskia Sassen-Koob and others suggest that San Francisco and other large cities are emerging as regional centers in the global economy for producing advanced corporate services in management, finance, and technical control functions (Sassen-Koob 1984; Mollenkopf 1983). Sassen-Koob argues that the economic growth generated by this type of regional specialization has created "an increased polarization in the income and occupational structure," the gradual elimination of middle-income white-collar and blue-collar jobs, and a large array of "mostly low-wage or very high-income" new jobs, the former attracting an influx of semi-skilled immigrants, the latter providing the "critical mass" needed for residential and commercial gentrification (Sassen-Koob 1984, 157-63).

There is evidence that such occupational and income polarization is occurring in San Francisco, creating a marginal economic base supporting a growing service class of blacks and recently arrived immigrants from

Southeast Asia and Central America. A recent projection by the Association of Bay Area Governments (ABAG) estimates that the number of lower-income service jobs in San Francisco will increase by 43 percent between 1980 and 2005, and the number of advanced corporate service jobs in finance, insurance, and real estate will increase by 18 percent. These two categories alone account for 74 percent of the projected increase of 119,500 jobs in San Francisco over the 25-year period (ABAG 1987, 158). Alarmed by these projections, the San Francisco Planning and Urban Research Association (SPUR) recently warned of the "danger of becoming primarily a service-oriented economy. . . . Instead of creating jobs that sustain a growing middle-class population, we could experience growth in high paying business service occupations, such as lawyers and accountants, and the kinds of low paying jobs protected by the state" (SPUR 1987, 2).

On the reasonable assumption that socio-economic conditions at least partially define a group's material interests and political objectives, what do these demographic and economic trends tell us about the likely voting behavior and coalitional propensities of San Francisco's major ethnic groups? First, Anglos and Asians (particularly Japanese and Chinese) should be conservatively aligned in their voting patterns on economic issues but more at odds on family life-style issues or race-specific issues involving clashing cultural traditions. Second, black and Hispanic voters should be progressively aligned on most economic issues and many family life-style issues. Third, Asians and Hispanics should vote alike on race-specific issues involving threats to ethnic cultural traditions but otherwise disagree. Fourth, blacks and Asians should display some degree of alignment in voting on family life-style issues but collide on economic matters. Fifth, the Asian population is much more socially stratified than blacks or Hispanics, implying greater obstacles in mobilizing ethnic solidarities around common political goals. Sixth, the huge socio-economic disparities noted in Table 1 lead us to expect the greatest amount of political conflict across the board between Anglos and blacks and between Anglos and Hispanics. Finally, the developing polarization of San Francisco's income and occupational structure as a consequence of regionally specialized economic growth is gutting the city's middle class and widening the gap between haves and have-nots. This might facilitate mobilization of "rainbow coalitions" (class-based alliances uniting people of all colors) and a resurgence of class conflict in local politics.

ETHNIC POLITICAL MOBILIZATION AND ELECTORAL ALLIANCES IN SAN FRANCISCO, 1979-1987

Three basic questions are addressed in this section: (1) How politically organized and mobilized are San Francisco's ethnic minority groups? (2) How progressively or conservatively do they vote relative to each other across a range of issues? (3) To what extent do voting patterns spring from ethnic solidarities per se rather than from class and status interests overlapping those of race?

Ethnic Political Power: Mobilization and Incorporation

There are many important elements to consider in trying to gauge the relative political power of San Francisco's ethnic minority populations. At the level of mass electoral participation, the key factors determining a group's "clout" in local elections and its ultimate impact on policymaking are its population size, voter registration and turnout rate, and degree of consensus or dissensus in supporting candidates and voting on the issues. At the level of elite political behavior, the key factors are a strong and unified leadership, efficient organization, control of resources, and inclusion in the city's dominant coalition (cf. Browning, Marshall, and Tabb 1984, 25).

Blacks. Blacks are now the smallest of the three ethnic minority groups in terms of population size, but they have mustered the highest rates of voter mobilization, ideological consensus, formal representation, and political incorporation. Supported by political organization and leadership at the state and national levels, San Francisco's black leaders have converted limited numbers and economic resources into a power bloc to be reckoned with in local politics. "Since at least the mid-1970s," writes political journalist Tim Redmond, "blacks have been a significant political force in San Francisco, wielding influence far greater than that enjoyed by other ethnic groups—Asians and Hispanics, for example." Redmond contrasts the political success of the black population with that of the Asian community, which is more than three times its size in terms of sheer numbers. "[B]lack representation in top policymaking posts dwarfs that of Asians," he points out, citing a long list of black supervisors, agency heads, board members, and commissioners under the Feinstein regime to compare with a very short one of Asians (Redmond 1986).

Despite their current political ascendancy among San Francisco's ethnic minority groups, there are signs that the black power base is eroding, mainly because of demographic attrition and developing schisms within the local black leadership over issues such as growth controls. Redmond quotes a local political analyst's view that black leaders are aware of the decline and feel threatened by the political emergence of other ethnic groups. "They see a Hispanic threat, and they see an Asian threat. . . . And that's logical, since the black population of the city is declining, while other minority groups are growing" (quoted in Redmond 1986). Black Supervisor Willie Kennedy recently remarked that "for years we were considered *the* minority. Then everyone else became a minority, and we started to get pushed back." She said that blacks "ought to be further advanced than these other groups, because we got here first" (quoted in Redmond 1986).

Hispanics. San Francisco's growing Hispanic population has only recently begun to translate its demographic potential into political power. According to Uhlaner et al., Hispanics throughout the state register and vote at about three-fifths the rate of Anglos and blacks (Uhlaner, Cain, and Kiewiet 1988). Grant Din cites studies estimating even lower rates of voter mobilization within San Francisco's Hispanic community, which has a very high proportion of noncitizens and formidable language barriers (Din 1984, 2).

Although the Hispanic community is divided on some issues (e.g., aid to the Contras, the death penalty), education "is the great unifier on which virtually all Latinos agree . . . , according to Louis Freedberg, who notes that nearly half of all Latino elected officials in the state are school board members (Freedberg 1987, 15). In San Francisco, Hispanic leaders have made their greatest political inroads in the education field, achieving the appointment of Ramon Cortines as school superintendent, placement of Chuck Ayala on the Community College Board, and the election of Rosario Anaya to the school board. With former Mayor Dianne Feinstein's appointments of Richard Sanchez to the Health Commission and Jim Gonzales to the Board of Supervisors (Gonzales was elected on his own in 1988), and with Mayor Agnos' appointments of Hispanics to the Police and Planning Commissions, the Hispanic community now has political representation in broader areas of public policy. Recently considered to be on the "periphery of San Francisco's dominant coalition" (Browning, Marshall, and Tabb 1984, 58), Hispanics under the Agnos regime are quickly closing the gap with blacks in the level of political incorporation. The Latino Democratic Club (LDC) has become one of the city's more influential political organizations and is working with other groups and committees to register voters and fund election campaigns. Near the end of Mayor Feinstein's administration, former LDC President Alfredo Rodriquez asked, rhetorically: "Do we have the political clout we should have? No. Are things happening to position ourselves to have that clout? Yes." (Freedberg 1986, 10). Under the progressive Agnos administration, things should happen even faster to make Hispanics a major force in San Francisco politics.

Asians. Asian Americans have been the "forgotten minority" in studies of urban ethnic politics (Din 1984, 26). Historical reasons for this include the lack of national visibility, limited political experience and sophistication relative to other ethnic groups in the rough and tumble of American politics, relative success compared with blacks and Hispanics in achieving economic advancement directly without resort to political mobilization, and a cultural disinclination to employ direct action tactics in sponsoring candidates, running campaigns, and mobilizing voters (Viviano 1988b). Thomas Hsieh, the Asian community's only representative on San Francisco's Board of Supervisors, explains:

> We found ourselves not particularly sophisticated on issues, or united on a national basis. I think the Asian/Pacific Americans finally realized that just providing the money, raising the money, and sitting on the sidelines is not what we want to see (Din 1984, 44).

Asian community political organizers face many of the same obstacles confronting the Hispanic community, including language barriers and lack of citizenship status, particularly among new arrivals. But times are changing.

Just in terms of numbers, the Asian population has become too large for politicians to ignore, particularly in San Francisco where they are now the single largest ethnic minority group. At the level of mass electoral participation, however, the Asian community still has a long way to go in converting its growing numbers into votes, as Din discovered in a careful study of voter registration rates of eligible adults in the three San Francisco neighborhoods with greatest concentrations of Chinese Americans (Chinatown, Richmond, and Sunset). Comparing Chinese and non-Chinese registration rates in November 1983, he found large disparities in all three areas: Chinatown, 23.1 percent vs. 60.2 percent; Richmond, 39.9 percent vs. 75.1 percent; Sunset, 29.0 percent vs. 65.7 percent, with a citywide average of 63.3 percent (Din 1984, 80). He notes that income levels "do not seem to be the main determinants of political participation," a finding corroborating Uhlaner et al.'s statewide survey results indicating that, "[e]ven with controls for demographic and other variables, Asian Americans are generally less active than non-Hispanic whites" (Uhlaner, Cain, and Kiewiet 1988, 33). Din concludes: "Asian/Pacific Americans appear to be grossly underrepresented in terms of their voting power in relation to their numbers in the population" (Din 1984, 86).

San Francisco's Asian community continues to be underrepresented on the Board of Supervisors, with Feinstein appointee Tom Hseih the only Asian member. Although incumbent Hseih was returned by voters to a full term in the most recent election, it is perhaps more significant and revealing that he was the only Asian candidate running for the board in a field of 24. In other areas of the city's political life, Asian leaders have made major inroads. Three have won posts on the Community College District Board, two on the Board of Education. Over 250 applied for positions on county commissions in 1988, "a vast increase over previous election years," according to Viviano (Viviano 1988b). Mayor Agnos' recent appointments of Asians to key commissions and administrative positions, as mentioned earlier, have accelerated this process of political incorporation.

It is important to note that nearly all of these political accomplishments were those of Chinese Americans, who make up about half of the total Asian population. Although some segments of the "other" Asian community, particularly Filipinos, have achieved greater visibility and clout in San Francisco, for the most part they lack political voice and exist at the periphery of city politics. It is doubtful that even the most committed pan-Asianists within the Chinese-American political elite can adequately represent the concerns and aspirations of all segments of San Francisco's large and diverse Asian community. Henry Der observes:

> In the last two decades people have come to this communi-
> ty from all over the place, from every part of China, Hong
> Kong and Taiwan, Vietnam, Laos, Cambodia, Thailand,
> Burma and Malaysia. The diversity of origins, opinions and
> belief systems is staggering. There's no way that any single
> organization can claim to represent "Chinese San Francis-
> co" (quoted in Viviano and Silva 1986, 74).

Table 2 provides a highly impressionistic summary of the relative political power of each major ethnic minority group in terms of the various indicators identified at the beginning of this section. If this summary may be used as a guide to the future of ethnic politics in San Francisco, the prospects look somewhat discouraging for blacks, encouraging for Hispanics, and very encouraging but more problematic for Asians. Black leaders will have to work harder and harder just to preserve their existing power base, coping with demographic erosion, leadership schisms, limited resources, and competition from other ethnic groups. Hispanic leaders must continue politicizing the influx of immigrants, accommodate their housing and employment needs to stabilize residency, and mobilize voters. Asian leaders must do the same but face a greater problem of creating political forms of racial-ethnic solidarity in a community riven by cultural and language differences, competing elites, and developing social class disparities.

Patterns of Ethnic Group Voting and Support for the Progressive Regime

A critical test of whether a true regime transformation took place with the Agnos victory in 1987 is the political longevity of the grass-roots multi-ethnic "rainbow" alliance of voters that brought him to power. Just as real rainbows are ephemeral, appearing one moment and dissipating the next, rainbow coalitions tend to disintegrate rather quickly in San Francisco's turbulent, "hyperpluralistic" political environment (cf. Wirt 1974; Castells 1983; Browning, Marshall, and Tabb 1984, 53-58). It is now well known in urban political studies that successful electoral coalitions do not necessarily translate into effective governing coalitions (Browning, Marshall, and Tabb 1984; Ferman 1985; Swanstrom 1988), and it might be that Mayor Agnos' ambitious progressive program will devolve into yet another centrist juggling act just to keep his various constituencies together under one political roof. Much depends on the compatibility of group goals and agendas within the progressive coalition, on the attractive force of progressive ideology in dislodging certain groups from their orbits around downtown business elites, and on the degree to which latent progressive support from low-income

Table 2:   *Impressionistic Summary of Political Power Indicators for San Francisco's Major Ethnic Groups*

	Blacks	Hispanics	Asians
Mass			
Numbers	Medium, shrinking	Medium, growing	Large, growing
Mobilization	High, stable	Low, increasing	Low, increasing
Consensus	High-moderate	Moderate	Moderate-low
Elites			
Leadership Unity	High-Moderate	High-Moderate	Moderate-low
Organization	High	Moderate	Moderate
Resources	Low	Low	Moderate-High
Incorporation	High	Moderate	Low

Source: Author. See main text.

ethnic minority subgroups on the periphery can be mobilized and incorporated under the new regime.

One useful approach to assessing the compatibility of ethnic group goals and agendas within the progressive coalition is an analysis of group voting propensities on a range of issues over the last decade. In what follows, we examine the voting patterns and alignments of San Francisco's major ethnic groups through an analysis of precinct electoral data on 24 state and local ballot propositions over the period 1979-1987. Although not a random sample, these propositions cover a wide range of issues: five different growth control measures, a rent control initiative, a local corporation tax measure, a proposal to study municipalization of utilities, a school bond measure, an environmentalist recycling proposal, handgun controls, a resolution to remove U.S. troops from El Salvador, two bilingual ballot repeal measures, a smoking ban referendum, a proposal to divest city pension fund investment in South Africa, a measure to limit property taxes, a state lottery initiative, a Republican-sponsored measure establishing a reapportionment commission, a Democrat-opposed campaign finance reform initiative, a proposal to cut state medical and public assistance programs, a resolution declaring San Francisco as a nuclear free city, a proposal for building a new downtown baseball stadium, and the last in a long line of initiatives to restore district elections. (A more detailed description of ballot propositions is available from the author on request.)

Our analysis proceeds in three stages. First, we use ecological regression to estimate the actual percentages of voter support within each major ethnic group for individual ballot propositions. Pairwise group comparisons are then made across the entire range of issues to identify similarities and differences in voting propensities. Second, we factor analyze the voting data, extracting three factors (interpreted as "liberalism," "populism," and "quality of life") related to separate dimensions of progressive ideology and voter support. Precinct factor scores are computed for each of these dimensions. Third, focusing on the progressivism factor scores, we re-estimate the model of ethnic group voting propensities, this time statistically controlling for possible confounding effects of social class, housing tenure, and sexual orientation on the vote. This analysis allows us to weigh the importance of ethnicity as a determinant of the vote relative to that of other social cleavages.

Patterns of ethnic voting on ballot issues: 1979-1987. Estimates of ethnic group voting rates supporting each of the 24 ballot propositions were made using ecological regression analysis of precinct electoral data and 1980 census tract information on race. (Methodological details are available from the author on request. For an introduction to ecological regression analysis, see Langbein and Lichtman 1978, 50-60.) Table 3 shows the results.

The tabular presentation allows a direct comparison of each ethnic group's voter support for each ballot measure. For example, the ecological regression model estimates that in 1979, 47 percent of Anglo voters, 41 percent of blacks, 60 percent of Hispanics, and 38 percent of Asians supported Proposition O, a local initiative to amend the city planning code to reduce building height limits and floor area ratios in the downtown area.

A graphical display of the same data allows overall patterns to be seen more clearly. Figure 1 shows scatter diagrams plotting one group's vote on a proposition against another's, six diagrams in all, one for each possible comparison. In each diagram a line of equality is drawn. If two groups voted identically on all the issues, all 24 data points would fall on the line of equality, suggesting perfect concordance in the voting patterns of the two groups. If two groups voted differently on some issues and similarly on others, the data points would be scattered across the chart. And if they voted in diametrically opposite ways on every issue, the chart would show a negative-sloping diagonal of data points cutting across the line of equality. The closer a data point is to the line of equality, the greater the agreement between the two groups on that issue. The farther away it is from the line of equality, the greater the disagreement. What do these charts tell us?

As predicted earlier, the highest level of concordance in voting patterns is seen for Anglos and Asians and for blacks and Hispanics. Anglos and Asians tend to vote alike, and blacks and Hispanics tend to vote alike, on most issues. (Cain and Kiewiet, 1984, discovered similar patterns in a California public opinion poll, as did Jackson, 1988, in a study of ethnic voting in Los Angeles.) There are mixed levels of interethnic agreement and disagreement shown in the other four comparisons (Anglo-Hispanic, Anglo-black, black-Asian, and Hispanic-Asian).

Figure 1: *Scatterplots of Ethnic Group Voting Rates on 24 San Francisco Ballot Propositions, 1979-1987.*

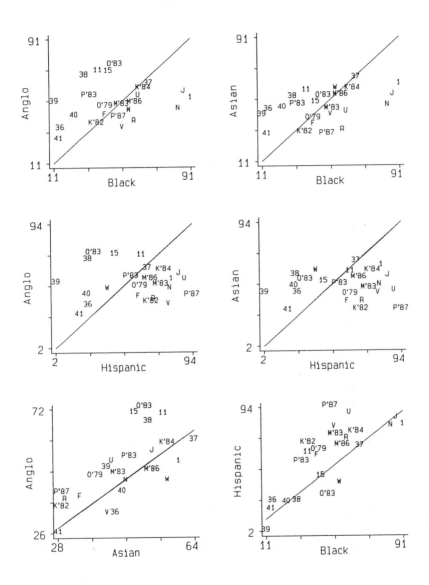

Source: Table 3.

Table 3:   *Ethnic Group Voting Patterns on 24 Ballot Propositions: San Francisco, 1979-1987[a]*

Proposition		Anglo	Black	Hispanic	Asian
O'79	(Highrise Growth Control)	47	41	60	38
R	(Rent Control)	37	58	68	30
V	(Tax Local Corporations)	33	51	78	41
K'82	(Public Ownership Utility)	36	36	67	29
1	(School Bonds)	52	91	80	60
11	(Beverage Container Refund)	70	37	60	56
15	(Handgun Control)	71	43	42	49
M'83	(Highrise Growth Control)	48	52	73	44
N	(Out of El Salvador)	45	84	79	46
O'83	(Repeal Bilingual Ballots)	72	47	28	51
P'83	(Prohibit Smoking Workplace)	54	32	53	47
K'84	(Shadow Ban)	59	64	75	57
J	(Anti-apartheid)	56	87	85	53
36	(Save Prop. 13—Limit Taxes)	33	15	24	43
37	(State Lottery)	60	66	64	64
38	(Repeal Bilingual Ballots)	67	29	24	52
39	(Reapportionment Commission)	50	11	2	41
40	(Campaign Finance Limits)	41	23	23	45
41	(Limit Public Assistance)	26	14	18	28
F	(Highrise Growth Control)	39	41	58	34
M'86	(Highrise Growth Control)	49	57	66	53
P'87	(District Elections)	40	49	94	28
U	(City Nuclear Free Zone)	52	60	89	42
W	(Build Baseball Stadium)	45	54	37	57

[a]Estimated percentage yes vote using ecological regression on precinct electoral and census tract data.

On four propositions, all of the racial groups voted pretty much the same way. There were majorities across the board favoring a ban on new buildings that would cast shadows on parks and recreation areas (Prop. K, '84). Strong majorities in all groups supported the state lottery (Prop. 37). All groups strongly opposed cuts in spending for medical and public assistance (Prop. 41). And there was fairly even voter support across all groups for the most recent growth control initiative (Prop. M, '86), reflecting an important shift favoring controls by blacks and Asians since the first such measure was proposed seven years earlier (Prop. O, '79).

Using a differential of 20 percent or more to indicate significant disagreement in the voting preferences of any two groups, we can easily spot in Table 3 those issues included in the analysis that cause greatest divergence in voting tendencies.

(1) Anglo and Asian voters disagreed most on handgun controls and repeal of bilingual ballots, Anglos being more supportive of both.

(2) Anglos more than Hispanics supported a reapportionment commission, repeal of bilingual ballots, and handgun controls. Hispanic voters, on the other hand, were more likely to support district elections, a nuclear free city, a local corporation tax, rent control, school bonds, South African divestment, troop withdrawal from El Salvador, municipalization of utilities, and growth controls (Prop. M '83).

(3) Anglos were more supportive than blacks of a reapportionment commission, repeal of bilingual ballots, bottle recycling, handgun controls, and an antismoking ordinance. Black voters were more likely to support school bonds, withdrawal from El Salvador, South African divestment, and rent control.

(4) Blacks and Hispanics disagreed on seven issues, Hispanic voters being more supportive of district elections, a nuclear free city, municipalizing utilities, taxing corporations, recycling bottles, limiting growth (Prop. M '83), and regulating smoking.

(5) Blacks more than Asians supported district elections, withdrawal from El Salvador, South African divestment, school bonds, and rent control. Asian voters were more likely to support a reapportionment commission, property tax restrictions, and campaign finance reform.

(6) Hispanics were more supportive than Asians of district elections, a nuclear free city, rent control, municipalization of utilities, corporation taxation, withdrawal from El Salvador, growth controls, South African divestment, and school bonds. Asians, on the other hand, were more likely to support repeal of bilingual ballots, campaign finance reform, and construction of a downtown baseball stadium.

These differences in policy orientation between ethnic groups are interesting to study from the point of view of identifying issues that might undermine future efforts to form ethnic coalitions. On only two issues did blacks, Hispanics, and Asians vote the same way against an opposite position by Anglos: handgun controls (Anglos for) and growth controls in 1986 (Anglos barely against). Thus, conflicts pitting Anglos against all people of color seem most unlikely.

On issues involving more radical proposals, such as local corporation taxes and municipalization of utilities, Hispanic voters are alone among racial minorities in their strong support. One exception is rent control, a perennially hot issue in San Francisco that opens a deep fissure between blacks and Hispanics on one side, Anglos and Asians on the other. This finding is consistent with figures reported earlier in Table 1 showing that many more Anglos and Asians earn income from interest, dividends, rent or royalties (42.0 percent and 37.1 percent) than do Hispanics and blacks (16.6 percent and 10.1 percent).

Proposals for modest economic redistribution in the tradition of Democratic party politics, such as public school financing, public assistance, and local property taxes, appear to group relatively liberal blacks and Hispanics against relatively conservative Anglos and Asians—emphasis on "relatively" because in San Francisco the whole ideological spectrum is left of center on these kinds of issues. Also reflecting underlying partisan cleavages is the gap in support between blacks/Hispanics and Anglos/Asians for a Republican-sponsored reapportionment commission and a Democrat-opposed campaign finance reform initiative.

Black voters stand alone *vis-à-vis* the other three ethnic groups in strongly opposing bottle recycling and smoking regulation, so-called "quality of life" regulatory measures. This finding suggests that black and Hispanic electoral alliances may have to be confined to policy areas of shared material concerns (jobs, housing, education) that are congruent with Democratic party politics. Blacks tend to be more narrowly "liberal," Hispanics more broadly "progressive," in the lexicon of San Francisco's political culture.

Three dimensions of progressivism in San Francisco politics. The tool of factor analysis makes it possible to sort out and identify the separate dimensions of progressivism implicit in the voting data and the patterns of ethnic group support associated with each. The strength of factor analysis in this context is its data reduction capability, i.e., its capacity to reduce a large amount of information to a smaller set of factors that can be interpreted as theoretically significant source variables accounting for observed relationships in the data.

The analysis identifies three principal factors underlying precinct voting patterns on the 24 ballot propositions. In our interpretation, each factor corresponds to a separate dimension of progressivism in San Francisco politics. The first and main factor we call "liberalism," the second "populism," the third "quality of life." Table 4 reports the factor loadings on each factor.

The highest positive loadings on the "liberalism" factor show strong voter support for public school spending, anti-apartheid measures, nonintervention in El Salvador, and residential rent control. The highest negative loadings tap voter opposition to the repeal of bilingual ballots, a Republican-sponsored reapportionment measure, limits on local property taxes, and reductions in public assistance expenditures. The underlying political cleavage reflected in this voting pattern is congruent with national partisan divisions on social welfare and foreign policy issues and with traditional liberal-conservative conflicts on matters involving racial discrimination and distributive justice.

The highest positive loadings on the "populism" factor indicate strong voter support for district versus at-large elections, municipal ownership of private utilities, severe restrictions on highrise office construction, and declaration of the city as a nuclear free zone. The highest negative loading taps voter opposition to building a new downtown baseball stadium. The underlying political cleavage reflected in this voting pattern is that of community versus capital, "use values" versus "exchange values," slow-growth versus pro-growth, neighborhood preservation versus downtown business development.

The highest positive loadings on the "quality of life" factor show strong voter support for an environmentalist beverage container refund measure, statewide handgun controls, and prohibition of smoking in office workplaces. These measures reflect a "public-regarding" ethos (Wilson and Banfield 1971) promoting government regulation of individual behavior to enhance the quality of life affecting public health, public safety, and the environment. The highest negative loading is on a proposal for a statewide lottery. The underlying political cleavage is that of public versus private interest, holistic versus individualistic concerns.

Of all the ballot propositions analyzed, the growth control measures (O '79, M '83, K '84, M '86, and F '85) as a group have the greatest factorial complexity, with substantial positive loadings on all three factors. This is important because, as will be argued later, growth control issues have dominated San Francisco's political agenda for a decade and were a fulcrum point for organizing the progressive coalition that came to power in 1987. In tracking voter support for growth controls over the three major initiatives (O '79, M '83, M '86), the factor loadings in Table 4 suggest that growth control has become less a quality of life issue and more a liberal-conservative issue as traditionally defined. This shift was a key element in mobilizing ethnic group support for the progressive coalition (DeLeon and Powell 1989).

The three factors extracted from our analysis of the ballot proposition data correspond to three independent dimensions of progressive politics in San Francisco: liberalism, populism, and quality of life. Viewed as components of a political ideology, these three dimensions are internally consistent and appear to capture the wide-ranging sweep of the new urban regime in San Francisco politics. Viewed as indicators of cross-cutting political cleavages in voting patterns, however, these same three factors by construction are independent of each other and are consistent with varying degrees of group support or opposition on each dimension. Considering just the first two factors, for example, certain precinct electorates might be strongly liberal yet antipopulist in their voting tendencies (let us call them "old liberals"), while others might be strongly conservative yet populist ("neighborhood parochials"). Liberal populist precincts ("progressives") and conservative antipopulist ones ("conservatives") illustrate instances of pure progressive and antiprogressive voting patterns. Indeed, given the likelihood of varying issue salience among different groups, one may conceive of pro-

Table 4:   *Progressivism in San Francisco: Factor Loadings on Three Dimensions of Voting on Ballot Propositions in San Francisco Precincts, 1979-1987*[a]

Ballot Proposition		Factor 1 "Liberalism"	Factor 2 "Populism"	Factor 3 "Quality"	h^2
1	School Bonds	.946	-.041	-.039	.90
J	Anti-apartheid	.938	.202	.016	.92
N	Out of El Salvador	.935	.158	-.030	.90
R	Rent Control	.805	.273	.071	.73
U	City Nuclear Free Zone	.789	.486	.125	.87
M'86	Highrise Growth Control	.781	.385	.233	.81
M'83	Highrise Growth Control	.772	.438	.314	.87
K'84	Shadow Ban	.766	.400	.262	.82
P'87	District Elections	.748	.586	-.025	.90
K'82	Public Ownership Utility	.741	.521	.293	.91
V	Tax Local Corporations	.708	.422	-.063	.68
O'79	Highrise Growth Control	.619	.445	.437	.77
F	Highrise Growth Control	.588	.512	.131	.63
11	Beverage Container Refund	.164	.449	.824	.91
15	Handgun Control	.155	.201	.872	.83
37	State Lottery	.116	.106	-.404	.19
W	Build Baseball Stadium	-.033	-.600	-.170	.39
P'83	Prohibit Smoking Workplace	-.041	.474	.590	.57
40	Limit Campaign Contributions	-.616	.129	.273	.47
41	Limit Public Assistance	-.804	-.078	-.004	.65
O'83	Repeal Bilingual Ballots	-.863	-.201	-.090	.79
36	Save Prop. 13—Limit Taxes	-.904	-.032	-.259	.88
39	Reapportionment Commission	-.913	-.199	.265	.94
38	Repeal Bilingual Ballots	-.949	-.062	.036	.91
Eigenvalues		14.26	3.19	.81	

[a]Principal components analysis with varimax rotation.

gressive electoral alliances whose members are "progressive" in only one dimension but not the others.

Factor index scores for the liberalism, populism, and quality of life factors were calculated for each precinct. These scores were standardized by setting lowest and highest scores on each index to 0 and 100, respectively. In the analysis that follows we will focus on these three factor indices as overall measures of ethnic group support for each separate dimension of the progressive agenda.

Minced cleavages: ethnicity, class, housing, and sexual identity as determinants of progressive voting in San Francisco. In our earlier socio-demographic profiles of San Francisco's major ethnic groups (see Table 1), we found strong relationships between ethnicity and socio-economic status. Anglos and Asians tend to be relatively more affluent, for example, and blacks and Hispanics relatively poorer. Later in our analysis, we discovered that Anglos and Asians tend to vote alike, blacks and Hispanics alike. Now we must ask: how do we know that racial-ethnic differences rather than social class differences account for the observed patterns in policy preference? If a wealthy Asian homeowner votes against rent controls and a poor Hispanic renter votes for them, how may we sort out the distinctively racial component of the voting decision from those of social class and housing tenure? A straightforward analysis of ethnicity and politics in San Francisco is confounded by these other factors that must be taken into account.

One potentially confounding factor is class. Charles Ragin writes:

> By most accounts, class and ethnicity are among the most incompatible affiliations. This is because classes are economically defined and often contain a variety of ethnic groups, while ethnic divisions usually cross-cut class divisions. Thus, a political actor may have difficulty supporting his or her class and ethnic group simultaneously. The former affirms the importance of occupationally based economic divisions; the latter denies them (Ragin 1986, 199).

The analytical problem addressed here has more than academic relevance. Ragin goes on:

> In fact, class mobilization often is successful only when ethnic antagonisms within classes can be disregarded or, better yet, forgotten altogether. Similarly, ethnic mobilization may require a submergence of class antagonisms within an ethnically defined collectivity (Ragin 1986, 199).

Those who attempt to mobilize class-based "rainbow coalitions" must solve the first kind of problem. Leaders of San Francisco's Asian-American community will be increasingly vexed by the second and eventually so too will black and Hispanic leaders as a paradoxical consequence of internal social stratifications generated by the economic success of their political programs.

Another important cleavage cross-cutting racial divisions is that of housing tenure (owners versus renters), which also cross-cuts social classes, as we saw earlier in our socio-demographic profile analysis. In recent neo-Weberian literature on urban political economy (Rex and Moore 1967; Castells 1983; Dunleavy 1979; Saunders 1984; Lowe 1986), housing tenure has been theoretically subsumed under the rubric of "consumption sectors" in contraposition to the neo-Marxist emphasis on production-based class relations (Katznelson 1981; Harvey 1985). Peter Saunders writes:

> Consumption sectors, which are constituted through the division between owners and non-owners of crucial means of consumption such as housing, crosscut class boundaries, are grounded in non-class-based material interests, and represent an increasingly significant form of social cleavage which may in certain circumstances come to out-weigh class membership in their economic and political effects (Saunders 1984, 23).

San Francisco has about three renters for every two homeowners. These housing tenure statuses are strongly correlated with what we call "family life-style" differences (see below), which are spatially configured in recognizable "turfs" throughout the city's many neighborhoods. San Francisco also is plagued by a perpetually low residential vacancy rate and a shrinking stock of affordable housing. The housing supply ebbs while the demand for it grows with each new wave of immigrants and with each new job added to the local economy. Nearly every major policy debate in San Francisco is shot through with some aspect of the housing crisis: AIDS, economic development, budget deficits, saving the Giants, homeporting the U.S.S. Missouri fleet, the proposed Mission Bay development, growth controls, etc. Consumption sectors organized around housing tenure and family life-style differences have a political life of their own in San Francisco, and they must also be taken into account when assessing the effects of ethnicity.

One final social cleavage to be considered in our analysis of ethnic politics is that of sexual orientation. The gay community in San Francisco is sizable (representing about 16 percent of adults, perhaps 20 percent of the registered voters), geographically concentrated, well-mobilized politically, and economically potent (Castells 1983, 355-59). Many gays in San Francisco are relatively affluent white male renters whose housing needs have produced significant gentrification over the last 20 years, in some cases displacing blacks and creating political friction between these groups (Mollenkopf 1983, 202-03). Gay voters are a major part of the progressive base, and their political power is respected by politicians. A columnist for a local gay newspaper writes: "We've got power here because we're great voters. Politicians can be destroyed by the gay vote. As long as we keep our vote, they're going to kiss our ass for a long time" (quoted in Roberts 1987a, 29).

To summarize, San Francisco's population is politically minced by four cross-cutting cleavages: ethnicity, class, housing tenure, and sexual identity. To isolate and weigh the political effects of ethnicity alone requires statistical controls adjusting for the potentially confounding influences of the other three factors. These controls can be achieved by including measures of socio-economic status, housing tenure, and sexual orientation along with ethnicity as independent variables in a linear-additive multiple regression model predicting precinct progressivism scores on the liberalism, populism, and quality of life indices.

Social status and housing tenure are measured on precincts using factor scores derived from a principal components analysis of socio-demographic census data and metrically converted to a 0-100 scale. (Statistical details of index construction are available from the author on request. See Appendix A for data sources.) High-scoring precincts on the socio-economic status index (SES) are those with high percentages of professional-managerial workers and high school graduates, high median rents and home values, high income per capita, and low levels of poverty and unemployment. High-scoring precincts on the housing tenure ("family life-style") index (FLS) are those with high percentages of homeowners, long-time residents, and children under the age of 18, and with low levels of poverty. (The poverty variable loaded high and negatively on both factors.) Precincts are classified as "gay" and assigned a value of 1 if they are located in census tracts with at least 30 percent single males where numbers of men also exceed women by 15 percent in the 25-44 age range. All other precincts are scored zero. This indicator is commonly used by San Francisco political consultants for polling and targeting purposes. The three ethnicity variables (percentage of blacks, Asian, and Hispanics) are measured as before. Table 5 reports the regression results.

Focusing first on the liberalism factor, we find that the effects of ethnic group voting are powerful, even controlling for other social structural variables. Black and Hispanic voting is strongly liberal on these types of issues, Asian voting also but weaker. Social class cleavages have limited impact on precinct liberalism scores when ethnicity and other factors are taken into account. The positive slope for SES does indicate some degree of conservative voting among working-class poor. Housing tenure, on the other hand, is an important factor shaping the vote on these types of issues, renters voting much more liberal than homeowners. Voters in gay precincts are clearly allied with renters and ethnic minority groups on this dimension of progressive voting. Even controlling for other factors, classification of a precinct as "gay" adds more than 10 points to the estimated liberalism score.

Regression results for the populism factor show a much different picture of structural influences on precinct voting. Voters in black and Asian precincts are strongly antipopulist in their voting tendencies, those in Hispanic precincts essentially neutral. Class conflicts are clearly activated by populist-type issues. Voters in poorer, working-class precincts support populist initiatives, those in more affluent, middle-class precincts oppose them. The forces of class and ethnicity collide on these kinds of issues, effectively neutralizing each other. What Ragin described as the "incompatibilities" of ethnic and class affiliations are experienced most powerfully by voters in working-class black and Asian precincts. Housing tenure, on the

Table 5:   *Regression Analysis of Progressive Voting as a Function of Social Class (SES), Housing Tenure (FLS), Sexual Orientation (Gay), and Race (Black, Hispanic, Asian): San Franciso Precincts, 1979-1987*

Independent Variables	Progressive Voting Factor Scores		
	"Liberalism"	"Populism"	"Quality"
Social Class (SES)	.115*	-.554**	.865**
Housing Tenure (FLS)	-.440**	.048*	-.523**
Gay (dummy)	10.216**	12.732**	-.437
Percent Black	.624**	-.724**	-.025
Percent Hispanic	.641**	.020	.199**
Percent Asian	.245**	-.509**	.375**
Constant	50.029**	103.678**	25.147**
S.E.E.	11.665	12.116	11.752
Adjusted R-SQR	.63	.48	.67

*p < .05
**p < .01

Source: Precinct electoral data, 1979-1987: Statements of Vote, San Francisco Registrar of Voters. Census tract data, 1980: U.S. Bureau of the Census.

other hand, has little independent effect on populist voting. Homeowners are revealed to be slightly more inclined than renters to support populist positions once other factors are statistically controlled—possibly reflecting antagonisms between neighborhood preservationists and downtown business elites. Voters in gay precincts are strongly populist in their voting behavior.

The results for the quality of life factor are very interesting and deserve extended discussion because they point to one possible future for San Francisco politics. Quality of life issues fall into the domain of what Inglehart has described as "postmaterialism"—a new political polarization found increasingly in advanced industrial societies that is value-based rather than class-based, in which voters are motivated more by "socio-tropic" concerns (e.g., environmentalism) than by egocentric pursuits. Inglehart argues that these types of issues "may stimulate a reaction in which part of the working class sides with the Right, to reaffirm the traditional materialist emphasis on economic growth, military security, and domestic order" (Inglehart 1987, 1297). In this view, the traditional "Left" versus "Right" vocabulary is slowly recalibrated so as to coincide with, and give familiar meaning to, the new axis of political polarization.

In San Francisco politics, the "materialist" Left versus Right cleavage is clearly evident in our findings for the liberalism and populism factors, although the Left position in the case of populism is undercut by opposition from blacks and Asians. The "postmaterialist" Left versus Right cleavage emerges in our results for the quality of life factor. There is middle-class renter support for these initiatives meeting with working-class homeowner opposition (strong positive slope for SES, strong negative slope for FLS). Among ethnic minorities, Asian voters are strong supporters of quality of life measures, Hispanics also but weaker. Map analysis (not shown here) identifies the Pacific Heights neighborhood—residential headquarters of the city's "new class" mobile, affluent, professional elite—as the top-scoring cluster of precincts on the environmentalism index. Lowest-scoring precincts are found in the Excelsior, Crocker-Amazon, Visitacion Valley, and Bayview-Hunter's Point working-class homeowner districts, the latter two with high concentrations of blacks. Precincts in the city's geographical progressive core—Haight-Ashbury, Noe-Eureka, Buena Vista-Duboce—score high on the index but cannot claim leadership in this domain.

In the context of this discussion, one implication of our factor analysis and regression results viewed as a whole is that at least three different Left-Right axes cross-cut each other in San Francisco's political space: liberalism (strongest), populism, and quality of life (weakest). Where the three polarities on the Left converge, that is what we have called "progressivism." The geographical point of greatest convergence is the Haight-Ashbury. These axes, however, are not static. Although liberalism and populism are currently dominant in shaping the content and character of San Francisco's political life, the postmaterialist quality of life axis will exert increasing hegemonic control over the city's political agenda if the demographic and economic trends discussed earlier continue—specifically, the bifurcation of the city's occupational structure, gentrification, and the rapid economic advancement of an expanding Asian population. If this line of speculative argument is plausible, San Francisco could be entering an extremely volatile and possibly dangerous period of political dealignment and polemical confusion, a period when "old class" citizens (particularly blacks and Hispanics) and their material concerns are shut out entirely from a local government agenda controlled by "new class" citizens preoccupied with the "socio-tropic" goals of making San Francisco a beautiful, safe, "world-class" city.

Returning to an interpretation of our regression results, perhaps the most important conclusion one can draw from Table 5 is that ethnicity remains a key factor influencing voter decisions on a wide range of issues, even when the effects of social class, housing tenure, and sexual orientation are statistically controlled. This generalization holds true especially for the liberalism and populism factor scores, less so for voting on quality of life issues. Thus, ethnic politics in San Francisco has a life of its own and is not merely the epiphenomenal manifestation of what some theorists (e.g., Harvey 1985, 61) believe are the submerged but more fundamental conflicts between economic classes.

There are those who concede the power of ethnicity in urban politics but lament the fact. Ira Katznelson, for example, brilliantly analyzes the "trenches" in American cities that establish "boundaries and rules that stress ethnicity, race, and territoriality, rather than class, and that emphasize the distribution of goods and services, while excluding questions of production and workplace relations" (Katznelson 1981, 6). Among the consequences, according to Norman Fainstein, are "racially and ethnically segmented communities and a local politics of particularistic exchange and ethnic symbolism. The urban politics that Americans take for granted simultaneously insulates capital from popular demands within cities and reproduces ethnic and racial, rather than class, solidarities" (Fainstein 1985, 561-62). The statistical evidence presented in Table 5 strongly supports this view—particularly regarding the liberal yet antipopulist voting behavior of blacks and Asians.

THE 1987 MAYORAL RACE:
SOCIAL AND IDEOLOGICAL BASES OF THE AGNOS COALITION

Now that we have explored ethnic group electoral support for the three-dimensional ideological framework of progressive politics in San Francisco, it is time to bring into sharper focus the contours of that support for Art Agnos himself as a candidate for mayor and as a leader of the city's progressive movement. Table 6 reports the results of regression analyses of the precinct vote for Agnos in his race against the other two leading mayoral candidates, John Molinari (progrowth moderate) and Roger Boas (progrowth conservative) in the November 3, 1987 election. In terms of numbers, Agnos received more votes (49 percent of the total) than Molinari (24 percent) and Boas (20 percent) combined. (Agnos went on to defeat Molinari 70 percent to 30 percent in the December run-off election.) Lacking detailed survey data, these equations provide at least a partial statistical summary of constituency support for Agnos after the dust had settled at the end of a hard-fought campaign. The first column of Table 6 reports regression coefficients for the social structural variables alone. The results suggest that low-income working class voters and renters strongly supported the Agnos candidacy (negative SES and FLS slopes). Voters in gay precincts provided Agnos with substantial support. Among ethnic groups, Hispanic voters gave Agnos strongest support, followed by blacks, with Asian voters far behind. The accompanying level-importance statistics shown in column two indicate that the housing tenure cleavage was the single most important determinant of the vote. Social class (8.11) and

Table 6: *Regression Analyses of Precinct Vote for Art Agnos in Mayoral Race, November 3, 1987 (Percentage of Total Votes Cast)*

	Social Structural Variables	Level-Importance Statistic[a]	With % Democratic	Political Ideology Variables
SES (Class)	-.156**	(8.11)	.027	—
FLS (Tenure)	-.220**	(11.44)	-.307**	—
Gay (dummy)	4.746**	(.35)	1.747	—
Percent Black	.105**	(1.26)	-.019	—
Percent Hispanic	.213**	(2.34)	.102**	—
Percent Asian	-.173**	(3.46)	-.103**	—
% Democratic Regis. 1982	—	—	.686**	—
Liberalism Factor	—	—	—	.525**
Populism Factor	—	—	—	.227**
Quality of Life Factor	—	—	—	-.013
Constant	68.08**	—	21.49**	8.18**
S.E.E.	8.86	—	7.82	5.62
Adjusted R-SQR	.50	—	.61	.79

*p < .05
**p < .01

[a]Absolute value of regression coefficient times mean of independent variable. (See Achen 1982, 71-73.)

ethnicity (1.26 + 2.34 + 3.46 = 7.06) had about the same impact. The gay/nongay cleavage had relatively little marginal effect on the outcome.

This first set of findings clearly demonstrates the importance of ethnic voting as an independent force in San Francisco's electoral politics. Black low-income renters, for example, were much more likely to vote for Agnos than Asian low-income renters or Anglo low-income renters. But the findings show just as clearly that social class and housing tenure "solidarities" (to use Fainstein's term) have their own political force and are not dissipated by cross-cutting ethnic affiliations. The regression coefficients tell us, for example, that black renters were much more likely to vote for Agnos than black homeowners.

Art Agnos came to the mayoral race as a well-known local Democratic assemblyman with strong support from the northern California Democratic leadership. Although the election was officially nonpartisan, the voters' partisan affiliations had an important mediating influence on the outcome. This can be seen in column three of Table 6, which shows a significant shift in the coefficients for social structural variables after statistically controlling for percent Democratic registration. The results suggest that the effects of social class cleavages on the vote were almost entirely mediated by the intervening variable of party affiliation. The effects of ethnicity also appear to have been mediated by partisanship, particularly in the case of blacks. (Blacks tend to be Democrats, and Democrats vote for Agnos.) These results imply that Mayor Agnos' strong connection with the Democratic party is the political glue binding some elements of his coalition to the others. The housing tenure cleavage, on the other hand, appears to have had an even stronger direct impact on the vote than what was estimated in column one. Evidently, many renters who voted for Agnos were motivated by ideological commitment or material self-interest rather than party loyalty.

The last set of findings, reported in column four of Table 6, gives insight into the ideological base of Agnos' victory. These coefficients were obtained by regressing the percentage Agnos vote on the three progressivism factors. The results indicate that traditional liberalism was the main ideological force determining the vote, buttressed by a high degree of urban populist sentiment. The coefficient for the quality of life factor is virtually zero, suggesting that the "postmaterialist Left" contributed little one way or the other to the Agnos victory. It is worth noting that just two numbers—the liberalism and populism factor index scores—explain nearly 80 percent of the precinct variation in the Agnos vote.

CONCLUSION: RAINBOW COALITIONS AND THE PROGRESSIVE URBAN REGIME UNDER MAYOR AGNOS

Based on the statistical findings and theoretical interpretations presented thus far, what are the prospects that Mayor Agnos can maintain and expand his base of support among San Francisco's voters? Considering the historic nature of the Agnos victory, perhaps a better formulation of the question is: how can Mayor Agnos build and solidify a *progressive* governing coalition—a coalition whose leaders will seek not only the political empowerment and economic advancement of their separate constituencies but also the broader transformation of the old urban regime? This paper will end with some brief speculative answers to that question.

The core of Mayor Agnos' electoral coalition includes renters, poor people, Hispanics, blacks, gays, and neighborhood populists. Although voters in these groups helped to bring a progressive mayor to power, relatively few of them (outside the Haight-Ashbury) embrace all the values of a progressive ethos. Particularly among low-income working-class voters, support for progressivism is at best one- or two-dimensional. Many blacks need jobs and affordable housing, for example, and do not take kindly to populist or environmentalist efforts to limit growth and economic development. Many Anglo neighborhood preservationists support restrictions on downtown highrise office construction, but do not take kindly to efforts by Asian property owners to raze Victorian houses, replacing them with more affordable multiple-unit dwellings to accommodate large extended families (Chung 1987). From the narrower perspective of any one of these groups, the progressive agenda may be viewed as an unstable compound of contradictory political goals. It can happen all too easily that some of the colors found in the Agnos rainbow coalition will fade away, both figuratively and literally, and the progressive electoral base will disintegrate. Blacks and Hispanics, in particular, will have to exit the city if Agnos fails in his promise to provide affordable housing and decent jobs for low-income residents. And they will take their votes with them.

To solve these problems would be difficult for Mayor Agnos under the best of circumstances, but to do so under the conditions of a $180 million budget deficit, a growing AIDS epidemic, continuing immigration flows into the city, a shortage of affordable housing, threats of disinvestment by large corporations, and financial abandonment by state and federal governments—to push even a few yards in the direction of regime transformation under these conditions might require miracles. "My curse is coming in as a liberal with no money to spend," complained Agnos recently, alluding to the deficit he inherited from the Feinstein administration (quoted in Garcia and Sward, 1988). Cleveland's populist mayor Dennis Kucinich failed to work such miracles and so have other big city mayors with progressive aspirations (Swanstrom 1985; Stone 1988; Reed 1988; Judd 1986). Why should Agnos succeed?

Here are six reasons, briefly stated.

(1) Mayor Agnos is an experienced and skillful politician. He is not likely to repeat Kucinich's mistake of alienating his own constituency (Swanstrom 1988, 132-35). He is nonconfrontational in his dealings with the business community and conservative neighborhood groups. Although pressed by supporters to consult less and lead more, Agnos has an explicit agenda (spelled out clearly in his widely distributed campaign book, "Getting Things Done") and the patience to implement it through consensus-building over the long term. "I didn't say I was going to do it all in 11 months or 12 months or 18 months," said Agnos recently. "If you look at those things, it takes more than that to put them in place" (quoted in Garcia and Sward 1988). Agnos has also moved quickly to incorporate progressive-minded blacks, Hispanics, and Asians within his administration, and he appears responsive to the material interests and concerns of their constituencies. Given the absence of state and federal urban programs, the mayor's appointive patronage is about the only game in town; political and ideological commitments can be exacted.

(2) A progressive policy "infrastructure" was already partially in place when Mayor Agnos assumed office, particularly in the area of growth management. No large American city has more stringent restrictions on commercial land use or highrise office construction. Further, the grip of progrowth ideology on blacks and the working class has softened as a cumulative consequence of repeated slow-growth initiative campaigns and the failure of downtown business to deliver on promises of jobs and housing (DeLeon and Powell 1989).

(3) The Board of Supervisors now has a progressive (or at least liberal) majority that is likely to work with Mayor Agnos rather than against him in the policymaking process.

(4) The growth-induced problems of daily urban life have become pervasive, omnipresent, and increasingly unbearable: traffic congestion, parking, skyrocketing rents. Arguments that the cure for growth is more growth sound hollow. The stock in community use values has gone up. The cleavage between community and capital is deepening, and it cuts across all other cleavages of race, class, and housing tenure.

(5) The San Francisco business community is divided (into "fractions" of capital, the neo-Marxists might say). Many owners of existing commercial real estate are delighted with the stringent growth controls; many developers and corporate investors, on the other hand, feel thwarted and frustrated by them. Many small businesses call for lease restrictions and commercial rent controls; big businesses resist them. Once again, given the absence of state and federal urban programs, and given the restrictions on local tax assessments, businesses are being made to pay the bills through linkage fees and similar devices, and the allocation of burdens is divisive. In the face of all this internal conflict, the Chamber of Commerce has retreated from visible leadership and appears to be hunkering down in political disarray (DeLeon and Powell 1989).

(6) In performing his roles as mayor and as leader of the progressive movement, Agnos has a tremendous asset: San Francisco itself. The city continues to be widely perceived as a desirable place to live and work and set up businesses—despite the congestion, highrises, and other problems. Daykin has argued that, in theory, "all cities can impose conditions on capital in exchange for access to their urban space. However, certain cities are strategically located to drive harder bargains than others" (Daykin 1988, 383). San Francisco is one of those cities.

With these factors in his favor, Mayor Agnos might well succeed in governing the city, preserving his electoral majority, and advancing the progressive agenda in all three directions at once: liberalism, populism, and quality of life. Under this new regime, leaders of the city's ethnic minority groups have an opportunity to pursue goals of empowerment and social mobility within a larger political vision of San Francisco becoming the nation's first world-class progressive city. Rainbows may last longer in such a regime.

REFERENCES

Achen, Christopher. *Interpreting and Using Regression*. Beverly Hills: Sage, 1982.

Association of Bay Area Governments (ABAG). *Projections—87: Forecasts for the San Francisco Bay Area to the Year 2005*. Association of Bay Area Governments, 1987.

Browning, Rufus P., Dale Rogers Marshall, and David H. Tabb. *Protest is Not Enough: The Struggle of Blacks and Hispanics for Equality In Urban Politics*. Berkeley: University of California Press, 1984.

Cain, Bruce, and Roderick Kiewiet. "California's Coming Minority Majority." *Public Opinion* (Feb./Mar. 1986): 50-52.

Castells, Manuel. *The City and the Grassroots*. Berkeley: University of California Press, 1983.

Chung, L. A. "Behind S.F.'s Neighborhood Building Wars." *San Francisco Chronicle*, Sept. 12, 1987.

Clavel, Pierre. *The Progressive City*. New Brunswick: Rutgers University Press, 1986.

Cordova, Carlos. "Undocumented El Salvadoreans in the San Francisco Bay Area: Migration and Adaptation Dynamics." *Journal of La Raza Studies* 1 (1987): 9-37.

Daykin, David S. "The Limits to Neighborhood Power: Progressive Politics and Local Control in Santa Monica." In *Business Elites and Urban Development*, edited by S. Cummings. Albany: State University of New York Press, 1988.

DeLeon, Richard E., and Sandra S. Powell. "Growth Control and Electoral Politics in San Francisco: The Triumph of Urban Populism." *Western Political Quarterly* 42 (1989): 307-31.

Din, Grant. *An Analysis of Asian/Pacific American Registration and Voting Patterns in San Francisco*. Master's thesis. Claremont Graduate School, 1984.

Dunleavy, Patrick. "The Urban Bases of Political Alignment: Social Class, Domestic Property Ownership, and State Intervention in Consumption Processes." *British Journal of Political Science* 9 (1979): 409-43.

Elkin, Stephen. *City and Regime in the American Republic*. Chicago: University of Chicago Press, 1987.

Fainstein, Norman. "Class and Community in Urban Social Movements." *Urban Affairs Quarterly* 20 (1985): 561-62.

Ferman, Barbara. *Governing the Ungovernable City*. Philadelphia: Temple University Press, 1985.

Freedberg, Louis. "Latino Power." *This World* (October 19, 1986): 9-11.

_____. "Latinos: Building Power from the Ground Up." *California Journal* (January 1987): 12-17.

Garcia, Dawn. "Who Holds the Keys to Power in San Francisco Under Agnos." *San Francisco Chronicle*, July 11, 1988.

Garcia, Dawn, and Susan Sward. "The Agnos Record a Year After Election." *San Francisco Chronicle*, December 16, 1988.

Godfrey, Brian. *Inner-City Neighborhoods in Transition: The Morphogenesis of San Francisco's Ethnic and Nonconformist Communities.* Ph.D. dissertation. Berkeley: University of California, 1982.

Harvey, David. *Consciousness and the Urban Experience: Studies in the History and Theory of Capitalist Urbanization.* Baltimore: The Johns Hopkins University Press, 1985.

Heskin, Allen. *Tenants and the American Dream: Ideology and the Tenant Movement.* New York: Praeger, 1983.

Inglehart, Ronald. "Value Change in Industrial Societies." *American Political Science Review* 81 (1987): 1289-1303.

Jackson, Byran O. "Ethnic Cleavages and Voting Patterns in U. S. Cities: An Analysis of the Asian, Black, and Hispanic Communities in Los Angeles." Paper presented at the Conference on Comparative Ethnicity, University of California at Los Angeles, June 1-3, 1988.

Jacobs, John. "Agnos Win Reflects Grass-Roots Strategy." *San Francisco Examiner*, November 15, 1987.

Judd, Dennis. "Electoral Coalitions, Minority Mayors, and the Contradictions in the Municipal Policy Agenda." In *Cities in Stress*. Beverly Hills: Sage, 1986.

Katznelson, Ira. *City Trenches: Urban Politics and the Patterning of Class in the United States.* New York: Pantheon Books, 1981.

Langbein, Laura, and Allan Lichtman. *Ecological Inference.* Beverly Hills: Sage, 1978.

Lowe, Stuart. *Urban Social Movements: The City After Castells.* New York: MacMillan, 1986.

McCarthy, Kevin. "San Francisco's Demographic Future." *In The City We Share*. San Francisco: San Francisco Forward, 1984.

McLeod, Ramon G. "Bay Area is Tops in Ethnic Diversity." *San Francisco Chronicle*, April 9, 1988.

Mollenkopf, John. *The Contested City.* Princeton, N.J.: Princeton University Press, 1983.

_____. "New York: The Great Anomaly." *PS* 19 (1986): 591-97.

Molotch, Harvey. "Strategies and Constraints of Growth Elites." In *Business Elites and Urban Development*, edited by S. Cummings. Albany: State University of New York Press, 1988.

Ragin, Charles. "The Impact of Celtic Nationalism on Class Politics in Scotland and Wales." In *Competitive Ethnic Relations*, edited by Susan Olzak and J. Nagel. Orlando, Florida: Academic Press, 1986.

Redmond, Tim. "Behind the Bitter Lobbying of Declining Power." *San Francisco Bay Guardian*, May 14, 1986.

Reed, Adolph, Jr. "The Black Urban Regime: Structural Origins and Constraints." In *Power, Community and the City*, edited by M. Smith, vol. 1. New Brunswick: Transaction Books, 1988.

Rex, J., and R. Moore. *Race, Community and Conflict*. London: Oxford University Press, 1967.

Roberts, Jerry. "Crossing the Bridge to the New San Francisco." *Golden State Report* (May 1987a): 24-30.

_____. "Assemblyman Gets 70% of Vote." *San Francisco Chronicle*, December 9, 1987b.

Sample, Herbert. "Black Political Power: As Asian and Latino Populations Expand, Will Black Political Power Fade?" *California Journal* (May 1987): 232-39.

San Francisco Planning and Urban Research Association (SPUR). "Vitality or Stagnation? Shaping San Francisco's Economic Destiny." Report No. 234. San Francisco: SPUR, 1987.

Sassen-Koob, Saskia. "The New Labor Demand in Global Cities." In *Cities in Transformation: Class, Capital, and the State*, edited by M. Smith. Beverly Hills: Sage, 1984.

Saunders, Peter. "Beyond Housing Classes: The Sociological Significance of Private Property Rights in Means of Consumption." *International Journal of Urban and Regional Research* 8 (1984): 202-22.

Starr, Kevin. "Art Agnos and the Paradoxes of Power." *San Francisco Magazine* (January/February 1988): 40-44, 157.

Stein, Arlene. "Agnos Did It the Grass-Roots Way." *The Nation* (February 1988): 156-58.

Stone, Clarence N. "Atlanta: Protest and Elections Are Not Enough." *PS* 19 (1986): 618-25.

_____. "Preemptive Power: Floyd Hunter's 'Community Power Structure' Reconsidered." *American Journal of Political Science* 32 (1988): 82-104.

Swanstrom, Todd. *The Crisis of Growth Politics: Cleveland, Kucinich, and the Promise of Urban Populism*. Philadelphia: Temple University Press, 1985.

_____. "Urban Populism, Uneven Development, and the Space for Reform." In *Business Elites and Urban Development*, edited by S. Cummings. Albany: State University of New York Press, 1988.

Uhlaner, Carole J., Bruce E. Cain, and D. Roderick Kiewiet. "Political Participation of Ethnic Minorities in the 1980s." Mimeo, 1988.

U.S. Bureau of the Census. *Census of Population and Housing, 1980: Public-Use Microdata Sample (PUMS): San Francisco, 5% Sample*. (Machine readable data file available through Computing and Communications Resources, California State University.) Washington, D.C., 1983.

Viviano, Frank. "The Long March." *Image* (May 11, 1986): 16-21.

_____. "Bay Area in 1990s—Preview of Big Changes." *San Francisco Chronicle*, December 5, 1988a.

_____. "In Politics, A Giant is Waking." *San Francisco Chronicle*, December 7, 1988b.

Viviano, Frank, and Sharon Silva. "The New San Francisco." *San Francisco Focus* (September 1986): 64-74.

Wilson, James Q., and Edward Banfield. "Political Ethos Revisited." *American Political Science Review* 65 (1971): 1048-62.

Wirt, Frederick. *Power in the City: Decision Making in San Francisco*. Berkeley: University of California Press, 1974.

Witteman, Paul A. "An Upstart Mayor, A Shaky Future." *Time Magazine* (December 21, 1987): 29-30.

APPENDIX A: DATA SOURCES

Sources of Census Tract Data

1980 Census of the Population and Housing, San Francisco-Oakland SMSA, Census Tracts, Two Parts, PHC 80-2-321:

(1) Percent Asian, Hispanic, Black: Tables P2-P6.

(2) Percent living in same house 1975: Table P-9.

(3) Percent high school graduates of persons 25 years or older: Table P-9.

(4) Percent of persons below 125% of the official poverty line: Table P-11.

(5) Percent unemployed of civilian labor force, persons 16 years or older: Table P-10.

(6) Percent managerial or professional occupations: Table P-15.

(7) Income per capita: Table P-15.

(8) Percent owner occupied: Table H-1.

(9) Percent individuals over age of 18: Table P-1.

(10) Gay dummy variable: tract classifications from David Binder, political consultant.

Note: Precincts classified as contained within a census tract were assigned the same values on these variables.

CHAPTER 9

BYRAN O. JACKSON
California State University—Los Angeles

Racial and Ethnic Voting Cleavages in Los Angeles Politics

INTRODUCTION

Immigration into the U.S. from countries in Latin and Central America and Asia is rapidly changing the ethnic and demographic composition of American cities. In Los Angeles alone, the Hispanic[1] population grew from 18 percent of the city's total population in 1970 to 28 percent in 1980. The Asian[2] population, while smaller in total size, rose from 5 percent in 1970 to 7 percent in 1980. As the new wave of immigrants grows in size, much attention in both the academic community as well as the mass public is being devoted to their impact on the social and political composition of the communities in which they reside.

The new wave immigrants pose new questions for research on ethnic politics. Most salient of these are the following: what form of political empowerment will take place in these ethnic communities? How adequate is the political assimilation model posed by Robert Dahl (1961) or the political incorporation model posed by Browning, Tabb and Marshall (1984) in explaining the political behavior of these ethnic groups? Given that new wave immigration is highly concentrated in American cities where black Americans have come to constitute sizeable proportions of both the population and political officeholders, what impact will the growing presence of new immigrants have on black political development?

This paper examines the political behavior of the Asian, black, and Hispanic communities of Los Angeles in a comparative context. Attention is focused on: (1) the extent to which each group forms an ethnic voting bloc in the city, (2) differences in comparative levels of local political

---

[1]The Hispanic population is broadly defined to include immigrants from Mexico, Cuba, Puerto Rico, and other countries in Latin and Central America.

[2]Broadly defined to include individuals of Chinese, Filipino, Japanese, Korean, and Vietnamese descent.

involvement and the forces responsible, and (3) the potential for interethnic coalition building among Asians, blacks, and Hispanics. The work assesses the adequacy of the Dahl ethnic political assimilation model to explain the political experiences of these new wave immigrants and discusses the nature and level of political incorporation within each group.

LITERATURE REVIEW ON ETHNIC POLITICAL PARTICIPATION AND VOTING PATTERNS

Ethnic Group Cohesion

In examining the literature on ethnic voting patterns in U.S. cities, one finds a number of competing theories linking ethnic group identity to ethnic voting behavior. For example, Dahl offers a comprehensive model of the ethnic political assimilation process in his work on New Haven, Connecticut (Dahl 1961). According to his thesis, ethnic politics is a "transitional phenomenon." In his analysis Dahl closely associates the socio-economic status of the ethnic group with their political behavior (Dahl 1961, 34-35). He argues that ethnic groups undergo three stages of political assimilation. In the first stage, members of the ethnic group are almost exclusively prole-tarian. Politically and socially group members are low in status, income, and influence. Dahl argues that these similarities generate an ethnic-based identity that leads to homogeneity in political attitudes and voting. Thus, he hypothesizes that political homogeneity is a function of socio-economic homogeneity.

In stage two of his model, ethnic groups become more heterogeneous socio-economically. Those group members with higher incomes are able to gain political influence outside their ethnic group. However, while this process undermines overall ethnic cohesion, it does not destroy it. At this stage, ethnic groups theoretically become open for coalition building with other groups.

In the third and final stage of the Dahl model, an ethnic group is highly heterogeneous socio-economically. Group members have thoroughly assimilated into diverse social and economic environments taking on new identities. Ethnic politics at this stage is often times viewed as "embarrass-ing or meaningless" to individual group members (Dahl 1961, 35).

While this model is comprehensive and intuitively appealing, it has not gone without its critics. More recent work on ethnic voting patterns has found cohesion in ethnic voting independent of the degree to which the group was socio-economically differentiated (see, for example, Wolfinger 1965). Wolfinger argues that ethnic voting is even more pronounced at the middle-income level. Furthermore, some scholars have observed a relation-ship between ethnic voting and ethnic concentrations in municipalities with nonpartisan elections (see Pomper 1966). They argue that such a relationship exists because of low levels of voter information on candidates and the lack of cues from political parties (see Pomper 1966). More recent studies in the political science and sociology fields report high correlations between ethnic identity and voting behavior (see London and Hearn 1977; Nelson 1979). Nelson's work (1979) in particular formalizes ethnic identity as a determinant of political behavior.

Another major criticism of Dahl's assimilation model involves his concept, assimilation. In his analysis, assimilation is defined as taking on the dominant group's values and culture. However, in other analyses the concept has been used to describe how the dominant group accepts minority groups' values and culture (see Gordon 1967). In this regard, we find that black Americans as an ethnic group failed to assimilate into New Haven society. While Dahl argues the contrary, his work fails to demonstrate convincingly that black Americans present in New Haven at the time of his analysis had successfully assimilated into the mainstream of the New Haven economy. His work actually demonstrates that blacks had been surpassed by ethnic groups later entering the New Haven economy. Nevertheless, he argues that the assimilation process held true for blacks as well.

Barnett and Pinderhughes both note this shortcoming in their critiques of the ethnic assimilation model as it relates to black Americans (see Barnett 1976; Pinderhughes 1987). According to Barnett, "blacks are external to the American ideological system and not effectively integrated into the political system" (Barnett 1976, 13). Pinderhughes demonstrates this point by comparing the political experiences of blacks, Poles, and Italians in the city of Chicago. She concludes that "black economic life supported politics of a very different character than that proposed by the pluralist theorist" (Pinderhughes 1987, 38).

White resistance to black candidates running for public office further illustrates how minorities are excluded from the political process. Empirical studies have shown white racial bloc voting irrespective of the socio-economic status of the black candidate (see Pettigrew 1967; Henry 1987; and Jackson 1987). In most of these cases, white voters have been unwilling to vote for black candidates for public office or have shown high resistance to a black candidacy (Jackson 1987). On the other hand, blacks have been found more often to support the candidacy of white candidates at the expense of black challengers (Jackson 1987). This hostility toward black candidates based on race has made the political assimilation of blacks difficult.

In sum, I argue that the major void in the ethnic voting literature is the lack of a theoretical explanation for ethnic voting. Is voting along ethnic lines truly a function of one's socio-economic status as argued by Dahl? If so, why does the Dahl thesis fail to explain middle income ethnic voting patterns observed by Wolfinger? Second, given that Dahl's assimilation model explained poorly the experience of black Americans, is it reasonable to assume that it will work in explaining the experiences of other non-European ethnics such as Asians and Hispanics?

There are lessons also to be learned about ethnic voting through critically examining Dahl's critics. For example, in the Wolfinger analysis, the standard criticism has pertained to his attempt to directly link ethnic vote cohesion to ethnic identity. While ethnic voting patterns may naturally be correlated with the presence of a particular ethnic group in a community, there is no reason to believe that one's ethnic identification directly leads to or solely determines his vote choice. Such a proposition precludes other factors (e.g., issue saliency, candidate appeal, social class) from being considered as determinants of an ethnic member's political behavior. Aggregate analyses of ethnic voting such as the work performed by Wolfinger tend to undermine these differences.

In short, theory development on ethnic group voting behavior has been largely descriptive, plagued with inference problems and confined to the European immigrant experience. While we know that voting along ethnic lines does occur, we don't know why or under what conditions. How do we explain cases where members of an ethnic group fail to vote along ethnic lines? Furthermore, how does one account for groups that find it difficult to assimilate in American society? These are definitely issues to consider as we explore the political experiences of new wave immigrants.

Ethnic Identity and Political Mobilization

With the advent of the Civil Rights Movement and the black Protest Movement of the 1950s and 1960s, black political participation in the American political system increased. In the early '70s the work on black group consciousness and political participation by Verba and Nie captured some of the dynamics of these changes. A major question posed by these scholars was whether black Americans could use "participatory mechanisms as a means of overcoming their deprived status in social and economic terms" (Verba and Nie 1972, 149).

As a group, the socio-economic status of blacks is depressed compared to American society as a whole. The Verba and Nie analysis demonstrates a high correlation between the socio-economic status of blacks and their representation in the various modes of political participation examined (voting, campaign activity, cooperative activity, and citizen initiated contact), thus explaining their low levels of participation. However, they found that when socio-economic status was controlled for, blacks were overrepresented in cooperative activity and campaign activity but remained underrepresented in voting and citizen-initiated contact. The major finding by Verba and Nie regarding black Americans was that blacks with a sense of group consciousness had average participation rates higher than their white counterparts (Verba and Nie 1972, 158-70).

In sum, these findings tend to suggest that while socio-economic status is important in determining level of political involvement, involvement can be stimulated by other sources such as ethnicity. This point was dramatized in the 1983 Chicago mayoral election where 84 percent of black voters turned out to vote compared to 82 percent of white voters.

A number of studies have been critical of the Verba and Nie analysis. For example, in a recent analysis of group identification and political behavior, Miller et al. (1981) rightfully criticize Olsen (1970) and Verba and Nie (1972) for attempting to directly associate "group identification" with "political group identification." Miller et al. (1981) draw a distinction between group identification and politicized group consciousness. They argue that "group identification connotes a perceived self-location within a particular social stratum along with a psychological feeling of belonging to that particular stratum." Group consciousness, on the other hand, "involves identification with a group and a political awareness or ideology regarding the group's relative position in society along with a commitment to collective action aimed at realizing the group's interest." The scholars note that there is no theoretical reason to expect a direct relationship between group identification and political participation (Miller et al. 1981, 495). They conclude:

> participation is not simply a reflection of the social condi-
> tions that people experience. How people perceive and
> evaluate their position is an important link between the
> experience of certain social situations and political partici-
> pation. If the experience is politicized through group
> consciousness and assessments of social justice, it can
> indirectly motivate social action (Miller et al. 1981, 503).

In other words, "politicized group consciousness" as opposed to "ethnic affinity" is important in determining ethnic political behavior.

Drawing from these studies on ethnic identification and political participation we ask under what conditions is ethnic identity likely to emerge as a force shaping an ethnic group member's political participation? Second, how does ethnic consciousness conflict with other forms of group identity (e.g., religion, gender, social class) in affecting political behavior? From the above discussion we learn that ethnic mobilization is not automatic, yet ethnic groups with ethnic group consciousness can be mobilized on ethnic related issues.

Coalitions and Ethnic Group Politics

Dahl raises another question on ethnic group behavior that deserves further exploration. He suggests that as ethnic groups improve their socio-economic status, they will attempt to coalesce as a group with other groups in society to improve their political condition. A number of studies have explored political coalitions within urban areas (see Holloway 1968; Henry 1980; Browning, Tabb, and Marshall 1984, 1986; and Sonenshein 1986).

Most of the early studies focused on the relationship between blacks and whites. For example, Harry Holloway provides three forms of black-white electoral coalitions based on experiences in southern cities: the conservative coalition, the independent power strategy and the liberal coalition. The conservative coalition according to Holloway, consists of the linkage between the black community and powerful white business and financial interests; the independent power strategy is one where black leaders exchange the black vote for political concessions; and the liberal coalition consists of blacks uniting with low-income whites, labor unions, Chicanos, and liberal whites. Using the cities of Atlanta, Memphis, and Houston respectively, he illustrates the formation of each of these strategies (Holloway 1968).

A recent work by Browning, Tabb, and Marshall has examined both black and Hispanic groups seeking political empowerment. Using a typology similar to Holloway's they outline the following forms of minority group mobilization: co-optation, protest and exclusion, weak minority mobilization, and political incorporation. According to these analysts, incorporation into a white liberal coalition was a precondition to minority group political success in the cities that they studied.

Based on these cases, it is clear that the form and character of urban ethnic coalitions vary from one urban context to another. Both the Holloway and Browning et al. work suggest that the political leadership found in urban areas as well as the "racial climate" impact upon the character of the political coalitions formed.

Internal differences with minority group communities have been found to undermine the development of coalitions. Social class differences and ideological differences within minority communities tend to weaken the unity of these communities and the external as well as internal coalition building process. Competition among ethnic leaders and organizations over scarce resources within minority communities have also been attributed to undermining the coalition building process (Holden 1973).

These concerns are important for this analysis for they provide a framework for examining the comparative political experiences of the ethnic groups under study. In this analysis we will seek to understand both the nature and character of coalition politics within ethnic Los Angeles communities.

A Comparative Framework for Studying Ethnic Political Behavior

From the literature above, questions arise about the future of new wave ethnic groups seeking to assimilate into the mainstream of American society. How closely will they follow the assimilation model laid out by Robert Dahl? What signs are there that ethnic groups will vote according to ethnic lines?   What is the relationship between ethnic identity and political mobilization?   What kind of political coalitions can one expect to emerge within and among these groups?

Answers to these questions are both basic to our understanding of ethnic political behavior and intricately linked to the more fundamental issue of the openness of our democratic political system.   That is, does the pluralist system in America provide access for all would-be competitors (Gamson 1975)?

ANALYZING ETHNIC VOTING IN LOS ANGELES

Social Setting

As of 1980, Asian and Hispanic immigrants represented over 3/4 of the immigrants entering the U.S.   In Los Angeles County the Asian population increased by 123 percent between 1970 and 1980 compared to 97 percent for the Hispanic population.   During the same period, the Anglo and black populations increased by 21 and 24 percent, respectively.

Generally, the majority of the Asian, black, and Hispanic populations of southern California are located in the Los Angeles County Region. According to a Southern California Association of Governments (SCAG) report, 75 percent of the Hispanic population and 90 percent of the black population of southern California (Imperial, Orange, Riverside, San Bernadino, Los Angeles, and Ventura Counties) reside in the central portion of Los Angeles County.   The same trend holds true for the Asian population with heavy concentrations of Asian residents in the cities of Los Angeles, Monterey Park, and Alhambra.

Examining the city of Los Angeles, Table 1 offers a comprehensive profile of the changes in the ethnic distribution of the city's population between 1970 and 1980.   While we find that whites constituted the largest proportion of the population in 1970 and 1980 (59 percent in 1970 and 48 percent in 1980), there has been a sharp decline in the growth rate of this group relative to Asian and Hispanic groups over the 10-year period under examination.   We also find that the relative size of the black population has remained about the same over the 10-year period (18 percent).

The Hispanic population grew from 18 percent of the total population in 1970 to 28 percent in 1980.   Within the Hispanic population we find that Hispanics of Mexican origin by far constitute the majority of the population (77 percent).

Among Asians, the Japanese, Chinese, Filipino, and Korean populations constitute the largest groups within the Asian Community.   As of 1980, the Japanese and Chinese represented the largest components of the Asian population in L.A.   They were also the first two Asian groups to settle in the southern California region (see Sowell 1970).

Table 1:   *Changes in the Ethnic Composition of the City of Los Angeles, 1970-1980*

Race	Population Size 1970	%Total	Race	Population Size 1980	%Total
Anglos	1,654,909	59.0%	Anglos	1,419,413	48%
Asian	129,683	5.0%	Asian	196,017	7%
Japanese	54,878		Japanese	49,335	
Chinese	27,345		Chinese	44,353	
Filipino	19,392		Filipino	43,713	
Other	28,068		Korean	33,066	
			Vietnamese	13,257	
			Other	12,293	
Blacks	503,606	18.0%	Blacks	495,723	16,7%
Hispanics[1]	518,791	18.5%	Hispanics	816,076	28%
			Mexican	615,887	
			Cuban	15,864	
			Puerto Rican	13,835	
			Other	170,490	
Native			Native		
Americans	9,172	.3%	Americans	14,731	.5%
Total	2,945,844		Total	3,954,053	

Sources: 1970 Ethnic Composition of Cities and Places-Los Angeles County, compiled by Los Angeles Regional Office of U.S. Census Bureau.

1980 Census of Population and Housing-Census Tracts: Los Angeles-Long Beach Washington, D.C.: U.S Government Printing Office.

[1]Not considered as a racial category by the U.S. Bureau of the Census. Persons of Hispanic origin have been extracted from racial categories in this table.

Table 2 summarizes basic economic and demographic characteristics of Anglos, Asians, blacks, and Hispanics in the area using 1980 census data. Here we find that the Anglo population is older compared to the other groups in Los Angeles. Eighteen percent of Anglos fall in the 16-24-year-old category compared to 35 percent of Hispanics, 25 percent of blacks and 21 percent of Asians. At the other extreme, we find 18 percent of Anglos are 65 years of age and above compared to half that amount for Hispanics. Blacks and Asians have 12 percent and 9 percent of their population groups represented in the 65 years and above category respectively.

There are also sharp differences in terms of education among the groups. While well over 50 percent of both the Anglo and Asian populations have a college education or better, only 35 percent of the black population and 14 percent of the Hispanic populations fall into this category.

Table 2: *Economic and Demographic Profile of Los Angeles Ethnic Communities*

	Anglos	Blacks	Hispanics	Asians
Tenure				
Homeowners	57%	43%	27%[1]	47%[2]
Renters	43	57	63	53
Poverty				
% 125 Below				
Poverty Line	11.5	30.4	33	19
Occupations				
% Managerial-Prof.	34	15	5	25
Tech, Sales-Adm.	38	35	17	36
Service	9	21	20	13
Farm, Forestry,				
Fishing	7	1.3	2.6	2.4
Craft	10	8.6	15.2	8.2
Laborers	9	18.3	38.5	14.9
Education				
% 8th Grade or				
Less	7	12	47	12
High School				
(9-12)	40	53	39	34
College	40	31	12	43
College +	14	4	2	12
Age				
16-24	18	25	35	21
25-32	18	19	27	22
33-40	13	14	14	17
41-48	10	11	9	12
49-56	12	10	—	12
57-64	11	10	7	8
65 & above	18	12	9	8

Source: U.S. Department of Commerce, Bureau of the Census, Census of Population and Housing 1980 Public-Use Microdata Samples-Los Angeles.

[1]43% of all Puerto Ricans were found to own thier own homes, 37% of Cubans, and 27% of Mexicans.

[2]56% of Japanese were found to own their own homes and 52% of the Chinese.

We also find that 47 percent of the Hispanic population has less than an 8th grade education.

These differences carry over to the relative economic positions of the groups in the city. For example, while 11.5 percent of the Anglo population and 19 percent of the Asian population fall 125 percent below the poverty line, 33 percent of Hispanics and 30 percent of blacks fall in this category.

In terms of home ownership we find that 57 percent of Anglos own their own homes compared to 47 percent of Asians, 43 percent of blacks and only 27 percent of Hispanics. Within the Asian community it is important to note that 56 percent of Japanese residents own their own home. Similarly, among Hispanic residents 43 percent of Puerto Ricans and 37 percent of Cubans compared to only 27 percent of Mexican Americans own their own homes.

Occupationally one also observes differences among the ethnic groups. Anglos are highly represented in professional and managerial positions and have lower levels of representation in service and manual labor jobs. Asians are similarly represented. On the other hand blacks and Hispanics are highly represented in service and manual labor jobs.

In sum, these data show significant differences in the socio-economic and demographic make-up of the ethnic communities in Los Angeles. The profiles discussed here are quite comparable to the ones described by DeLeon (1988) for the city of San Francisco.

The Anglo population is older, well educated and socio-economically well off. The Asian population, while younger, is also highly educated and socio-economically well off. However, blacks and Hispanics are the least well off of the groups under investigation. Members from both groups are comparatively younger and on average less educated than Anglos and Asians. Both groups also have high levels of poverty and underrepresentation in the major income earning professions. Taking these differences into consideration, we now turn our attention to the ethnic political assimilation process in Los Angeles.

Study Design

The data for this analysis were obtained primarily from election result files maintained by the Los Angeles County voter registrar's office. From these data a special data set was created using voter turnout data, vote outcomes for the 1982 and 1986 California governor races, and three state and local ballot initiatives from the 2,500 voting precincts in the city of Los Angeles. These data were aggregated to the census tract level. Demographic information identifying the socio-economic and ethnic composition of these precincts has been added based on the census tracts in which each precinct falls. The state and local initiatives that will be used are: (1) the 1982 gun control initiative, (2) 1982 local rent control measure, and (3) the 1986 Proposition 63 (English-only Proposition). The following section will briefly describe each proposition.

Background and Analysis Plan

The 1982 and 1986 California gubernatorial elections offer an excellent opportunity to explore ethnic voting patterns at both the state and local level. In both elections, Tom Bradley, a black Democrat from Los Angeles, was defeated by George Deukmejian, a white Republican.

In 1982, two ballot initiatives at the state and local level generated divisions across both ethnic and class lines. These measures were a statewide initiative calling for the registration of handguns (gun control) and a local measure calling for rent control.

In 1986, Proposition 63, another ballot initiative that proved controversial was voted upon. Proposition 63 called for the use of English Only as the official language of the state of California. The initiative passed by a large margin.

Taken together the vote for governor and the vote on each of the propositions provide a basis for exploring the levels of ethnic group cohesion both within the Asian, black, and Hispanic communities as well as among the communities. Furthermore, it provides a basis for evaluating how cross-cutting cleavages such as social class can undermine ethnic cohesion.

Data Analysis

Ethnic Identity and the Bradley Vote. Figure 1 illustrates the 1982 gubernatorial vote for Bradley by income and ethnicity. As shown in Figure 1, blacks gave Bradley 90 percent or more of their vote. We also find that within the black community, no substantial variation of the vote by income existed.

In terms of the Hispanic communities examined, the Bradley support was high but not as strong as in the case for blacks. On average, Bradley received roughly 70 percent of the vote in predominately Hispanic communities. However, it is interesting to note the variation in the Hispanic vote by the income of the neighborhoods. Here we find that the percent for Bradley was negatively related to the income level of these communities.

The Anglo vote for Bradley in 1982 was strong but divided. His support in these communities ran across class lines. In this regard, it is important to note the strong support his candidacy received in relatively low-income Anglo communities.

Taken together these findings illustrate the diversity in voting patterns found in the Los Angeles electorate. Clearly, ethnic identity among blacks played a tremendous role in the Bradley vote. However, the Hispanic vote illustrates how the vote could be explained by not only "ethnic pride" but also by group interest. That is, Tom Bradley was perceived as being able to represent the interests of the Latin community better than George

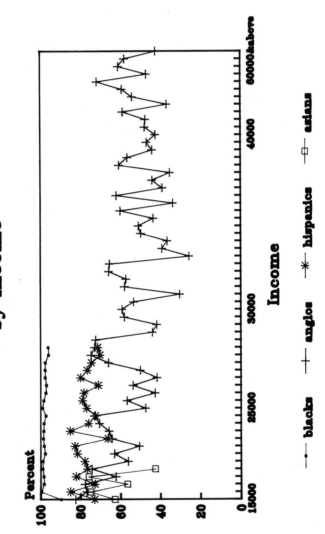

Figure 1

1982 Gubernatorial Vote for Bradley
by income

Dukmejian. Certainly such a perception by blacks could also aid in explaining the black vote as well.

Bradley's second attempt for governor was met with skepticism over his ability to win, demoralization from those who thought he should have won in 1982, and a lack of enthusiasm from those who saw very little change in his 1982 and 1986 strategies. Old allies such as the Jewish community were found distant to his candidacy due to problems with the Louis Farrakahn visit and Bradley's apparent reversal on oil drilling in the Pacific Palisades. Moreover, many speculated that the black community was also disenchanted with Bradley for failing to explicitly include issues relevant to the black community on his campaign agenda.

Figure 2 outlines the effects of these speculated defections by examining the percentage decrease in the Bradley vote between 1982 and 1986. Here we see that the black community was clearly Bradley's strongest ally with the average defection rate around 1.5 percent, followed by the Hispanic community. Among whites the defection rate was as high as 15 percent and on average approximately 7 to 10 percentage points in each census tract.

Table 3 attempts to capture more precisely the ethnic differences in support for Bradley in 1982 and 1986. In addition, party affiliation, income, and issues are taken into consideration. In both cases the level of support for Bradley in each neighborhood was estimated as a function of the ethnic composition of the neighborhood (black, Hispanic, and Asian with whites as the excluded category), the percentage of democrats in the neighborhood, the median income of the neighborhood, and issues that Bradley supported in each gubernatorial campaign (gun control, 1982, and regulation of toxic waste, 1986).

From the analysis, we find that ethnic cleavages far outweigh other factors in determining the level of Bradley support. Social class measured in terms of median income turns out to be statistically insignificant.

Issue Voting in Ethnic Communities. In order to investigate further the effects of ethnicity on voting behavior in the city, an analysis on voting on selected ballot propositions from the 1982 and 1986 elections was performed. The following propositions were examined: the 1986 English only proposition and the 1982 rent control and gun control measures. Figure 3 represents voting patterns on the 1986 English-only proposition. As pointed out earlier, this proposition called for the use of English only as the official language of the state of California and established measures to prevent the displacement of this objective. As expected, we find that this measure was highly voted against in the Hispanic community. However, Hispanics in higher-income neighborhoods were more likely to support the measure than those in low-income neighborhoods.

Black communities voted solidly against the English-only proposition as well. While the vote was not as strong as found in the Hispanic community,

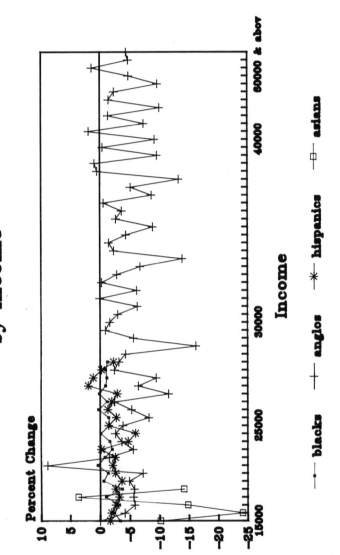

Figure 2
%Difference in Brad Vote 82–86
by income

Table 3: *Regression Analysis of Ethnic Vote for Tom Bradley in 1982 and 1986*

1982 Variables	1986 Variables	Parameter Estimate 82	Parameter Estimate 86
Intercep	Intercep	-5.50	-17.04
		(2.87)[1]	(4.39)
		(.057)[2]	(.0002)
Median Income	Median Income	-.00003	-.00002
		(.00003)	-.00003
		(.354)	(.337)
Black Neighborhood	Black Neighborhood	27.39	25.54
		(2.60)	(3.74)
		(.0001)	(.0001)
Hispanic Neighborhood	Hispanic Neighborhood	10.06	4.50
		(1.96)	(1.56)
		(.0001)	(.005)
Asian Neighborhood	Asian Neighborhood	3.84	2.72
		(2.57)	(3.66)
		(.14)	(.345)
Percent Democrat	Percent Democrat	.63	.82
		(.0598)	(.064)
		(.0001)	(.0001)
% Yes Gun Control	—	.43	
		(.0457)	
		(.0001)	
—	% Yes on Toxic Reg.		.27
			(.0812)
			(.0011)
		R^2 .97	R^2 .97

[1]Standard Error
[2]Significance Level

it is far different from voting in the Anglo community. In most Anglo neighborhoods, the measure passed by a solid majority.

From the analysis thus far one can see distinct patterns of voting found in each ethnic community, which is characteristically distinct from the Anglo community. While there have been slight variations in social class within the black and Hispanic communities, class voting among Anglos has not appeared to manifest itself.

The rent control measure was selected precisely for this reason. On issues that affect one economically, does class supersede race and ethnicity

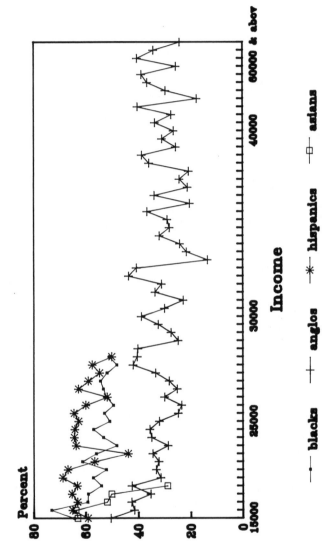

Figure 3

Percent No on English Only Proposition by income

in determining one's voting behavior? The 1982 rent control measure, which was adopted by citizens in the city of Los Angeles, shows an interesting configuration of voting patterns. Figure 4 outlines these patterns. Here we find ethnicity and class operating simultaneously. For example, while black communities were overall more supportive of the measure compared to other groups, support declined in the black community as income increased. The same pattern existed in Latin neighborhoods. Nevertheless, overall support for the measure in the Hispanic community was far less enthusiastic than in the black community.

Support for the rent control measure increased with income in the predominately Anglo neighborhoods. This could suggest a number of things. For example, home ownership rates among Anglos at the lower levels of income could have been higher than in the case of black and Hispanic neighborhoods at the same level. Or the vote may have been ideological, suggesting that this group was more ideologically opposed to the government intervening in the market place in this fashion. Also, the Anglos at this income level could more often than not be landlords themselves and voted to protect their economic interest. Richard DeLeon has found support for this latter hypothesis through his San Francisco analysis.

The 1982 gun control initiative produced still another configuration of voting patterns that demonstrated polarized voting based on group interest. Figure 5 shows that while the Anglo community voted widely in support of the gun control measure across class lines, the black community was strongly opposed to this measure. There is reason to believe that voting on this measure may have been related to the level of crime found in the communities. In black communities where crime is high and police protection is perceived as low, guns are viewed as necessary for self-protection. Therefore, the voting patterns appear to represent a clear difference in the Anglo and black communities. Latin voters were also found to be in opposition to gun control; however, less so than blacks.

The general assessment that evolves from this analysis is that there is extreme polarization between the black and white communities of Los Angeles, which manifests itself in terms of voting behavior. The Latin community also demonstrates a distinct pattern of voting that falls in between blacks and whites but patterns black voting behavior.

In examining the Dahl and Wolfinger argument concerning the role of social class versus ethnicity in determining one's political behavior, we find both forces at work. While ethnic identity is found to set the general ideological context in which voting takes place (e.g., blacks overall liberal, whites overall more conservative), social class within the black community moderates this behavior. That is, high-income blacks are shown to vote differently from low-income blacks. As in the case of rent control, this voting pattern could be based on economic interest.

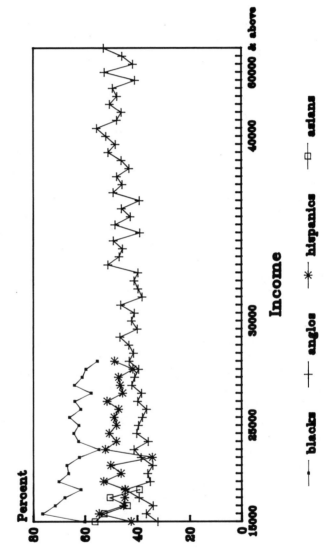

Figure 4
Percent Yes on Rent Control
by income

Figure 5

Percent Yes on Gun Control
by income

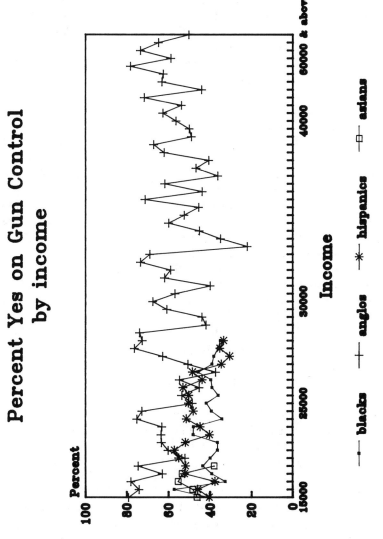

These issues will be addressed more fully later in this paper. At this point, however, we turn our attention to political mobilization defined in terms of voter turnout.

Mobilizing the Minority Vote. Socio-economic status has been the major variable used in explaining levels of citizen participation in the U.S. As pointed out earlier, ethnicity has been added to this model as a determinant of levels of political involvement. While the data available do not allow for an extensive analysis of political participation in the ethnic communities under investigation, they do show comparative differences in the area of voter turnout. Controlling for income, what effect does ethnicity have on turnout?

Table 4 estimates the difference in turnout rates for Asians, blacks, and Hispanics relative to Anglos in the 1982 and 1986 California gubernatorial campaigns within Los Angeles city neighborhoods. As shown in Table 4 the black turnout rate in both elections is not significantly different from Anglo turnout. However, for both Hispanic and Asian communities the turnout rate was substantially lower than the Anglo's rate.

In 1986 the Asian turnout rate was 27 percentage points lower than the rate for Anglos, which represented a further decrease from 1982 of 14 percentage points. The rate for Hispanics fluctuated only slightly between 1982 and 1986 (15 percent less to 13 percent less).

In sum these findings support the notion that ethnic identity is related to political involvement. In the case of blacks, it is "politicized group consciousness." For Hispanics and Asians, the findings represent a lack of politicization. While the data are insufficient to make a strong assessment, it is worthwhile to note that Asians are the most affluent of the ethnic groups but the least active politically.

Conclusions and Political Implications

The analysis presented here points to some interesting trends in terms of ethnic voting patterns. It is important to review the findings in light of the theoretical concerns and the initial questions raised at the outset of this work. The leading theoretical question is does economic differentiation lead to political differentiation among ethnic voters? How accurate is the Dahl model in explaining the political assimilation of ethnic groups?

Certainly, with the data available one cannot address this question at the individual level, however, the aggregate level data offer some insight. In this analysis we find that black and Hispanic voters form distinct ethnic communities with voting patterns different from the Anglo community. Generally, if we were to use the concept liberal and conservative loosely to describe the communities, we would find blacks at the liberal end of the spectrum and Anglos at the conservative end. Hispanic voters would fall in

Table 4: *Regression Analysis of Los Angeles Voter Turnout for the 1982 and 1986 Gubernatorial Elections*

1982 Variables	1986 Variables	Parameter Estimate 82	Parameter Estimate 86
Intercep	Intercep	74.28	73.04
		(12.26)[1]	(12.36)
		(.0001)[2]	(.0001)
Median Income	Median Income	.0004	.0001
		(.0001)	(.00001)
		(.0005)	(.19)
Black Neighborhood	Black Neighborhood	-2.17	-.97
		(10.03)	(7.45)
		(.83)	(.89)
Hispanic Neighborhood	Hispanic Neighborhood	-14.97	-12.63
		(6.37)	(6.24)
		(.02)	(.05)
Asian Neighborhood	Asian Neighborhood	-13.97)	-27.33
		(7.94)	(11.6)
		(.08)	(.02)
Percent Democrat	Percent Democrat	.23	-.24
		(.18)	(.18)
		(.19)	(.19)
% Yes Gun Control	—	-.28	
		(.13)	
		(.03)	
		R^2 .33	R^2 .31

[1]Standard Error
[2]Significance Level

between. Within each ethnic community we find more homogeneity in the vote in black and Hispanic neighborhoods than in Anglo neighborhoods.

Given the general socio-economic status of the two groups, support is found for Dahl's ethnicity, social class, and vote thesis (also see more recent work by Gilliam and Whitby 1987). That is, given the relative homogeneity of these groups along economic lines one would expect homogeneity in terms of political behavior within them. This turns out to be the case.

Furthermore, examining behavior within ethnic neighborhoods we find class trends emerging. Higher-income black and Hispanic neighborhoods voted differently as a whole from low-income neighborhoods on issues such as rent control. The higher the income of the neighborhoods, the lower the support for rent control. For Hispanics, this behavior also manifested itself in voting for Bradley. Higher-income Hispanic neighborhoods were less likely to support Bradley than low-income neighborhoods.

The general shortcoming of the Dahl model is what it fails to address. Roughly 80 to 90 percent of blacks in Los Angeles reside in racially homogenous neighborhoods. With the many exclusionary devices used in the past to restrict the movement of blacks to other areas, social integration has been severely hampered. Social isolation, along with slow economic advancement makes assimilation difficult if not impossible for members of this ethnic group.

Likewise, while Hispanics and Asians are more geographically dispersed than blacks, communities both within Los Angeles as well as on the periphery have become known as Asian and Hispanic enclaves (e.g., Korea Town, Little Tokyo, China Town, Monterrey Park, Rosemead, East Los Angeles, and Alhambra.) Unlike European immigrants, the process of suburbanization does not appear to bring assimilation. Consequently, the prospect for ethnic voting within these communities is likely to remain undaunted, thus casting doubt on Dahl's assimilationist thesis.

Turning to ethnic mobilization, we find that ethnic identity can make a difference in terms of political mobilization. Blacks in Los Angeles seem to have reached a stage of "politicization" so that the turnout rate in black communities is comparable to the rate found in Anglo communities when income is controlled for. Furthermore, we find that the Asian and Hispanic turnout levels are much lower than those of blacks and Anglos.

Finally, what are the prospects for interethnic coalitions emerging in the city of Los Angeles? According to Charles Hamilton and Stokely Carmichael, the following factors are preconditions for a coalition between blacks and other groups in society:

• the recognition by the parties involved of their respective self-interest,

• the mutual belief that each party stands to benefit in terms of that self-interest through joining with the other or others,

• the acceptance of the fact that each party has its own independent base of power and does not depend for ultimate decision making on a force outside itself,

• the realization that the coalition deals with specific and identifiable as opposed to general and vague goals (Hamilton and Carmichael 1967, 79-80).[3]

The voting data presented here clearly demonstrate the prospect for a coalition forming between the black and Hispanic communities of Los Angeles. However, as Henry points out, the suspicion of one group

---

[3]Charles Henry uses these criteria in assessing the general prospects of a national Chicano-Black coalition (Henry 1980, 224).

exploiting the other as well as competition and conflict over inducements offered by whites both serve as major obstacles in this process.

For example, the issue of redistricting of county supervisorial districts and city council seats sets the stage for struggle between these two groups as one group attempts to gain its fair share of representation (Hispanics) while the other group seeks to maintain its share. Conflict over job opportunities in the public and private sector also serve as sources of conflict (see Johnson and Oliver).

Nevertheless, there is no reason to believe that these groups are not capable of recognizing their common interests and acting upon them. This is particularly true given that both groups occupy similar economic positions in the city. Black support for the defeat of Proposition 63 and Hispanic support for Bradley are examples of working on behalf of a common interest.

REFERENCES

Barnett, Marguerite Ross, and James A. Hefner. *Public Policy for the Black Community: Strategies and Perspectives.* New York: Alfred Publishing Company, 1976.

Browning, Rufus, Dale Rogers Marshall, and David Tabb. *Protest is Not Enough: the Struggle of Blacks and Hispanics.* Berkeley: University of California Press, 1984.

_____. "Minority Power in City Politics." *PS*, vol. 19, no. 3 (Summer 1986): 573-81.

Cain, Bruce, and Roderick Kiewiet. "Ethnicity and Electoral Choice: Mexican American Voting Behavior in the California 30th Congressional District." *Social Science Quarterly* 65 (June 1985): 315-27.

Carmichael, Stokely, and Charles V. Hamilton. *Black Power.* New York: Random House, 1967.

Crenson, Matthew A. "Social Networks and Political Processes in Urban Neighborhoods." *American Journal of Political Science* 22 (August 1978): 289-95.

Dahl, Robert. *Who Governs?* New Haven: Yale University Press, 1961.

De la Garza, Rodolfo. "As American as Tamale Pie: Mexican-American Political Mobilization." In *Mexican-Americans in Comparative Perspective,* edited by Walker Connor. Washington, D.C.: Urban Institute Press, 1985.

DeLeon, Richard. "Race and Politics in San Francisco." Paper delivered at the annual meeting of the Western Political Science Association. San Francisco, California, March 10-12, 1988.

Erbring, Lutz, and Norman H. Nie. "Electoral Participation in America: Looking Back." Paper prepared for the Conference Analyzing Declining Voter Turnout in America. University of Chicago, April 1984.

Gabriel, Richard. "A New Theory of Ethnic Voting." *Polity,* vol. 4 no. 4 (1972): 405-28.

Gamson, William A. *The Strategy of Social Protest.* Homewood, Illinois: The Dorsey Press, 1975.

Gilliam, Frank. "Race, Class, and Mass Attitudes: An Ethclass Interpretation." Paper delivered at the annual meeting of the Midwestern Political Science Association, 1987.

Glazer, Nathan, and Daniel P. Moynihan. *Beyond the Melting Pot: The Negroes, Puerto Ricans, Jews, Italians and Irish of New York City.* Cambridge, Mass.: MIT Press, 1963.

Gordon, Milton. *Assimilation in American Life.* New York: Oxford University Press, 1964.

Greeley, Andrew M. *Why Can't They Be Like Us?* New York: E. P. Dutton, 1971.

Hahn, Harlan, and Timothy Almy. "Ethnic Politics and Racial Issues: Voting in Los Angeles." *Western Political Quarterly* 24 (1971).

Hahn, Harlan, David Klingman, and Harry Pachon. "Cleavages, Coalitions, and the Black Candidate: The Los Angeles Mayoral Elections of 1969 and 1973. *Western Political Quarterly* 28 (December 1976): 507-20.

Halley, Robert M. "Ethnicity and Social Class." *Western Political Quarterly* (1975).

Henry, Charles P. "Blacks-Chicano Coalitions: Possibilities and Problems." *Western Journal of Black Studies* (Winter 1980).

Holloway, Harry. "Negro Political Strategy: Coalition or Independent Power Politics?" *Social Science Quarterly* 49 (December 1968): 534-47.

Huckfeldt, Robert. "Political Participation and the Neighborhood Social Context." *American Journal of Political Science* 23 (August 1979): 579-614.

_____. *Politics in Context: Assimilation and Conflict in Urban Neighborhoods*. New York: Agathon, 1986.

Jackson, Byran O. The Effects of Racial Group Consciousness on Political Mobilization in American Cities." *Western Political Quarterly* 40 (December 1987): 631-47.

Lovrich, Nicholas P., and Otwin, Marenin. "A Comparison of Black and Mexican American Voters in Denver: Assertive versus Acquiescent Political Orientations and Voting Behavior in an Urban Electorate." *Western Political Quarterly* 29 (June 1976): 284-94.

Miller, Abraham. "Ethnicity and Political Behavior: A Review of Theories and an Attempt at Reformulation." *Western Political Quarterly* 24 (1971): 483-500.

Miller, Arthur H., Patricia Gurin, Gerald Gurin, and Oksana Malanchuk. "Group Consciousness and Political Participation." *American Journal of Political Science* 25 (1981): 495-511.

Mollenkopf, John. "On the Causes and Consequences of Political Mobilization." Paper prepared for presentation at the annual meeting of the American Political Science Association. New Orleans, 1973.

Nelson, Dale C. "Ethnicity and Socioeconomic Status as Sources of Participation: The Case for Ethnic Political Culture." *American Political Science Review* 73 (December 1979): 1024-38.

Oliver, Melvin, and James H. Johnson, Jr. "Inter-Ethnic Conflict in an Urban Ghetto: The Case of Blacks and Latinos in Los Angeles." *Research in Social Movements, Conflict and Change* 6 (1984): 57-94.

Olsen, Marvin. "Social and Political Participation of Blacks." *American Sociological Review* 35 (1970): 682-96.

Pachon, Harry P. "Political Mobilization in the Mexican-American Community." In *Mexican-Americans in Comparative Perspective,* edited by Walker Connor. Washington D.C.: The Urban Institute Press, 1985.

Parenti, Michael. "Ethnic Politics and the Persistence of Ethnic Identification." *American Political Science Review* 59 (1965): 717-26.

Pinderhughes, Dianne M. *Race and Ethnicity in Chicago Politics: A Reexamination of Pluralist Theory.* Chicago: University of Illinois Press, 1987.

Shingles, Richard D. "Black Consciousness and Political Participation: the Missing Link." *American Political Science Review* 75 (1981): 76-91.

Sonenshein, Raphe. "Biracial Coalition Politics in Los Angeles." *PS,* vol. 19, no. 3 (Summer 1986): 582-90.

Sowell, Thomas. *Ethnic America.* New York: Basic Books, 1981.

Verba, Sidney, and Norman Nie. *Participation in America: Political Democracy and Social Equality.* New York: Harper and Row, 1972.

Wolfinger, Raymond E. "The Development and Persistence of Ethnic Voting." *American Political Science Review* 59 (1965): 896-908.

Wilson, William J. *The Declining Significance of Race.* Chicago: The University of Chicago Press, 1978.

V. ETHNIC PARTICIPATION IN PARTY POLITICS

CHAPTER 10

WILLIAM J. MIDDLETON
Attorney

The Impact of Party Reform in California on Minority Political Empowerment

Worried about elections, parties are responsive. They respond particularly to demands voiced by large numbers of people. This characteristic has made parties the special agency of the poor and disadvantaged. Those who have wealth, education, and other privileges can often make their own way political-ly. . . .

Parties seek votes and ultimately do not care if the hands that move the levers are black or white, male or female, or rich or poor. Parties, more than any other U.S. institution, accept our national premise, namely, that "all men are created equal."

Gerald M. Pomper[1]

INTRODUCTION

When properly functioning, political parties are ideal institutions for protecting and advancing the interests of the economically disadvantaged and minority groups in America. One of their central functions is to aggregate and articulate the political interests of the electorate.[2] These interests take the form of political candidacies or policy choices. Parties are the principal

---

[1]Gerald M. Pomper, "The Contributions of Political Parties in American Democracy," in *Party Renewal in America: Theory and Practice*, edited by Gerald M. Pomper (New York: Praeger Publishers, 1980), 8, 9.

[2]Gerald M. Pomper, "The Contributions of Political Parties in American Democracy," in *Party Renewal in America*, 5-6; See also, Ruth K. Scott and Ronald J. Hrebenar, *Parties in Crisis: Party Politics in America* (New York, John Wiley & Sons, 1984), 6.

agencies of interest aggregation.[3] This aggregative function is a primary associational right[4] of political parties since it is used to reconcile conflicting interests. Reconciling conflict among their various constituencies or promoting compromise is necessary to arrive at a political consensus. Such reconciliation is significant because parties have a vested interest in creating consensus. Their central purpose is to win elections.[5] All of the constituents of a political party coalition, including minorities, have a stake in the outcome of elections. This creates an incentive to compromise and in turn strengthens political parties.

Minority groups within political party coalitions benefit because they are generally assured by the party leaders that their interests will be protected and advanced by the "party line," or platform.

Without the unifying mechanisms of the party, political campaigns become divisive controversies between racial, religious, ideological, and national minorities.[6] But with them, parties can become very powerful vehicles for unifying, protecting, and promoting disparate minority interests. Historically, immigrant groups identified with and relied on the political parties as their entree to the American political process.[7] When parties fail to provide effective vehicles for participation in the political process, minority groups inevitably resort to unofficial political associations to influence the electoral process.[8] This experience teaches the importance

---

[3]Dennis S. Ippolito and Thomas G. Walker, *Political Parties, Interest Groups and Public Policy: Group Influence in American Politics* (Englewood Cliffs, New Jersey: Prentice Hall, Inc., 1980). Ippolito and Walker observe "the party still represents the most important vehicle for electorate mobilization; no other organization can match its capacity to aggregate masses of individuals and a diversity of groups," 5.

[4]The First Amendment liberty of political association is the cornerstone of the political parties right to exist.

[5]Pomper, *op. cit.,* 6

[6]Pomper, *op. cit.,* 6.

[7]Mark R. Levy and Michael S. Kramer, *The Ethnic Factor: How America's Minorities Decide Elections* (New York: Simon & Schuster, 1973); Raymond E. Wolfinger, "The Development and Persistence of Ethnic Voting," in *The Ethnic Factor in American Politics,* edited by Brett W. Hawkins and Robert A. Lorinskas (Columbus, Ohio: Charles E. Merrill Publishing Co., 1970), 101-23; Daniel N. Gordon, "Immigrants and Urban Governmental Forms in America," *The Ethnic Factor in America Politics,* 142.

[8]Charles V. Hamilton, *The Black Experience in American Politics* (New York: G. P. Putnam's Sons, 1973); Hans Walton, Jr., *Black Political Parties* (New York: The Free Press, 1972); Raphael J. Sonenshein, "Black Factions and the Origins of Biracial Coalitions," prepared for presentation at the Annual Meeting of the American Political Science Association, September 2, 1990.

of the role of parties in securing the political interests of racial and ethnic minorities and the economically disadvantaged.

Yet, political parties have been severely undermined in many states in America by an electoral system that fosters direct democracy,[9] as opposed to representative government. Such systems adversely affect the political interests of minorities[10] and the economically disadvantaged and create significant constitutional dilemmas for the American political system. Robert A. Dahl recognized the constitutional foundations of political parties when he observed:

> whatever the intentions of the Founding Fathers may have been, their Constitution, if it were kept to, made political parties not only possible but inevitable. With the Bill of Rights the Constitution made parties possible; with the institutions of representation and elections designed in Articles I and II, made parties inevitable.[11]

The reforms of the early 20th century adversely impact fundamental tenets of American democracy—the First Amendment liberties of freedom of speech and assembly (political association). These liberties find their highest manifestation in the functions of political parties. Government regulation

---

[9]Pomper, *op. cit.*, 13; see also, Willis Hawley, *Nonpartisan Elections and the Case for Party Politics* (New York: John Wiley, 1973).

[10]Samuel P. Hays, "The Politics of Reform in Municipal Government in the Progressive Era," *Pacific Northwest Quarterly* 55 (October 1964): 157-89; Robert Lineberry and Edmund Fowler, "Reformism and Public Policies in American Cities," *American Political Science Review* 61 (September 1967): 715; Theodore Robinson and Thomas Dye, "Reformism and Black Representation on City Councils," *Social Science Quarterly* 63 (March 1982): 99-114; Tari Renner, "Municipal Election Processes: The Impact on Minority Representation," in *The 1988 Municipal Yearbook* (Washington: The International City Management Association, 1988).

[11]Robert A. Dahl, *Pluralist Democracy in the United States: Conflict and Consent* (Chicago: Rand McNally & Co., 1967), 210. For thorough discussions of the development and importance of political parties, see: E. E. Schattschneider, *Party Government* (New York: Holt, Rinehart and Winston, 1942); Everett Carll Ladd, Jr., *American Political Parties: Social Change and Political Response* (New York: W. W. Norton & Co., 1970); Richard Hofstadter, *The Idea of a Party System* (Berkeley, California: University of California Press, 1969); for a thorough discussion of political organizations and parties that predate the drafting of the U.S. Constitution, see Jackson Turner Main, *Political Parties before the Constitution* (New York: W. W. Norton & Co., Inc., 1973). Although parties were not mentioned in the Constitution, this book provides a wealth of historical information on the political organizations, political parties, and their leaders that dominated the political landscape in America prior to the adoption of the Constitution. In this regard, see also, Austin Ranney and Willmoore Kendall, *Democracy and the American Party System* (New York: Harcourt, Brace and Company, 1956) 95-98.

of these functions, therefore, is an infringement on the exercise of these quintessential democratic liberties.[12] The late U.S. Supreme Court Justice Robert H. Jackson has been reported as stating:

> The very purpose of a Bill of Rights was to withdraw certain subjects from the vicissitudes of political controversy, to place them beyond the reach of majorities and officials and to establish them as legal principles to be applied by the courts. One's right to life, liberty, and property, to *free speech*, a free press, freedom of worship *and assembly*, and other fundamental rights may not be submitted to vote; they depend on the outcome of no elections.[13]

Justice Jackson's conclusion that these liberties may not be subjected to the political process suggests that the political imposition of the reforms of the Progressive Era, although popular with voters, went too far. In addition, the constitutionally protected right to vote for racial minorities,[14] it has become clear, has also been adversely impacted by the reforms.

The principal purpose of the Progressive Era reforms was to eradicate corruption in California politics by eliminating the domination of political parties by political "machines" and party "bosses." Its target was the Southern Pacific Railroad, which controlled the state legislature through the political parties. The reformers' efforts resulted in statutory enactments and constitutional amendments, which gutted the role of political parties in California. These reforms—the direct primary, the initiative, referendum, and recall processes, the institution of nonpartisan offices, at-large election districts, and their progeny, such as prohibitions against party endorsements in partisan and nonpartisan elections—determined the course of politics in California until recently.

---

[12]In the last three decades, the courts have begun to define the parameters of the First Amendment rights of political association and political speech. See, *Eu v. San Francisco County Democratic,* 109 S. Ct. 1013 (1989); *Tashjian v. Republican Party,* 479 U.S. 208 (1986); *Democratic Party v. Wisconsin,* 450 U.S. 107 (1981); *Cousins v. Wigoda,* 409 U.S. 477 (1975); *Williams v. Rhodes,* 393 U.S. 23 (1968); *NAACP v. Alabama,* 357 U.S. 449 (1958); *Geary v. Renne,* Case No. 88-2875, opinion filed August 14, 1990, 9th Cir., *In Banc,* 1990; *Ripon Society v. Republican Party,* 525 F.2d 567 (1975).

[13]Norman Dorsen, *Frontiers of Civil Liberties* (New York: Pantheon Books, 1968), 4.

[14]The 14th and 15th Amendments to the U.S. Constitution form the operative constitutional protections of the right to vote for racial minorities. Congress enacted a statutory protection in the Voting Rights Act, as amended in 1982 [42 U.S.C. 1973].

These structural reforms did not cure the evils they were intended to cure, on the one hand.[15] And on the other hand, they opened the door to sophisticated forms of electoral systems that adversely impact the political influence of the economically disadvantaged and racial minorities.

Political and social scientists have devoted a considerable amount of their research to the impact the electoral structure of at-large and nonpartisan offices have had on the electoral successes of minority candidates.[16] This research has resulted in a body of knowledge used by individual, as opposed to party, plaintiffs to support their legal challenges to particular electoral systems. The traditional basis for such challenges has been alleged violations of Section 2 of the Voting Rights Act, as amended in 1982.[17] The Voting Rights Act is simply a codification of existing constitutional guarantees in the Bill of Rights and the 14th and 15th Amendments to the U.S. Constitution. The 15th Amendment is specifically referenced in the Voting Rights Act and has an enabling clause granting to Congress the right

---

[15] Political corruption continues to dominate the headlines of the news media. See, "Carpenter Convicted of Corruption," *Los Angeles Times*, September 18, 1990, (State Board of Equalization member and former state senator, Paul Carpenter, was convicted on two counts of extortion, one count each of conspiracy and racketeering); "Senator Montoya Indicted on 10 Counts of Corruption," *Los Angeles Herald Examiner*, May 18, 1989; and "Montoya, Ex-Aide Indicted on Multiple Felony Counts," *Los Angeles Times*, May 18, 1989; "Vast Investment in State Politics By Keating Told," *Los Angeles Times*, November 23, 1989.

[16] Jeffrey S. Zax, "Election Methods and Black and Hispanic City Council Membership," *Social Science Quarterly* (June 1990): 339-55; Kenneth R. Mladenka, "Blacks and Hispanics in Urban Politics," *American Political Science Review* 83 (March 1989): 165-91; Richard L. Engstrom and Michael D. McDonald, "The Election of Blacks to City Councils: Clarifying the Impact of Electoral Arrangements on the Seats/Population Relationship," *American Political Science Review* 75: 344-54; Tari Renner, "Municipal Election Processes: The Impact on Minority Representation," *Municipal Yearbook* (Washington, D.C.: International City Manager's Association, 1988); Albert K. Karnig and Susan Welch, "Electoral Structure and Black Representation on City Councils," *Social Science Quarterly* (March 1982): 99-114; Albert K. Karnig and Susan Welch, *Black Representation and Urban Policy* (Chicago: University of Chicago Press, 1980); Theodore Robinson and Thomas Dye, "Reformism and Representation on City Councils," *Social Science Quarterly* 59 (June 1978): 133-41; Clinton Jones, "The Impact of Local Election Systems on Black Representation," *Urban Affairs Quarterly* 11 (March 1976): 345-56.

[17] See James Blackshear and Larry Menefee, "At-Large Elections and One Person, One Vote: The Search for the Meaning of Racial Vote Dilution," in *Minority Vote Dilution*, edited by Chandler Davidson (Washington, D.C.: Howard University Press, 1984), 203-48.

to legislate voting rights protections.[18] Therefore, without the Voting Rights Act, the courts could and have protected the constitutional liberties embodied in the right to vote.[19]

The parties have successfully challenged, and the courts have held that California's prohibitions against the parties endorsing or supporting candidates in nonpartisan and partisan elections violated the parties' First Amendment rights to political speech.[20] The author has not discovered any legal challenge to nonpartisan at-large electoral systems based on violations of an individual citizen's First Amendment right of association, and neither has a political party lodged such a challenge. The parties have successfully challenged the state's role in regulating the nomination process through the direct primary, based on the right of association.[21] The literature on the direct primary focus mainly on the rights of political parties, as opposed to individual voters, and take the form of legal analyses, as opposed to empirical social science studies. In addition, the courts have held that in certain circumstances the initiative process is a proper subject for judicial review.[22] But the literature on the initiative process reveal very little empirical data on the impact such processes have on racial minorities or

---

[18]The 15th Amendment provides:

  Section 1. The right of citizens of the United States to vote shall not be denied or abridged by the United States or by any State on account of race, color, or previous condition of servitude.

  Section 2. The Congress shall have power to enforce this article by appropriate legislation.

[19]See, *The White Primary Cases*: *Nixon v. Herndon*, 273 U.S. 536 (1927); *Nixon v. Condon*, 286 U.S. 73 (1932); *Smith v. Allwright*, 321 U.S. 649 (1944); *Terry v. Adams*, 345 U.S. 461 (1953); *Gray v. Sanders*, 372 U.S. 482 (1962). [Yet the Courts have been reluctant to find effective constitutional standards for reviewing voting rights cases, as witnessed by the decision in *City of Mobile v. Bolden*, 446 U.S. 55 (1980), and its progeny, as well as the strong dissenting opinions in *Baker v. Carr* and *Reynolds v. Sims*.

[20]See, *Eu v. S.F. County Demo. Cent. Committee*, 109 S. Ct. 1013 (1989), [State prohibition against party endorsement in partisan elections was unconstitutional.]; *Geary v. Renne*, Case No. 88-2875, opinion filed August 14, 1990, 9th Cir., In Banc. [State prohibition against party endorsement in nonpartisan elections was unconstitutional on free speech grounds. There was no challenge to the constitutional efficacy of the "at large" or "nonpartisan" nature of the electoral system.

[21]See for example, *Wigoda v. Cousins*, 419 U.S. 477 (1975); *Williams v. Rhodes*, 393 U.S. 23 (1968); *Democratic Party v. Wisconsin*, 450 U.S. 107 (1981).

[22]See *Reitman v. Mulkey*, 387 U.S. 369 (1967); *Hunter v. Erickson*, 393 U.S. 385 (1969); See also, Julian N. Eule, "Judicial Review of Direct Democracy," *Yale Law Journal* 99 (June 1990): 1503; Derrick Bell, "The Referendum: Democracy's Barrier to Racial Equality," *Wash. L. Rev.* 54 (1978): 1.

political parties, but what exist are instructive.[23] But the political and social science literature on nonpartisan/at-large elections provide sufficient data for the comparative analysis of this article. The operative issue is the same—the adverse impact on minority groups' voting franchise.

This essay examines the nature of these reforms, the legal, political, and social science literature concerning the impact they have had on minority political influence, political parties, and the constitutional dilemmas they created.

NONPARTISAN ELECTIONS AND AT-LARGE DISTRICTS

In 1913, at the urging of the reformers,[24] California adopted a nonpartisan system of government at the county and municipal levels for the offices of sheriff, assessor, judge, members of the county boards of supervisors, mayor, members of the school board and city council. Again, their primary argument in favor of these reforms was, ostensibly, the prevention of political corruption. In addition to making certain municipal and county offices nonpartisan, the reformers imposed a system of jurisdictionwide election districts, commonly known as "at-large" election districts. In *general law cities*, the councilmanic districts are at-large districts. *Charter cities* determine their own election districts, and they vary from at-large to mixed to single member districts. All county offices are at-large districts, except for members of the boards of supervisors in some of the larger counties. Nonpartisan offices are synonymous with at-large districts in the majority of California cities.

Yet, there is a clear distinction between each type of electoral system, and the courts have treated the distinction accordingly. For example, in *Geart v. Renne*, the 9th Circuit Court of Appeals held that California's prohibition against political parties endorsing or supporting candidates in nonpartisan elections was unconstitutional. It violated the parties' First

---

[23]See Elaine B. Sharp, "Voting on Citywide Propositions: Further Tests of Competing Explanations," *Urban Affairs Quarterly* 23 (December 1987): 233-48; Gerald Benjamin and Robert Marcus, "Minority Non-Voting in the New York City Charter Referenda: Does the Voting Rights Act Reach the Referendum Process, and Should It?" Prepared for presentation at the annual meeting of the American Political Science Association, September 2, 1990; Julian N. Eule, "Judicial Review of Direct Democracy," *Yale Law Journal* 99 (June 1990): 1503; Derrick Bell, "The Referendum: Democracy's Barrier to Racial Equality," *Wash. L. Rev.* 54 (1978): 1, 22-28.

[24]For a thorough discussion of the development of nonpartisanship, see Eugene Lee, *The Politics of Nonpartisanship* (Berkeley: University of California Press, 1960) and Willis Hawley, *Nonpartisan Elections and the Case for Party Politics* (New York: Wiley, 1973).

Amendment rights of free speech.[25] The Court did not consider the question of whether "nonpartisan electoral systems," themselves, were unconstitutional. And in *Gomez v. City of Watsonville*, the 9th Circuit Court of Appeals held that the at-large electoral system in the city of Watsonville, California, discriminated against Latinos and therefore violated the Voting Rights Act.[26] Again, the Court did not consider the question of whether the nonpartisan nature of the city's electoral system was invalid under the Voting Rights Act, the First, Fourteenth, or Fifteenth Amendments.[27]

This treatment, by the courts, raises significant concerns for legal scholars, political and social scientists who deal with these issues. While there is sufficient social science data and legal standards to test the validity of at-large systems, they do not settle several nagging questions regarding nonpartisanship, per se.

First, does nonpartisanship adversely affect minorities? Some studies answer this question in the affirmative.[28] But most of these studies predate the congressionally mandated standards set forth in the Voting Rights Act, as amended in 1982. Second, does nonpartisanship adversely affect political parties? Most of the studies answer this question in the affirmative. But most of these studies predate the recent court decisions in which the issue of nonpartisan elections have been raised. Third, why do the courts avoid the issue of the validity of nonpartisan electoral systems? Could it be that the existing data are insufficient? Would the remedy be too harsh (i.e., the wholesale invalidation of nonpartisan electoral systems)? Or, could it be that the issue is not justiciable because it presents a "political question?" In any event, there is a dearth of data addressing these questions and, therefore, more exploration is needed. This essay does not attmpet to answer these questions. Its purpose is a modest attempt to begin an exploration of them.

How Do Nonpartisan/At-Large Electoral Systems Effect Minorities and the Economically Disadvantaged?

It has been observed that cities with nonpartisan elections devote less attention to the needs of the economically disadvantaged in the areas of

---

[25]See, *Geary v. Renne*, Case No. 88-2875 (opinion filed August 14, 1990). 9th Cir., In Banc).

[26]*Gomez v. City of Watsonville*, 863 F.2d 1407 (9th Cir., 1988).

[27]The plaintiffs lodged in the trail court a claim alleging a voting rights violation based on the Fifteenth Amendment but abandoned this claim on appeal.

[28]For one of the more recent studies, see, Davidson and Fraga, "Slating Groups as Parties in a 'Nonpartisan' Setting," *The Western Political Quarterly* 41 (June 1988): 373-90.

social services, housing, and employment.[29] This observation is consistent with the mainstream literature.[30]

In their study, Davidson and Fraga, concluded:

> While research has established the deleterious effects of nonpartisanship on the representation of social minorities and Blacks in particular, this fact has received less attention than the consequences of nonpartisanship regarding social class, ideology, and party. Scholars are virtually unanimous that nonpartisan systems in general disadvantage the poor, the working classes, liberal voters, and Democrats. What explains this effect? One answer is that nonpartisan systems are tied to other forms whose bias is known. At-large elections, for example, which are typical of such systems, disadvantage racial minorities.[31]

Moreover, from an electoral standpoint, minorities have a more difficult time electing representatives from their respective groups than the majority population.[32] Nevertheless, a few scholars have concluded that "at-large" districts do not adversely effect the electoral success of minorities.[33]

---

[29]Willis Hawley, *Nonpartisan Elections and the Case for Party Politics* (New York, New York: Wiley, 1973), Chap. 6.

[30]Chandler Davidson and Luis Ricardo Fraga, "Slating Groups as Parties in a 'NonPartisan' Setting," *The Western Political Quarterly*, vol. 41, no. 2 (June 1988); Chandler Davidson and George Korbel, "At-Large Elections and Minority-Group Representation: A Re-examination of Historical and Contemporary Evidence," *Journal of Politics* 43 (1981): 982-1005; Albert K. Karnig and Susan Welch, *Black Representation and Urban Policy* (Chicago: University of Chicago Press, 1980).

[31]Chandler Davidson and Luis Ricardo Fraga, "Slating Groups as Parties in a 'Nonpartisan' Setting," *The Western Political Quarterly* 41 (June 1988): 373-90.

[32]See Susan Welch, "The Impact of At-Large Elections on the Representation of Blacks and Hispanics," paper prepared for presentation at the annual meeting of the American Political Science Association, August 1990, San Francisco, California; Susan Welch and Timothy Bledsoe, *Urban Reform and its Consequences: A Study in Representation* (Chicago: The University of Chicago Press, 1988); Timothy Bledsoe, "A Research Note on the Impact of District/At-Large Elections on Black Political Efficacy," *Urban Affairs Quarterly* 22 (September 1986): 166-74; Richard L. Engstrom and Michael D. McDonald, "The Effect of At-Large Versus District Elections on Racial Representation in U.S. Municipalities," in *Electoral Laws and their Political Consequences*, edited by Bernard Grofman and Arend Lijphart (New York: Agathon Press, Inc. 1986), 203-25.

[33]See Susan MacManus, "At-large Elections and Minority Representation: An Adversarial Critique," *Social Science Quarterly* 60 (November 1979): 338-40; Susan MacManus, "City Council Elections Procedures and Minority Representation," *Social Science Quarterly* 59 (June 1978): 153-61; Leonard A. Cole, "Electing Blacks to Municipal Office: Structural and Social Determinants," *Urban Affairs Quarterly* 8

Others take a middle of the road position.[34]   Susan MacManus and
Leonard A. Cole, using *subtractive and ratio measurements* in their methodology, conclude that socio-economic variables have not been sufficiently
factored into most *regression* analyses of this issue. This view is commonly
referred to as the revisionist position,[35] in that it challenges the traditional
evidence.[36]

Lineberry and Fowler concluded:

> The introduction of at-large, nonpartisan elections has at
> least five consequences for [minority] groups. First, they
> remove an important cue-giving agency—the party—from the
> electoral scene, leaving the voter to make decisions less on
> policy commitments . . . of the party, and more on irrele-
> vancies such as ethnic identification and name familiarity.
> Second, by removing the party from the ballot, the reforms
> eliminate the principal agency of interest aggregation from
> the political system. . . . Moreover, nonpartisanship has the
> effect of reducing the turnout in local elections by working
> class groups, leaving officeholders freer from retaliation by
> these groups at the polls. Fourth, nonpartisanship may also
> serve . . . [to increase] the relative political power of . . .
> the local press. And when nonpartisanship is combined
> with election at-large, the impact of residentially segregat-
> ed groups· or groups which obtain their strength from

(1974): 17-39.

[34]Carol A. Cassell, "The Nonpartisan Ballot in the United States," in *Electoral
Laws and their Political Consequences*, edited by Bernard Grofman and Arend Lijphart
(New York: Agathon Press, Inc., 1986), 226-41.

[35]Susan Welch, "The Impact of At-Large Elections on the Representation of
Blacks and Hispanics," paper prepared for and presented at the annual meeting of the
American Political Science Association, August 1990 (forthcoming in *Journal of
Politics*, November 1990); Richard L. Engstrom and Michael D. McDonald, "The
Election of Blacks to City Councils: Clarifying the Impact of Electoral Arrangements
on the Seats/Population Relationship," *The American Political Science Review* 75
(1981): 344-54.

[36]Kenneth R. Mladenka, "Blacks and Hispanics in Urban Politics," *The American
Political Science Review* 83 (March 1989): 165-91; Rufus P. Browning, Dale Rogers
Marshall, and David H. Tabb, *Protest is Not Enough: The Struggle of Blacks and
Hispanics for Equality in Urban America* (Berkeley: University of California Press,
1984); Robert L. Lineberry and Edmund P. Fowler, "Reformism and Public Policies
in American Cities," *The American Political Science Review* 61 (1967): 701-16.

voting as blocs in municipal elections is further reduced.[37]

H. Eric Schockmann has made similar observations with respect to the
California experience and has written:

> The solution [to Los Angeles' transportation and political
> ethics problems] is not at-large elections. These only breed
> underrepresentation of minorities. What we need is to
> return to partisan elections in the existing district system,
> and rekindle party organizational checks that would prevent
> the balkanization of Los Angeles.... Any reformist ground
> swell in Los Angeles must first do away with nonpartisan
> local elections.[38]

To the extent that the revisionist position is correct in concluding that
certain socio-economic factors are also relevant, it is important to briefly
examine them. One factor has received considerable attention: money
raised and spent in political campaigns. At-large districts require candidates
to raise enormous sums of money to be competitive. Incumbents vastly
outspend challengers. In the city of Los Angeles, for example, incumbents
account for 76 percent of campaign expenditures while challengers spend
only 18 percent. In San Francisco, incumbents account for 85 percent of
campaign expenditures.[39] In the county of Los Angeles, incumbents
account for 90 percent. Hence, it is easy to conclude that a challenge to a
well-financed incumbent is almost insurmountable and therefore to
discourage any serious opposition. This suggests that high spending
incumbent campaigns generally guarantee success.[40] And since minorities
tend to be challengers, this would suggest that they have very little
probability of influencing the outcome of nonpartisan and at-large elections
in California. While money has always been a factor, the amount of money
presently used in nonpartisan elections may be much more significant than
in the past. Further research in this area would be useful and instructive,
because the revisionists conclude that the existing empirical data, on the
question of whether incumbents holding nonpartisan office are more likely

---

[37]Robert L. Lineberry and Edmund P. Fowler, "Reformism and Public Policies in
American Cities," *The American Political Science Review* 61 (1967): 715-16.

[38]H. Eric Schockmann, "Nonpartisan City Elections Produce a Leaderless Ship,"
Los Angeles Times, February 4, 1990.

[39]The Los Angeles City County Council and San Francisco Board of Supervisors
districts are not at-large districts, but the offices of mayor, city attorney, city controller
are city-wide districts.

[40]California Commission on Campaign Financing, *Financing California's Local
Elections: Money and Politics in the Golden State* (Los Angeles: Center For
Responsive Government, 1989), 66.

to be reelected than incumbents holding partisan office, are not conclusive.[41] Yet, the recent data compiled by the California Commission on Campaign Financing suggest otherwise.[42]

Minorities have used these existing data to successfully challenge at-large electoral systems, in the courts, pursuant to Section 2 of the Voting Rights Act. The most recent California case is *Gomez v. City of Watsonville*.[43] The court held that the at-large districts in the city of Watsonville discriminated against Latinos. The court listed the seven congressionally mandated factors that are usually "probative" of Section 2 violations. They are: (1) a history of official discrimination in a political subdivision that touched the right of a minority group to vote or participate in the democratic process; (2) racially polarized voting; (3) unusually large elections districts; (4) a "slating process" that denies minorities access; (5) the effects of discrimination in health, education, and employment that bears on a minority group's ability to participate effectively in the political process; (6) campaigns characterized by overt or subtle racial appeals; and (7) electoral success of minority groups. In the leading case of *Thornburg v. Gingles*,[44] the U.S. Supreme Court reminds us that this list is neither comprehensive nor exclusive. This suggests that other factors may be used.

A substantial volume of the social science literature deals with *racial polarization*.[45] Some deal with *slating groups*.[46] Others deal with racial segregation and the *electoral success of minority groups*.[47] Another compares electoral success to public benefits such as employment.[48]

---

[41]Carol A. Cassel, "The Nonpartisan Ballot in the United States," in *Electoral Laws and their Political Consequences*, edited by Bernard Grofman and Arend Lijphart (New York: Agathon Press, Inc., 1986), 232-33.

[42]California Commission on Campaign Financing, *Financing California's Local Elections: Money and Politics in the Golden State* (Los Angeles: Center For Responsive Government, 1989).

[43]See, 863 F.2d 1407 (9th Cir., 1988).

[44]*Thornburg v. Gingles*, 478 U.S. 30, 106 S. Ct. 2752 (1986).

[45]The court, in *Thornburg v. Gingles*, cited with approval, Richard L. Engstrom and Michael D. McDonald, "Quantitative Evidence in Vote Dilution Litigation: Political Participation and Polarized Voting," *Urban Lawyer* 17 (1985): 369. See also, Engstrom and McDonald, "Quantitative Evidence in Vote Dilution Litigation, Part II: Minority Coalitions and Multivariate Analysis," *Urban Lawyer* 19 (1987): 65-75.

[46]Chandler Davidson and Luis Ricardo Fraga, "Slating Groups as Parties in a 'Nonpartisan' Setting," *The Western Political Quarterly* 41 (June 1988): 373-90.

[47]Jeffrey S. Zax, "Election Methods and Black and Hispanic City Council Membership," *Social Science Quarterly* 71 (June 1990): 339-55.

[48]Kenneth R. Mladenka, "Blacks and Hispanics in Urban Politics," *American Political Science Review* 83 (March 1989): 165-91.

While each of these factors are "probative" of Section 2 violations, they may also be probative of violations of the 14th and 15th Amendments of the U.S. Constitution or the First Amendment right of association, which encompass voting rights. Chief Judge Bazelon, in his dissent in *Ripon Society v. National Republican Party*,[49] drew the constitutional parallel in voting rights cases:

> These cases were as much "right to vote" cases as they were racial discrimination cases and as such formed part of the express doctrinal basis for *Reynolds v. Sims*, (citation omitted). The subject matter of *Reynolds* and the present litigation is territorial discrimination against the right to vote of certain citizens. *Reynolds* teaches that such discrimination is forbidden by the same constitutional structure that forbids racial discrimination against the right to vote of certain citizens.

In other words, discrimination that implicates the right to vote is governed by the same constitutional doctrine. Part of the doctrine may be emphasized more than another depending on the particular case. The First Amendment's associational rights also implicate the right to vote. It follows, therefore, that such rights are also governed in similar fashion by the same constitutional doctrine. And when the right to vote is implicated, it triggers the highest standard of judicial scrutiny.

This means that the state may not impose a discriminatory electoral system unless it can justify that such imposition was necessary to protect a "compelling state interest," which could not be achieved by a less restrictive means. The alternatives to "single-member" districts or "mixed" districts make it difficult to justify the necessity of a nonpartisan/at-large electoral system.

However, it is instructive to note that federal appeals court Justice Pamela Rymer, in a forceful dissent, in *Geary v. Renne*,[50] argued that California had a "super-compelling interest" in choosing the nonpartisan nature of its electoral system. She argued that this interest is rooted in Article IV, Section 4, of the U.S. Constitution,[51] and means that California has a right to choose a nonpartisan system of government if it so desires. She concludes that such a right is an interest that is "super compelling," and therefore justifies an infringement on the parties' First Amendment rights.

---

[49]*Ripon Society v. National Republican Party*, 525 F.2d 567 (1975). Judge Bazelon was referring to the "state action" cases cited in the majority decision.

[50]See *Geary v. Renne*, No. 88-2875 (9th Cir., filed August 14, 1990).

[51]Section 4, Article IV, provides that: "The United States shall guarantee to every state in this Union a Republican Form of Government, and shall guarantee to protect each of them against invasion; and on application of the legislature, or of the executive (when the Legislature cannot be convened), against domestic violence."

This argument, however, did not persuade the eight justices subscribing to the majority opinion.[52]

These observations illustrate, in a summary manner, the problems minorities encounter in their quests to influence the electoral and public policy outcomes of nonpartisan/at-large electoral systems. They also illustrate, based on the existing social science data, that the challenges to such electoral systems may not be exhausted by the Voting Rights Act and other legal bases for voting rights challenges such as those based in the Bill of Rights, and the 14th and 15th Amendments.[53]

How Do Nonpartisan Electoral Systems Effect Political Parties?

Critical to this analysis is the observation the courts have held that the political parties have a right to assert, on behalf of their membership, First Amendment associational rights.[54] Thus, government regulation that implicates these rights is subject to challenge by the parties.

Certainly, the voters are entitled to know which candidates share their party's viewpoints and are committed to their party's platforms, including the initiative measures on nonpartisan ballots that are supported or opposed by their party. Nonpartisan elections make it difficult for individual voters to receive this information.[55] Adrian has observed that nonpartisan systems encourage candidates to avoid issues of policy in campaigns. Nonpartisanship frustrates protest voting. Thus, when the voters are disgruntled with the state of political affairs and want to "throw the rascals out," they don't.

---

[52]*Geary v. Renne*, No. 88-2875 (9th Cir., filed August 14, 1990). The court held that California's prohibition against parties endorsing or supporting candidates in nonpartisan elections violated the free speech guarantee of the First Amendment. However, the court did not rule that nonpartisan elections, per se, were unconstitutional. That issue was not before the court. At the time of this publication, this decision has been appealed to the U.S. Supreme Court.

[53]In *Gomez v. City of Watsonville*, the plaintiffs lodged, in their complaint, a 15th Amendment claim, but abandoned it on appeal.

[54]See *Sweezy v. New Hampshire*, 354 U.S. 234 (1957). The court stated:
Exercise of these basic freedoms in America has traditionally been through the media of political associations. Any interference with the freedom of a party is simultaneously an interference with the freedom of its adherents." at p. 250.
And in *NAACP v. Alabama*, 357 U.S. 449 (1958), the court recognized the right of the association to exercise these rights on behalf of its membership. See discussion in: Note, "Primary Elections and the Collective Right of Freedom of Association," *Yale Law Journal* 94 (1984): 117.

[55]See Charles R. Adrian, "Some General Characteristics of Nonpartisan Elections," *The American Political Science Review* 46 (1952): 766-76.

The reason is simple. It is not as easy to vote against an individual human being whom you know, than an inanimate object—a political party. This strengthens individual incumbencies. The voter has no way of knowing, in nonpartisan, issueless campaigns, whether the candidate who seeks to replace an incumbent will follow policies the voter desires.

But do parties have a right to disseminate such information? And if so, do nonpartisan/at-large electoral systems deny them this right? Enrolled party members usually rely upon and expect guidance from their party in deciding electoral issues. That is a traditional role of the party. When the party fails to provide such information, it has abrogated a responsibility to its membership. On the other hand, when a party is impeded in disseminating that information, by the state removing party labels, the state has infringed, however minimally, upon the voter's franchise and First Amendment associational rights.

In *Tashjian v. Republican Party*, the U.S. Supreme Court recently stated:

> To the extent that party labels provide a shorthand designation of the views of party candidates on matters of public concern, the identification of candidates with particular parties plays a role in the process by which voters inform themselves for the exercise of the franchise.[56]

This suggests that party labels are important in communications between the parties and their membership. Thus, prohibiting party labels from the ballot may well violate the First Amendment rights of both association and speech.

Second, the absence of party labels from the ballot makes it difficult for parties to recruit candidates to run for partisan and nonpartisan office under their banners.[57] Exceptional campaigners, who have held nonpartisan office, are recruited by both parties. This creates competition for good campaigners. Party regulars resent recruiting candidates for partisan office who are not party regulars. Thus, nonpartisan officeholders are not available, generally, for partisan office. On the other hand, partisan officeholders do not seek nonpartisan office because of the stigma attached to having been a partisan officeholder. Each of these phenomenon makes it difficult for the parties to recruit candidates for partisan and nonpartisan offices, according to Adrian. This makes it difficult for parties to develop slates of candidates that will adhere to the parties' policy positions, and therefore, perform their function of "interest aggregation," which is one the parties' associational rights.

Third, the effectiveness of political parties, to a large extent, depends on the loyalty of the voters. Nonpartisan electoral systems undermine the

---

[56]*Tashjian v. Republican Party*, 479 U.S. 208, 220, 107 S. Ct. 544 (1986).

[57]Charles R. Adrian, "Some General Characteristics of Nonpartisan Elections," *The American Political Science Review* 46 (1952): 766-76.

loyalty of voters to political parties. Party loyalty is essential to the ability of a party to adequately plan and develop electioneering strategies. Parties have a right to rely on party loyalty in their electioneering efforts.

Nonpartisan Elections Encourage Candidates to Mislead Voters with Respect to Their Party Affiliation

Fourth, when parties are not able to effectively inform their membership of a candidate's party affiliation, inscrutable candidates and political entrepreneurs who prepare, for profit, "slate mailers," can mislead the voters with respect to a candidate's party affiliation.[58] This practice undermines the effectiveness of the electioneering efforts of political parties, as well as impunges the integrity of the elctoral process.

Nonpartisan Elections Make It Difficult for Parties to Raise Money to Engage in Ordinary Electioneering Efforts on Behalf of Nonpartisan Candidates

Fifth, electioneering efforts involve fund raising for voter registration, absentee voter campaigns and "get-out-the-vote" (GOTV) efforts. It is more difficult to raise money for nonpartisan elections because contributors cannot be certain that their money will be used for candidates who support their political values and policies.

In summary, while it is well settled that the standards of Section 2 of the Voting Rights Act are applicable to at-large electoral systems, when they adversely effect minority groups, at-large/nonpartisan systems are not immune to attack under the Bill of Rights or the 14th and 15th Amendments to the U.S. Constitution primarily because they impact the voting franchise. Moreover, the political parties may have an interest in challenging at-large nonpartisan elections under the First Amendment right of association since they reduce voter turnout and eliminate the principal agency of interest aggregation—the political party.

INITIATIVE, REFERENDUM, AND RECALL

California enacted the initiative, referendum, and recall processes in 1911. The referendum process allows the electorate to confirm or reject

---

[58]See, Dick Lloyd, "Party Power Figures in 'Non-Partisan' City Elections," *Pasadena Star News*, March 21, 1983 [In the 1983 Pasadena municipal elections, misleading political advertisements were used by candidates. One candidate, Maria Low, permitted her name to be used on mailings by groups purporting to represent both the Democratic and Republican parties.

measures passed by the state legislature. The initiative process is used by the voters to directly enact legislation or constitutional amendments. The recall process of elected officials also included the recall of judicial officers. The reformers felt that in order to ensure that the results of the initiative were guaranteed, it was essential that the voters retain the ability to recall judicial officers who might invalidate their popular decisions.[59] These are forms of direct democracy.[60]

How Does the Initiative Affect Parties and the Governmental Process?

The initiative process adversely affects the roles and functions of political parties, and thus the right of political association. It also impacts the governmental process. It affects political parties in each of the following ways.

First, parties play little or no role in initiative campaigns. These campaigns are usually conducted by hired political consultants who engage in fund raising and other electioneering activities. Parties are not involved. Campaign support is usually provided by the proponents or special interest groups most affected by or concerned about a particular initiative. Because of the large number of signatures necessary to qualify a measure for the ballot, proponents generally hire professional signature gathering firms, which makes it a very expensive undertaking.[61] If the initiatives are hotly contested, the proponents and opponents must raise large sums of money to gather signatures, wage extensive media campaigns in newspapers, billboard advertisements, radio and television appeals, and utilize direct-mail solicitation of the voters.

Second, political parties are not ordinarily involved in drafting initiatives[62] or in formulating ballot arguments provided in the voters'

---

[59]See *California Secretary of State; Proposed Amendments to the Constitution of the State of California with Legislative Reasons For and Against Adoption Thereof* (October 1911). See also, *California Secretary of State, Statement of the Vote of California* 5 (October 1911).

[60]See Julian N. Eule, "Judicial Review of Direct Democracy," *Yale Law Journal* (May 1990): 1555.

[61]Berg and Holman, "The Initiative and Its Agenda-Setting Value," *Law and Policy* 11 (October 1989): 459. The use of direct mail to gather signatures costs approximately $2.00 per signature, as opposed to $.53 per signature gathered using the door-to-door method.

[62]David B. Magleby, *Direct Legislation: Voting on Ballot Propositions in the United States* (Baltimore: Johns Hopkins University Press, 1984).

pamphlets. This practice impedes the ability of political parties to effectively communicate their positions on ballot measures to their members.[63]

Third, initiative campaigns have the potential for undermining the campaigns of candidates of political parties. Issues that are strongly associated with a political party's position have the potential for negatively or positively influencing the campaigns of candidates of a particular party.

Fourth, initiative campaigns reinforce the belief that political parties are not significant actors in the legislative process, and therefore, result in a loss of respect for parties causing a decline in party loyalty. A decline in party loyalty, it has been noted, causes low voter turnouts.[64]

As early as 1965, Governor Edmund G. "Pat" Brown, in his message to the legislature, expressed concern about the influence of special interest groups in the initiative process. He sought legislation to "prevent special interests from turning the initiative to private gain through the use of professional petition circulators and large sums of money." Governor Brown's warning is manifestly prophetic in light of the most recent initiative campaigns.[65]

Early opponents of the initiative process argued that such a process weakened state legislatures, causing a loss of respect for those institutions, and resulted in legislators being less responsive to the electorate. They argued that legislators may conclude that any legislation they pass—good or bad—may be overridden by an initiative. This argument was also prophetic. Ironically, modern day proponents of the initiative argue that the legislature has abrogated its responsibility to enact laws, particularly on controversial matters. In either case, the result is the same.

When the legislature is not responsive to the electorate and leaves policymaking to plebiscite, special interest groups play a disproportionate role. Special interest groups, such as the oil and gas industry, insurance and banking industries, teachers, doctors, lawyers, realtors, environmentalists,

---

[63]The California secretary of state recently has decided to solicit the positions of the political parties on ballot measures, although the California Elections Code does not require it.

[64]See Gerald M. Pomper, "The Contributions of Political Parties in American Democracy," in *Party Renewal in America*, 9.

[65]Berg and Holman, "The Initiative Process and Its Declining Agenda-setting Value," *Law and Policy* 11 (October 1989): 465. The authors concluded:

> Today, a viable qualification effort requires exorbitant financial resources, professional administration, and access to sophisticated campaign technology. The initiative industry had developed to such an extent that all the services needed for a place on the ballot simply can be purchased. Affecting public policy through the initiative process is by far the greater domain of the very special interest groups the process originally intended to restrain.

public employee unions, prohibitionists, liquor interests, the tobacco industry, tax crusaders, and consumer organizations all have used the initiative process to support or oppose ballot measures. They have sponsored tax reform measures, legislative reform, campaign finance and ethics reform, education funding, revenue raising measures, environmental protection reforms, health care and housing initiatives, insurance reform, criminal procedure reform, reapportionment reform, and earthquake bond measures.

Other critics of the initiative argue that it is an "inherently defective" method of legislating.[66] First, they have noted that the electorate cannot function effectively as a deliberative body because voters do not have an opportunity to develop expertise on the subject matter of initiative measures and, therefore, may enact laws that do not reflect the public will. Second, the high abstention rate of voters in initiative elections permits small segments of the electorate to have a disproportionate impact on legislation, and therefore, undermine the true public sentiment. Third, initiative legislation is generally not subject to the veto power of the executive branch of government[67] and often prohibits amendment of the legislation even when there are excesses or mistakes in the legislation. Fourth, the separation of powers principal is proscribed by the use of the initiative.[68]

The initiative also adversely impacts the courts and the legislature, according to Professor Preble Stolz.[69] In addition, plebiscites eliminate the "checking" function of political organizations, as envisioned by James Madison, in American democracy.[70] By eliminating this function, the initiative process invites the abuses most feared by the founding fathers, namely: majoritarian oppression, which may result in depriving minority groups of fundamental rights.

---

[66]See, Note, "Initiative and Referendum—Do They Encourage or Impair Better State Government," *Florida State Univ. L. Rev.* 925 (1977): 941.

[67]See, Note, "Constitutional Constraints on Initiative and Referendum," *Vanderbilt L. Rev.* 32 (1979): 1143, 1146.

[68]*Ibid.*, 11.

[69]See Preble Stolz, "Say Good-Bye to Hiram Johnson's Ghost," *California Lawyer* (January 1990): 44-46. Stolz argues that the initiative effects the courts when the measures mandate application of U.S. constitutional standards in evidentiary matters involving criminal cases. Government by initiative crowds out other matters that might be on the California Supreme Court's agenda. Cases that result from initiatives are the "big cases" that require the court's attention, thereby effectively crowding out other cases since the court can only decide about 140 cases per year. He further argues that judicial preoccupation with initiative measures will increase with the increasing utilization of this process by ballot proponents.

[70]Federalist No. 10.

How Does the Initiative Affect Minorities and the Poor?

The social science literature on the effect the initiative process has had on minorities is not as vast or as persuasive as the literature on the nonpartisan/at-large electoral systems.[71] It is instructive to note, however, that one legal scholar has drawn a direct comparison to both issues. Professor Derrick Bell has concluded:

> Referenda and initiatives are "at-large elections" on issues instead of candidates. Just as multimember districts have the potential of minimizing or cancelling out the voting strength of racial or political groups in the election of officials, referenda and initiatives have a similar effect on direct legislation. In both cases the strength of the minority will be diluted.[72]

Julian N. Eule, another legal scholar, reviewed the social science and census data used by David Magleby, Raymond Wolfinger and S. Rosenstone, T. Cronin, W. Burnham, S. Verra and N. Nie, in their studies, and concludes:

> Minorities, the poor, and the uneducated are thus doubly underrepresented in the plebiscite. They are both less likely to turn out and less likely to vote on propositions if they do.[73]

And since voters with less education rely more on the political parties for their voting cues,[74] they are less able, on complex and technical issues, to translate their political preferences into votes.[75]

---

[71]A couple of the most extensive studies on the initiative process have been conducted by Professors David Magleby and Thomas Cronin. See David Magleby, *Direct Legislation: Voting on Ballot Propositions in the United States* (Baltimore: Johns Hopkins University Press, 1984); and Thomas Cronin, *Direct Democracy: The Politics of Initiative, Referendum, and Recall 79* (Cambridge: Harvard University Press, 1989). Magleby concludes that legislatures are more sensitive to the concerns of minorities than the results of the initiative process, but Cronin does not.

[72]Derrick A. Bell, Jr., "The Referendum: Democracy's Barrier to Racial Equality," *Wash. L. Rev.* 54 (1978): 1, 25.

[73]Julian N. Eule, "Judicial Review of Direct Democracy," *Yale Law Journal* 99 (1990): 1503, 1515.

[74]David Magleby, *Direct Legislation: Voting on Ballot Propositions in the United States* (Baltimore: Johns Hopkins University Press, 1984).

[75]See Julian N. Eule, "Judicial Review of Direct Democracy," *Yale Law Journal* 99 (1990): 1515.

Most of the social and political science literature focus on education and housing issues.[76] This evidence demonstrates that the initiative process works to the disadvantage of the poor and minority groups.

Professor Bell suggests that the courts, in reviewing the efficacy of the initiative process, should apply the same standards used in reviewing "at-large" elections.[77] This is a powerful suggestion because of the potential for challenging the initiative process under the Voting Rights Act with its well-defined standards. And since this list is neither comprehensive nor exclusive, the initiative process, as an electoral mechanism, may be tested for adverse or discriminatory affects against minorities using standards and methodologies for examining the data that are well defined.

There are a few social and political science studies that have examined the impact of the initiative process on minorities[78] and one that addresses the particular issue of the Voting Rights Act.[79] Benjamin and Marcus examined the referendum process in the city of New York in elections between 1975 and 1989. They utilized a multivariate regression methodology and came to a conclusion similar to Elaine Sharp's, that there is racial polarity in voting on initiative measures. That being the case, they further conclude that the courts could apply the Voting Rights Act to the referendum process.

The cost of conducting an initiative campaign is prohibitive. It precludes effective participation by the average voter. Because racial minorities tend to be financially less well off, they are less inclined to be involved in initiative campaigns. In 1988, special interest groups raised and spent more than $110 million on statewide, county, and city ballot measures in the general election. Sponsors and opponents of the five insurance measures spent more than $83 million, which is more than the total spent by the

---

[76]Howard D. Hamilton, "Direct Legislation: Some Implications of Open Housing Referenda," *The American Political Science Review* 64 (1970): 124-37; Raymond E. Wolfinger and Fred I. Greenstein, "The Repeal of Fair Housing in California: An Analysis of Referendum Voting," *The American Political Science Review* 62 (September 1968): 753-69.

[77]See Derrick A. Bell, Jr., "The Referendum: Democracy's Barrier to Racial Equality," *Wash L. Rev.* 1 (1978): 22-28.

[78]Elaine B. Sharp, "Voting on Citywide Propositions: Further Tests of Competing Explanations," *Urban Affairs Quarterly* 23 (December 1987): 233-48; [Among Sharp's findings was a conclusion that racial polarization existed in the vote on ballot propositions.] See also, E. Cataldo and J. Holm, "Voting on School Finances: A Test of Competing Theories," *Western Political Quarterly* 36 (1983): 619-31.

[79]Gerald Benjamin and Robert Marcus, "Minority Non-Voting in the New York City Charter Referenda: Does the Voting Rights Act Reach the Referendum Process, and Should It?" Prepared for presentation at the annual meeting of the American Political Science Association, September 2, 1990.

presidential candidates on their national campaigns that year. The tobacco industry spent $22 million on a losing cause. The sponsors and opponents of the county and city ballot measures spent approximately $10 to $15 million. According to campaign statements filed with the California Secretary of State, the insurance companies who sponsored the defeated no-fault insurance measure, alone, spent $57 million.

The consulting firm, headed by Clinton Reilly, managed the campaign on behalf of the insurance industry and received $22,038,730. The direct-mail firm, BFC Direct Marketing Firm, received $1,124,580. The signature gathering firm, American Petition Consultants, received $706,389. Two law firms received a total of $626,910. Another direct-mail firm, Direct Communications of San Francisco, received $391,897. Even a law professor from the University of Virginia, Jeffrey O'Connell, received $103,632. Radio and television stations received more than $11 million, newspapers more than $3.3 million, and more than $2.7 million was spent on billboard advertising.[80]

Notwithstanding the popularity of the initiative, referendum, and recall processes, there has not been a recent challenge to their constitutional validity. This is significant because the early constitutional challenges did not consider the recent doctrines of political association, or the Voting Rights Act. And until the initiative is tested against these standards, its legal efficacy will continue to be clouded.

DIRECT PRIMARY

Traditionally, political parties nominated their candidates at party conventions, raised campaign funds, and conducted the campaigns. These are some of the most important functions of political parties. These practices prevailed, in California, prior to the Progressive Era. The reformers convinced the electorate that eliminating these practices would abolish political corruption, democratize the electoral process, and make government accountable to the people. They proposed, as an initial solution, the direct primary for nominating candidates for public office.

The direct primary allows voters to choose candidates without the input from their official party organizations. It was designed to give the individual voter a direct voice in the selection of his or her party's nominees for public office.

California enacted the modern day direct primary in 1908, after the court had invalidated prior primary laws. The primary significance of the California courts' early decisions invalidating the direct primary laws is the recognition that the political parties' associational rights were recognized by

---

[80]*Id.*

the courts more than half a century before the commonly discussed genesis of the doctrine, at least in California.[81] Recently, the courts have applied the doctrine of political association to strengthen the role of political parties in the nomination process[82] but have not invalidated the direct primary as an institution. However, the courts have not applied the standards of the Voting Rights Act to direct primary cases.

The arguments used by the reformers to support the direct primary system are interesting but not persuasive in view of recent evidence. For example, while primary elections prevent party leaders from influencing candidate selection, the direct primary encourages candidates to resort to media politics that require them to raise large sums of money from political

---

[81]In 1896, the California Supreme Court, in *People v. Cavanaugh,* 112 Cal. 674, held that the Purity of Elections Act did not require the political parties to hold primary elections in that "political parties are a law unto themselves as to the conduct of primary elections," p. 676. On March 13, 1897, the state legislature enacted a direct primary law. The court invalidated 11 provisions of this act, in *Speier v. Baker,* 120 Cal. 370 (1898), as violative of the rights of political parties. On March 3, 1899, the state legislature enacted another primary election law, and the Supreme Court immediately invalidated that law in *Britton v. Board of Elections Commissioners,* 120 Cal. 337 (1990), as an infringement of the constitutional rights of minor political parties. Justice Temple, in his concurring opinion, wrote:

> A political party is an association of citizens who agree on certain lines of policy; and the purpose for which it exists is to impose that policy upon the government. This can only be done by electing to office those who are in favor of such policy. It is for this that conventions are held and candidates selected. . . . To deprive the party of this power [to exclude those who do not share its views of policy] is to destroy it." (at p. 347)

The court noted, in *Britton,* that the California Constitution protects political conventions through its declaration of the Bill of Rights, which provides that "the people have the right to assemble freely, to consult for the common good, to instruct their representatives, and to petition the legislature for redress of grievances." (at pp. 342-43)

So while the early decisions invalidating the direct primary laws as invasions of the political parties constitutional rights, the court upheld the 1908 primary law in *Katz v. Fitzgerald,* 152 Cal. 433 (1908). Ironically, the *Katz* decision was authored by Justice Henshaw, who also wrote the principal opinion in *Britton.* It is difficult to see how he could reconcile the logic in both decisions. Nevertheless, the courts, after *Katz,* have uniformly accepted the validity of primary laws. Yet, that does not mean that primary laws don't infringe the parties' right of association.

[82]See *Eu v. San Francisco County Democratic Central Comm.,* 109 S. Ct. 1013 (1989); *Democratic Party v. Wisconsin,* 450 U.S. 107 (1981); *Wigoda v. Cousins,* 419 U.S. 477 (1975); *Williams v. Rhodes,* 393 U.S. 23 (1968); *Ripon Society v. Republican Party,* 525 F.2d 567 (1975).

action committees or special interest groups. This practice favors incumbents and creates the perception of corruption.[83] Such perception creates mistrust of politicians and impugns the integrity of the electoral process.[84] Moreover, the evidence of actual corruption, in modern day politics, illustrates the failure of the reformers' central argument, as well as their purposes.

The necessity of raising money for campaigns, by candidates, sometimes involves practices of "vote trading," or, in other words, legislative corruption. For example, former state Senator Joseph Montoya was convicted, in April 1990, of legislative corruption charges. It was reported that Montoya, a social worker by profession, accumulated after he was first elected to the California state legislature, real estate holdings with an estimated value of two million dollars.[85] This practice is so well accepted that some special interest contributors believe they have a right to special treatment. Charles H. Keating, Jr., the owner of the scandal-plagued Lincoln Savings and Loan made handsome contributions to several U.S. senators, who reportedly intervened on behalf of Lincoln with federal savings and loan regulators. When asked if he expected his contributions to influence those senators, he stated:

> One question, among many raised in recent weeks, had to do with whether my financial support in any way influenced

---

[83]Report of the California Commission on Campaign Financing, *Money and Politics in the Golden State* (Los Angeles: Center For Responsive Government, 1989), 14-15.

[84]See Joe Scott, "Truth and Consequences," *Los Angeles Herald Examiner*, June 2, 1989 (Citing a *Washington Post*-ABC News Poll) See also, "Poll on Lobbyists and Lawmakers," *Pasadena Star News*, June 24, 1990, reporting on a poll conducted by Media General-Associated Press of 1,071 adults. In response to the question: "Which of these do you think is more important to most state lawmakers: passing good laws, or raising money for their reelection campaign?" 51 percent cited "money," and 42 percent cited "laws." In response to another question: "Do you think state lawmakers sometimes vote the way lobbyists want them to in exchange for gifts from lobbyists?" 81 percent responded "yes," and 9 percent responded "no." And finally, in response to the question: "Do you think your state government should limit the amount of money candidates can spend to run for state office?" 89 percent said "yes," and 7 percent said "no."

[85]See "Montoya Known in Capitol Circles as a Strong-willed, Combative Loner," *Los Angeles Times*, May 18, 1989; and see "Nothing Polite About Montoya's Political Style," *Los Angeles Herald Examiner*, May 18, 1989.

several political figures to take up my cause. I want to say
in the most forceful way I can, I certainly hope so.[86]

These two examples illustrate the extent to which the practice of campaign fund raising infects the legislative process, in the absence of political parties. Thus, the central purpose of the direct primary—eliminating political corruption—has not been accomplished. Yet, it has an adverse impact on political parties and minorities.

What Impact has the Direct Primary had on Parties?

The California Elections Code provides that the primary function of the state committees is to conduct the campaigns of its candidates.[87] However, this law is meaningless because candidates prefer to run their own campaigns. The parties have little or no influence in or responsibility for their candidates' electioneering efforts. The candidates invariably hire their own campaign consultants. These professional entrepreneurs perform the services that political parties traditionally performed, such as fund raising and electioneering. The interests of these consultants do not necessarily coincide with the interests of a political party's members or constituents. Some of them work for Democratic and Republican candidates and have no political, philosophical bent. These entrepreneurs engage in preparing slates of candidates that are mailed to the electorate purporting to represent, in appearance, the official "slates" of a particular political party. They often include names of candidates of the opposing party.[88] The only qualification for inclusion on these "slate-mailers" is the payment of a fee to the political

---

[86]See "Vast Investment in State Politics By Keating Told," *Los Angeles Times*, November 23, 1989. This article also details extensive contributions by Keating, his family and associates, to elected officials, including California Governor George Deukmejian. Keating even employed key Deukmejian supporters and appointees.

[87]See Elections Code, Section 8776 provides: "This committee shall conduct party campaigns for this party and in behalf of the candidates of this party. It shall appoint committees and appoint and employ campaign directors and perfect whatever campaign organizations it deems suitable or desirable and for the best interest of the party." This provision applies solely to the Democratic State Central Committee. Elections Code, Section 8940, provides the language for Democratic County Committees. Section 9819 deals with the conduct of campaigns by the Peace and Freedom Party (uses same language as 8776). Section 9688 deals with campaigns for the American Independent Party, and Section 9740, for AIP, County Committees. For the Republican Party, see Section 9276 (state committee) and Section 9440 (county committees).

[88]An example of practice was the "slate-mailer" distributed by political consultant, Basil Kimbrew, in the June 1990 Democratic primary. It was purported to be a Democratic slate, but a registered Republican judicial candidate bought onto the slate, which was sent to Democratic voting households.

consultant. Party officials have expressed outrage with entrepreneurial slate mailers that imply political party endorsements of the candidates promoted on them.[89] This practice may be equated to voter fraud, which ultimately impugns the integrity of the electoral process. Unlike the political party, political consultants do not seek to reconcile conflicting interests of constituent groups within a party coalition to win elections and, therefore, have no need to seek the voice of minorities or views of any other groups in primary elections.

Second, the direct primary takes control of the nomination process from the party. This makes it difficult for the parties to create "balanced tickets," or slates of candidates reflective of the ethnic, religious, and ideological groups that comprise a party's constituents.[90] The more control a party's leadership has over the nomination process, the easier it is to form and maintain party coalitions.[91] Professor Weisburd argues persuasively that a party's associational rights are implicated in the nomination process.[92]

Third, just as in nonpartisan elections, the direct primary makes it difficult for parties to recruit candidates who share the views and party platform of the party.

Fourth, until recently,[93] California law prohibited the political parties from endorsing or supporting candidates in partisan primaries and nonpartisan elections. These prohibitions forced party activists to establish unofficial party organizations for the purpose of endorsing and supporting candidates. Some of these groups, historically, have been more instrumental in the success of candidates than the official party organizations.[94]

---

[89]See "Political Mailer Criticized," *Long Beach Press Telegram*, June 5, 1988, C5.

[90]Dennis S. Ippolito and Thomas G. Walker, *Political Parties, Interest Groups and Public Policy: Group Influence in American Politics*, 177.

[91]Arthur M. Weisburd, "Candidate-Making and the Constitution: Constitutional Restraints on and Protections of Party Nominating Methods," *S. Cal. L. Rev.* 57 (1984): 213. Party leaders are able to obtain compromises between different groups in the party, develop a "party line," or coherent policy positions, and require discipline of elected officials.

[92]*Ibid.*

[93]See *Eu v. San Francisco County Democratic Central Comm.*, 109 S. Ct. 1013 (1989) [The U.S. Supreme Court held that California's prohibitions on party endorsements in partisan primaries violated the First Amendment rights of association and speech.]; *Geary v. Renne*, No. 88-2875 (9th Cir., filed August 14, 1990). [The Ninth Circuit Court of Appeals invalidated California's constitutional prohibition against parties endorsing in nonpartisan races as a violation of the First Amendment of the U.S. Constitution.]

[94]For a thorough discussion of the unofficial party organizations, see James Q. Wilson, *The Amateur Democrat* (Chicago: University of Chicago Press, 1962).

California Republican Assembly. In March 1934, the California Republican Assembly (CRA) was founded after the 1932 defeat of Republican President Herbert Hoover by Franklin Delano Roosevelt. The Democrats, riding on Roosevelt's "coattails," won a majority of California's congressional delegation for the first time in this century. Democrats made significant inroads into the Republican controlled state assembly.

The CRA sought to reassert "progressive" Republicanism, under the leadership of Earl Warren, Goodwin Knight, and Richard Nixon. They believed that the leadership of the Republican party was too conservative and too old.

The formation of the CRA was a direct challenge to the official Republican party organization. This was a telling moment, a "watershed" if you will, for all political parties in California. For the first time, it demonstrated the extent of the impotence of the political parties in California, after institution of the Progressive Era reforms.

CRA succeeded in restoring Republican dominance in California politics. Nearly all candidates endorsed by the CRA won the Republican primary. In 1942, all CRA endorsed statewide candidates won in the primary and went on to win the general elections. CRA did not endorse in the race for attorney general, and a Democrat won that office.

In 1964, the CRA abandoned its moderate image and endorsed Arizona Senator Barry Goldwater over New York Governor Nelson Rockefeller for president. At this time, members of the John Birch Society were gaining in influence within the CRA. This led to the CRA adoption of conservative "antiminority" positions. In fact, there were frequent clashes between the moderate leadership of the CRA and the archconservative Birchers. This more conservative position was not enough for some of the Goldwater supporters who bolted CRA to form another organization.

In 1990, the CRA refused to endorse the gubernatorial candidacy of U.S. Senator Pete Wilson because of his proabortion and environmental positions. Yet, the CRA refused to endorse Dr. William Allen, a conservative African-American candidate, who opposed Wilson and supported the abortion and environmental positions of the CRA. The CRA's failure to endorse Dr. Allen, a Claremont College professor and ideological soulmate of the conservatives within that organization, indicates that minorities continue to have difficulty influencing the deliberations of the Republican party political associations.

The United Republicans of California. In 1963, Goldwater Republicans felt the CRA was too liberal and formed the United Republicans of California (UROC). This organization endorsed and supported the victories of Ronald Reagan for governor in 1966, and the primary election of arch-conservative senatorial candidate, Max Rafferty, in 1968, over incumbent U.S. Senator Thomas Kuchel.

The California Republican League. In 1964, Nelson Rockefeller Republicans, who considered the CRA and UROC organizations too conservative, formed the California Republican League (CRL). The CRL remains the most liberal of the Republican party organizations. It enjoyed it greatest prominence in 1974 when the Republicans nominated their most liberal slate of candidates.

The California Democratic Council. The California Democratic Council (CDC) was formed in 1953 by the grass-roots Democratic clubs. Alan Cranston, the present senior U.S. senator, was elected CDC's first president. It's effectiveness was immediately apparent. In 1954, every CDC endorsed statewide candidate won their respective primary races. In 1958, CDC's influence was at an all-time high. Every CDC endorsed candidate was successful in the primary election, and each of them won the general election, except Henry P. Lopez, the Democratic nominee for secretary of state. This exception was and is significant because it demonstrates that racial minority candidates require more than ordinary support from their political parties because discrimination against racial minorities, in the electorate, remains formidable. When political parties ignore this fact, they do it to the party's peril. If the parties do not provide extraordinary support to their minority candidates, they unwittingly contribute to the defeat of their minority candidates.

Minorities have historically had little influence in the CDC. Nate Holden, who is a black Los Angeles city councilman, was elected president of the CDC. Quincy Beaver, a longtime CDC activist, has served in high level positions for more than a decade. With these exceptions, minorities have not had considerable impact on the activities of the CDC.

What Impact has the Direct Primary had on Minorities?

As previously noted, minorities have had little or no influence on the electioneering efforts of the political consultants or the candidate selection, endorsement, and electioneering processes of the unofficial political party organizations in California.

Black Political Associations. In the early 1960s, Los Angeles Congressman Augustus Hawkins and Oakland Assemblyman Byron Rumford founded the Negro Political Action Association of California (NPAAC). The impetus for the formation of NPAAC was the defeat of Assemblyman Rumford for a state senate seat in Alameda County, the passage of Proposition 14, a measure supportive of housing discrimination against minorities, and dissatisfaction with the results of the 1961 reapportionment process under the Democrats. NPAAC was successful in its efforts to elect Reverend James E. Jones to the Los Angeles Board of Education in 1965. Four years later, Reverend Jones was defeated by Ralph Poblano, a Mexican American, when the organization split and two of its most prominent members—Los Angeles City Councilman Billy Mills and Assemblyman Mervyn Dymally—backed

Poblano. This split sealed the fate of African-American united support for black candidates for more than a decade.

The Black American Political Association of California, (BAPAC), under the leadership of Assembly Speaker Willie L. Brown, was founded in the 1970s. BAPAC has functioned as an arm of Speaker Brown's political operation. It has chapters throughout the state where there are significant numbers of black voters. While it endorses candidates, it can not claim to have been primarily responsible for the success of any particular candidate—unlike the victory of NPAAC in Reverend Jones' 1965 race.

Of course, organizations such as the National Association for the Advancement of Colored People (NAACP), Congress of Racial Equality (CORE), the Urban League, the Student Non-Violent Coordinating Committee (SNCC), and the Southern Christian Leadership Conference (SCLC) have had some minimal impact on the political process through their civil rights activities. Since they are legally prohibited from engaging in political activities, they are not expected to impact the electoral process. *Mexican American Political Associations.* During the early part of the 20th century, Latino political power was systematically decimated by electoral reforms. Frustrated by these reforms, they organized the Community Service Organization of Los Angeles (CSO) and in 1949 elected Edward R. Roybal to the Los Angeles City Council. Chapters of the Texas-based veterans organization, GI Forum, operate in California's Mexican-American community encouraging and supporting candidates for office. Another Texas-based organization, the Southwest Voter Registration Project, engages primarily in voter registration drives to enlist Latinos on the voter rolls in California, as well as other southwestern states.

The most visible Latino political association is the Mexican American Political Association (MAPA). It was founded in 1959 by Edward Quevedo and Bert Corona. The impetus for forming MAPA was the 1958 defeat of Henry P. Lopez, the Democratic party's candidate for secretary of state. He was the only statewide Democratic party candidate defeated in that election. Latinos felt that the Democratic party's leadership did not give Lopez the support he needed to win. MAPA is the largest and best organized ethnic political organization in the state. It recruits candidates and engages in voter registration and get-out-the-vote drives. It takes stands on issues and lobbies government agencies and officials on behalf of Latinos.

In summary, a cursory view of California's experience with the direct primary demonstrates that it weakens the political parties by denying them the right to exercise their traditional functions in a number of areas. They are even curtailed in their ability to perform the one function specifically sanctioned in the Elections Code—running the political campaigns of their candidates. It also impedes the ability of minority groups to influence the direct primary candidate selection and electioneering processes because of an inordinate reliance on professional campaign consultants.

And while the courts have begun to restore some of the traditional functions of political parties by applying the doctrine of association, they have not applied the standards of the Voting Rights Act to the direct primary. Since an historical survey of discrimination in California, as the court laid out in *Gomez v. City of Watsonville*, meets one of the tests of the Voting Rights Act, it should not be difficult to prove, at least one of the other tests such as polarized voting in the direct primary. When that is done, a case can be made that the direct primary is subject to challenge under the Voting Rights Act.

CONCLUSION

The failure of the Progressive Era reforms have been a costly lesson for American democracy in that they undermined fundamental democratic values that are embodied in the role and functions of political parties. They have also undermined the electoral influence of minorities and the economically disadvantaged. And while these values—freedom of speech and association—coupled with the voting franchise are enshrined in the Constitutions of the United States and California, only recently have scholars and the courts begun to grapple with the significance of these liberties to the ability of political parties to perform their natural functions, and to assess the impact these reforms have had on the franchise of racial minorities. In the process of dealing with these issues, certain conclusions are unavoidable.

First, the arguments used to support the reforms of the Progressive Era are no longer valid, if they ever were. Although it is difficult to compare the extent of corruption when the reforms were adopted with that of today, it is quite clear that the problem of corruption remains a very serious issue. It may even be argued that the present system encourages corruption.

Second, political parties have become so weak they cannot perform the functions of helping the economically disadvantaged and minorities, and even if they could, minorities have had little or no influence in their decision-making processes. The functions of political parties are largely performed by political consultants who are usually hired by individual candidates or proponents of ballot initiatives. These consultants are political entrepreneurs who do not seek to reconcile conflicting interests of constituent groups of a political party. This usually results in minorities not being consulted about their views on a particular candidate or ballot measure. Additionally, minorities cannot compete with the special interest groups who infuse such enormous sums of money into the electoral process, making their effective participation almost prohibitive.

Third, in California's experience, the nonpartisan/at-large electoral systems demonstrate their adverse impact on the ability of political parties to perform their natural functions, and on the political interests of the economically disadvantaged and racial minorities.

Fourth, the direct primary weakens political parties and impedes the ability of minorities to influence the candidate selection and electioneering processes of primary elections.

Fifth, minorities have had to resort to their own political associations to advance and protect their interests, and they have had only limited success.

Sixth, while the courts have begun to restore some of the rights of political parties by applying the First Amendment doctrine of association in direct primary cases, this doctrine should also be applied in cases involving the initiative process and at-large/nonpartisan electoral systems. On the other hand, the courts have applied the tests of the Voting Rights Act primarily to cases involving at-large/nonpartisan systems, but it should also apply these tests in cases involving the initiative process and direct primary.

REFERENCES

Adrian, Charles R. "Some General Characteristics of NonPartisan Elections." *American Political Science Review* 46 (1952): 766-81.

Banfield, Edward, and James Q. Wilson. *City Politics.* Cambridge, Ma.: Harvard University Press, 1966.

Barker, Lucius J., and Jesse J. McCorry, Jr. *Black Americans and the Political System.* Boston: Little, Brown and Co., 1980.

Bell, Derrick A., Jr. "The Referendum: Democracy's Barrier to Racial Equality," *Wash. L. Rev.* 54 (1978): 1.

Benjamin, Gerald, and Robert Marcus. "Minority Non-Voting in the New York Charter Referenda: Does the Voting Rights Act Reach the Referendum Process, and Should It?" Prepared for the annual meeting of the American Political Science Association, September 2, 1990.

Berdon, Robert I. "The Constitutional Right of the Political Party to Chart its own Course: Defining Its Membership Without State Interference." *Suff. Univ. L. Rev.* 22 (1988): 933.

Berg, Larry L., and Craig B. Holman. "The Initiative Process and its Declining Agenda-Setting Value." *Law & Policy* 11 (October 1989): 451.

Bledsoe, Timothy. "A Research Note on the Impact of District/At-Large Elections on Black Political Efficacy. *Urban Affairs Quarterly* 22 (September 1986): 166-74.

Browning, Rufus P., Dale Rogers Marshall, and David H. Tabb. *Protest is Not Enough: The Struggle of Blacks and Hispanics for Equality in Urban America.* Berkeley: University of California Press, 1984.

California Commission on Campaign Financing. *Money And Politics In The Golden State.* Los Angeles: Center For Responsive Government, 1989.

Caltado, E., and J. Holm. "Voting on School Finances, etc." *Western Political Quarterly* 36 (1983): 619-31.

Cassel, Carol A. "The Nonpartisan Ballot in the United States." In *Electoral Laws and their Political Consequences*, edited by Bernard Grofman and Arend Lijphart. New York: Agathon Press, Inc., 1986, 232.

Converse, Phillip E. *The Dynamics of Party Support: Cohort-Analyzing Party Identification.* Beverly Hills: Sage Publications, 1976.

Cornwell, Elmer E. "Ethnic Group Representation: The Case of the Portuguese." *Polity* 13 (1980): 5-20.

Cronin, Thomas. *Direct Democracy: The Politics of Initiative, Referendum, and Recall.* Cambridge: Harvard University Press, 1989.

Crouch, Winston W., John C. Bollens, and Stanley Scott. *California Government and Politics.* Englewood Cliffs, New Jersey: Prentice-Hall, Inc., 1981.

Dahl, Robert A. *Pluralist Democracy in the United States: Conflict and Consent.* Chicago: Rand McNally & Co., 1967.

_____. *Polyarchy: Participation and Opposition.* New Haven: Yale University Press, 1971.

Davidson, Chandler, and George Korbel. "At-Large Elections and Minority-Group Representation: A ReExamination of Historical and Contemporary Evidence." *Journal of Politics* 43 (1981): 982-1005.

Davidson, Chandler, and Luis Ricardo Fraga. "Slating Groups as Parties in a 'NonPartisan' Setting." *Western Political Quarterly* vol. 41, no. 2 (June 1988).

Dorsen, Norman. *Frontiers of Civil Liberties.* New York: Pantheon Books, 1968.

Engstrom, Richard, and Michael McDonald. "The Election of Blacks to City Councils: Clarifying the Impact of Electoral Arrangements on the Seats/Population Relationship." *American Political Science Review* 75 (June 1981): 344-55.

_____. "The Effect of At-Large versus District Elections on Racial Representation in U.S. Municipalities." In *Electoral Laws and their Political Consequences,* edited by Bernard Grofman and Arend Lijphart. New York: Agathon Press, 1986.

Eule, Julian. "Judicial Review of Direct Democracy." *Yale Law Journal* 99 (May 1990): 1555.

Fallon, Richard H., Jr. "What is Republicanism And Is It Worth Reviving?" *Har. L. Rev.* 102 (1989): 1695.

Gillette, Clayton P. "Plebiscites, Participation, and Collective Action in Local Government Law." *Mich. L. Rev.* 86 (1988): 930.

Gordon, Daniel N. "Immigrants and Urban Governmental Forms in American Cities, 1933-60." In *The Ethnic Factor in American Politics,* edited by Brett W. Hawkins and Robert A. Lorinskas. Columbus, Ohio: Charles E. Merrill Publishing Co., 1970.

Gottlieb, Stephen E. "Rebuilding the Right of Association: The Right to Hold A Convention as a Test Case." *Hofstra L. Rev.* 11 (1982): 191.

_____. "Government Allocation of First Amendment Resources." *Univ. of Pitt. L. Rev.* 41 (1980): 205.

Grofman, Bernard, and Arend Lijphart. *Electoral Laws and their Political Consequences.* New York: Agathon Press, Inc., 1986.

Gurin, Patricia, Shirley Hatchett, and James S. Jackson. *Hope & Independence: Blacks' Response to Electoral and Party Politics.* New York: Russell Sage Foundation, 1989.

Guttman, Julia. "Primary Elections and the Collective Right of Freedom of Association." *Yale L. J.* 94 (1984): 117.

Hamilton, Charles V. *The Black Experience in American Politics.* New York: G. P. Putnam's Sons, 1973.

Harvey, Richard B. *The Dynamics of California Government and Politics.* Belmont, California: Wadsworth Publishing, 1971.

Hawkins, Brett W., and Robert A. Lorinskas. *The Ethnic Factor in American Politics.* Columbus, Ohio: Charles E. Merrill Publishing Co., 1970.

Hawley, Willis. *Nonpartisan Elections and the Case for Party Politics.* New York: John Wiley, 1973.

Hays, Samuel P. "The Politics of Reform in Municipal Government in the Progressive Era." *Pacific Northwest Quarterly* 55 (October 1964).

Hofstadter, Richard. *The Idea of a Party System.* Berkeley, Ca.: University of California Press, 1969.

Hyink, Bernard L., Seyom Brown, and Ernest W. Thacker. *Politics and Government in California.* New York: Thomas Y. Crowell Company, Inc., 1975.

Ippolito, Dennis S., and Thomas G. Walker. *Political Parties, Interest Groups and Public Policy: Group Influence in American Politics.* Englewood Cliffs, N.J.: Prentice Hall, Inc., 1980.

Jones, Clinton. "The Impact of Local Election Systems on Black Representation." *Urban Affairs Quarterly,* 11 (March 1976).

Karnig, Albert K., and Susan Welch. *Black Representation and Urban Policy.* Chicago and London: University of Chicago Press, 1980.

_____. "Electoral Structure and Black Representation on City Councils." *Social Science Quarterly* 63 (March 1982).

Karnig, Albert K. "Black Representation on City Councils: The Impact of District Elections and Socioeconomic Factors." *Urban Affairs Quarterly* 12 (December 1976): 223-42.

Kenney, Patrick J. "Sorting Out the Effects of Primary Divisiveness in Congressional and Senatorial Elections." *Western Political Quarterly* 41 (December 1988).

Key, V. O. *American State Politics: An Introduction.* New York: Knopf, 1956.

Ladd, Everett Carll, Jr. *American Political Parties: Social Change and Political Response.* New York: W. W. Norton & Co., 1970.

Lane, Robert E. *Political Life: Why People Get Involved in Politics.* Glenco, Ill.: Free Press, 1959.

Lawson, Kay, and Peter Merkl. *When Parties Fail: Emerging Alternative Organizations.* Princeton: Princeton University Press, 1988.

Lee, Eugene C. *The Politics of Nonpartisanship.* Berkeley and Los Angeles: University of California Press, 1960.

_____. "Hiram Johnson's Great Reform is an Idea Whose Time has Passed." *Public Affairs Report,* Institute of Governmental Studies, University of California, Berkeley, July 1990.

Levy, Mark R., and Michael S. Kramer. *The Ethnic Factor: How America's Minorities Decide Elections.* New York: Simon & Schuster, 1973.

Lineberry, Robert, and Edmund Fowler. "Reformism and Public Policies in American Cities." *American Political Science Review* 61 (September 1967).

Lovrich, Nicholas P., Jr., Charles H. Sheldon, and Erik Wasmann, "The Racial Factor in NonPartisan Judicial Elections: A Research Note." *Western Political Quarterly*, vol. 41, no. 4 (September 1988).

Lowi, Theodore J., and Benjamin Ginsberg. *American Government: Freedom and Power*. New York and London: W. W. Norton & Co., 1990.

MacManus, Susan. "City Council Election Procedures and Minority Representation." *Social Science Quarterly* 59 (June 1978): 153-61.

_____. "At Large Elections and Minority Representation: An Adversial Critique." *Social Science Quarterly* 60 (November 1979): 338-40.

Main, Jackson Turner. *Political Parties Before the Constitution*. New York: W. W. Norton & Co., Inc., 1973.

Madison, James. *National Gazette*. 1792.

_____. *Note to Speech on the Right of Suffrage*. Ca. 1821.

Magleby, D. B. *Direct Legislation: Voting on Ballot Propositions in the United States*. Baltimore: Johns Hopkins University, 1984.

Miller, Phillip L. "The Impact of Organizational Activity on Black Political Participation." *Social Science Quarterly* 62 (March 1982).

Mladenka, Kenneth. "Blacks and Hispanics in Urban Politics." *American Political Science Review* 83 (March 1989b): 165-91.

Morrison, K. C. Minion. *Black Political Mobilization*. Albany: State University of New York Press, 1987.

Owens, John R., Edmond Costantini, Louis F. Weschler. *California Politics and Parties*. Canada: The MacMillan Company, 1970.

Parenti, Michael. "Ethnic Politics and the Persistence of Ethnic Identification." *American Political Science Review* (19..): 717-26.

Piven, Frances Fox, and Richard A. Cloward. *Why Americans Don't Vote*. New York: Pantheon, 1988.

Polsby, Nelson W. *Consequences of Party Reform*. New York: Oxford University Press, 1983.

Pomper, Gerald. "Ethnic and Group Voting in Nonpartisan Elections." *Public Opinion Quarterly* (Spring, 1966): 95.

_____. "The Contribution of Political Parties to American Democracy." In *Party Renewal in America: Theory and Practice*, edited by Gerald M. Pomper. New York: Praeger Publishers, 1980.

Ranney, Austin. *Curing the Mischiefs of Factions: Party Reform in America*. Berkeley: University of California Press, 1975.

Ranney, Austin and Willmoore Kendall. *Democracy and the American Party System*. New York: Harcourt, Brace and Company, 1956.

Renner, Tari. "Municipal Election Processes: The Impact on Minority Representation." In *The 1988 Municipal Yearbook*. Washington: The International City Management Association, 1988.

Richards, David A. J. "A Theory of Free Speech." *UCLA Law Rev.* 34 (1987): 1837.

Riker, William H. *Democracy in the United States*. New York: The MacMillan Company, 1953.

Robinson, Theodore, and Thomas Dye. "Reformism and Black Representation on City Councils." *Social Science Quarterly* 63 (March 1982).

Sabato, Larry. *The Rise of Political Consultants*. New York: Basic Books, 1971.

Schattschneider, E. E. *Party Government*. New York: Holt, Rinehart & Winston, 1942.

Schockman, H. Eric. "Nonpartisan City Elections Produce a Leadership Ship." *Los Angeles Times*, February 4, 1990.

Scott, Gary L., and Craig L. Carr. "Political Parties Before the Bar: The Controversy Over Associational Rights." *Univ. of Puget Sound L. Rev.* 5 (1982): 267.

Scott, Ruth K., and Ronald Hrebenar. *Parties in Crisis: Party Politics in America*. New York: John Wiley & Sons, 1984.

Sharp, Elaine B. "Voting on Citywide Propositions: Further Tests of Competing Explanations." *Urban Affairs Quarterly* 23 (December 1987): 233-48 .

Sonenshein, Raphael J. "Black Factions and the Origins of Biracial Coalitions." Paper prepared for presentation at the annual meeting of the American Political Science Association, August 1990.

Sorauf, Frank J. *Political Parties in America*. Boston: Little, Brown and Company, 1984.

Sunstein, Cass R. "Interest Groups in American Public Law." *Stan. L. Rev.* 38 (1985): 29.

_____. "Beyond the Republican Revival." *Yale L. J.* 97 (1988): 1539.

Trilling, Richard J. *Party Image and Electoral Behavior*. New York: John Wiley & Sons, 1976.

Turner, Henry A., and John A. Vieg. *The Government and Politics of California*, 4th ed. New York: McGraw-Hill, Inc., 1971.

Verba, Sidney and Norman Nie. *Participation in America*. New York: Harper and Row, 1972.

Walton, Hans, Jr. *Black Political Parties*. New York: The Free Press, 1972.

Wattenberg, Martin. *The Decline of American Political Parties*. Cambridge, Ma.: Harvard University Press, 1986.

Weisburd, Arthur M. "Candidate-Making and the Constitution: Constitutional Restraints on and Protections of Party Nominating Methods." *S. Cal. L. Rev.* 57 (1984): 213.

Welch, Susan. "The Impact of At-Large Elections on the Representation of Blacks and Hispanics." Paper prepared for presentation and presented at the annual meeting of the American Political Science Association, August 1990.

Welch, Susan, and Timothy Bledsoe. *Urban Reform and its Consequences: A Study in Representation.* Chicago, Ill.: The University of Chicago Press, 1988.

Welch, Susan, and Eric H. Carlson. "The Impact of Party on Voting Behavior in a Nonpartisan Legislature." *American Political Science Review* 72 (1973).

Wilson, James Q. *The Amateur Democrat.* Chicago: Univ. of Chicago Press, 1962.

Wolfinger, Raymond E. "The Development and Persistence of Ethnic Voting." In *The Ethnic Factor in American Politics,* edited by Brett W. Hawkins and Robert A. Lorinskas. Columbus, Ohio: Charles E. Merrill Publishing Co., 1970.

Zax, Jeffrey S. "Election Methods and Black and Hispanic City Council Membership." *Social Science Quarterly* 71 (June 1990).

CHAPTER 11

DWAINE MARVICK
University of California at Los Angeles

Ethnic Officeseeking and Party Activism in Los Angeles

Why do some minority ethnic groups take greater advantage of the political route to power and success than others? In Los Angeles, as elsewhere, the inclusion of ethnic minorities in the ranks of elected officialdom has been structured by opportunities keyed to vacancies, political boundaries, and minority electoral clout. Not only must the political geography be conducive to success but effective minority candidates and supportive campaign activists must also exist.

Nothing succeeds like success, of course. Once a candidate succeeds, he or she is *ipso facto* viewed as effective and formidable. Getting reelected is relatively easy; stepping up to a higher office is a plausible option, should opportunity arise.   Still, the tempo of success varies from minority to minority, and much depends on the track record of earlier fellow minority aspirants.[1]

The chances for an ethnic officeseeker to use the elected route to power are also shaped by the presence of fellow ethnics in the active political stratum and particularly in the party organizational life of the locally dominant party. In activist circles, if such an officeseeker lacks enthusiastic support from fellow ethnics, he or she is not likely to be taken seriously.

Apart from the question of how effective the various minority-status groups have been in supporting and advancing political careers for their own spokesmen and leaders, it matters also whether the grooming and sponsorship has come from Republicans, Democrats, or from group coalitions of various kinds. Notably different track records have characterized various groups of elective officeseekers in Los Angeles County in the years 1960 through 1985.[2]

---

[1]Fernando J. Guerra, "Ethnic Officeholders in Los Angeles," *Sociology and Social Research*, vol. 71, no. 2 (Jan. 1987): 89-94.
[2]*Ibid.*

Further analysis of their selection as candidates and of the campaign events that highlighted each step in their political careers is needed to clarify among other things the relative significance of ethnic community support, on the one hand, and sponsorship by partisan leaders and resources, on the other.

To explore some of the ways in which ethnic and partisan subcultures are interrelated, one presently available point of ingress is to examine the participation patterns and attitudes of Los Angeles party activists who have specific ethnic cultural affiliations. This paper follows that line of investigation. Using interview data with Democratic and Republican activists throughout Los Angeles County gathered periodically since 1968, it is possible to compare the attitudes and participation levels of blacks, Latinos, Jews, and others under notably contrasting political conditions. Moreover, within each of these ethnic subcommunity categories it is possible to distinguish officeseekers from other activists.

To anticipate our findings, three significant contrasts can be observed—in income levels, ideological stance, and ethnic-religious affiliation. Overall, annual incomes are about $4,000 higher for Republicans than for Democrats. But other social characteristics vary more by ethnic and religious types regardless of party.

Ideologically, most Republicans call themselves conservatives; the rest say they are moderates. Most Democrats consider themselves liberals; and, again, the rest call themselves moderates. But as we shall see, "moderate" means something quite different in terms of issue preferences when Republicans and Democrats use the term. And, however they characterize their own ideological viewpoint, the minority activists in both parties are distinctive—both when their views on minority-sensitive issues are examined and also when questions of defense, environment, and inflation are raised.

In Los Angeles, it has often been said that the rival major parties differ more in terms of religious composition than ethnicity. Only in a relatively small number of state legislative districts do blacks and Latinos respectively dominate the grass-roots party machinery of both parties and also control nonpartisan city politics in those locales. On the other hand, Jews appear to dominate the Democratic apparatuses in many districts of Los Angeles while white Christians wield power disproportionately in most Republican local and district-level units.

On some counts—certain policy questions, campaign tactics, and political beliefs—ethnic groups in both cities do register quite distinctively. Nevertheless, it is clear that on most counts the behavior and outlook of party activists do not vary systematically along either ethnic or religious lines. Rather, certain ideological, programmatic, and stylistic hallmarks of Democratic and Republican party life are present regardless of the ethnic or religious composition of the party's local organizational roster. Evidently, political subcultures can largely—though not entirely—override ethnic and religious socialization patterns, at least on the range of questions to be examined here. It is to such an analysis that we now turn.

UCLA PARTY ACTIVIST PROJECT

Since 1968 the UCLA Party Activist Project has been studying those who serve on the Los Angeles County committees of the two major parties. We have not been studying what the county committees do, but what kinds of people serve on them. Indeed, for our research purposes, the two major party county committees are simply legally prescribed composite structures that are convenient grids for sampling *equivalent* rosters of Republican and Democratic party activists. However, a word about the political significance of the two county committees is necessary.

Whether the work of either party's county committee is important today or has been so in the past is a rather complicated question. The two major parties are not alike. Each in the past has developed a county-level organization that was influential for a time at fund raising, candidate recruitment, and campaign coordination. For the past several decades, each party's county committee (and its secretariat) has been a rather unwieldy unit, which many activists feel is too large and too faction-ridden to provide effective coordination for the various campaigns mounted throughout the county every two years. In practice, moreover, these campaigns are independently mounted by those directly involved at the district and locality levels of party life.

By law, all parts of Los Angeles County are represented on each party's county committee. Each of the (currently) 27 assembly districts sends a delegation of seven, elected at primary time for two-year terms.[3] Rather spirited contests occur. In both parties, it is not uncommon for 10 to 15 people—many of them presidents or active figures in local party clubs—to compete for the county committee member positions. In a number of districts, rival slates recurrently are fielded by intraparty factions. Turnover is substantial; in 1978 and 1980, for example, approximately 40 percent of the incumbents who sought reelection were not successful, which is a considerably higher attrition rate than incumbent aspirants for state or national legislative office face.

For academically oriented research purposes, the county committees do provide an excellent sample frame. In 11 surveys since 1963, the UCLA project has used the rosters of the Republican and Democratic county committees as legally prescribed composite assemblies that are convenient

---

[3]Since 1980, a number of districts have straddled county lines, partly in Los Angeles county, partly in Orange, or Ventura, or Riverside. Accordingly, delegations from these districts have been proportionately smaller than seven.

grids for sampling *equivalent* sets of rival party activists. Not only does this sample frame guarantee geographic diversity, but it also mirrors (with equivalent weight built in for each party) the varied patterns of apathy, rivalry, and complacency to be found in different localities. And delegations from politically sure territory, doubtful areas, and lost terrain are represented on each party's county committee roster in due proportions.

POLITICAL COMPLEXION

Our surveys show that under one-third in each party describe their home district as Republican territory while nearly three-fifths say they live in Democratic terrain. Only about one-tenth consider their home district to be competitive ground.

As Table 1 discloses, blacks and Latinos are much less likely than their fellow activists to think of their home districts as Republican terrain and much more likely to report living in Democratic strongholds. Parenthetically, when pre-1976 responses are contrasted with those made from 1976 on, there are signs that some activists in both groups are changing their minds, that is, they are slightly less likely to view their neighborhoods as sure territory for Democrats, either because they live in less segregated areas now or because loyalty to the Democratic party is seen as having declined somewhat.

In Table 1 and all other tables of this article, Jews as well as blacks and Latinos are reported separately. Just as growing up in a black or Latino neighborhood shapes the outlook of those ethnic activists, so also we expect to find certain patterns of behavior and belief that reflect the secular and subcultural features of Jewish life styles, features that are part of the early family and neighborhood socialization experiences. In our tables, the categories do not overlap; that is, blacks and Latinos are first defined, and the rest are then classified as Jewish or other.

ETHNIC ENCLAVES

Only 14 percent of our informants say their home districts have no minority voter blocs. Certain assembly districts (roughly one-fourth) are overwhelmingly black or Latino in Los Angeles County, and delegations from these areas add quite a few blacks and Latinos to each party's county committee. At the same time, it is rare for the makeup of a seven-person district delegation to reflect the presence of minorities proportionately. About 30 percent in each party say their legislative district includes large minority voter blocs. But much larger proportions of black and Latino activists in both parties report that their home districts have such an ethnic character. However, not all minority-status party activists agree that their home district is an ethnic enclave. Table 2 summarizes the picture as

Table 1: *Ethnicity By Political Character of Assembly District*
"In Partisan Terms, How Would You Describe Your State Assembly District?"

	Republican Activists				
	Republican Locale %	Competitive Locale %	Democratic Locale %	Total 100%	N
Black	10	9	81	4.3	77
Latino	25	12	63	3.3	60
Jewish	38	9	63	4.5	81
Other	34	12	54	87.9	1,585
	32	12	56	100.0	
N	(583)	(207)	(1,013)		(1,803)

Gamma: -.29

	Democratic Activists				
	Republican Locale %	Competitive Locale %	Democratic Locale %	Total 100%	N
Black	9	4	86	10	194
Latino	20	11	70	9	172
Jewish	28	9	63	28	536
Other	42	12	46	40	1,016
	32	11	57	100.0	
N	(620)	(202)	(1,096)		(1,918)

Gamma: -.40

assessed by individual activists, when they are asked the ethnic character (as generally understood) of the home districts in which they work.

Asked to appraise the ethnic composition of their home district, about one-third of the 4,600-plus party activists in our 1968-1988 database said that it included large minority enclaves. For seven districts out of the 31 in Los Angeles County, our informants agreed to that description by better than two to one. Table 2 shows the large percentages among blacks in both parties (65 percent R, 65 percent D) who considered the legislative district

Table 2:   *How Party Activists Characterize the Ethnic Composition of Home District*

| | Republican Activists | | | | |
| | Home District Has | | | | |
	Large Ethnic Blocs %	Small Ethnic Blocs %	Almost No Ethnic Blocs %	Total 100.0	N
Black	65	26	9	4.2	74
Latino	39	46	15	3.5	61
Jewish	25	34	41	4.4	77
Other	31	40	29	87.8	1531
	32	39	28	100.0	
N	(564)	(684)	(295)		(1,743)

Gamma: -.21

| | Democratic Activists | | | | |
| | Home District Has | | | | |
	Large Ethnic Blocs %	Small Ethnic Blocs %	Almost No Ethnic Blocs %	Total 100.0	N
Black	65	25	10	10.1	190
Latino	48	35	17	9.0	169
Jewish	29	40	31	28.0	529
Other	27	41	32	52.9	998
	33	39	28	100.0	
N	(630)	(732)	(524)		(1,886)

Gamma: -.26

in which they were active to include a large minority community. Somewhat less segregated were the Latinos in both parties, somewhat under half of whom (39 percent R, 48 percent D) said that large minority blocs characterized their home district. No significant differences on this count seem to mark the response patterns of Jews and others among our activist-informants.

Using this as a basis for classifying localities, it can be said that in both parties, three-fourths of the activists worked in districts that were generally considered by activists to consist largely of a single ethnic or religious subculture. Relatively few blacks, either Republican or Democratic, were active in Jewish or Anglo neighborhoods. A majority were found in black enclaves and more than a quarter in Latino-dominated localities. The Latino pattern is rather different. On the one hand, more than one in four in each party worked in Latino enclaves. But very few Republican Latinos worked in areas not dominated by any single ethnic group, while almost one-fourth of Democratic Latinos did so.

AGE, MARITAL STATUS, GENDER, YEARS OF RESIDENCE

The two party organizations in Los Angeles County both draw heavily upon middle-aged, middle-class men and women whose voluntary commitment to party work both during and between campaigns is often both constant and great, although their ranks have thinned in recent years. In each party, nearly two-thirds are married with dependent-age children. About three-fourths are men. On average, both committees are getting older. In the years before 1976, the average Republican was 47 and the typical Democrat was 44. Since 1976, the age of a typical worker has jumped three years in both parties.

On average, they have lived for more than 30 years in California and for about 17 years at their current address. Los Angeles County for years has experienced a constant influx of newcomers, but the party activists of both parties, in ethnic enclaves as well in more diversified neighborhoods, are long-time residents. See Table 3.

SES, EDUCATION, INCOME, AND OCCUPATION

Whatever their ethnic or religious community status, a clear majority of party activists in Los Angeles are comfortable, well-off, middle-class citizens. Overall, Republicans enjoy a modest income advantage—about $4,000 a year—over their Democratic counterparts. In both camps, the most affluent were Jewish. The average Jewish Republican activist earned about $17,000 more a year than his black or Latino co-workers. The edge was less marked among the Democrats, but Jewish activists in that party also averaged $7,000 to $8,000 more than did their black or Latino co-workers.

Table 3:   *Family Status of Ethnic Party Activists in Los Angeles County*

| | Republican Activists | | | | | |
	Single, No Kids %	Single, Some Kids %	Married, No Kids %	Married, Some Kids %	Total	N
Black	18	13	5	64	4.4	98
Latino	21	5	5	69	3.5	77
Jewish	26	4	20	50	4.5	99
Other	18	7	9	66	52.0	1,154
	19	7	9	65	100.0	
N	(424)	(153)	(210)	(1,458)		(2,220)

Gamma: .09

| | Democratic Activists | | | | | |
	Single, No Kids %	Single, Some Kids %	Married, No Kids %	Married, Some Kids %	Total	N
Black	15	11	15	59	10.0	223
Latino	17	6	7	70	8.5	190
Jewish	26	5	8	60	27.5	613
Other	22	8	9	61	54.0	1,205
	21	7	10	62	100.02	
N	(486)	(161)	(211)	(1,373)		(2,231)

Gamma: .26

Both recently and in the earlier years, about two-thirds of our Republican activists and Democratic activists alike are college graduates. In both periods, Democrats and Republicans are equally likely to have gone on to graduate or professional schools. In both parties a mix of executive and professional jobs predominates, with Republicans slightly less likely to be doctors or lawyers, and a bit more likely to hold executive posts. Few sales

Table 3: *Age-Sex Characteristics of Ethnic Party Activists (continued)*

	Younger Male %	Younger Female %	Older Male %	Older Female %	Total	N
	Republican Activists					
Black	14	5	52	29	4.4	98
Latino	43	9	39	9	3.5	77
Jewish	48	7	27	18	4.5	99
Other	35	8	35	22	52.0	1,152
	35	8	36	21	100.0	
N	(775)	(182)	(806)	(480)		(243)

Gamma: -.01

	Younger Male %	Younger Female %	Older Male %	Older Female %	Total	N
	Democratic Activists					
Black	28	13	39	20	10.0	223
Latino	36	15	34	15	8.5	190
Jewish	43	12	29	16	27.5	613
Other	35	9	39	17	54.0	1,203
	37	11	36	17	100.0	
N	(818)	(246)	(794)	(371)		(2,229)

Gamma: .03

or clerical workers and even fewer blue-collar workers are active in either party. See Table 4.

POLITICAL PARTICIPATION

For the most part, these men and women who make up the organizational cadres of the two major parties in Los Angeles County are volunteers. For ethnic minorities as well as majoritarian stock, more than half say they

Table 4:   *Social Characteristics of Los Angeles Activists*

Life Cycle Characteristics of Ethnic and Religious Types, by Party

	Age (average)		Years in Calif. (average)	
	R.	D.	R.	D.
Black	57	47	33	28
Latino	46	45	33	34
Jewish	45	44	32	29
Other	48	48	35	32
All respondents	49	46	34	31

Socio-Economic Status Characteristics of Ethnic Activists, by Party*

	Low SES		Full College	
	R. %	D. %	R. %	D. %
Black	44	46	52	61
Latino	43	56	62	44
Jewish	24	26	72	76
Other	37	39	64	69
All respondents	37	38	64	68

are very active in the grass-roots clubs that exist in virtually every neighborhood. During campaign weeks, in all parts of the county, activists in both parties average about 29 hours a week of campaign effort. Moreover, as Table 5 shows, these activists have been constant for many years in their partisan work; 17 is the average number of years of active party participation.

Still, it should be noted that politics in southern California is not entirely an unpaid hobby for the activists. About one-fourth of the Republicans acknowledge having held a patronage position (that is, a paid noncivil-service government job). A closer look shows this to be true for

Table 4:   *(continued)*

Life Cycle Characteristics of Ethnic and Religious Types, by Party

Years at Same Address (average)		Women		Married with Children	
R.	D.	R.	D.	R.	D.
		%	%	%	%
23	15	34	33	64	59
20	19	18	30	69	70
17	15	25	28	50	60
18	17	30	26	66	61
18	16	30	28	65	62

Socio-Economic Status Characteristics of Ethnic Activists, by Party

Income (000's)		Exec. or Prof. Occupation		Cases	
R.	D.	R.	D.	R.	D.
		%	%		
28	27	52	60	99	223
27	25	63	48	77	190
45	34	70	71	102	613
33	28	59	62	1,966	1,205
33	29	60	63	2,244	2,231

Note: Socio-Economic Status (SES) is measured by trichotomizing three variables—income, education, and occupational stress—and giving them equal weight in a composite index called SES.

only 20 percent of the Jewish activists but for 48 percent of the blacks and 33 percent of the Latinos in organized Republican ranks. By comparison, only 33 percent of Democratic blacks could match them, a proportion rather similar to the patronage levels enjoyed by other Democratic activists.

Table 5:   *Political Participation of Ethnic and Religious Activists*

	Years Active (average)		Campaign Work Hours/Week (average)		Very Active in Local Party	
	R.	D.	R.	D.	R. %	D. %
Black	23	17	32	29	66	63
Latino	13	15	26	29	60	48
Jewish	15	16	27	30	50	49
Other	16	18	29	28	53	50
All respondents	16	17	29	29	53	51

	Patronage Job Held		Cases	
	R. %	D. %	R.	D.
Black	48	33	99	223
Latino	33	28	77	190
Jewish	20	27	102	613
Other	25	31	1,966	1,205
All respondents	26	30	2,244	2,231

ETHNIC COMPOSITION OF RIVAL MAJOR PARTIES

Table 6 summarizes the composition of rival major party ranks in Los Angeles, by time period, in terms of the four ethnic cultural groupings found in both parties. It further subdivides each of these groupings into those who have sought and/or held elective public office and those who have never done so, thus distinguishing what will be called "officeseekers" from "organizational activists."

The ethnic makeup of the two major parties is sharply different, with only token representation of blacks, Latinos, and Jews in the Republican party, where seven out of eight come from majoritarian backgrounds. The contrast between parties is striking. The Democratic ranks give significantly larger representation to Jews (27 percent), Latinos (9 percent), and blacks (10 percent). Within each party the profiles of ethnic and religious representation are remarkably constant, whether one is comparing the early and later time periods or whether one is seeking to contrast party activists

Table 6: *Ethnic and Religious Composition of Party, by Time Period and Public Office Records*

	Republicans			Democrats		
	1968-74 %	1976-88 %	All %	1968-74 %	1976-88 %	All %
Black	5.4	3.5	4.4	9.2	10.6	10.0
Latino	3.8	3.1	3.4	9.9	7.4	8.5
Jewish	3.5	5.5	4.5	26.8	28.0	27.5
Other	87.3	87.9	87.7	54.1	56.0	56.0
Cases	(1,066)	(1,178)	(2,244)	(980)	(1,251)	(2,231)

A. Among Those Who Never Sought or Held Public Office

	Republicans			Democrats		
	1968-74 %	1976-88 %	All %	1968-74 %	1976-88 %	All %
Black	4.4	3.2	3.7	10.0	10.9	10.6
Latino	4.8	2.0	3.1	10.2	7.0	8.2
Jewish	3.9	6.0	5.2	29.3	29.3	29.3
Other	86.9	88.8	88.0	50.5	52.8	51.9
Cases	(482)	(745)	(1,227)	(420)	(716)	(1,136)

B. Among Those Who Have Sought or Held Public Office

	Republicans			Democrats		
	1968-74 %	1976-88 %	All %	1968-74 %	1976-88 %	All %
Black	7.1	3.9	5.3	9.0	10.3	9.7
Latino	3.9	4.8	4.4	11.5	8.0	9.5
Jewish	3.2	4.6	4.0	25.5	26.2	25.9
Other	85.8	86.7	86.3	54.0	55.5	54.9
Cases	(309)	(433)	(742)	(400)	(535)	(935)

who have personally sought public office and those who never have done so. Among Republicans, the activist ranks are overwhelmingly majoritarian; only 3 or 4 percent are blacks, Latinos, or Jews. Quite different is the makeup of the Democratic roster. More than twice as many blacks and Latinos and six times as many Jewish activists are found in the Democratic camp. In both parties, activists with majoritarian credentials still predominate, although they are barely a majority among Democrats, and Jews account for better than one in every four active Democrats.

Essentially, it is the absence of noteworthy differences in Table 6 that calls for comment. Apparently the ethnic composition of the major party activist rosters in Los Angeles County is quite stable over several decades. Not only is this true of each party's officeseekers then and now, but it also holds for those party organizational personnel who have never sought public office.

Tables 7 and 8 probe the party office and public office patterns more closely, looking at the records of those ethnic activists in each party who have ever (a) held neighborhood club (7 in every 10) or district committee (4 in every 10) party organization offices and (b) ever sought schoolboard, city council, or legislative public office (true for about 1 in every 8, on all three counts).

In the Republican party, voluntary organizational officeholding at the *neighborhood* level is discernibly higher for Latinos than for the other minority types, while among Democrats only the blacks are somewhat underrepresented as club leaders.

The composition of party councils at the legislative *district* level shows discernibly high Latino figures and somewhat diminished representation for blacks in both major parties. As much as anything, this is probably a structural consequence of the way Los Angeles party organizations have long been fashioned to fit assembly-district boundaries.

As for public office seeking, Table 8 shows that—for school board posts, city council seats, and state legislative or congressional offices alike—both parties have in their activist ranks about 1 in every 8 who has aspired to incumbency. Nearly every fifth Republican black has sought a school-board post, while Latinos in both parties are especially interested in city council posts.

When the two parties are contrasted in terms of the ethnic and religious affiliations of the legislative aspirants among their activist ranks, it is noteworthy that blacks and Latinos are substantially more likely to have run under Republican auspices while majoritarian-status Democrats have proportionately better chances of Democratic sponsorship. On the one hand, this may reflect a willingness to sponsor blacks and Latinos in certain "lost" districts where no Republican has much chance to win; on the other hand, it may reflect an unwillingness among Democrats to back minority candidates in the kind of ethnically diverse districts in which mainstream

Table 7:   *Party Officeholding Records Among Ethnic and Religious Activists*

	Held Local Party Office		Held District Party Office		Would Accept Key Party Post		Cases	
	R.	D.	R.	D.	R.	D.	R.	D.
	%	%	%	%	%	%		
Black	61	59	33	27	79	85	83	211
Latino	73	70	44	41	78	72	71	182
Jewish	64	76	39	49	74	71	91	575
Other	70	75	44	45	67	67	1,068	814
All respondents	69	73	43	44	68	70	1,945	2,058

Table 8:   *Public Office Records Among Ethnic and Religious Activists*

	Sought School Board Office		Sought City Council Office		Sought Legislative Office		Cases	
	R.	D.	R.	D.	R.	D.	R.	D.
	%	%	%	%	%	%		
Black	18	9	11	12	24	12	84	211
Latino	10	8	19	18	28	18	71	182
Jewish	11	9	6	12	13	17	94	575
Other	10	8	12	18	14	22	1,720	1,103
All respondents	11	9	12	16	15	20	1,969	2,071

nominees have a good chance to win. The patterns are complex and require closer analysis keyed to the kind of district involved.

PATTERNS OF POLITICAL SOCIALIZATION

Table 9 discloses that, for our composite 1968 through 1988 samples of major party activists, one in every five Republicans and Democrats alike grew up in a family environment in which the parents were active in party affairs and/or active in community affairs. The rest were reared in less politicized homes. A rather different pattern emerges when we look at the current friendship circles of party activists; more than one-half in both parties report having many friends who are also active in politics. Party activists, in other words, typically live in a social context where many of their daily associates are also greatly concerned with politics and public affairs. In a sense, their social circles as well as their party activist efforts work to set

Table 9:   *Patterns of Political Socialization Among Ethnic and Religious Activists*

	Parents Active In Party Work		Parents Active In Civic Work		Friends Active in Organized Politics		Cases	
	R.	D.	R.	D.	R.	D.	R.	D.
	%	%	%	%	%	%		
Black	35	22	38	26	59	62	45	146
Latino	14	24	7	28	47	56	38	100
Jewish	9	16	15	16	43	58	63	383
Other	18	19	20	19	52	60	1,156	759
All respondents	18	19	20	19	52	59	1,302	1,388

them apart from ordinary citizens, whose political thoughts and actions are lukewarm and indifferent.

When the differences among ethnic and religious types are examined, however, some noteworthy points emerge. First, nonminority activists in both parties closely reflect the 1-in-5 ratio on all three counts. Second, blacks in both parties are most likely to have been reared in politicized homes. Third, Republican Latinos and Jews tend to report apolitical parental examples while their Democratic counterparts (especially Latinos) more frequently had activist parents. Fourth, Republican Jews are notably unlikely to have politically active friends while blacks in both parties are just the opposite. Finally, although these differentials suggest interesting lines of inquiry, it should be noted that *most* party activists in all categories appear to have rather impoverished histories of political socialization and about one-half spend the bulk of their adult daily lives in social circles peopled by largely apathetic citizens.

APPRAISALS OF MANIPULATORY TACTICS

Regularly since 1968, the UCLA party activist surveys have included a battery of questions asking informants to assess how well various controversial campaign tactics are likely to work, if directed at the local Republican and Democratic voters in their home legislative district.

Several points emerge when these data are examined. Table 10 reflects only the down side of the picture, by reporting what percentages of our activist informants *deny* that emotionalizing, personalizing, negativizing, counter-smearing, and stressing self-interest rather than community needs would be efficacious campaign tactics where they live. Among Republican activists, an average of 51 percent deny that such tactics would work, while a slightly lower level of tactical rejection (44 percent) comes from our

Table 10: *Denial of the Efficacy of Manipulative Campaign Tactics (in percentages)*

	Blacks		Latino		Jews		Other		All Respondents	
	R.	D.	R.	D.	R.	D.	R.	D.	R.	D.
In my home district, it is *poor* tactics to . . .										
Personalize the choice	53	42	46	39	42	38	44	36	44	38
Emotionalize the choice	52	48	59	51	51	51	57	52	56	51
Countersmear	45	46	60	56	43	43	53	49	53	48
Negativize the choice	61	47	45	45	36	41	48	47	48	45
Stress self-interest	40	41	56	44	41	41	50	43	49	42
Index (Avg)	50	45	54	51	40	40	51	45	51	44
Cases	88	195	64	167	76	487	990	717	1,844	1,821

Democratic informants. Jews in both parties are somewhat more likely to assess such tactics as effective ones. Latinos are especially negative about the use of countersmears as a way of meeting rival charges; Republican blacks do not like the idea of stressing the rival's bad record instead of one's own performance and plans. Apart from these special points, the pattern that Table 10 discloses is remarkably alike for each party and for each manipulative tactic—namely, a substantial level of negative evaluations on count after count.

PARTISANSHIP AND IDEOLOGY

Among party activists, one might suppose that feelings of strong partisanship would be widespread. Since 1968, the UCLA surveys have included a self-anchoring 8-point scale ranging from "strong" to "weak," and our informants have been asked to rate themselves. Perhaps surprisingly, only about half in each party rate themselves at the strongest end of the scale. As Table 11 shows, with minor variations, the same proportions are found when a breakdown by ethnic and religious types is made. Jews are a little low (48 percent) and Democratic blacks rather high (59 percent), but these levels may simply reflect vagaries in our samples. More surprisingly, perhaps, no substantial findings have come from a systematic effort to establish whether strength of partisanship among party activists works in ways analogous to its importance in guiding the political behavior and outlook of ordinary voters. From our data, it does not significantly help to predict greater levels of participation or involvement, more substantial conformity to party norms, heightened acceptance of the modal policy stands espoused by one's party, or any of a range of similar propositions keyed to the notion of partisanship in the voting behavior literature. Further analysis may cause revision of such a conclusion, but evidently once activated as a party worker, a different set of dynamics takes over, shaping how active one is, how zealous, how orthodox, how militant. Asking party activists to rate their own partisanship does not produce a variable that has great analytical power.

Quite different is the consequence of asking party activists to characterize themselves ideologically. As Table 11 dramatically shows, Republicans call themselves "conservatives" rather than "moderates" by 2-to-1 margins, and rarely use the term "liberal"; Democrats choose "liberal" by a similar margin and avoid the word "conservative." Each party has two remarkably stable ideological wings.

Looking at the ethnic breakdown introduces a few wrinkles worth mentioning. Among Republicans, Jews and Latinos are somewhat less likely to call themselves conservatives, and blacks are decidedly unlikely to do so, but there are relatively few minorities in that party. Among Democrats, it is Latinos that tend to call themselves moderates (40 percent) almost as

Table 11: *Partisanship and Ideology Among Ethnic and Religious Activists*

| | Self-Styled Strong Partisan | | Self Characterization of Ideology | | | | | | | |
| | | | Republicans | | | | Democrats | | | |
	%	%	Csv. %	Mod. %	Lib. %	Cases	Csv. %	Mod. %	Lib. %	Cases
Black	52	59	21	58	20	96	4	37	59	212
Latino	57	47	63	37	0	73	6	40	54	185
Jewish	49	48	64	33	7	93	2	20	78	596
Other	51	48	52	41	3	1,118	5	36	59	848
All	51	49	61	35	4	2,153	3	32	65	2,145

frequently as liberals (54 percent), while 78 percent of the Jews choose the word "liberal" to describe themselves.

ISSUE PREFERENCES

In each survey since 1968, the Los Angeles activists were asked what role the federal government should take in coping with various policy issues. On question after question, *each* ideological type—both the dominant wing and its moderate counterpart in each party—has a distinctive pattern of issue preferences that runs across foreign and domestic, defense, environmental, economic, and social welfare foci.

As the breakdowns in Table 12 for each of seven questions show, a fourfold spectrum of emphasis on the desirability of federal intervention persists. Overall, the ideologically dominant wings in each party are almost as different from their party's moderate wing as one party's moderates are from the other party's moderates. The ideological cleavages within each party appear to be almost as marked as the gulf between their moderates.

The various issues summarized in Table 12 can be divided into a set of three *minority-sensitive questions* and a set of four *mainstream problems*. Specifically, the latter focus on nuclear disarmament, defense spending, environmental pollution, and the cost of living—issues that have ideological overtones not distinctively keyed to minority status. The minority-sensitive questions are somewhat different—opportunities for the poor, desegregation of schools and housing, and *not* trying to solve inner-city problems simply by "getting tough" with urban violence.

Table 12: *Public Issue Preferences Among Ethnic and Religious Activists By Affiliation with Ideological Party Wing*

A. Want federal government to do more about nuclear disarmament

	Republican		Democratic	
	Conservatives %	Moderates[a] %	Moderates[b] %	Liberals %
Black	46 (13)	51 (57)	67 (81)	81 (110)
Latino	29 (41)	22 (23)	60 (78)	80 (95)
Jewish	16 (45)	22 (41)	73 (119)	90 (435)
Other	20 (1,018)	36 (562)	64 (417)	89 (626)
All respondents	20 (810)	36 (683)	66 (695)	88 (1,266)

B. Want federal government to do more about controlling the cost of living

	Republican		Democratic	
	Conservatives %	Moderates[a] %	Moderates[b] %	Liberals %
Black	50 (16)	73 (63)	79 (84)	85 (110)
Latino	49 (41)	60 (25)	70 (80)	83 (92)
Jewish	30 (43)	49 (39)	70 (119)	79 (424)
Other	41 (1,019)	54 (566)	74 (415)	83 (620)
All respondents	41 (1,119)	56 (693)	74 (698)	82 (1,246)

C. Want federal government to do more about cutting defense spending

	Republican		Democratic	
	Conservatives %	Moderates[a] %	Moderates[b] %	Liberals %
Black	25 (12)	41 (51)	58 (74)	73 (106)
Latino	15 (33)	40 (20)	47 (62)	85 (82)
Jewish	7 (42)	16 (37)	61 (104)	89 (397)
Other	10 (935)	21 (515)	56 (366)	86 (577)
All respondents	10 (1,022)	23 (623)	56 (606)	86 (1,162)

Table 12: *(continued)*

D. Want federal government to do more to stop air and water pollution

	Republican				Democratic			
	Conservatives %		Moderates[a] %		Moderates[b] %		Liberals %	
Black	50	(12)	85	(53)	78	(49)	86	(103)
Latino	41	(34)	70	(20)	84	(62)	95	(81)
Jewish	33	(39)	53	(34)	79	(104)	94	(392)
Other	36	(885)	49	(502)	76	(362)	92	(562)
All respondents	36	(970)	53	(609)	77	(602)	92	(1,138)

E. Want federal government to do more to expand opportunities for the poor

	Republican				Democratic			
	Conservatives %		Moderates[a] %		Moderates[b] %		Liberals %	
Black	80	(15)	78	(64)	90	(83)	94	(114)
Latino	40	(43)	46	(24)	74	(81)	87	(95)
Jewish	21	(44)	48	(40)	69	(117)	94	(432)
Other	19	(1,011)	34	(559)	66	(418)	90	(629)
All respondents	20	(1,113)	39	(687)	70	(699)	91	(1,270)

F. Want federal government to do more to desegregate housing and schools

	Republican				Democratic			
	Conservatives %		Moderates[a] %		Moderates[b] %		Liberals %	
Black	36	(14)	70	(63)	77	(83)	88	(113)
Latino	12	(43)	33	(24)	44	(78)	65	(95)
Jewish	0	(44)	18	(40)	43	(118)	79	(430)
Other	5	(1,022)	14	(555)	35	(414)	70	(623)
All respondents	5	(1,123)	20	(682)	42	(693)	75	(1261)

Table 12:　*(continued)*

G. Want Federal Government *not* to do more to get tough with urban violence

| | Republican | | Democratic | |
	Conservatives %	Moderates[a] %	Moderates[b] %	Liberals %
Black	27　(15)	26　(62)	25　(83)	30　(105)
Latino	17　(42)	17　(24)	30　(79)	45　(93)
Jewish	18　(45)	39　(38)	30　(118)	53　(408)
Other	23　(1,035)	24　(561)	33　(404)	52　(595)
All respondents	23　(1,137)	26　(685)	32　(684)	50　(1,201)

ABCD: Composite Leftist Averages on Four Mainstream Issues:

| | Republican | | Democratic | |
	Conservatives %	Moderates[a] %	Moderates[b] %	Liberals %
Black	43	63	71	80
Latino	34	48	65	86
Jewish	22	35	71	88
Other	27	40	68	88
All respondents	27　(1,032)	42　(652)	70　(650)	87　(1,203)

EFG. Composite Leftist Averages on Three Minority-Sensitive Issues:

| | Republican | | Democratic | |
	Conservatives %	Moderates[a] %	Moderates[b] %	Liberals %
Black	48	58	64	71
Latino	23	32	49	66
Jewish	13	35	47	75
Other	16	24	45	71
All respondents	16　(1,056)	28　(685)	48　(692)	72　(1,244)

---

[a]Includes a few liberals.
[b]Includes a few conservatives.

By averaging the *leftist* response on each item for the two sets of issues, and plotting the results separately for blacks, Latinos, Jews, and Others who have been classified according to *which ideological* wing of the Republican and Democratic party they belong to, two points are clarified. First, in every case, the ideological slope as one moves from RC to RM to DM to DL is discernible, although it is strongest for Jews, somewhat foreshortened for Latinos, and notably high and almost flat for blacks. Second, in every case, including the blacks, there is less enthusiasm for the leftist response on the minority-sensitive questions than on the mainstream issues.

CONCLUSION

This article has made an inventory of the backgrounds and views of organizational activists and officeseeking activists in the Republican and Democratic partisan ranks of Los Angeles County.

1. There is clear evidence that blacks and Latinos work largely in districts that are minority enclaves and that also are seen as Democratic strongholds.

2. Regardless of ethnic or minority affiliation, activists in Los Angeles are middle-aged, middle-class men and women, married and long settled in their communities. In both parties, they are well educated, often in professional or executive occupations, and with typical incomes of $35,000 to $45,000. But it is perhaps noteworthy that Democratic activists have typically been somewhat poorer—averaging $4,000 a year less than their Republican counterparts.

3. From the ranks of Republican and Democratic party workers, about one in five have aspired to local school board or city council seats, or have run for the state legislature or Congress. Of our activist informants, substantial majorities in all ethnic and religious types have held voluntary party club offices, and about two in every five have served at the translocal district level of party affairs.

4. Only a minority of our informants (one in five) grew up in politically attuned family environments. For the rest, their parents were neither active in party politics nor civic affairs. As for their current daily associates, the same ratio applies; only one in five say most of their friends are also active in politics. Again, the patterns disclosed for ethnic and religious minorities are not strikingly different from those of majority stock men and women.

5. In compositional terms, it has often been noted that the rival parties in Los Angeles differ more along religious than ethnic lines. Only in the seven or eight assembly districts out of 30 that are either largely black or largely Latino do activists and elected officials with appropriate ethnic credentials dominate the grass-roots party machinery of both parties and also control the nonpartisan municipal politics of the area.

6. Ideologically it is abundantly clear that each party has a dominant wing flanked by a smaller moderate wing. Across the party ideological space from Republican conservatives through moderates to Democratic liberals, there is clear evidence of ideological consistency on a range of persistent domestic and foreign issues. Perhaps the most surprising pattern apparent is one that shows a slightly weaker ideological pattern on three "minority-sensitive questions" than is to be found on four "mainstream problems." This is true across all five ethnic and religious categories used in the present analysis.

7. On some counts, such as specific policy issues, campaign tactics or officeseeking focus, the different ethnic groups do register quite distinctively. Still, it is necessary to say that on most counts neither the behavior nor the outlook of party activists seem to vary systematically either along ethnic or religious lines. Rather, certain ideological, programmatic, and stylistic hallmarks of Republican and Democratic party life are present. As noted earlier, evidently political subcultures can largely override ethnic and religious socialization patterns, at least on the range of questions reviewed here.

Figure 1: *Mainstream Issue Views Ethnic and Religious Party Activists (by Ideological Wings of Rival Parties)*

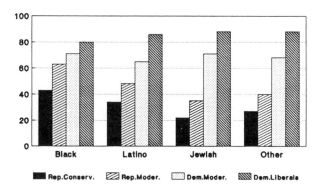

Leftist Percentage on Four-Issue Index

Figure 2: *Minority-Sensitive Issue Views Ethnic and Religious Party Activists (by Ideological Wings of Rival Parties)*

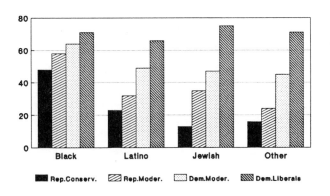

Leftist Percentage:Three-Issue Index

CHAPTER 12

RICHARD SANTILLAN
California State Polytechnic
FEDERICO A. SUBERVI-VÉLEZ
University of Texas—Austin

Latino Participation in Republican Party Politics in California

On November 8, 1988, Vice-President George Bush received a significant share of the Mexican-American vote in California, which contributed to his overall victory against Democratic challenger Governor Michael Dukakis of Massachusetts. Estimates of the actual percentage of the Mexican-American vote for Bush in California range between 25 percent and 40 percent.[1] Regardless of the final tally, the unmistakable fact remains that the Republican party continues to make important inroads among Mexican Americans who have often been viewed as faithful supporters of Democratic presidential candidates.

The unexpected nationwide Latino turnouts for both President Ronald Reagan and George Bush throughout the 1980s have caught many Democratic leaders by surprise, but a closer examination of this electoral turnabout plainly reveals that for nearly four decades the GOP has been methodically chipping away at this formerly solid block of loyal Democrats. This increasing Latino support for Republican presidential candidates cannot be merely dismissed as a political fad, but rather must be seen as the continuation of a detailed Republican blueprint conceived during the 1952 Eisenhower campaign to establish a new voting arrangement between the GOP and Latinos. These ongoing Republican efforts are, in large part, a direct political response to the increasing importance of the Latino vote in several key electoral states.

During the past four years, the authors of this article have interviewed over 200 Latino Republican leaders nationwide regarding the campaign strategies and public relations activities of the Republican party. In addition, the authors have closely scrutinized GOP materials and files which,

---

[1]Steve Tamaya, "Dukakis big winner among state's Hispanics," *The Inter-City Express*, December 22, 1988. Also, telephone interview with Susan Gonzales, former vice-chair of the Republican National Hispanic Assembly of San Diego, February 8, 1989, Washington, D.C.

when pieced together, provide an extraordinary insight into the Republican master plan to develop a political partnership with specific sectors of the Latino community in the critical swing states of California, Texas, and Florida.[2]

This article will explore two dimensions regarding the developing affinity of some Mexican Americans with Republicanism in California. The first part presents an historical overview of the Republican party's presidential strategies between 1952 and 1988 to attract Mexican-American voters into its ranks. The political cornerstone of this strategy is that the GOP views the Latino community as a socially and economically diversified community, whereas the Democratic party continues to politically treat the Latino community as a homogeneous interest group. As a result of these opposing political frames of mind, Republican presidential candidates, more so than their Democratic counterparts, have been relatively more politically flexible in keeping pace with the fundamental demographic changes taking place inside the Mexican-American and Latino communities. Mexican-American voters, nevertheless, have developed a pattern of switching back and forth between both parties depending on the issues, strategies, and the amount of attention committed by the presidential candidates. Democrats and Republicans have experienced both positive and negative feedback from the Latino electorate during the past 40 years. This ongoing political tug-of-war by both parties for Latino votes during presidential campaigns is the central theme of this first section.

The second part examines a critical element of these outreach programs—public relations and the use of the mass media. Historically, the Republican party has suffered from a negative image problem among many Mexican Americans, based largely on its economic elitism and genuine lack of social and cultural sensitivity towards ethnic and racial groups. In order to try and change this unfavorable perception, the Republican party, especially since the 1972 Nixon campaign, has invested both a considerable amount of time and millions of dollars in its marketing efforts to create the impression of political respectability among certain elements of the Mexican-American population. This section will trace the five distinct stages of these GOP public relations activities. Finally, the conclusion will assess the impact that these Republican campaign strategies and public relations have had on Mexican-American voters in California. It appears that while the GOP has made substantial gains among Latinos for presidential campaigns in recent elections, it has fallen short of most of its political objectives.

The Republican party's "Southwest Strategy," nevertheless, has been a contributing electoral factor in promoting   the recognition of Latino

---

[2]Personal files of Henry Ramírez and Manuel Ruíz, Jr. The files trace back the Republican outreach programs in detail since 1952.

political visibility in the United States. The Republican party, for example, has raised the political stakes against the Democratic party by selecting three Latinos to serve in President Bush's cabinet.

Before our discussion begins, some preliminary comments are required. Prior to the Great Depression of the 1930s, large segments of the Mexican-American community identified with the Republican party. In New Mexico, for example, the Republican party was known as the Hispano party until the early 1930s. In California and Colorado, nearly half of the Mexican-American elected officials between 1860 and 1910 were Republicans.[3] At one time, the GOP was considered to be more socially progressive than the southern-based Democratic party on the issues of civil rights, electoral reform, women's suffrage, and regard for family-oriented farms and small businesses. The Depression was widely viewed, however, as marking the failure of Republican economic policies. Herbert Hoover, the Republican president at the time, made the political mistake of blaming the crisis on the world depression, and believed the solution lay in reducing federal spending. Among his drastic actions was the federal implementation of the Repatriation Program under which thousands of Mexicans (many American citizens) were forcefully deported from the United States.[4] Many of those who remained in the country confronted prejudice and discrimination, and they suffered from the severe social and economic hardships resulting from the lack of steady work.

The election of Democrat Franklin Delano Roosevelt in 1932, and the inauguration of his New Deal, were viewed by many Mexican Americans as a refreshing alternative to Hoover and his unfair policies, and thus, the idea was born that Republicans were solely for the rich, while the Democrats were for the common people. In the 1930s, many Mexican Americans found employment in federal job programs that also deepened their attachment to the Democratic party.

Certain sectors of the Mexican-American community in the 1930s, however, did not have to depend on the federal government for work. Both Mexican-American farmers and businessmen were self-employed and,

---

[3]Fernando V. Padilla and Carlos B. Ramírez, "Patterns of Chicano Representation in California, Colorado, and Nuevo Mexico," *Aztlán: Chicano Journal of the Social Science and the Arts* (Spring and Fall 1974): 189-234. Also, interview with Fernando V. Padilla, December 28, 1988, Los Angeles, California.

[4]Abraham Hoffman, *Unwanted Mexican-Americans in the Great Depression: Repatriation Pressures, 1929-1939* (University of Arizona Press, Tucson, 1974); Neil Betten and Raymond A. Mohl, "From Discrimination to Repatriation: Mexican Life in Gary, Indiana During the Great Depression," *Pacific Historical Review* vol. 42, no. 2 (August 1973) and Daniel T. Simon, "Mexican Repatriation in East Chicago, Indiana," *The Journal of Ethnic Studies* vol. 2, no. 2 (Summer 1974).

therefore, had less reason to shift their political allegiance. As a consequence of this economic self-reliance, Mexican Americans in certain parts of Arizona, New Mexico, and Colorado have tended to remain loyal Republicans over the span of several generations. The majority of these Mexican-American Republicans continue to identify themselves with the moderate wing of the party.[5]

Finally, it should be noted that both World War II and the Korean War tended further to consolidate Mexican-American support for Democratic administrations, largely because of the nationalistic pride of the country and the distinguished service record of Mexican Americans during the terms of Democratic presidents. Furthermore, the G.I. Bill, which was passed during a Democratic administration, made it socially possible for many Mexican-American veterans to purchase homes outside the barrios and to attend school for new job skills. These newfound economic opportunities further cemented the political bond between the Democratic party and the majority of Mexican Americans residing in both the Southwest and the Midwest. In the 1952 presidential campaign, however, the Republican party, then in the hands of the moderates, took the first systematic step toward bringing Mexican Americans back into its political camp after an absence of 20 years.

The presidential campaigns of 1952 and 1956 matched two very different men. General Dwight D. Eisenhower had been a professional soldier all his life, whereas Adlai Stevenson was a career politician and diplomat. In California, Mexican Americans formed a group called Latin-American Veterans and Volunteers for Eisenhower-Nixon.[6] William (Bill) Orozco, who was then the Los Angeles chairman of the group, recalled that it was not difficult finding Mexican-American men to support Eisenhower because many of them had served under General Eisenhower during the war. Many of these veterans were convinced that Eisenhower's military experience and leadership could help end the war in Korea. Henry Ramírez, who later

---

[5]The moderate wing has tended to advocate some federal assistance to combat poverty and housing discrimination, support voting rights, and a diplomatic approach with communist nations. Over the decades, the moderates have included such people as Hiram Johnson, Jacob Javits, Charles Percy, Nelson Rockefeller, Richard Nixon, Lowell Weicker, and George Bush. The conservatives, on the other hand, view the federal government with suspicion and believe that the private sector can solve the social issues plaguing the nation. The conservatives also push for a harder line against communist countries. Historically, this group has been represented by Warren Harding, Herbert Hoover, Robert Taft, Barry Goldwater, Ronald Reagan, and Jack Kemp.

[6]Interview with William (Bill) Orozco, November 16, 1984, Los Angeles, California. Orozco served as the Los Angeles Chairman of the Latin-American Veterans and Volunteers for Eisenhower-Nixon in 1952. In addition, the authors had access to Mr. Orozco's personal files.

served in both the Nixon and Ford administrations, observed that Richard Nixon helped the ticket since Nixon had already attracted some Mexican-American support in California during his early political campaigns for the Congress and U.S. Senate.[7]

Orozco and other Mexican-American organizers, Republican and Democratic, traveled throughout California during both presidential campaigns speaking before sympathetic Mexican-American audiences. Mexican-American involvement in the two Eisenhower campaigns was primarily limited to local efforts in California, Texas, New Mexico, and Illinois. As for Stevenson, there appears to have been no organized Mexican-American outreach programs in either of his California campaigns.[8] Thus, the GOP in the 1950s, moved slightly ahead of the Democratic party in California regarding the recognition of Mexican Americans as part of its overall presidential strategy. The Democratic party in the next two presidential campaigns, however, recaptured the political momentum from the Republican party and further tightened its electoral grip on the Mexican-American community.

The 1960 and 1964 presidential races were political disasters for the Republican party because of the divisive philosophical and platform disagreements between moderates and conservatives within the party.[9] Vice-President Nixon had a lock on the GOP nomination in 1960, but two other Republican leaders, U.S. Senator Barry Goldwater of Arizona and New York Governor Nelson Rockefeller, played prominent roles at the GOP convention. The lack of Republican unity largely contributed to the Democratic victories of John F. Kennedy in 1960 and Lyndon B. Johnson in 1964 and represented a major setback for the Republican effort to effectively reach out to Mexican-American and Puerto Rican voters. This division within the leadership of the GOP also resulted in a lack of unity among some Latinos to back one Republican candidate. Conservative Cuban Americans, for instance, a small but rapidly emerging new group inside the GOP partly blamed the moderate Eisenhower-Nixon administration for losing Cuba to the communists and, therefore, were attracted to Goldwater's staunch anticommunism. Several prominent Cuban Americans of California, for example, provided only lukewarm support for Nixon in his presidential bid against Kennedy in the general election.[10] Furthermore, a sizeable group of moderate Republican Mexican Americans in the Southwest and

[7]Interview with Henry Ramírez, September 2, 1984, Washington, D.C.

[8]Interviews with Nell Soto, January 26, 1986, and Hope Mendoza Schectner, February 4, 1986, Los Angeles, California. Both women walked precincts for the Stevenson campaign in California.

[9]Interview with Manuel Ruíz, Jr., May 21, 1985, Los Angeles, California.

[10]Interview with Henry Ramírez, September 4, 1984, Washington D.C.

some Puerto Ricans on the East Coast threw their support for Rockefeller in both 1960 and 1964. Mexican-American and Puerto Rican Republican leaders were deeply impressed with Rockefeller's knowledge of Latin American culture and his fluency in Spanish. Rockefeller's business investments in Latin American also helped his political campaign because some Mexican-American businessmen believed that Rockefeller as president could provide them economic opportunities in this geographic region. Another major obstacle to Nixon's campaign was that many Mexican-American Democrats, who had supported the Eisenhower-Nixon ticket in the previous two elections, had abandoned Nixon for Kennedy.

Senator Kennedy held several distinct cultural advantages over Nixon in attracting Mexican-American voters in California and elsewhere, including his Catholic and immigrant background, the ability of his wife to speak basic Spanish, and the large and extended families within the Kennedy clan.[11] In addition, Kennedy's war record as a hero appealed to many newly established Mexican-American organizations, the majority of which had been founded by World War II veterans. More important, the 1960 Democratic convention was hosted by the city of Los Angeles, which provided the Mexican-American leadership, especially delegates and leaders of California, access to Kennedy's campaign staff. This political dialogue eventually led to the creation of the "Viva Kennedy" clubs in 13 states representing the regions of the Southwest, the Midwest, and the East Coast.

Nixon really never had an adequate opportunity for incorporating Mexican-Americans and other Latino groups into his 1960 campaign as a result of the aforementioned rift inside the Republican party. The only hint of any active participation of Mexican Americans was strictly limited to several chapters of the "Arriba Nixon" clubs in the southern California region. Kennedy carried nearly 75 percent of the Mexican-American vote in California but lost the state by a very slim margin, made extra close by the high turnout of Mexican-American voters.[12] Nixon received only 13 percent of the nationwide Latino vote.[13] See Table 1.

---

[11]Interview with Bert Corona, July 15, 1974, Los Angeles, California. Corona was one of the founders of the Mexican-American Political Association during the late 1950s in California, and he was very active in the "Viva Kennedy" campaign in Los Angeles. Also, interviews with Joseph Ramírez, June 16, 1986, Omaha, Nebraska; Dante Navarro, August 27, 1986, Milwaukee, Wisconsin; and Jesse Villapando, July 2,1986, Griffith, Indiana. All three men were active in the 1960 "Viva Kennedy" movement in the Midwest.

[12]Mark R. Levy and Michael Kramer, *The Ethnic Factor: How American's Minorities Decide Elections* (New York: Simon and Schuster, 1974), 77-78.

[13]Personal files of Henry Ramírez.

Table 1: *Estimated Percentage of Latino Votes for Presidential Candidates in 1960*

	Kennedy	Nixon
California	75	25
Arizona	75	25
Colorado	75	25
New Mexico	70	30
Texas	91	9
Nationwide	—	—

Source: Mark R. Levy and Michael Kramer, *The Ethnic Factor: How America's Minorities Decide Elections* (New York: Simon and Schuster, 1974), 77-78.

Many of the internal factors that had seriously undermined the Republican party's Latino outreach program in 1960 reappeared in the 1964 presidential race. Once again, the ongoing struggle between both wings of the GOP had split Latino Republicans along ideological and platform differences. Goldwater's Latino support in California came from a small group of conservative Mexican Americans and Cuban Americans. The Cuban community was very determined to help elect Goldwater, especially after the Bay of Pigs fiasco during the Kennedy administration. Moderate Mexican Americans, who labeled themselves as middle-of-the-road Republicans, considered Goldwater's political positions as too extreme. In addition, Mexican-American Republicans in California made several attempts to meet with Goldwater in late 1963 and early 1964 without any real success. Nearly all these proposed meetings did not materialize, including the failure of having Goldwater ride in the traditional September 16 parade through East Los Angeles. Nelson Rockefeller, on the other hand, made several exploratory campaign trips to California in the early 1960s to test the political waters by meeting with some Mexican-American Republican leaders. These informal meetings between Rockefeller and Mexican-American Republicans eventually led to the creation of a national group called Latin Americans for Rockefeller, which maintained a central office in Los Angeles.[14]

---

[14]Interviews with Gabriel R. Guardarramas, February 24, 1985, New York City, New York. The Latin American for Rockefeller organization also had chapters in Arizona, Colorado, Illinois, New Mexico, New York, Pennsylvania, and Texas. Personal files of Manuel Ruíz, Jr.

Goldwater, nevertheless, won a bitter victory over Rockefeller at the 1964 Republican convention held in San Francisco. A Californian, Manuel Ruiz, Jr., was asked to direct the national Latino effort for the Goldwater-Miller ticket. In California, several groups were formed including the Mexican-American Committee for Goldwater-Miller, Latin Americans for Goldwater, Hispanic Citizens for Goldwater, and Latino Youth for Goldwater.

In contrast to the 1960 Kennedy campaign, Mexican-American support for President Johnson in California and elsewhere can best be described as politically soft even with the establishment of the national "Viva Johnson" campaign. The tragic assassination of President Kennedy in November 1963 had dampened Latino support for the 1964 contest and the expected Johnson victory, unlike the close race in 1960, seemed to minimize the national importance of the Mexican-American and Puerto Rican vote. As predicted, President Johnson won in a massive landslide over Barry Goldwater. A postelection study conducted by the Democratic party, revealed that Goldwater did more poorly among Latino voters than Nixon had in 1960.[15] What cannot be overlooked, however, is that the Democratic party as early as 1964 showed some interest regarding Republicanism and the Latino vote. The Democrats believed that the low numbers of Latinos for Goldwater in 1964 did not warrant serious concern for future elections. This political misjudgment would eventually hurt the Democratic party in 1966.

In retrospect, the Kennedy and Johnson "Viva" movements in the early 1960s introduced a new era in the evolutionary development of Mexican-American politics in the United States. Whereas the GOP Latino efforts were primarily limited to a few scattered states in the 1950s, the Kennedy and Johnson campaigns viewed the Latino community as a national constituency from coast to coast. President Johnson, for example, established the Inter-Agency on Mexican-American Affairs, the first federal agency designed to provide policy guidance to congressional lawmakers and the White House concerning the needs of Mexican Americans. Not surprisingly, most of the key staff of the Inter-Agency were chosen from California and Texas, possibly as a tactic to off-set the GOP efforts in these

---

[15]The Democratic Party studied nine wards in Chicago and found Goldwater's electoral strength between 12 percent and 36 percent, compared with 14 percent and 47 percent for Nixon in 1960. In Detroit, six wards presented Goldwater with percentages ranging between 5 percent and 30 percent in contrast to Nixon's 15 percent to 43 percent. This particular study also included the cities of Los Angeles, New York, Philadelphia, Milwaukee, and San Francisco. The major drawback of this election analysis is that while the wards surveyed were predominantly Latino, the majority of the voters were non-Latinos. Authors' personal files.

two vital states. In addition, the Johnson administration made a handful of Mexican-American appointments to subcabinet positions. In general, Mexican-American leaders applauded these federal actions as long overdue. As a consequence of these policies and appointments, the Republican party fell further behind in the early 1960s to the Democrats in its efforts to attract Latino support for GOP candidates.

Ironically, both the Kennedy and Johnson administrations eventually came under political fire from a growing list of Mexican-American Democratic leaders for a host of reasons, including the failure to make higher level appointments of Mexican Americans, a string of broken campaign promises, the lack of adequate federal funds to remedy the pressing problems plaguing the barrios, and the breakdown of communication between the White House and some Mexican-American national organizations. The Johnson administration, as a result of this political pressure, hosted a national conference on Mexican-American issues in El Paso, Texas in 1967.[16] The conference was clearly designed by the Democratic party to diffuse this volatile situation with the Mexican-American leadership, particularly with the 1968 presidential election around the corner. This perceived political neglect by the Democratic party was viewed by some of the party's strongest Mexican-American supporters as "taking the Mexican-American vote for granted" syndrome. By dropping the Mexican-American political football in the mid-1960s, the Democrats generously gave the GOP a second chance to narrow the partisan gap in the presidential contest for Latino votes. The Republican party, the beneficiary of this newfound political fortune, wasted no time in taking the initiative by establishing the now famous "Southwest Strategy" in 1966.[17]

The 1960 federal census had revealed to Republican strategists that a small but flourishing Mexican-American middle-class was emerging in the key electoral states of California and Texas, and they could possibly be persuaded to vote for GOP candidates. The Republican leadership theorized that as Mexican Americans moved upward on the economic ladder, they would most likely identify more with the economic views of the GOP because of their higher social status. The 1966 campaigns of Ronald Reagan for California governor and John Tower for the U.S. Senate seat in Texas

---

[16]Interview with Juan Acevedo, January 22, 1986, and Fernando del Rio, January 21, 1986, Los Angeles, California. Several Democratic Latinos denounced Latino Republicans for distorting the Kennedy-Johnson appointment record. Acevedo, a Kennedy organizer, called GOP Hispanics "phonies" for supporting Eisenhower, Nixon, and Goldwater. Acevedo added that Kennedy had appointed seven California Latinos to federal posts.

[17]Interview with Tirso del Junco, May 2, 1986, Los Angeles, California, and Brownie Trevino, April 24, 1985, Dallas, Texas.

were viewed as a political litmus test regarding this GOP assumption concerning the Mexican-American middle-class voter.

Both campaigns made several political overtures aimed directly at two target groups within the Mexican-American community: white-collar professionals and business owners. Reagan and Tower spoke openly about how Mexican Americans assumed personal responsibility for their economic well-being and were, by nature, opposed to the welfare programs advanced by the Democratic leadership. Both candidates appeared before numerous Mexican-American civic groups repeating the themes of the work ethic and the entrepreneurial spirit of the Mexican-American culture.

The public appearances of Reagan and Tower before Mexican-American audiences were a not-so-subtle warning to the Democratic party that the GOP would now openly challenge the Democrats inside these traditional Democratic strongholds. Several key Mexican-American Democratic leaders had warned their party for many years about these Republican activities and the need to counteract these efforts. Their pleas for technical support and funds for a viable Mexican-American strategy, however, fell on deaf ears at Democratic headquarters. Reagan and Tower each received nearly 30 percent of the Mexican-American vote in California and Texas, which contributed to their victories, including the upset of an incumbent Democratic governor in California.[18]

As expected, the GOP was politically ecstatic regarding its ability to attract a high percentage of middle-class Mexican-American voters in the two critical states of California and Texas. The Democratic leadership , on the other hand, simply dismissed once again the GOP gains as nothing more than a temporary setback and accused the Republican party of engaging in a political slight-of-hand with regards to Mexican-American voters. Nevertheless, the Republican party felt in 1966 that it had established a political beachhead among the Mexican-American middle-class and moved rapidly to widen its geographical base for the upcoming 1968 presidential election.

The 1968 presidential campaign was the next logical step for the GOP to field test its "Southwest Strategy" nationwide after its successful utilization two years earlier in California and Texas. Nixon had not forgotten the

---

[18]The Latin-American State Advisory Committee and the Mexican-American Republicans of Texas (MART) helped Tower win the Senate seat with 25-30 percent of the Mexican-American vote. The "Viva Reagan" clubs were organized in California in 1965-66 and played an instrumental role in Reagan's victory over Democratic incumbent Edmund "Pat" Brown. Interviews with Henry Ramírez, September 2, 1984, Washington, D.C., and Celso Moreno, March 31, 1985, Minneapolis, Minnesota. Also see Armando B. Rendón, *Chicano Manifesto* (Collier Books: New York, 1971), 241-75.

pivotal role that Mexican-American and Puerto Rican voters had played in Kennedy's narrow victory in 1960 and, therefore, named Celso Moreno of Texas and Alex Armardariz early in his campaigns as his national directors for the 1968 and 1972 Latino outreach programs respectively. Several state directors were hired in both campaigns to coordinate "Viva Nixon" operations nationwide, including the key states of California, Texas, Florida, and Illinois.[19]

The Democratic party, meanwhile, found itself seriously divided between the hawks and doves regarding the war in Vietnam. Rank-and-file Mexican-American Democrats were also split in both 1968 and 1972 by age and ideology. The assassination of U.S. Senator Robert Kennedy in 1968, for example, stifled the hopeful spirits of many young Chicanos who viewed the Democratic candidate Hubert Humphrey in 1968 as part of the old-guard whereas, many middle-class Mexican Americans viewed George McGovern as too liberal in 1972. Indeed, the ill-fated welfare program proposed by McGovern served only to reinforce the social fears held by some middle-class Mexican Americans regarding Democratic "hand-outs" to the poor.

The Humphrey and McGovern campaigns did establish "Viva" outreach programs, and both men promised to appoint Mexican Americans to key positions in their administrations. In reality, however, the activities and campaign promises by the Democrats in 1968 and 1972 were merely token gestures. Also hurting the Democratic party's chances was the emergence of La Raza Unida Party in the late 1960s and early 1970s.[20] La Raza Unida party members in California publicly jeered several Democratic leaders in the East Los Angeles area including John Tunney, Edmund Muskie, and Edward Kennedy. These incidents received widespread news coverage throughout the nation because Democratic leaders were not

---

[19]Interview with Alex Armandariz, September 6, 1984, Washington, D.C. Also the personal files of Celso Moreno.

[20]El Partido de La Raza Unida was first established in Texas in 1969 and eventually spread to 18 states. A major factor for the creation of this third-party movement was the "take-the-Mexican-American-vote-for-granted" attitude by the Democratic party. The party was successful in electing some candidates in Texas, New Mexico, and California. See the following publications for the history and contributions of La Raza Unida Party: John Stamples Shockly, *Chicano Revolt in a Texas Town* (Notre Dame: Notre Dame Press, 1974); Tony Castro, *Chicano Power: Emergence of Mexican-America* (New York: Saturday Review Press, 1974); Alberto Juarez, "The Emergence of El Partido de La Raza Unida: California's New Chicano Party," *Aztlán: Chicano Journal of the Social Science and the Arts* (Fall 1972); Carlos Muñoz, Jr., and Mario Barrera, "La Raza Unida Party and the Chicano Student Movement in California," *The Social Science Journal* vol. 19, no. 2 (April 1982); and Richard Santillan, *The Politics of Cultural Nationalism: El Partido de La Raza Unida in Southern California, 1968-1978* (Ph.D. dissertation, Claremont Graduate School, 1978).

accustomed to unfriendly Mexican-American crowds. La Raza Unida leaders accused the Democratic party of appearing in the Mexican-American neighborhoods only during election times while ignoring the community's concerns afterwards.

The Republican party, at the same time, was spending considerable amounts of money and time for the Latino vote throughout the nation, principally during the 1972 election. President Nixon received 13 percent and 30 percent of the Latino vote in 1968 and 1972, which helped further consolidate the GOP electoral bond with certain elements of the middle-class, although Nixon also did well in the blue-collar areas of East Los Angeles and South Texas in 1972. See Table 2.

The Democratic party failed to seriously recognize Republican inroads into the Mexican-American community and again simply dismissed the notion of a new realignment taking place in the sunbelt states. The GOP during the 1970s took further political advantage of Democratic inaction and significantly expanded its Latino electoral base by introducing a series of innovative tactics designed to carefully fine-tune the "Southwest Strategy." The first tactic under the Nixon administration was the highly heralded appointments of Mexican Americans to head the U.S. Treasury, the Office of Economic Opportunity, and the Small Business Administration. Several other federal appointments went to Mexican Americans, most of whom resided in California and Texas, the twin pillars of the Republican Latino agenda. A number of Mexican-American Democrats charged the Nixon administration with engaging in blatant tokenism with these selections, but other loyal Mexican-Americans Democrats reluctantly applauded the choices as drastic improvements from previous Democratic administrations.

A second strategy in 1971 was the renaming of the Inter-Agency of Mexican-American Affairs to the Committee of Spanish-Speaking Affairs. This name change was obviously designed to broaden Nixon's political base with the Puerto Rican and Cuban communities. Both Latino groups had felt unfairly excluded and overshadowed by the political spotlight given Mexican Americans during the Kennedy and Johnson years. Concomitant to the name change, the Nixon White House recruited and appointed a number of Puerto Ricans and Cuban Americans to serve in the federal bureaucracy, mainly in the field of international relations.

Third, the GOP offered to subsidize Mexican-American redistricting activities with technical resources and financial assistance in the early 1970s.[21] The Republican party clearly understood that redistricting is an issue that has historically strained the delicate relationship between Mexican Americans and the leadership of the Democratic party. The traditional

---

[21]Richard Santillan, "Latinos in State and Congressional Redistricting: 1961-1984," *Journal of Hispanic Politics*, Harvard University, vol. 1, no. l, 1985.

Table 2:   *Estimated Percentage of Latino Votes for Presidential Candidates, 1968 and 1972*

	1968		1972	
	Humphrey	Nixon	McGovern	Nixon
California	80	20	74	26
Arizona	77	23	—	—
Colorado	75	25	—	—
New Mexico	73	27	57	43
Texas	83	17	80	20
Nationwide	—	—	73	27

Source: The Cabinet Committee on Opportunities for Spanish-speaking People: An Overview (December 15, 1972); *The Electoral College and the Mexican-Americans: An Analysis of the Mexican-American Impact on 1972 Elections,* prepared by the League of United Latin-American Citizens and the Mexican Bar Association (June 1971). Authors' personal files.

Democratic practice during redistricting is to fragment the Mexican-American community into as many districts as possible in order to insure several Anglo incumbents of Mexican-American votes. This policy of dilution of potential Mexican-American voting power by the Democratic party leadership has seriously foreclosed the political ability of Mexican Americans to elect themselves to state and congressional offices.

The GOP recognized this inherent conflict and saw a golden opportunity to take advantage of the situation by offering to help Mexican-American organizations spearheading the redistricting battles in California and Texas. The Republican tactic was to drive a political wedge between the Democratic party and Mexican-American organizations over the hotly contested issue of malapportionment. The Mexican-American leadership of both states, however, rejected the GOP offer, mainly because of the political mistrust among Latino community leaders regarding the interior motives of the Republican party in establishing an alliance with them concerning reapportionment.

The Mexican-American communities in California and Texas were, despite Democratic guarantees, politically sliced-up again in the 1970s without any regard to their political aspirations. This action by the Democratic party would eventually push many Mexican-American organizations during the 1980s reapportionment battles to openly forge a political partnership with the GOP in several states. Furthermore, the increasing attention being given to the Latino community by the GOP had finally convinced some long-time and frustrated Mexican-American Democratic leaders to change their political affiliation. During the Nixon years such conversions were strategically showcased. At one time, Mexican-American Republicans were considered political outcasts in the community, but by 1974, Republicanism was viewed by some Mexican-American leaders as a legitimate vehicle for political advancement. These political defectors rationalized their partisan fresh start by stating that they were tired of Democratic promises and felt Latino presence in both parties would help escalate Latino political influence because neither party could no longer afford to take the Latino vote for granted. The recruitment of disgruntled Mexican-American Democrats by the GOP conveyed the idea that Latino voters who cast their ballots for Republican candidates should no longer be viewed as disloyal to their community but rather as individuals enhancing the political influence of the Latino community. A related point to these political defections was that the GOP made it perfectly clear to Mexican Americans and other Latinos that they would have first priority to high-level positions inside the Republican party and administrations. Latino Democratic leaders in particular were constantly being reminded by GOP Latino recruiters that Mexican Americans and Puerto Ricans were always being overshadowed by the Democratic appointments of blacks, Jews, women, and other interest groups within the party.

The Republican National Committee established the Republican National Hispanic Assembly (RNHA) as part of its local and national structures.[22] These assemblies were founded in many states, including California, Texas, Florida, New York, and Illinois. The official establishment of the RNHA within the party structure was clearly another signal to some in the Latino communities that the GOP seriously viewed them as an integral part of the national political scene. Much of the hard work and results invested during the Nixon era by the Republican party regarding Latinos, however, was nearly lost under the Ford administration.

President Gerald R. Ford was sworn into office after the resignation of Richard Nixon in August 1974. For most of his political life, President Ford, unlike Nixon, Goldwater, and Rockefeller, had minimal social interaction with Latinos. Furthermore, Ford had opposed bilingual education and minority voting rights legislation when he served in the Congress. He was convinced by his White House advisors in 1975, however, to reverse his opposition to these two key Latino issues because Latinos

---

[22]Interview with Benjamín Fernandez, December 26, 1984, Los Angeles, California. Fernández was one of the key founders of the Republican National Hispanic Assembly in 1974.

could possibly play a pivotal role in a tight 1976 election.[23]   Latino advisors to Ford also persuaded him to adopt the term "Hispanic" for federal record keeping hoping that this new designation of inclusion would attract Puerto Ricans, Cubans, and other Latin Americans to the Ford campaign.

Ford's already slim chance to win over Latino voters was seriously crippled by several factors, and in some cases, outright political blunders. The GOP, as was the case in the early 1960s, was divided between the moderate and conservative factions.   Naturally, this ideological bickering inside the party leadership also served to disunite Latino Republicans. Ronald Reagan had established strong links with the Republican Latino community nationwide while serving as governor of California between 1966 and 1974.   During the primaries, some of Reagan's Latino spokespersons challenged Ford's poor record on Latino issues and his lack of appointments of Latinos to federal positions. Ronald Reagan campaign's against President Ford in the Republican primaries left bitter feelings between Latino Republicans on both sides.   Many Ford supporters believed that the harsh tone of the Reagan campaign contributed to Ford's defeat against Jimmy Carter in the general election.

The Democratic party took advantage of this Republican in-fighting by repeating the Reagan charges against Ford in the general election. Furthermore, Ford was blamed by many moderate Republican Latinos for his lack of serious intervention to save the Committee on Spanish-Speaking Affairs from congressional budget cuts.   Democratic lawmakers viewed the committee as nothing more than a propaganda arm for the "Southwest Strategy" and refused to provide funds for 1976.   There were also serious questions raised by the Democrats regarding the relationship of the committee and the Watergate scandal.[24]   Moderate Latino Republicans believed, nevertheless, that Ford had waited too late to rescue the commit-

---

[23]Interviews with Fernando de Baca, September 4, 1984, Washington D.C., and Alberto Zapanta, August 22,1984, Tulsa, Oklahoma. Zapanta served as the Southwest Latino coordinator for the Ford campaign.

[24]Interviews with Henry Ramírez, September 2, 1984, Washington D.C.; Benjamín Fernández, December 26, 1984, Los Angeles, California; and William (Mo) Marumoto, September 6, 1984, Washington, D.C. All three men appeared before the Senate Watergate Committee. For a detailed report concerning these allegations, see U.S. Congress, Senate, 93rd Congress, *1st Session, Hearing Before the Select Committee on Presidential Campaign Activities, Watergate, and Related Activities*, vol. 13 (Washington, D.C.: U.S. Government Printing Office, 1973). According to Ramírez, the allegations of wrongdoing were initiated by Latino Democrats as a means to discredit the Latino Republican leadership in order to prevent further inroads by the GOP.   Vicente Ximenes who headed the Inter-agency on Mexican-American Affairs during the Johnson administration, however, blamed Latino Republicans for the demise of the committee. See *Agenda*, vol. 5, no. 2 (February 1975), and vol. 3, no. 6 (August 1973).

tee, and as a result, the only federal agency advocating on behalf of Latinos no longer existed.

This political self-destruction among Latino Republicans during the 1976 campaign also resulted in a major blunder that divided Latino Republicans along the lines of ethnicity. The Ford campaign established a Latino outreach program, which in reality was a Southwest Mexican-American strategy concentrating on the states of California, Texas, and New Mexico. This decision to narrowly focus on Mexican Americans by the Ford strategists angered and alienated many Puerto Ricans, Cubans, and Latin Americans away from the Ford campaign.

On the Democratic side, Jimmy Carter, unlike previous Democratic presidential candidates, enjoyed overwhelming support from a broad base of Latino voters including some second-generation Cuban Americans. The Carter campaign established a national Latino effort with state offices in over 20 states.[25] The Latino campaign by the Democrats completely eclipsed the Republican Latino effort, and as a result, Carter captured nearly 85 percent of the Latino vote nationwide and in California. The Carter landslide victory in Mexican-American and Puerto Rican precincts dealt a serious blow to the "Southwest Strategy," which was left in shambles by the internal GOP battles and by an effective Latino outreach program by the Democrats. Some Democratic leaders went as far as declaring the "Southwest Strategy" as political history. Unfortunately for the Democratic party, this political obituary was premature because Ronald Reagan announced his third try for the White House in 1979.

Reagan was clearly the political beneficiary of three decades of Latino outreach efforts by the GOP. The Reagan campaigns of 1980 and 1984 borrowed several successful strategies from past Republican campaigns, including the endorsements of disgruntled Latino Democrats, a direct appeal to the Cuban community and middle-class Mexican Americans, the use of Latino film and television personalities for political advertising, and reaching out to the Latino business sector.[26]

---

[25]Interview with U.S. Congressman Esteban Torres, January 18, 1985, Los Angeles, California.

[26]Interview with Alex Armandariz, September 6, 1984, Washington, D.C., and Robert Estrada, August 22,1984, Dallas, Texas. Armandariz served as the 1980 Latino national coordinator while Estrada headed the 1984 "Viva Reagan-Bush" campaign. Also, see the following: Haynes Johnson and Thomas B. Edsall, "Hispanic Star Ascending," *The Washington Post*, March 25, 1984; Albert Frias, "GOP Working to Draw More Hispanics Into Party," *San Gabriel Valley Tribune*, March 20, 1983; Kenneth C. Burt, "Competing With the Democrats for the Growing Hispanic Vote," *California Journal* (May 1983); and, David Hoffman, "A Preview of Hispanic Strategy," *The Washington Post*, August 10, 1983.

Reagan's appeal for Latino votes in general and Mexican-American votes in particular was primarily based on ideology rather than on campaign pledges for more federal programs and appointments. Ironically, Reagan opposed, for example, many federal programs supported by the Latino business sector including set-aside legislation and the Small Business Administration. The Republican party in 1980 made the political decision that the Reagan campaign, more so than that of Nixon or Ford, could enlarge its Latino base with a set of policy positions on several emotional issues instead of programmatic promises.

This particular strategy focused on three main themes. The first theme centered around religious issues. The Reagan camp repeatedly endorsed prayer in public schools, tax credits for private educational institutions, and opposition to both abortion and federal funding for family planning programs. These issues were selected, in part, by the GOP to take cultural advantage of the perceived religious conservatism among many Latino Catholics.[27] The second theme promoted the virtues of patriotism and the necessity for a strong defense. Reagan appealed to the Cuban community with his anti-Castro speeches and the Soviet threat in Central America.[28] Furthermore, Reagan continuously praised and honored several Mexican-American Medal of Honor winners at the White House and along the

---

[27]Republican National Hispanic Assembly, The Reagan Campaign 1980: Hispanics Can Make a Difference (July 1980). The study listed several traits that made Latinos a prime target for the GOP recruitment efforts, including individualism, honesty, belief in the virtues of hard work, and a sincere devotion to religion. Authors' personal files. Also, see John L. Korey and Jose M. Vadi, "Political Attitudes and electoral Choices Among California Hispanics," paper presented at the Western Political Science Association, March 26, 1981, Denver, Colorado.

[28]On May 20, 1983, President Reagan spoke in Miami, Florida, to celebrate Cuban Independence Day. He talked about how Cubans had arrived in this country poor and through hard work and dedication had achieved success. The president mentioned his Cuban-American appointments and strongly stressed his opposition to Fidel Castro. He concluded: "We are, by and large, people who share the same fundamental values of God, family, work, freedom, and justice. Perhaps the greatest tie between us can be seen in the incredible number of cathedrals and churches found throughout the hemisphere. Our forefathers took the worship of God seriously." *Presidential Documents,* vol. 19, no. 21 (May 20, 1983). In addition, one week prior to his Miami visit, President Reagan pardoned Eugenio R. Martínez, one of the five men convicted for the Watergate break-in. Some Democrats expressed suspicion between the pardon and Reagan's stop in Florida. Democratic Governor Toney Anaya of New Mexico said: "If it appears that the pardon was related to any political effort to appeal to Hispanics, I think it will simply backfire and turn most Hispanic stomachs." "Democrats Hint that Pardon is Tied to Bid for Latino Votes," *Los Angeles Times,* May 15, 1983. See also "Polls Shouldn't Mix Latinos Together," *Hispanic Link Weekly Report,* July 29, 1985.

campaign trail also and used these occasions to depict the Democrats as being soft toward communism.

The final Reagan theme was that Latino culture rested on the twin pillars of the work ethic and an entrepreneurial spirit—a successful theme he used during his 1966 campaign for California governor. During both the 1980 and 1984 campaigns, Reagan appeared before numerous Mexican-American organizations, especially in California and Texas, encouraging the establishments of small business ventures and enterprise zones as a means for achieving economic prosperity.[29]

These three GOP campaign themes were selected, in large part, as a result of Republican pre-election surveys designed to measure the political pulse of the Latino community. The studies also revealed to the GOP specific issues not to discuss among Latinos during the campaign, including proposed cutbacks and opposition to Social Security, veteran benefits, bilingual education, and voting rights legislation—issues that suffered during the Reagan era.[30]

The Reagan campaign took a major step toward expanding further its Latino base by appealing to women and college students. Several Latinas played key roles in both campaigns, and several women were appointed to serve in various capacities in the Reagan administrations. In fact, Reagan appointed more Latinas than men to his administrations than any previous Republican or Democratic president.[31] The appointments of Latinas by

---

[29]On August 25, 1983, President Reagan visited Los Angeles and spoke to 800 Latino business people. Reagan continued to repeat his basic Latino themes: "There are people in America today who feel that expression of love for country and family are old-fashioned. They squirm and get uneasy when we talk about pride in neighborhood and work or speak of religious values. Yes, there are people like that. But you won't find many of them in the Hispanic business community. To every cynic who says the American dream is dead, I say, 'Look at the Americans of Hispanic descent who are making it in the business world with hard work and no one to rely on but themselves'. . . . We believe in the dignity of work and we believe in rewarding it." George Skelton, "Latinos Applaud Reagan's Praise of Hard Work," *Los Angeles Times*, August 26, 1983. Also, see Ruben Castaneda, "Cheers from L.A. Hispanics," *Los Angeles Herald-Examiner*, August 26, 1983, and "Republicans Launch New Hispanic Efforts," *Hispanic Link Weekly Report*, November 28, 1983.

[30]Interview with Mike Martínez, August 22, 1984, Dallas, Texas. Martínez was one of the key architects for the 1984 Latino outreach program. For the Democratic Strategy, see Cara J. Abeyta, "Hispanic Force '84: Collective Symbolism or Political Reality," paper presented at the annual meeting of the American Political Science Association, September 2, 1984, Washington, D.C.

[31]Interviews with Laura Reyes Kopack, June 25, 1984, Detroit, Michigan; Sylvia Hernández Maddox, September 11, 1984, Dallas, Texas; Ana Rodríquez Bartash, September 6, 1984, Alexandria, Virginia; Arnhilda Gonzales-Quevedo, July 6, 1984,

the Reagan White House were clearly based on the electoral data that revealed that since the early 1980s Latinas are registering and voting in a larger percentage than men.

Several Latino college students, including many Mexican-American students on California campuses, were the target of the GOP college recruitment efforts. Many Latino students openly endorsed Reagan and many worked as volunteers for the Republicans. It appears that many members of this new generation of college students of the 1980s were attracted to the Republican philosophy of individualism, wealth, and status.[32] Furthermore, unlike their parents' and grandparents' generations, Mexican-American youth of today are not emotionally attached to the nostalgic memories of FDR and JFK. Unfortunately for the Democrats, many of today's Mexican-American college students have based their negative judgment of the Democratic party on the lackluster performance of former President Jimmy Carter.

The Democratic party, both in 1980 and 1984, was in a very weak position to commit technical and financial assistance for an effective Latino outreach program to offset the impressive efforts by the GOP. Both Democratic campaigns were marred by divisive primary races and bitter convention floor fights among delegates over platform issues, candidates, and party rules.

Mexican-American Democrats found themselves almost politically voiceless in these two elections because they were fragmented among numerous camps including those of Edward Kennedy, Jimmy Carter, Walter Mondale, John Anderson, Jesse Jackson, and Jerry Brown. The consequence of this internal political scrabbling was that both Carter in 1980 and Mondale in 1984 could not launch an effective Latino agenda. As a result, Reagan gained the highest voting percentage among Latinos of any other Republican presidential candidate since the 1930s. In the 1980 election, for example, Carter's popularity among Latino voters dropped nearly 25 points between 1976 and 1980, a defection greater than any other voting group.[33]

Miami, Florida; Graciela Beecher, February 23, 1984, Ft. Wayne, Indiana; and Carmen Mancera, January 24, 1986, Los Angeles, California.

[32]Interviews with Anna Vega, August 23, 1985, Los Angeles, California; Laura Simon, February 18, 1986, Los Angeles, California; and Frank Darrell Castillo, April 24, 1985, Dallas, Texas. All three individuals are very active in Republican politics.

[33]Roger Langley, "Hispanics More Than Any Other Group Deserted Jimmy Carter," *Arizona Republic*, November 30, 1980. Throughout the campaign, Latino Republicans hit hard at both the high unemployment rate of Mexican Americans and the lack of key Latino appointments to the Carter administration. Also, George Bush always reminded Mexican-American audiences about President Carter's remark about "Montezuma's Revenge" during a speech in Mexico. Bush said the reference was in bad taste and one that Carter apparently never apologized for.

The major reasons for significant Latino support for Reagan appeared to be basically the same factors that influenced many non-Latino voters: the Iranian hostage situation and problems with the economy. See Table 3.

The post-1984 election saw President Ronald Reagan enjoying the highest level of Latino support of any recent Republican president, including Eisenhower, Nixon, and Ford. This unprecedented Latino support, however, began slowly slipping away by Reagan's second-term. A growing number of Latino Republican leaders openly expressed extreme disappointment with Reagan's poor record of Latino appointments, with none serving in his cabinet. In addition, the Republican National Committee with the president's approval eliminated all funding for special interests in the party structure including the National Republican Hispanic Assembly.

The majority of Latino Republicans describe themselves as moderates who generally support such issues as affirmative action, voting rights, fair housing and health care, bilingual education, federal assistance to the poor, and federal support for minority economic development. The Reagan cutbacks in many of these areas further alienated many disappointed Latinos away from the Reagan White House. Many moderate Mexican-American and Puerto Rican Republicans made it no political secret that they couldn't wait for the Reagan era to end in order to support Vice-President George Bush in 1988.

George Bush has enjoyed a good amount of support among Mexican-American Republicans since the early 1970s when he served as Chairman of the Republican National Committee. During his tenure at the RNC, Bush worked hard along with Latinos in implementing several creative reforms within the party structure, including financial support for the Republican National Hispanic Assembly, funding for a Latino Republican newsletter, campaign assistance for Latino candidates, support for voter registration programs, and an aggressive affirmative action program for more Latino delegates and officials at both the state and national levels.[34]

Several key Mexican-American and Puerto Rican Republicans supported Bush in 1980 when he ran against Ronald Reagan in the GOP primaries. In addition, Bush's son, Jeb, has been very active with the RNHA for many years and is fluent in Spanish. Jeb Bush also worked as the campaign coordinator for his father in Puerto Rico in 1980 and 1988. President Bush has made it quite clear that he supports the admission of Puerto Rico as the 51st state and echoed this sentiment during his first State of the Union address to the Congress.

---

[34]Interviews in Washington, D.C., with Henry Ramírez, September 2, 1984, and with Fernando de Baca, September 4, 1984. Also, see Christine Marie Sierra, "Chicano Politics After 1984," paper presented at the 13th Annual Conference of the National Association for Chicano Studies, March 21-23, 1985, Sacramento, California.

Table 3:   *Estimated Percentage of Latino Votes for Presidential Candidates, 1980 and 1984*

	1980		1984	
	Carter	Reagan	Mondale	Reagan
California	78	22	65	35
Arizona	76	24	70	30
Colorado	—	—	67	23
Florida	41	59	35	65
New Mexico	70	30	65	35
Texas	80	20	80	20
Nationwide	—	—	—	—

Source: The Latino Vote in the 1980 Presidential Election, Southwest Voter Registration Education Project, January 1981, San Antonio Texas; Robert R. Brischetto, "Latinos in the 1984 Election Exit Polls: Some Findings and Some Methodological Lessons," in *Ignored Voices: Public Opinion Polls and the Latino Community*, edited by Rodolfo O. de la Garza (Austin, Texas: Center for Mexican American Studies, 1987).

The 1988 Latino Bush-Quayle campaign was organizationally structured somewhat differently from previous Republican campaigns. In the past, Latino outreach programs were either centralized or decentralized by the GOP. The 1988 Latino presidential campaign program was an unique combination of both strategies.[35]   Each state party, for example, had control over its Latino component as a way to mold the outreach to the specific concerns and issues of each distinct Latino community. At the same time, the Republican National Committee was responsible for promoting the virtues of the party to Latinos while the Bush-Quayle ticket campaigned in several Latino communities from coast to coast.

Vice-President Bush, like Reagan in 1980 and 1984, did not openly speak out on specific Latino issues including his position on bilingual education, voting rights legislation, the English-only movement, immigration, and Central America. Instead, Bush spoke about the general themes of a strong defense, the war against crime and drugs, and the need for a "kinder nation." A number of campaign materials designed for Latino voters by the

---

[35]Telephone interview with Ernesto Olivas, February 8, 1989, Washington, D.C.; he currently works with the Republican National Committee. Also, see Marta Varela, *Report on the Activities of New York State Hispanics for Victory '88, The Hispanic Coalition of the Bush Campaign in New York State, November 8, 1988*, from authors' personal files.

Bush campaign echoed many of President's Reagan's sentiments about the Latino community: "Family values. Conservative. Anti-communist. Hard-Working. These are the characteristics of an ethnic group known as Hispanic Americans. . . . The attraction Hispanic Americans have for America coincides with their industriousness, desire for self-improvement, and a desire to provide for their families."[36]

The Dukakis campaign, on the other hand, did not have a strong national Latino effort. Most of the Latino outreach was spearheaded by elected and appointed Latino Democratic officials. This strategy may have backfired because many of these officials were very busy with their own elections and, thus, did not have the time or resources to devote fulltime to the Dukakis campaign. In addition, many key Latinos nationwide supported the grass-roots campaign of Jesse Jackson who they felt spoke directly to the issues confronting many in the Latino community. Furthermore, many of Jackson's Latino supporters were angered by the way the Dukakis campaign treated Jackson after the Democratic convention and chose not to volunteer for the Dukakis campaign, which clearly hurt the Democrats in the Mexican-American and Puerto Rican communities. See Table 4.

Also, the Democrats did not take political advantage of Bush's blunder when he referred to his Mexican-American grandchildren as the "little brown ones." In fact, Latino Republicans defused this potential embarrassment by declaring that Bush's comments were affectionate in nature.

The Republican party's public relations and mass media outreach efforts directed at Latinos are worthy of separate attention for at least two reasons. First, these undertakings have been a central and integral part of the evolving strategy to make inroads with this ethnic population. And second, the public communication strategies during the last few years have become ever more complex and have taken on a life of their own. Today there exist well-planned state and national public relations as well as mass media strategies. These are aimed at winning the allegiance—and votes—of the Latino electorate. Particularly notable at the presidential campaign level, efforts have evolved from the simple bilingual pamphlets and flyers of the Goldwater campaign of 1964 to the sophisticated multimedia plan of the 1988 Bush campaign.

While much has been written about the mass media and politics especially during election campaigns, there is a lack of public documentation that would allow us to fully reconstruct and comprehend Republican—or Democratic—party communication strategies aimed at Mexican Americans in California or Latinos elsewhere. Both parties have failed to keep complete records of such efforts and researchers have not systematically

---

[36]Pamphlet entitled *Hispanic Americans: The Key to the GOP Victory in '88*, authors' personal files.

Table 4:   *Estimated Percentage of Latino Votes for Presidential Candidates in 1988*

	Dukakis	Bush
California	75	25
New Mexico	69	31
Texas	83	17

Source: Southwest Voter Research Institute, Inc., *Special Edition: California Exit Poll Results*, vol 2, no. 7 (September-December 1988).

studied or analyzed those communication activities. Nevertheless, in this section we reconstruct and describe various stages of the Latino-oriented public relations and mass media outreach efforts of the Republican party.

STAGE ONE

From Traditional Pamphlets to Ethnic Directed Propaganda

The Eisenhower (1952 and 1956) and Nixon (1960) presidential campaigns did not include distinct national efforts to win over Latino voters. Most of the Latino-oriented activities were carried out at the local and county levels with a limited amount of bilingual materials—usually traditional pamphlets translated to Spanish—distributed in New Mexico and South Texas.

The Goldwater (1964) and Nixon (1968) presidential campaigns, however, did include national outreach programs specifically aimed at the Latino electorate. Both campaigns hired Latino staff members and printed bilingual campaign material to attract Latino voters. For example, a bumper sticker that proclaimed "Goldwater es mi gallo" was distributed in California. Bilingual campaign material, however, was in short supply in that campaign.[37] The other avenue the GOP had as early as 1963 for reaching some Latinos and other minorities was the newsletter *Nationalities Reporter*, which reported on Republican appointments and events related to ethnic populations. The September 29, 1964 edition of that newsletter, for instance, featured a front page picture of candidates Goldwater and Miller wearing Mexican sombreros and clasping hands with Hispanic-American director Robert B. Robles and *Nationalities* Director L. Dobriansky. Also

---

[37]Personal files of Manuel Ruíz, Jr., national coordinator for the Goldwater-Miller ticket, presently a Los Angeles Attorney.

of notice was that during the primaries at least one presidential hopeful, Nelson Rockefeller, spoke to Latinos in Spanish on Spanish-language television—channel 34 of Los Angeles. This was probably the first time a presidential candidate had intentionally used Spanish-language television for reaching the Mexican-American population.

For the 1968 Nixon campaign, Celso Moreno was selected as the National Director of Spanish-speaking affairs, and bilingual material was produced and widely distributed as part of the centralized strategy. The nationwide mailings produced that year were targeted to three specific Latino groups: businessmen, conservative Democrats, and Latinos living outside the barrios.[38] There is no documented evidence, however, telling us if and how the Republicans tried to use the mass media in Spanish or English to specifically reach the Latino communities.

STAGE TWO

Early Recognition of the Potential Power of Latino Voters and the Need for their Integration

After his narrow victory in 1968, there is evidence to suggest that President Nixon and others within the highest circles of the Republican party recognized the growing political value of the Latino vote and that the mass media were key instruments to mobilize this ethnic population for the GOP's political purposes.[39] There are numerous references to memos, for example, stating that specific messages aimed at Latinos should be produced by the various administration and party offices. It was also suggested in these documents that a person who could reach the Latino public be included in strategic planning of public relations and other outreach efforts.

As the 1972 presidential campaign period approached, the Latino middle class was courted with messages of "traditional" values such as strong family bonds, prayer in public schools, the work ethic, patriotism, and respect for law and order.[40] For the campaign, separate informational materials were published for each of the major Latino groups. Nixon's record on bilingual education and Latino employment were highlighted in brochures for Mexican Americans, whereas his pro-statehood and anti-Castro positions were respectively stressed in materials directed to Puerto Ricans and Cubans.

---

[38]Interview with Celso Moreno, March 3, 1985, and Manuel Ruíz, Jr., May 21, 1985, Los Angeles, California.

[39]Tony Castro, *Chicano Power* (New York: Saturday Review Press, 1974).

[40]Interview with Alex Armandariz, national Latino coordinator for the Nixon 1972 campaign, September 6, 1984, Washington, D.C.

By the early 1970s the GOP *Nationalities Reporter* newsletter had been replaced with *Spanish-Speaking News* published monthly by the Inter-Agency on Spanish-speaking affairs. This newsletter was later renamed *Hoy* and lasted until 1975, when the Republican National Assembly was formed. Later, the Republican National Committee issued the monthly *El Republicano*, which continues to this day. All such publications, however, have been English-language publications, usually four, letter-size pages long highlighting Republican programs, grants, and appointments of Latinos.

Furthermore, the campaign staff sought to skillfully utilize the talents of several Latino media personalities such as Cesar Romero and Desi Arnaz.[41] The defection of longtime Latino Democrats to the GOP was also displayed with much fanfare to the media.[42] It is not known, however, if these Democrats appeared in political advertisements aimed at Latinos in the Spanish-language or English-language media. Finally, while there are no records of Republican presidential commercials in Spanish-language broadcast media, at least one Nixon ad was published in *La Opinión*, a Spanish-language daily newspaper from Los Angeles, California.[43]

The Ford campaign of 1976 did not come close to the high level of Latino participation as achieved by the two preceding Nixon campaigns. Nevertheless, Ford utilized bilingual campaign materials and appointed several Latinos to his campaign staff. Little is known about what the GOP did regarding outreach via specialized brochures and Spanish-language and/or English-language media directed at Latinos during the Ford campaign.[44]

---

[41]Lorenzo Ramírez, "Mexican-Americans: Natural Republicans." Strategy proposal submitted to the Republican party, circa February 1972. Strategy recommendation number 15, p. 46, reads:

> Mexican-American artists (i.e., movie stars, television personalities, professional athletes, etc.) should be contacted and used as participants in planned community activities. Their presence will add to the validity of the Party and create a communications bridge with the community.

[42]"Six Latino Democrats Bolt to Nixon, Claiming Party Rebuffed Them," *Arizona Republic*, July 28, 1972; "Texas GOP Aims for Mexican Vote," *San Antonio Express*, August 13, 1972.

[43]The full page ad in this standard size newspaper had a picture of the president, which covered the top half of the page and under it the banner read "Necesitamos al Presidente Nixon!" Text and graphics with propaganda followed, and the bottom banner read "HISPANOS CON NIXON." *La Opinión*, November 1, 1972, part 1, p. 3.

[44]The authors are currently trying to gather information on this topic.

STAGE THREE

Sophistication and Specialization

According to Carol Vernon, Director of Outreach Communications for the Republican National Committee, the GOP began to look more seriously at the Spanish-language media during the late 1970s through the early 1980s as an invaluable vehicle to reach out to the Latino population.[45] What started out with a radio program by Kathryn Murray developed into a specialized media outreach office, which in 1985 began a concerted effort to keep the Spanish-language media abreast on all information about the issues and events related to the Republican party. This activity currently includes providing taped interviews of Republican party officials or elected officials with whom the stations would not otherwise be able to interview because of the lack of personnel and time.

While there is limited public knowledge about such media and public relations efforts during the Reagan-Bush 1980 campaign, a lot more can be written about the 1984 campaign. The most revealing information stems from what appears to have been the Republican party's blueprint to capture the Latino vote: "Hispanic Victory Initiative '84. A proposed strategy for the Reagan-Bush '84 Hispanic campaign."[46] Various pages in this highly detailed document specify the plan for advertising, public relations, and publicity, as well as the importance of the mass media, particularly the Spanish-language print and broadcast outlets.

The advertising strategy, for example, outlines the importance of designing original ads with which Hispanics can relate. It further recommends against settling for English translations and proposes strong local media action in these publicity activities. After considerable space specifying media and creative strategies, as well as the importance of monitoring activities of the Democrats, the document concludes, "In summary, let the Democrats register all the Hispanics they want. The battle for the hearts and minds of Hispanic voters will be fought in the media."[47]

Based on our assessment of the campaign that year it seems that the recommendations were implemented because the Republican party significantly expanded its efforts in seeking more news exposure in the English-language and Spanish-language media. For example, advertising was produced to air in English-language television but intentionally aimed at

---

[45]Interview with Carol Vernon, in Washington, D.C., December 9, 1988.

[46]Mike Martínez, "Hispanic victory initiative '84: A proposed strategy for the Reagan-Bush '84 Hispanic campaign," authors' personal files. See also "GOP Confident of Attracting Latino Vote," *Hispanic Link Weekly Report*, August 20, 1984.

[47]*Ibid.*, p. 51.

Latinos. This innovation was not whimsical; it was largely based on the application of acculturation theory from which Republican advertising strategists extrapolated that many potential Latino voters could be better reached via English-language television. This would be especially so for programs that TV ratings indicated high Latino viewership.[48]

Furthermore, the GOP sought extensive use of both free and paid Spanish-language media, which the aforementioned document indicated was the fastest and most effective means to reach and convince the bulk of the Latino electorate to vote Republican. The GOP media strategy recognizes that English-language media are important sources from which Latinos get their news, but also acknowledges that "these do not always focus on issues and topics of interest to Hispanics."[49] That document exposes the GOP media strategists' thinking about the importance of the Spanish-language media as it states that: "you may be able to reach them [Latinos] in English, but you have to convince them in Spanish."[50]

In the only study on how the Spanish-language press covered a presidential campaign, it was quite evident that four of the six daily papers in four cities (Los Angeles, New York, Chicago, and Miami) gave preferential coverage to the Republicans in 1984.[51] This partisanship, however, is as much a reflection of the conservative leaning of the newspaper owners or publishers as it may be of the GOP's public relations efforts.

One measure of the seriousness of this Republican master plan proposal to win Hispanic votes was its budget of $4.850 million. Of this total, $3.994 million were to be designated for advertising for distribution as follows: $2.162 million for television, $1.295 million for radio, $.226 million for newspapers, $.108 million for magazines, and $.203 million for outdoor. An additional $100 thousand was recommended for Latino campaign literature, an equal amount for voter registration support, and $450 thousand for direct mail. When expenditures at the state and local levels are combined, the $6 million figure could easily have been exceeded.[52] The amount of money that went to the various English-language *vis-à-vis* Spanish-language media is unknown.

---

[48]For a detailed analysis of the Republican party's TV theoretical-acculturation—strategy and discussion of the advertisements aimed at Latinos in 1984, see Federico A. Subervi-Vélez, Richard Herrera, and Michael Begay, "Toward an understanding of the role of the mass media in Latino political life," *Social Science Quarterly*, vol. 68, no. 1 (March 1987), 185-96.

[49]M. Martínez, 1984, *op. cit.*, 52.

[50]*Ibid.*

[51]Federico A. Subervi-Vélez, "Spanish-language daily newspapers and the 1984 elections," *Journalism Quarterly* vol. 65, no. 3 (Fall 1988): 678-85.

[52]Subervi-Vélez, Herrera, and Begay, *op. cit.*

Our investigation of the 1984 political advertising expenditure records kept by Spanish-language radio and television stations in Los Angeles, New York, Chicago, Miami, and San Antonio, however, suggests that in these media outlets the Republican party spent $217,925 (in contrast to the Democrats' $94,742) in ads for all the federal races, including president and vice-president, Senate, and House (see Tables 5 and 6).[53]

For example, as indicated in Table 5, in Los Angeles from September 1 through November 6, 1988, the Republican party spent at least $38,845 for 92 political spots (30 seconds each); these were aired on channel 34, the local affiliate of SIN (*Spanish International Network*, which is currently *Univisión*). The same records indicate no advertising expenditures by the Mondale-Ferraro campaign. Moreover, the Los Angeles Spanish-language radio station records show (Table 6) that $34,930 (for 847 spots) were spent by the Republicans versus $17,620 (for 440 spots) by the Democrats for the presidential campaigns.

The Republican party continued its use of newsletters including *Comentario* and *Hispanics for Reagan & Bush*, which were produced by the RNC. These and other types of publications have had more life and dis-

---

[53]The data presented in Tables 5 and 6 were gathered by making personal visits to seven television stations, and 18 AM and four FM radio stations in the indicated cities. At the time of the visits [dates indicated in brackets] these stations transmitted primarily (i.e, most of the broadcast time) in Spanish; there may have been some changes since then. The cities and their stations visited were as follows: Chicago: WCIY-TV (channel 26), WBBS-TV (channel 60), WSBC-AM, WCRW-AM, WOJO-FM [August 1985]. New York: WNJU-TV (channel 47), WXTV-TV (channel 41), WADO-AM, WSKQ-AM, WKDM-AM, and WJIT-AM [August 1985]. San Antonio: KWEX-TV (channel 41), KCOR-AM, KXET-AM, KFHM-AM, and KEDA-AM [October 1985]. Los Angeles: KMEX-TV (channel 34), KALI-AM, KTNQ-AM, KLVE-FM, and KWKW-AM [January 1986]. Miami: WLTV-TV (channel 23), WRHC-AM, WOCN-AM, WSUA-AM, WQBA-AM & FM, and WCMQ-AM & FM [February 1986]. Data were obtained by inspecting the stations' public files with records of political advertisements.

The Federal Communications Commission requires that stations maintain such files and that these be open for public inspection. The dollar figures collected from those records represent gross expenses by the political candidate and/or his/her representative. However, the figures reported here may underestimate political advertising in the Spanish-language broadcast media because some stations have poor record-keeping procedures and do not keep in their public files copies or records of all accounting transactions related to political advertising. Also, some of the records observed were incomplete; for example, dollar figures did not specify if expense was for gross or net costs. Net cost is gross cost minus the commission (usually 15 percent) that goes to the person who secured the ad for the station. If the candidate used an advertising agency, or a representative of the broadcast station, the 15 percent goes there; if the candidate acts as his/her own agent, he/she keeps the commission.

Table 5: *Number of Political Advertising Spots and Expenditures in Spanish-Language Television Stations by Candidates Running for National Office*

City	Democrats				Republicans			
	House		Pres/V.P.		Senate		House	
	#	$	#	$	#	$	#	$
Los Angeles	—	—	92	38,845	—	—	—	—
Chicago	—	—	69	17,515	—	—	16	930
Miami	28	14,160	—	—	—	—	53	16,890
New York	20	3,680	142	30,700	—	—	—	—
San Antonio	—	—	80	13,080	110	18,100	—	—
Total	48	17,840	355	75,275	110	18,100	69	17,820

Total Expenses   Democrats: $17,840   Republicans: $111,195

Note: Data from September 1, 1984 through November 6, 1984.

Table 6: *Number of Political Advertising Spots and Expenditures in Spanish-Language Television Stations by Candidates Running for National Office*

City	Democrats						Republicans					
	Press/V.P.		Senate		House		Press/V.P.		Senate		House	
Los Angeles	440	17,620	—	—	30	1,200	847	34,930	—	—	70	3,140
Chicago	92	4,968	346	6,456	—	—	—	—	—	—	468	15,580
Miami	—	—	—	—	262	6,720	—	—	—	—	—	—
New York	199	13,777	—	—	—	—	—	—	—	—	—	—
San Antonio	338	10,400	447	15,761	—	—	506	19,825	367	8,390	—	—
Total	1069	46,765	793	22,217	292	7,920	1,353	54,755	367	8,390	538	18,720

Total Expenses   Democrats: $76,902   Republicans: $81,865

Note: Data from September 1, 1984 through November 6, 1984.

persion than other conventional forms of mass media. A distinct tactic of the 1980s was the decentralization of such efforts—each state chapter of the Republican National Hispanic Assembly was commissioned to publish its own newsletters, which reflected the GOP philosophy of state autonomy in the matters related to Hispanic-oriented political propaganda.

In 1986, the Republican National Committee allotted $350,000 for a "get-out-the-Republican-vote" campaign carried out through Spanish-language radio ads during the last week prior to election day.[54]

For the 1988 campaign, the GOP most certainly upped the political ante in the battle for the Latino vote. Although our data collection and analysis about that campaign are still in process, we can report that early in the campaign the Republican National Committee commissioned an in-depth study on the Latino voting community to Lance Tarrance & Associates of Houston, Texas. The survey went further in detail than the "Victory 84" in magnitude and focused on the media habits and socio-political concerns of this electorate in order to recognize the specific message, vehicle, and messenger for the various Latino markets.[55] The findings were later used to segment the increasingly specialized messages to Mexican Americans in California and the Southwest, Puerto Ricans in the Northeast, and Cubans in Miami as well as to all mixes of Latinos in small and large communities across the nation.

The pollsters for the Republican party have most certainly analyzed the various angles regarding how all these public relations efforts and the mass media messages influenced Latinos' political attitudes and/or voting behaviors. Yet there are no reliable public records to that effect. Thus, while Republicans claim significant inroads in the Mexican-American electorate in California and elsewhere, Democrats counter this claim by pointing out that Democratic candidates continue to receive the majority of the Latino vote nationwide, with the exception of Florida. It would certainly be interesting to scrutinize the survey results on which each party supports their claim of making the best of the Mexican-American vote in California and the other Latino votes in the U.S.

The real electoral outcome notwithstanding, the data we have collected certainly suggest that the Republican party has worked hard with its sophisticated and specialized public relations and mass media outreach efforts to reach deep into the Spanish-speaking community and win the Latino electorate.

---

[54]Interview with Carol Vernon, December 9, 1988.
[55]*Ibid.*

CONCLUSION

There is sufficient evidence that the Republican party has made some impressive inroads in the Latino community. But even this emerging Latino support for the party remains politically soft and could easily turn toward Democratic presidential candidates in future elections. On the positive side, the GOP has clearly been successful in establishing political ties with the vast majority of Cuban Americans, significant numbers of middle-class Mexican Americans, the Latino business community, and increasing numbers of professional women and college students. A critical advantage for the GOP is that these particular groups have a stronger record of electoral participation than the Latino groups that continue to support the Democratic party, e.g., union members, social service agencies, community-based organizations, and the socially disadvantaged.

Also boosting the Republican party's reputation are its key appointments of Latinos to federal posts. Some Democratic officials dismiss these appointments as mere tokenism. Since 1960, however, Republican administrations (Nixon, Ford, Reagan, and Bush) have a slight edge over the Democrats (Kennedy, Johnson, and Carter) regarding Latino appointments. One major factor for this disparity in Latino appointments between both parties is that Democratic administrations have often given more political attention to other interest groups inside the party, which has resulted in Latinos being repeatedly overlooked. Yet a number of key Latino Republicans have openly expressed disappointment with the GOP's poor record of Latino appointments and broken promises. This frustration is not new and can be traced back to the 1950s when Latino Republicans criticized the party for ignoring the Latino community.[56] During the Nixon-Ford years, the party moderates, who controlled the RNC, attempted to broaden

---

[56]Latino Republican leaders since the 1950s have repeatedly warned the GOP regarding the lack of real commitment to Latino issues and concerns. Many Latino Republicans, for example, were disappointed with Eisenhower's poor record regarding Latino appointments and programs during the 1950s. In 1971, Lorenzo Ramírez, who helped formulate part of the "Southwest Strategy" wrote: "The Republican Party must discontinue the verbalization of their desires to win strong support from Mexican-Americans and display their intentions with action. Continued inactivity will indicate a negative response to the question of the party's intent . . . the Mexican-American is waiting and watching."

Finally Fernando Oaxaca, a Reagan campaigner and former chair of the RNHA, warned in 1980 that Latinos could not be counted on to remain loyal to the GOP unless concrete programs and appointments were implemented. Authors' personal files. Also see Frank del Olmo, "Taking on GOP's Unwanted Wizard," *Los Angeles Times*, February 28, 1989; and "Few Hispanics Found in Presidential Campaigns," *Hispanic Link Weekly Report*, January 18, 1988.

the GOP base by appealing to ethnic minorities and women. In the 1980s, however, the GOP has come under the leadership of the conservatives, who have successfully purged most of the moderates from the party structure. As a consequence of this ideological coup, most Latino gains and influence inside the party have been dramatically reduced. Needless to say, many Latino Republicans feel politically betrayed by the GOP.

More recently, however, the Republican party has gained some political points with Latinos as a consequence of the Justice Department's intervention in a number of voting rights cases. In fact, the GOP itself has joined forces with civil rights groups in some court challenges.[57] These legal challenges, regardless of the motives behind them, are viewed by the overall Latino community as major steps to eliminate the unfair practices of racial gerrymandering and at-large district elections system. More often than not, Latinos have found themselves on the same side with the Justice Department against Democratic elected officials.

Yet, despite all of these positive signs, including the Latino turnouts for Reagan and Bush in 1980, 1984, and 1988, the GOP's "Southwest Strategy" has yielded few other political dividends. A close examination would reveal that recent Latino support for the GOP during presidential elections is primarily based on personalities, more so than on ideology and issues. Moreover, GOP gains among some Latinos appear to have been in direct proportion to the continued political carelessness manifested by the Democratic party towards Latino voters. Republican registration figures, for example, have not significantly increased in the past two decades among Latinos. Although increasing numbers of Latinos have been backing Republican presidential candidates, their political convictions do not seem strong enough to encourage changes in party affiliation. The significant Latino turn-outs for Nixon (1972), Reagan (1980 and 1984), and Bush (1988) did not substantially benefit numerous Latino Republican candidates at the state or local levels hoping to ride the political coattails of a popular president.

Latino voting patterns show that Latinos still continue to view themselves primarily as Democrats. What has changed over the past several elections is that Latinos are splitting their votes between Republican presidential candidates and Democrats seeking state and congressional seats. This ticket splitting can be attributed in large part to the failure of the Democratic party to field fresh candidates with exciting ideas and programs. Latino voters seem to have indicated that McGovern, Carter, Mondale, and Dukakis were poor substitutes for the likes of Franklin Roosevelt, Harry

---

[57]Paul Taylor, "GOP Will Aid Civil Rights Groups in Redistricting," *The Washington Post*, April 1, 1990, A-6. See also, James A. Barnes, "Minority Map Making," *National Journal*, April 7, 1990.

Truman, and John Kennedy. Another way of demonstrating this point is that Latino support for GOP candidates in nonpresidential elections is dismal. Latino voters overwhelmingly endorsed Democratic candidates in 1974, 1982, and 1986.

It is therefore evident that both major parties and the Latino community presently find themselves at an important crossroad. Latinos and their leaders have long experienced broken campaign promises, neglect, and the lack of key appointments from both parties. So once again, as a new decade begins, Latinos are anxiously waiting to see which of the two political organizations takes major steps toward appointing Latino leaders to positions of power and truly integrating Latino concerns as a vital part of the national agenda. The 1990s could bring either a continuation of the history of general neglect or a significant change that transcends cosmetic and temporal accommodations of Latinos and their agenda.

As alluded to above, in terms of appointments, the Bush administration has taken some visible and important steps with three cabinet level Hispanics: Dr. Lauro Cavazos, Secretary of Education; Manuel Luján, Secretary of Interior; and Dr. Antonia Novello, Surgeon General. A fourth Latina appointed at the top level is Catalina Villalpondo as U.S. Treasurer. According to Roberto de Posada, Deputy Director of Outreach Communications for the RNC, there have also been 37 high-level presidential appointments that are not just staff assistant positions; and, in addition, there have been over 150 other appointments.[58] Furthermore, the GOP has established a Latino advisory board in order to learn more about the issues that concern the Latino community.[59]

The Democratic party, even though lacking the advantages of presidential and other executive level offices, has also made some notable gestures to the Latino communities in terms of appointments. For example, it too has established a Latino advisory board with duties similar to the GOP's advisory board.[60] In addition, the DNC has placed four Latinos in important positions: Gilberto Ocañas, Director of the Office of Voter Participation; Jack Otero, Vice-Chair of Voter Participation and Registration; Carmen Pérez, Vice-Chair of the DNC in charge of Hispanic Political Development and Census Reapportionment; and María T. Cardona as the Communications Outreach Coordinator.[61] One of Ms. Cardona's duties is to make better use of the Spanish-language media for the party's political goals. It will be interesting to observe how she and her staff develop and implement strategic plans to use the various Spanish-language (and maybe

[58]Telephone interview with Roberto de Posada, May 23, 1990.

[59]"Attuned to Hispanic Voices," *Vista*, April 22, 1990.

[60]*Ibid*.

[61]Telephone interview with María T. Cardona, May 24, 1990.

English-language media oriented at Hispanics) in the party's attempts to win the votes of Latinos.

These steps seem to be in the right direction, and they may be a result of sincere interest in integrating Latinos at all levels of the party and administration. But the changes may also be a response to the growing political demands and needs of organized Latino leaders and communities. For example, on February 28, 1990, representatives of 30 Latino national organizations met with White House staff to discuss the insufficient numbers of Latinos in the Bush administration. At the time there were only 116 appointees out of 3,317 positions, or 3.5 percent.[62]

During the 1990s, however, there is yet an even more important issue to watch closely; one that goes beyond the numbers game and the activities of token appointments and advisory boards. The issue is not just the integration of Latinos into American politics but the integration of the diverse Latino agendas into mainstream politics. While in these pages we cannot venture to identify or define those agendas, it is certain that there are problems, concerns, and issues of particular importance for Latinos of diverse national origins, regional locations, and social classes. Redistricting, bilingual education, and immigration are just three of the most visible, but there are others as well. It will be extremely important to scrutinize if the Latino appointees in the Bush administration, the GOP, and the Democratic party bring those issues to the forefront where they can be discussed and acted upon as part of the American political and social system. Otherwise we may find that in the process of the personal integration and political assimilation of Latino appointees and politicians, the distinct and vital Latino agendas are ignored and forgotten. At the present time, it appears that neither party is willing to make this bold move.

---

[62]"Group to Call for Posts," *Hispanic Link Weekly Report*, February 26, 1990.

VI. POLITICAL COALITIONS AND CONFLICTS AMONG CALIFORNIA ETHNIC MINORITIES

CHAPTER 13

CHARLES HENRY AND CARLOS MUÑOZ, JR.
University of California at Berkeley

Ideological and Interest Linkages in California Rainbow Politics

In 1967, Martin Luther King, Jr. argued that Negroes are traditionally manipulated because the political powers take advantage of three major weaknesses. The first weakness involves the selection of Negro leaders by white leadership. The "black masses were generally suspicious of these manufactured leaders," said King, who spent little time in persuading the black community that they embodied personal integrity, commitment, and ability. These Negro politicians offered few programs and less service. They were figureheads for old regimes rather than fighters for progress. Second, in order to develop genuinely independent and representative political leaders, King believed Negroes must master the art of political alliances. "The future of the deep structural changes we seek will not be found in the decaying political machines," said King, but "lies in new alliances of Negroes, Puerto Ricans, labor, liberals, certain church and middle-class elements."[1] Such alliances must be based upon some self-interest of each component group as well as a common interest into which they merge. Finally, King attacked the general reluctance of the Negro to participate fully in political life. While King did not believe the ballot had magical powers, he did think that its full and creative use would help to achieve many far-reaching changes. Moreover, a decade of civil rights activity can be used to overcome the deep sense of futility that many northern Negroes feel.

King's views in *Where Do We Go From Here: Chaos or Community?* echo those of Stokely Carmichael and Charles Hamilton, which were published the same year in *Black Power*. After critiquing the myths of coalition—that what is good for America is automatically good for black people, that a viable coalition can be affected between the politically and economically secure and the politically and economically insecure, and that political coalitions are or can be sustained on a moral, friendly, sentimental basis; by

---

[1]Martin Luther King, Jr., *Where Do We Go From Here?* (New York: Harper & Row, 1967), 150.

appeals to conscience—they offer four grounds for viable coalitions: (1) the recognition by the parties involved of their respective self-interests; (2) the mutual belief that each party stands to benefit in terms of that self-interest from allying with the other or others; (3) the acceptance of the fact that each party has its own independent base of power and does not depend for ultimate decision making on a force outside itself; and (4) the realization that the coalition deals with specific and identifiable—as opposed to general and vague—goals.[2] The National Rainbow Coalition is the best example to date of an attempt to enact the remarkably similar political principles of King, Carmichael, and Hamilton at a society-wide level.

A national coalition government composed of groups embodying the class and racial consciousness of the 1960s along with the environmental and consumer consciousness of the 1970s and 1980s would seem to be a logical outgrowth of the type that King, Carmichael, and Hamilton were proposing. In fact, Rev. Jesse Jackson's articulation of a national rainbow coalition builds directly on this political vision.

Jackson's understanding of coalition politics involves three concepts that are crucial: interests, reciprocity, and leverage. He believes that America's rejected hold the keys to progressive political change. If they recognized their own self-interest, they would not only gain self-respect but also recognize what they share in common with others. There must be a relationship of reciprocity rather than of domination if coalition politics are to work. Too often, argues Jackson, race has been used to obscure the interests of the disinherited. In terms of leverage, Jackson contends that the Rainbow Coalition must become a "third force" in American politics, pressuring Republicans from the outside and Democrats from the inside.[3]

Jackson's efforts to sustain and build a rainbow coalition raise a number of issues that have received little attention in the literature on mass mobilization and coalition building. First, to what extent do Jackson's ideological and symbolic appeals to racial participation and mobilization spillover to other nonwhite racial groups? There is a great deal of literature on black-white biracial coalitions, but very little on coalitions of people of color or multiracial coalitions. Second, to what extent did Jackson's appeal to and incorporation of specific group interests attract multiracial support? Finally, if ideology and interest are not enough to sustain a rainbow coalition, how was it built in the first place? To answer this question, we will briefly explore the organizational histories of coalition leaders and the incorporation of multiracial leadership into decision making. Discussion of

---

[2]Stokely Carmichael and Charles V. Hamilton, *Black Power* (New York: Vintage, 1967), 79-80.
[3]Roger D. Hatch, *Beyond Opportunity* (Philadelphia: Fortress Press, 1988), 124-25.

all three questions will focus on the nation's largest and most diverse state—California.

MASS MOBILIZATION

Cross-cultural studies of political participation patterns in the United States have produced confusing results at best. For example, some studies report that black participation rates lag significantly behind white participation rates while other studies have shown the exact opposite. The few studies conducted of blacks, Latinos, and Anglos' political participation have not produced consistent results. Moreover, when other forms of political participation, (e.g., contributions, campaigning, etc.) or social participation patterns are considered, the picture becomes even more muddled.[4] In general, these studies have produced two types of theories. Those studies finding less black participation have suggested that blacks are isolated from mainstream politics. Structural obstacles, overt repression, and cultural inhibition are cited as reasons for low black participation. Indeed, from this isolation perspective, any significant increase in electoral activity might be regarded as threatening to whites (negative). Studies showing greater participation among blacks than whites, even when socio-economic and educational status are held constant, have usually suggested that ethnic community identification is responsible. These studies suggest that blacks compensate for their oppression through increased political and social activity. The ethnic (read racial) community explanation tends to see such activity as a positive development and recent elections involving high levels of black participation have given more weight to earlier research.

To date, there are two possible explanations for differences in black and Latino political participation. George Antunes and Charles M. Gaitz contend that higher levels of black participation are triggered by greater perceived levels of social distance held by blacks. That is, when blacks are asked about white attitudes towards blacks, they predict a greater amount of white discrimination than indicated by white responses to questions about their attitudes toward blacks. Chicanos, on the other hand, hold views about

---

[4]See Thomas M. Guterbock and Bruce London, "Race, Political Orientation, and Participation: An Empirical Test of Four Competing Theories," *American Sociological Review* 48 (August 1983): 439-53; Patricia Klobus-Edwards et al., "Differences in Social Participation," *Social Forces* 53 (1978): 1035-52; Steven Martin Cohen and Robert E. Kappis, "Participation of Blacks, Puerto Ricans, and Whites in Voluntary Associations: A Test of Current Theories," *Social Forces*, vol. 56, no. 4, 1978; and George Antunes and Charles M. Gaitz, "Ethnicity and Participation," *American Journal of Sociology*, vol. 80, no. 5, 1975.

white attitudes toward them that are significantly closer to the actual white responses.[5]

Richard D. Shingles has provided an important elaboration of ethnic community theory. Although omitting an examination of Latinos, he has cast the social distance explanation in a more proactive direction. Shingles argues that black consciousness contributes to political mistrust and a sense of internal political efficacy, which, in turn, promotes policy-related participation. This results in greater political involvement on the part of blacks than whites of comparable status.[6] A later Shingles study found that black men were more active than any other group, even higher status white men. He also finds that while in 1967 black women expressed higher internal political efficacy than black men, the findings were reversed for 1987.[7]

A second possible explanation for differential rates of ethnic participation may rest in the political climate of each city or region. Nicholas L. Danigelis believes that both the isolation and ethnic community theories may be correct depending on the specific political climate. During periods of overt repression visible black political participation may be low with blacks isolated from conventional activity. At times when blacks are receiving some external support, high participation may result in and produce conditions conducive to ethnic community politics. According to Danigelis, a neutral or ambiguous political climate should produce black levels of political participation similar to those of whites.[8]

A political climate theory of minority participation would appear to be a variant of resource mobilization theory. Although resource mobilization has been developed to explain the rise of social movements, it might be particularly useful in minority electoral campaigns, which often resemble social movements.[9] Early resource mobilization theorists tended to emphasize the dependence of social movements led by minorities and the

[5]Gaitz, *op. cit.*

[6]Richard D. Shingles, "Black Consciousness and Political Participation: The Missing Link," *American Political Science Review*, vol. 75, no. 1 (March 1981): 76-90.

[7]Richard D. Shingles, "A Black Gender Gap in Political Participation?" a paper presented at the annual meeting of the National Conference of Black Political Scientists, Baton Rouge, Louisiana, March 7, 1989.

[8]Nicholas L. Danigelis, "A Theory of Black Political Participation in the United States," *Social Forces*, vol. 56, no. 1, 1977.

[9]Charles P. Henry and Carlos Muñoz, Jr., "Minority Power and Urban Reform: The Case of Black and Chicano Mayors," a paper presented at the annual meeting of the American Political Science Association, New Orleans, Louisiana, August 1984.

poor on external resources, such as sympathetic whites and the press.[10] However, more recent theorists, such as Doug McAdam, have focused on the internal factors as well as the opportunities presented by the political system in general. Ronald Walters has applied McAdam's analysis of the civil rights movement to the 1984 Jackson campaign to demonstrate a class dynamic in the mobilization of support for Jackson in the black community. Walters contends that [s]ince the blacks were beginning to respond to Reagan long before black leaders began to consider a black candidacy, the emergence of the Jackson campaign clearly confirmed the thesis that it responded to a popular mobilization already building."[11] While the work of McAdams and Walters tends to support ethnic community theory and corrects an early overemphasis on external support by resource mobilization theory, it does not explain how other elements of the rainbow coalition were activated.

INCORPORATING IDEOLOGY AND INTERESTS

In their pioneering study of black and Latino electoral participation in 10 northern California cities, Rufus Browning, et al., adopt a variation of the political climate theory to explain differences among blacks and Latinos. They argue that the dominant coalitions in these cities have diverse orientations toward minorities and their interests. They attempt a balanced approach using the characteristics of minority mobilization as well as the ideology and interests of the dominant coalition.[12]

The work of Browning, et al., is especially significant because they attempt to move beyond minority mobilization to develop a theory of incorporation. Incorporation means more than getting elected. Minorities must become part of a coalition, according to Browning, and the coalition must be dominant if the interests of minority groups are to influence policy.[13]

---

[10]See John D. McCarthy and Mayer N. Zald, "Resource Mobilization and Social Movements: A Partial Theory," *American Journal of Sociology*, vol. 82, no. 6 (May 1977): 1212-39; and Marvin E. Olson, "Social and Political Participation of Blacks," *American Sociological Review* 72 (1966): 32-46.

[11]Ronald W. Walters, *Black Presidential Politics in America* (Albany: State University of New York Press, 1988), 48.

[12]Rufus P. Browning, Dale Rodgers Marshall, and David H. Tabb, *Protest is Not Enough* (Berkeley: University of California Press, 1984), 240-41.

[13]Richard A. Keiser argues that political competition is the crucial variable in promoting minority incorporation. See his "Amicability or Polarization? Patterns of Political Competition and Leadership Formation in Cities with Black Mayors," unpublished paper presented at the annual meeting of the Midwest Political Science Association, Chicago, 1987. It should also be noted that a high degree of organization may lead to fragmentation, e.g., as in New York.

According to the theory, three factors shape local mobilization: (1) the size of the minority population, (2) the amount of support for minority interests among the rest of the electorate, and (3) the organizational development and political experience of the group. The theory of incorporation emphasizes the relevance of ideology in making coalitions work to the benefit of minority interests. In particular, the importance of liberal white coalition partners is seen as essential to minority incorporation.[14] This emphasis on ideology as the glue that binds successful biracial coalitions together is supported in Raphael Sonenshein's analysis of New York, Chicago, and Los Angeles. Interests are given only a secondary role since racial attitudes are likely to prevent poor or working class whites from uniting with blacks of similar status in a coalition leading to black incorporation. Thus, coalitions of liberal, well-educated whites with blacks in pursuit of status rather than welfare goals seem to have the best chance for success.[15]

This argument is fine as far as it goes. However, it does not go far enough in explaining the multiracial nature of such coalitions. If black-white coalitions based on the economic interests of blacks and whites from the same class background are impossible because of racial prejudice, then ideology alone is left to sustain coalitions between blacks and whites with different economic interests. When black interests come into conflict with those of liberal whites, as Sonenshein suggests is the case in New York, liberal sentiments are not enough to sustain a coalition. In New York, this conflict has resulted in tension between the black and Jewish communities. Black-Jewish conflict involves elements of subordination and domination characteristic of the historic relationship between blacks and whites.[16] This relationship is a vertical one in which Jews are represented as storekeepers, landlords, and employers while blacks are seen as customers, tenants, and domestics. This economic conflict is exacerbated by cultural factors. Black novelist Richard Wright, for example, has stated that, "All of us black people who lived in the neighborhood hated Jews, not because they've exploited us, but because we have been taught at home and in Sunday School the Jews were 'Christ-killers.'" On the other hand, Jews have experienced a long history of discrimination in the United States and were

---

[14]Browning, *op. cit.*, 240-49.

[15]Raphael J. Sonenshein, "Biracial Coalitions in Big Cities: Why They Succeed, Why They Fail," in *Racial Politics in American Cities*, edited by Rufus P. Browning, et. al. (New York: Longoan, 1990), 193-96.

[16]See, for example, George M. Frederickson, *White Supremacy* (New York: Oxford University Press, 1981) and Hubert M. Blalock, *Toward a Theory of Minority Group Relations* (New York: Wiley and Sons, 1967).

active supporters of the civil rights movement. Thus, they are susceptible to liberal ideological appeals.[17]

As Sonenshein notes, a liberal coalition of blacks and Jews has dominated Los Angeles politics for the last 17 years. Yet this fragile alliance is beginning to show signs of strain both because of divergent economic interests among the principal partners and because of increasing demands on the part of Asian Americans and Latinos. Both of these latter minority groups differ significantly from blacks and whites in terms of ideology and interests.[18]

Korean Americans, for example, have a much more horizontal relationship with blacks than do Jews. Although Korean Americans, like Jews, are often seen as a "model minority" and have replaced Jewish storeowners in many black neighborhoods, the dynamic is different. Korean immigrants are not white and have not been a part of the historic white domination of black communities. Their businesses are more marginal than Jews, and they have less political power than blacks. While Korean immigrants are likely to be fundamentalist Christians, they are also venture capitalists who are strongly anti-Communist and anti-Socialist. They have no first-hand experience of the black struggle for civil rights and are suspicious of liberal economic demands.[19]

While Browning et al., indicate that black mobilization appears to facilitate Latino mobilization, they also point out some basic differences. First, Latinos do not suffer the stigma of blackness and many consider themselves whites of Hispanic origin. Second, there is greater cultural and socio-economic diversity among Latinos (such as Cubans, Puerto Ricans, Dominicans, and Mexicans) than blacks.[20] Third, they are more likely to be Roman Catholic and therefore less likely to see political action as a preferred means of improvement than blacks. On the other hand, the Mexican-American community, in particular, has a long history of colonial conflict with white America, and the Chicano power movement drew direct support from the black power movement.[21]

---

[17]Edward Chang, "Black-Korean Conflict in Los Angeles" (Berkeley: Ethnic Studies Department, unpublished Ph.D. dissertation, 1990).

[18]Raphael J. Sonenshein, "Biracial Coalition Politics in Los Angeles" in Browning (1990), *op. cit.*, 44.

[19]Chang, *op. cit.*, and Edna Boracich, "Making It in America," *Sociological Perspective*, vol. 30, no. 4 (October 1987): 446-48.

[20]Browning (1984), *op. cit.*, 220. Also see Kenneth R. Nladenka, "Blacks and Hispanics in Urban Politics," *American Political Science Review*, vol. 83, no. 1 (March 1989): 165-91.

[21]See Carlos Muñoz, Jr., *Youth, Identity, Power* (London: Verso, 1989).

Based on this brief overview of multiracial relationships, we might suggest that blacks and Latinos are the most likely coalition partners followed by Asians and Anglos in that order. Indeed, a recent *Los Angeles Times* poll supports this ranking. Their survey of southern California residents found that Anglos were seen as looking least favorably on blacks (44 percent), followed by Latinos (38 percent), and Asians (24 percent). Respondents thought blacks most disliked Anglos (40 percent), Asians (23 percent), and Latinos (19 percent). In fact, the poll suggests that the greatest potential for coalition may lay with Asian Americans and Latinos if attitudes are any guide.[22]

ORGANIZATIONAL LINKAGES

The importance of political organization in overcoming ideological and interest differences is illustrated by a brief look at the organizational history of key rainbow coalition leaders in California. A key spinoff of the industrial workers movement was the development of the field of community organizing. The key innovator in this area, Saul Alinsky, grew up in the 1930s in Chicago and gained his reputation by changing the focus of organization from the factory to the neighborhood. When he formed the Woodlawn Organization in a black ghetto in Chicago in the late 1930s, he successfully combined the skills of social work and union organizing. In 1940, he founded the Industrial Areas Foundation to train other community organizers. According to Alinsky, the minority organizer must always work within definite ideological constraints imposed by (1) the ideas and beliefs of his/her constituency; (2) the rules, values, and organization of the dominant authority; (3) the possibility of attracting third parties to the dispute; and (4) the rules and condition of coverage by the public media.[23]

One of Alinsky's basic rules was that the organizer must learn the concerns of one's constituency and never step outside their experience. One of the earliest Industrial Areas Foundation projects was a community-based organization for the Chicano community in California, the Community Service Organization. This organization was headed by Fred Ross, a staff veteran of the Dust Bowl Era farm labor camps and the World War II Japanese-American relocation camps. Through his work in the Community Service Organization, Ross met Delores Huerta. Also through Ross, Huerta met Cesar Chavez and later helped to establish the United Farm Workers in 1962. Huerta was a major Chicano supporter of the Jackson campaign

---

[22]Kevin Roderick, "Times Poll Shows That Southern Californians Think Prejudice Is Still Common, But Subtle," *Los Angeles Times*, February 13, 1989, 3, 9.

[23]See Saul D. Alinsky, *Rules For Radicals* (New York: Vintage, 1972).

in California while Chavez promoted Dukakis (this division explains the UFW's official neutrality during the campaign).

Highlander Folk School (HFS) was founded in 1932 by Myles Horton. Horton had been influenced by Danish folk schools (which also influenced Booker T. Washington) and by Jane Addams' Hull House. Highlander, however, was based in the American South with the goal of promoting social change by bringing black and white farmers and factory workers together to discuss and solve their problems. It viewed itself as providing the radical training for labor leaders that neither the AFL nor the Communist Party could provide. In 1953, Highlander anticipated the Supreme Court decision on school desegregation by conducting its first workshops on desegregation.

Among the early participants was Rosa Parks, who was active in the Montgomery NAACP before the bus boycotts. Martin Luther King also attended sessions at Highlander. According to sociologist Aldon Morris, the Highlander Folk School was to play three important roles during the civil rights movement:

> First, before and during the movement, the HFS assisted in pulling together black leadership. Second, as an institution it provided a visible and successful model of a future integrated society. Finally, the HFS developed a successful mass education program that was later transferred to the Southern Christian Leadership Conference (SCLC), along with three trained staff members. That program was revolutionary from an educational, political, and social standpoint and was directly involved in the mobilization of the civil rights movement.[24]

Of course, Jesse Jackson was given his first national exposure as a staff member of SCLC. When placed in charge of their Chicago office, Operation Breadbasket, he adopted both the tactics of The Woodlawn Organization and the political education programs of Highlander Folk School.[25]

Mabel Teng, a Jackson delegate and a leader in Chinese-American politics in northern California, decided to support Jackson after he publicly drew attention to Vincent Chin's murder in Detroit in 1983. Her work on the Chin case was representative of the work she had done with the Chinese Progressive Association (CPA). This group was first formed in 1973 to protest an alleged attack by San Francisco police against Harry Wong, a Chinatown book seller whose offerings included Mao's Little Red Book and other communist literature. Before moving to San Francisco, Teng had

---

[24]Aldon D. Morris, *The Origins of the Civil Rights Movement* (New York: The Free Press, 1984), 141.

[25]Charles Henry attended a number of Operation Breadbasket political education meetings from 1969-1971.

helped found a CPA in Boston. In Boston, she had become politically sensitized by the Vietnam War and taught in Boston's schools during the busing controversy. Teng believes that Jackson did not give the highest priority to Asian-American concerns such as immigration, bilingual education, hate crimes, or university admission quotas; he was the only candidate to treat that community as more than a fund-raising source.[26]

MULTIRACIAL INCORPORATION

These institutional/individual linkages are important in demonstrating the continuity of social movements and the ripple effects of key institutions across racial and cultural groupings. These linkages, along with general ideological appeals and specific interest group appeals, help explain the limited success of the rainbow coalition at the electoral level in California. However, they do not provide a blueprint for multiracial incorporation in decision making that has been largely absent in the rainbow.

Charles Henry and Carlos Muñoz employ this approach in their examination of black and Latino support for minority mayors in San Antonio, Denver, Chicago, and Philadelphia. They conclude that the influx of blacks, Latinos, and other racial minorities into urban areas, along with white flight to suburbia, have made the traditional class-defined models of upper- and middle-class white Protestant reform and white ethnic machines obsolete. Their analysis suggests that any new model of urban politics must take into account several points: (1) high levels of minority participation across all class lines tend to support the ethnic community theory rather than the social isolation theory; (2) less white support for black mayoral candidates as compared to Latino mayoral candidates may confirm that black perceptions of greater social distance between blacks and whites are correct; (3) less Latino support for Latino candidates as compared to black support for black candidates may reflect less distrust or lower feelings of efficacy (an earlier stage of political mobilization); (4) external black support, which made Philadelphia and Chicago "national campaigns," may help explain higher levels of black participation and may demonstrate that black consciousness is not dependent on local leadership style; and (5) both Philadelphia and Chicago have long histories of black electoral mobilization, while in San Antonio and Denver, one must distinguish between older Mexican-American elites who have long been active and the more recent Latino residents from working-class backgrounds.[27]

---

[26]Laird Harrison, "Mabel Teng Rises to the Top With Jackson Campaign," *Asian Week*, vol. 9, no. 45 (June 17, 1988): 16-17.

[27]Charles P. Henry, *op. cit.*

The notion that emerges from the Henry and Muñoz study that racial minorities support each other's mayoral candidates to a greater extent than whites but not as much as the candidate's own racial group is supported by political scientist Byran Jackson's study of ethnic cleavages in California. He reports that the 70 percent support black gubernatorial candidate Tom Bradley received in 1982 from the Latino community in Los Angeles was significantly higher than Bradley's Anglo support but less than the 90 percent support Bradley achieved in the black areas of Los Angeles. Latinos held this middle ground in the 1986 gubernatorial election as Bradley lost support among all three groups. Moreover, Jackson extends his analysis of ethnic voting patterns to issue voting with similar results. For example, his analysis of voting for the 1986 English-only proposition in California found that black communities occupied the middle ground voting solidly against the proposition but not as strongly as the Latino community. Most Anglo neighborhoods, on the other hand, supported the measure.[28] In terms of mobilization, the Latino and Asian voter turnout lagged significantly behind that of blacks and Anglos.

When we look at polling data for the 1988 Democratic primary in California, we find additional support for a middle ground model of interracial support among minority groups for minority candidates. A California poll taken of Dukakis-Jackson preferences by Democratic sub-groups just before the election found that while only 20 percent of whites supported Jackson, 35 percent of Latinos and 84 percent of blacks supported him.[29] These findings were reinforced by a *Los Angeles Times* poll in California, which revealed a 22 percent white vote for Jackson, a 36 percent Latino vote and a 95 percent black vote. Among Asian Americans, Jackson won an impressive 46 percent of their vote. See Table 1.

Table 2 compares Jesse Jackson's statewide vote total by ethnic groups to Tom Bradley's voting totals in his two campaigns for governor of California. With the exception of the American Indian vote for Jackson in 1988, the percentage of racial minorities voting for the black candidates is higher than the Anglo vote for the black candidates.

In moving from group identification to political awareness, Jackson's position on the issues most relevant to each racial group was seen as crucial. A campaign letter from "Latinos for Jackson" emphasized his opposition to the Simpson-Rodino immigration bill and his support for bilingual educa-

---

[28]Byran O. Jackson, "Ethnic Cleavages and Voting Patterns in U.S. Cities: An Analysis of the Asian, Black and Hispanic Communities of Los Angeles," a paper presented at the Conference on Comparative Ethnicity, Los Angeles, California, June 1-3, 1988, 19-21.

[29]Mervin Field, "Dukakis Leads Jackson by a 57% to 28% Margin Among California Voter," *The California Poll*, May 25, 1988.

Table 1:   *How California Ethnic Groups Voted (1988 Primary)*

	Dukakis	Jackson
Anglo	73%	22%
Black	4%	95%
Asian	50%	46%
Latino	59%	36%
American Indian	80%	17%

Source: *Los Angeles Times* poll July 8, 1988.

Table 2:   *How California Democrats Voted by Ethnic Group for the Two Black Candidates*

	Bradley 1982	Jackson 1984	Bradley 1986	Jackson 1988
Anglo	42%	8%	33%	22%
Black	95%	80%	91%	95%
Asian	60%	NA	39%	46%
Latino	70%	17%	52%	36%
American Indian	NA	NA	NA	17%

Source: *Los Angeles Times* poll January 1, 1988; Thomas F. Pettigrew and Denise A. Alston, *Tom Bradley's Campaigns for Governor* (Joint Center for Political Studies 1988).

tion.   It highlighted his active participation in the Watsonville canning strike, the Phelps Dodge strike, and the Campbell's soup boycott. His visits with the leaders of Nicaragua, Mexico, and Cuba as well as the barrios of East Los Angeles were mentioned.[30]

Jackson also did substantial amounts of campaigning in Asian-American communities. He outlined a specific plan for attacking anti-Asian violence by enforcing laws, "sensitizing the American people to the historical contributions, culture, needs, and concerns of Asian Pacific Americans in order to break historic stereotypes by using public education" and public hearings on violence and harassment. Jackson also demonstrated his commitment to Asian-American appointments by naming four high level Asian staff members while Dukakis had none. The only issue on which

[30] "Form Letter," Latinos for Jackson, San Francisco, California, January 27, 1988.

Dukakis and Jackson clearly split was on the Immigration Reform and Control Act of 1986, which Jackson opposed and Dukakis supported.[31]

If these appeals to group interests had been combined with more multiracial incorporation into decision making, a true grassroots organization might have developed. However, Armando Gutierrez, a staff member with the 1984 Jackson campaign, in which Jackson's major opponent was then Vice-President Walter Mondale, reports on the problems he faced in gaining access to Jackson during a crucial period. Gutierrez had "virtually total access" to Jackson prior to the 1984 Democratic convention and convinced Jackson to embark on a trip to Central America over the objections of higher campaign officials. During the convention, however, he had to fight to be housed in the same hotel with Jackson and had no access to the floor on which the candidate was staying. Gutierrez believed that Mondale's refusal to publicly condemn the Simpson-Mazzoli immigration bill represented an opportunity for Jackson to win over Latino delegates pledged to Mondale. He obtained a list of these nearly 300 Latinos but could not reach Jackson to set up a strategy for approaching them. "All of the key campaign 'heavyweights' (Marion Berry, Richard Hatcher, Walter Fauntroy, California Assemblywoman Maxine Waters, and others) had sequestered Rev. Jackson," said Gutierrez, "and controlled access to him."[32]

Another problem stemmed from a lack of effective contact between African-American and Latino leaders at the national, state, and local levels. Black Jackson officials made the mistake of assuming titular leadership in the Latino community implied real leadership. According to rainbow coordinator Shelia Collins, this led to the appointment of Latinos to the campaign with either no grassroots organizing experience or activists who were divisive and sectarian in their politics.[33]

In 1988, Jackson attempted to rectify this past mistake by appointing Mario Obledo, a former president of the League of United Latin American Citizens (LULAC), and Toney Anaya, former governor of New Mexico, as two of his top advisors. Chicano political scientist and activist Carlos Muñoz, Jr., was appointed Latino issues advisor to the campaign staff, and activist Gene Royale was appointed to head the grassroots "Latinos for

---

[31]Laird Harrison, "Yellow Stripe in Jackson's Rainbow," *Asian Week*, May 20, 1988.

[32]Armando Gutierrez, "The Jackson Campaign in the Hispanic Community," in *Jesse Jackson's 1984 Presidential Campaign*, edited by Lucius J. Barker and Ronald W. Walters (Urbana: University of Illinois Press, 1989), 125. Carlos Muñoz, Jr., co-chair of University of California at Berkeley Faculty and Staff for Jackson, reports that while the 1988 campaign was better organized in the Latino community than the 1984 campaign, many of the same problems of access to Jackson and the top elite remained.

[33]Collins, *op. cit.*, 186.

Jackson" organization. Outside the campaign structure, Jackson named Obledo as president of the National Rainbow Coalition and appointed several other Latinos, Mexican Americans, and Puerto Ricans, to the organization's board of directors.

Collectively, those appointments represented an improvement over the 1984 campaign experience, but Gutierrez remained the only paid Latino staff member in the national campaign structure, and again in the lower echelon. As had been the case in 1984, Latinos were largely excluded from direct access to the campaign decision-making process.

At the campaign voter mobilization level, only one "Latinos for Jackson" group actually emerged, and that was in California. The group's effectiveness was limited due to lack of funding support, and most unfortunately, lack of direct access and communication with the statewide campaign leadership. Furthermore, the "Latinos for Jackson" group, mostly active in northern California, suffered from internal divisions between Latino members of two Marxist left subgroupings, the League of Revolutionary Struggle (LRS) and the Line of March organization. The basis of division was ideological and due to the perceived exclusion of the latter from the "Latinos for Jackson" group and the campaign as a whole.

Collins states that similar problems plagued Jackson's efforts to organize women as a special constituency within the rainbow. While Jackson had the most progressive position on all of the traditional "feminist" issues, such as the Equal Rights Amendment (ERA), freedom of reproductive choice, equal pay for equal work and work of comparable worth, and affirmative action, Jackson officials sought to mobilize the wing of the feminist movement most likely to support Mondale. To head the women's desk they chose Barbara Honegger, largely for her name recognition. Honegger had been a policy analyst in the Reagan administration who was fired in 1983 when she revealed that Reagan's ERA alternative was a sham. Lacking organizing ability or credibility within the feminist community, she was largely ignored after the press attention surrounding her initial appointment faded.[34]

These appointments of minority and women campaign officials and staff for their titles or press worthiness represent a real organizational problem. Symbolic ties at the elite level are used as a substitute for grassroots organizing at the mass level. Given a lack of resources and a lack of contacts in these communities by Jackson and his inside advisors, the mistakes described above are understandable. However, many of these mistakes were repeated during the 1988 campaign.[35] In large part, they reflect the contradiction of trying to develop a democratic, grassroots

---

[34]*Ibid.*, 196.
[35]Elizabeth O. Colton, *The Jackson Phenomenon* (New York: Doubleday, 1989), 184-86.

organization of divergent interests at the bottom with a charismatic leader of one core constituency at the top. Political scientist Manning Marable describes this problem as "the messiah complex." Black political organizations led by such a charismatic leader usually reflect a pyramidic top-down organizational structure in which all key decisions are made by the leader and his (almost always male) coterie of political lieutenants. "The branches or local organizations," says Marable, "recruit new members in large measure on the popularity and charisma of the national spokesperson, rather than on the basis of an agenda or political program." A second tier of leadership is developed on the criteria of loyalty to the leader rather than political or technical expertise. Marable states that Jackson did not consult with leaders of the rainbow before making such key decisions as meeting with George Bush after the 1988 election, or pursuing the vice-presidential nomination in June and July of 1988 or not running an independent campaign in the 1988 general election.[36]

These problems are manifest in the internal organization of the National Rainbow Coalition. Following the 1988 general election, Jackson proposed a restructuring of the organization. This restructuring was to make the organization more representative while at the same time, tightening control over decisions and appointments at the top. A comparison of the 1987 bylaws of the National Rainbow Coalition to the proposed 1989 bylaws is instructive. Many powers that were once the province of the convention, like amending the bylaws, electing officers, and electing the board, are now delegated to the National Rainbow Coalition Board. Powers once reserved for the NRC Board, such as the appointment of vice-presidents, nonboard officers, and the executive director, are now to be exercised solely by the president (Jackson). In addition, the president may now appoint NRC committee chairs and advisory council members from outside the NRC, establish state chapters or congressional district chapters, and appoint or remove their leaders. The national convention would convene every four years instead of every two years, and the NRC Board would meet every two years instead of annually.[37] These changes obviously centralize power in Jackson and, to a lesser extent, the NRC Board, which is self-perpetuating. While the new bylaws (to be adopted without a convention) may allow for more representative local leadership selected by national leaders, it does so at the expense of democratic participation.

---

[36]Manning Marable, "The Rainbow's Choice: The Man or The Movement," syndicated column, n.d.

[37]"Rainbow Restructuring," internal memo from Rev. Jackson to Jim Zogby and Lawrence Landry, February 18, 1989.

CONCLUSION

Both Tom Bradley's campaigns for governor and Jackson's campaigns for president suggest an inability to construct a broad-based progressive political coalition in California. Running a traditional, heavily financed, media-oriented campaign dependent on party leadership, Bradley narrowly lost in 1982. In 1986, he launched a more grassroots-oriented campaign, but lacking both charisma or a galvanizing issue(s), Bradley lost by a 2-to-1 margin.

Bradley sought to reconstruct his successful Los Angeles coalition of liberal whites and blacks at the statewide level. With a smaller black base of support (7 percent vs. 17 percent) and a smaller liberal base in the white community, Bradley sought to diffuse racial attitudes by positioning himself as a moderate. As a moderate, however, he found little to distinguish himself from his equally moderate Republican rival. In the end, Bradley's moderation helped to deactivate liberal and minority support while his race served to activate conservative opposition.[38]

Jackson ran a campaign that varied greatly from Bradley's. Rather than campaigning on the basis of a few general issues, he made specific appeals to groups based on their racial, ethnic, and political interests. Little money was spent on paid advertisements, but Jackson obtained a great deal of local coverage as he crisscrossed the state making many appearances. Those activists attracted to Jackson because of his position on issues found themselves welcomed to the campaign in a visible way but without real access to decision making. The diverse historical and individual links to the campaign were not harnessed in an efficient or systematic way. In some cases, previous organization loyalties led to fragmentation and in-fighting.

The major obstacle to the realization of a "rainbow coalition" rests in the nature of its leadership. A true coalition rests on democratic participation and shared decision making. A symbolic coalition relies on public endorsements, token representation, and charisma. Even if such a symbolic coalition should succeed electorally, there is little hope of it governing effectively without some resolution of the multiple interests represented among its multiracial supporters. In short, multiracial incorporation is essential to successful governing.

---

[38]Charles P. Henry, "Why Bradley Lost," in Michael Preston, et al., eds., *The New Black Politics* (New York: Longman, 1987).

CHAPTER 14

CAROLE J. UHLANER
University of California at Irvine

Perceived Discrimination and Prejudice and the Coalition Prospects of Blacks, Latinos, and Asian Americans

Ethnicity and race have historically served as a basis for coalition formation in American politics. The Democratic New Deal coalition can be understood in part as an alliance of European immigrants and their children with northern blacks (Anderson 1979; Petrocik 1981). Over the last few decades, changing immigration patterns and birthrates have led to a substantial increase in the number of Latinos and Asian Americans. The shift has arguably been most notable in California, where the proportion of non-Hispanic whites in the population dropped from 87 percent in 1960 to 67 percent in 1980 and 58 percent in 1990 and is expected to fall below 50 percent by the year 2010. Will these "new" groups join each other in a political coalition? Will they join blacks in a larger "minority" coalition? These questions are of substantial importance to political analysts (see Jackson, Gerber, and Cain 1991). Clearly a number of political commentators and actors anticipate that these groups will come together as a political force. Recall, for example, Jesse Jackson's talk of a Rainbow Coalition in the 1984 campaign. In light of the size of these populations in California, the future evolution of politics in the state will depend to a large extent upon the fate of these potential alliances.

At its most practical, the question about coalitions translates into the question of whether citizens from any or all of these groups will support a candidate from another group. Will the combined numbers of voters from minority groups translate into the election of minority officials? A descriptive notion of representation underlies this concern. Although descriptive representation captures only a portion of the concept (Pitkin 1967), voter behavior suggests that people do care about being represented by people "like them." Studies of policy outcomes suggest minority

Data collection for this research was funded by a grant from the Seaver Institute to the California Institute of Technology. Bruce E. Cain and D. Roderick Kiewiet were principal investigators in the overall project.

representation has real consequences for minority communities (Browning, Marshall, Tabb 1984). However, simply being other than non-Hispanic white may not be sufficient to make a candidate an adequately descriptive representative for persons who are also not non-Hispanic white but of different backgrounds. It depends upon how individuals categorize their world. Beyond descriptive representation, however, voters select officials to look out for their interests. Thus, cross-group support may derive from shared interests. Clearly, a coalition of minorities must rest on some common ground.

Shared interests in bald material terms may not be a sufficient basis for unity among these groups, as blacks, Latinos, and Asian Americans in California face different circumstances. Variations in objective economic standing, place of residence, educational attainment, and cultural traditions suggest possibilities for divisiveness rather than cooperation. As reported in Shastri (1986), in 1980 blacks in California were more likely than either of these other groups to have incomes below the poverty line, be unemployed, and use welfare and social services programs heavily. Latinos were only slightly more affluent than blacks and also used welfare programs heavily. However, they were much less likely to use social programs such as foster care and elderly services. Asian Americans had the highest income and lowest poverty and unemployment rates of these three groups, and a substantially higher proportion of their families than in any other group contained two or more workers. They made the least use of welfare and social service programs. The differences may lead individuals from each group to respond to others as competitors or just fail to see them as potential allies. On the other hand, since all three groups shared a lower standard of living than non-Hispanic whites, they may join together in demands for greater affluence. Even if potential partners do not share similar objective circumstances, they may have compatible interests.

Shared perceptions and experiences of discrimination provide an alternative, although related, possible common ground for a coalition. To the extent that people believe that the "majority" society is prejudiced against them based upon their race or ethnicity and that the opportunity structure of American society contains inequities, they may consequently believe that others who are "minorities" are politically like them. Perceived prejudice provides a particularly potent basis for a coalition, as the relevant political information—discriminatory experience—is acquired incidentally during the course of daily life. Much of the discussion of coalitions of minorities seems implicitly to assume that the belief that the dominant society treats minorities unfairly would provide the driving force behind joint action. Under this view, it makes sense to consider Asian Americans as possible coalition members, despite their objectively better economic circumstances, to the extent that discrimination limits their opportunities. Other relatively affluent groups that have experienced discrimination have previously entered similar coalitions. Daniels and Kitano (1970) suggest that discrimination in the U.S. reflects a two-category system of stratification, where "white" is presumed superior to "non-white." Thus persons of color, having suffered similar prejudice, may fight back collectively.

However, perceptions of discrimination and lack of opportunity need not necessarily lead to cooperation. Instead of sympathy towards others, someone who suffers from prejudice may instead feel competition, especially if they feel that they are particularly disadvantaged. Thus, discriminatory experiences might produce antagonisms instead of coalitions.

One factor that may affect a person's experience of prejudice is being native born versus being an immigrant. The experiences of white ethnic immigrants in the last century attest to the virulence of nativist sentiments at times in the United States. Substantial proportions of Latinos and Asian Americans are immigrants; many more are the children of immigrants. Beyond the issue of discrimination, and even in tolerant periods, immigrants confront different problems than the native born. Learning a new language, dealing with new customs, and negotiating the intricacies of the immigration and naturalization process itself present a set of experiences that may generate common interests that bring immigrants together. For example, language use is directly relevant to certain issues, such as bilingual services. Paradoxically, the newest immigrants may be most insulated from perceived discrimination, for example if they live within ethnic enclaves.

Up to this point, ethnic and racial groups have been discussed as though all possible members identified with them equally. However, individuals vary substantially both in their ethnic or racial identity and in the extent to which they believe that such an identity is linked to specific interests. Ethnically specific interests can provide a basis for alliance or for competition with others. Moreover, the perception of such interests may itself serve as an indicator of the salience and the potential political relevance of the ethnicity. The belief that one has both group-specific problems and a strong ethnic identity may enhance the ability to perceive prejudice. Conversely, the experience of prejudice reinforces a sense of ethnic identity. Keefe and Padilla (1987, 192) conclude that in their study of Chicanos, "perceived discrimination is a major contributory force in the maintenance of ethnic loyalty across our four generations of respondents." There is evidence that ethnic identity and perceived group problems are related to increased political activity. Whether they inhibit coalition formation—by leading to a focus on the problems of one's own group—or enhance it—by spotlighting the relevance of ethnicity as an organizing principle—remains unclear.

Ethnic identity and perceived inequity come together in the concept of group consciousness. Gurin and her collaboraters argue that a crucial prerequisite for group identity to produce political consequences is the linking of ethnic identity with a political consciousness of the external structures producing the group's circumstances (Gurin and Epps 1975;

Miller, Gurin, Gurin, and Malanchuk 1981; Gurin, Miller, and Gurin 1980; Gurin, Hatchett, and Jackson 1989). Group identification denotes a subjective sense of similarity to others. Group consciousness denotes political beliefs that arise from the identity, including, although not limited to, the sense that the group's condition is illegitimately inferior to that of others in society. The experience of prejudice should increase a sense of group consciousness. It reinforces a sense of ethnic identity. More crucially, this experience provides a tutorial in the lesson that one's group is treated unfairly. However, perceived prejudice is not identical with the perception of structural inequality. That further step, which is an important element of group consciousness, may be encouraged by the experience of prejudice, but need not necessarily follow. Whether group consciousness leads to a coalition may well depend upon whether structural inequality is seen as limited to one's own group or as a general condition affecting other groups as well. In the latter case, cooperation may well appear useful.

THE APPROACH

This paper examines perceived prejudice among California blacks, Mexican Americans, and Asian Americans and considers the possibilities for building a coalition upon this perception. It will also examine other aspects of possible shared experiences, as discussed above, as they may contribute to perceptions of prejudice and affect the likelihood of alliance.

Thus, data will first be presented on the degree to which these groups contain immigrants and to which their members identify problems specific to their ethnicity. Next, the distribution of perceived prejudice, as personally experienced, as perceived towards one's own group, and as projected into the future will be examined. An attempt will be made to locate those factors that correlate with higher or lower perceptions of bias.

As noted in the discussion of group consciousness, a perception of discrimination can exist without individuals believing that their group holds an illegitimately depressed structural position, that is, that it receives fewer opportunities than it deserves. Moreover, a belief that others also receive fewer opportunities may be key to the formation of a coalition. Thus, data on this set of beliefs, and the factors associated with them, are examined.

While eventually any coalition will have to deal with concrete political issues, any particular set of issues may prove irrelevant. Issues change over time, and their salience and interpretation change even more rapidly. Nonetheless, it is useful to consider whether these groups do share some issue preferences and whether perceptions of structural inequity and prejudice enhance or diminish similarities.

The data on which these analyses are based are drawn from a statewide telephone survey of Californians undertaken in late 1984. The study yielded completed interviews with 574 Latinos, 308 Asian Americans, 335 blacks, and 317 non-Hispanic whites of voting age, including noncitizens. The Latino sample includes 61 individuals of national origin other than Mexican. They are excluded from the analyses that follow, leaving 513 Mexican-American respondents.[1] In order to sample each of these four populations, rather than the state population, we overweighted certain census tracts, to locate blacks, and applied surname dictionaries to telephone listings, to locate Latinos and Asian Americans. Residential dispersion coupled with relatively low numbers in the population makes other techniques of locating respondents in these last two groups prohibitively expensive. As with most similar surveys, the resulting sample is somewhat more educated than the population as a whole but otherwise matches census data fairly well. Further details on the sampling design can be found in Uhlaner, Cain, and Kiewiet (1989, Appendix A). For ease of exposition, non-Hispanic whites are referred to in the text that follows as "Anglos," Asian Americans are referred to as "Asians," and Mexican Americans are referred to as "Mexicans."

Since this paper focuses on the prospects for a coalition among blacks, Mexicans, and Asians, many of the analyses will be restricted to them. However, for some analyses it will be useful to look at the Anglos for comparison.

IMMIGRATION AND GROUP PROBLEMS

As discussed in the introduction, substantial numbers of Asians and Mexicans in California share the experience of recent immigration. This may contribute to experiences of prejudice, and likely leads to some shared concerns. Table 1 shows that 40 percent of the Mexicans and 63 percent of the Asians were born abroad. Less than 10 percent of Anglos or of blacks were foreign born. In fact, 96 percent of blacks are third generation or more—their parents were born in the U.S. About a quarter of all three of the other groups are second generation citizens—persons whose parents were born abroad but who themselves were born in the U.S. Lower citizenship rates and a greater propensity to use a language other than English go along with the high proportion of recent immigrants among the Mexicans and

---

[1]Restricting the analysis to Mexican Americans avoids problems of interpretation that arise from the variety of countries and circumstances that characterize the other Latino respondents, at no real cost in statistical power as the number of Mexican Americans is very large. Although the Asian Americans come from a variety of countries, and thus lumping them into a single group is not optimal, there are too few from any single country to permit independent analyses. In other studies done with these data, however, it appears that this strategy has not produced serious distortions (see Uhlaner, Cain, Kiewiet 1989; Cain, Kiewiet, Uhlaner 1991).

Table 1:   *Immigration and Language Characteristics of Racial/Ethnic Groups*

	Anglo	Black	Mexican	Asian
Respondent Born Abrcad	9%	3%	40%	63%
Not citizen[a]	52 (15)[b]	44 (4)	71 (138)	47 (84)
Citizen[a]	48 (14)	56 (5)	29 (56)	53 (94)
Parents Born Abroad	22	2	29	22
Parents Born in U.S.	69	96	31	15
N	314	315	498	285
Not citizen	5%	1%	28%	30%
Citizen	95	99	72	70
N	314	317	493	283
Primary language English	92%	98%	46%	53%
Primary language not English	8	2	54	47
N	317	335	513	308

[a]As percentage of those born abroad.
[b]Actual number of cases in category.

Asians. Over one-fourth of the persons in these groups are not citizens, and only about one-half use English as their primary language.

Persons who believe that they have problems specific to their racial or ethnic group may have a stronger sense of ethnic identity, but in any event clearly identify ethnic interests. The following questions were used to locate respondents who perceive such interests and to assess which interests were most salient:

> Do you think there are problems today of special concern to [. . .] Americans? [respondent's race/ethnicity obtained in a previous question was inserted automatically.] [Anglo respondents were asked,
> Do you think there are problems today of special concern to people of your racial or national background?]
> Thinking of those problems which are of special concern to [. . .] Americans, what would you say is the most important? [respondent's race/ethnicity inserted automatically].
> [Anglo respondents were asked,
> Thinking of those problems which are of special concern to people of your racial or national background, what would you say is the most important?]

As indicated by the figures in Table 2, blacks were considerably more likely than either Anglos or members of other minority groups to name a particular problem of special concern to them as members of a racial/ethnic/national group. Sixty-five percent of the blacks in the survey said there was a problem of special concern, while only 24 percent of the white respondents did so. It is also clear that unemployment stood out in blacks' minds as especially troublesome for the black community. Over three out of 10 blacks cited this problem, compared with 10 percent of the Mexicans and only a handful of Anglos and Asians. Mexican respondents were notable for their relatively high propensity to refer to education. Blacks were more likely than respondents from other groups to refer to race relations, but not by a large margin. Asians stand out in their concern with loss of ethnic heritage, or such ethnically-specific problems as the Philippines or World War II reparations. The primary message of this table, however, is that blacks see themselves as more adversely affected by unemployment and other problems than do other Americans, including other minorities.

PERCEPTIONS OF PREJUDICE

Is the concern with ethnic/racial problems paralleled in perceptions of discrimination?[2] The most immediate impact of prejudice comes through personal experiences of discrimination. These perceptions were elicited by the following questions:

> Have you, yourself, personally experienced discrimination because you are [. . .]? (The respondent's race/ethnicity was inserted automatically at this point by the computer).

> (If "yes" to the previous question) Thinking of the most serious discrimination you have experienced . . . was it in getting a job, or getting into school, in getting a house or apartment, in a social situation, or in some other respect?

---

[2]Many survey researchers believe that blacks and members of other minority groups are frequently reluctant to discuss matters of race and ethnicity with white interviewers and that whites are reticent about expressing racist views that are no longer socially acceptable. Although many of the interviewers were Asian American or Latino (bilingual interviewers conducted interviews in Spanish), matching the race/ethnicity of respondents with the race/ethnicity of interviewers was not feasible. Thus, prejudice may be underreported in these results.

Table 2:   *Problems of Special Concern to One's Racial/Ethnic Group*

Problem Reported	Race/Ethnicity of Respondent			
	Anglo	Black	Mexican	Asian
None	76%	35%	54%	63%
Unemployment	1	31	10	4
Education	0	3	9	2
Crime, Gangs, Drugs	1	4	3	3
Race Relations/Discrimination	7	12	10	8
Loss of Ethnic Heritage/ Ethnic Issues	1	0	0	7

Anglo respondents were not asked these questions about personal experiences of prejudice. Table 3 reports the responses to these questions by the respondents' race/ethnicity.

As these figures indicate, the degree and nature of personally experienced discrimination reported in the survey varied dramatically across groups. Not only were blacks more likely to report personally experienced discrimination (62 percent), the discrimination they cited was largely economic in nature—over half reported that the discrimination involved a job. Although Asians perceived Americans in general as less prejudiced than did Mexicans, they were more likely to report having personally experienced discrimination (46 percent to 36 percent). In contrast with blacks, over half of the Asians who reported being personally discriminated against referred to social situations—possibly snubs, misguided attempts at ethnic humor, or insults—but not something that was obviously economically injurious. Only a quarter reported discrimination involving a job. Mexicans fell between these extremes, with a third reporting job discrimination and 40 percent reporting prejudice in a social situation. Mexicans were more likely than those in either of the other groups to report serious discriminatory experiences involving education or housing, although even for them these reports involved substantially fewer respondents than the job and social situation categories.

Perceptions of group interests and experiences of discrimination are not necessarily independent. For example, Mexicans were more likely than others to cite education in both contexts. Individuals who have experienced discrimination may differ from those who have not in their perceptions of the existence and nature of group interests. Conversely, those who have a keen sense of group interests may be more ready to perceive prejudice.

Table 3: *Personally Experienced Discrimination Reported by Blacks, Mexican Americans, and Asian Americans*

	Race/Ethnicity of Respondent		
	Black	Mexican	Asian
Respondent Personally Experienced Prejudice	62%	36%	46%
As Percentage of Those Who Said Yes, Most Serious Discrimination Personally Experienced:			
Social Situation	26	40	55
Job	52	32	23
Education	7	13	7
Housing	7	12	6

When respondents' characterizations of the most important problem facing their group are tabulated by whether or not they report a personal experience of discrimination, it becomes clear that individuals who report personal experience of prejudice were much more likely than those who did not to report a problem that they viewed to be of special concern to their group. The salience of race relations and discrimination is higher—by a factor of two—among those who have had such experiences themselves than for others in each ethnic/racial group. Within each minority group, one other issue area stands out by receiving substantially more mentions from those who report experiences of prejudice. Blacks with such experiences are half again as likely as other blacks to name unemployment as a problem. Three times as many Mexicans who report prejudice name education as a major problem area. Asians who say they have experienced prejudice are much more likely than other Asians to spotlight crime as a problem.

As discussed above, the experience of prejudice may also differ for the native born as distinct from immigrants. Asian and Mexican respondents' personal experiences of prejudice did vary as a function of how long their families had been in the United States. (Virtually all of the blacks were third generation; Anglos were not asked about personal experiences of prejudice.) The pattern, however, was an uneven one. Reports of personally experienced discrimination *increased* from the immigrant to the second generation (those who were born in the United States, but whose parents were not) and then declined for third and later generations (those whose parents were born in the United States), for both groups. The first part of the pattern is consistent with data reported by Portes and Bach

(1985) that Cuban and Mexican immigrants to the U.S. perceive more discrimination after three years in the country than when they first arrive. The situations in which prejudice is perceived vary from generation to generation. For both the Mexicans and Asians, the incidence of job-related prejudice decreases with generation in the country, although the dramatic drop occurs between the immigrant and second-generation respondents. On the other hand, for respondents from both groups, discrimination in social situations increases from the immigrant to the second generation. Third-generation Asians report still more social prejudice. Whatever the generation, Mexicans are almost equally likely to point to education as a problem area, while for Asians mention of this as an area where discrimination occurs drops after the immigrant generation. On the other hand, problems with housing are greater for second-generation Asians than for immigrants or those in the third generation, while for third-generation Mexicans housing problems diminish. Overall, Asian experiences of prejudice were likely to be in the social sphere, and increasingly so with time in the country; fully three-quarters of those third-generation Asians who experienced discrimination did so in a social situation. On the other hand, for the immigrant generation in both groups, jobs and education frequently presented the occasion for bias.

In addition to direct reports of personal experience, people form general views of the extent to which others think of them in discriminatory fashion. Thus, another aspect of perceived prejudice can be tapped by asking respondents what they believe to be the attitude of other Americans toward someone of their race or ethnicity. Such perceptions were tapped with the following question:

> As you mentioned previously, you are [. . .] [respondent's race/ethnicity inserted automatically by the computer]. Do you think most Americans are prejudiced against [. . .], only some Americans are prejudiced, or that most Americans are not prejudiced?

Table 4 reports the answers by the respondent's race/ethnicity.

Compared with Mexicans and Asians, blacks perceive Americans in general to be considerably more prejudiced. Asians perceive less prejudice than Mexicans. Asians, in fact, were twice as likely as blacks (42 percent compared with 21 percent) to report a belief that most Americans were not prejudiced against them.

However, differences between the groups were substantially less when respondents were asked about their expectations for future racial and ethnic relations. Respondents were asked:

> Do you think that over the next 10 years or so Americans will become more prejudiced against [. . .] [respondent's race/ethnicity inserted automatically by the computer], less

Table 4:   *Degree of Prejudice and Future Amount of Prejudice Directed Toward One's Racial/Ethnic Group*

	Race/Ethnicity of Respondent		
	Black	Mexican	Asian
American's Degree of Prejudice:			
Most Are Prejudiced	17%	10%	5%
Some Are Prejudiced	63	54	52
Most Are Not Prejudiced	21	36	42
America's Degree of Prejudice in 10 Years:			
More	8	9	11
Won't Change Much	48	46	48
Less	44	45	41

prejudiced, or do you think that their attitudes probably won't change much?

The responses, by ethnicity, are reported in the bottom half of Table 4. Despite the fact that, as shown by the previous tables, blacks perceive more prejudice in contemporary American life than do members of the other two groups, there is little difference across groups in their perceptions of the future. Members of all groups display optimism, with very few respondents anticipating more prejudice in the future, and close to one-half in each group expecting to see less.

To assess which factors are associated with perceived prejudice for each group, the three measures discussed here—self experience, prejudice towards the group, expected future prejudice—were combined in a simple additive scale of overall prejudice. This scale was then regressed on a number of variables capturing the respondents' citizenship and immigration status and on a variable reflecting whether or not they identified a group-specific problem. A number of other variables were controlled for: the respondents' age, party identification, education, and a measure of issue attentiveness (the number of items in the issue battery to which the respondent gave a yes or no—rather than don't know—response). The last two items relate to the ability and willingness to process political information. Age may reflect accumulated wisdom or simply different life experience, and party may shape a person's views. Table 5 reports the models estimated for each racial/ethnic group after variables with no effect were dropped.[3]

The first column reports the estimation for blacks. Perceptions of prejudice were lower among the handful of blacks who were foreign born or second generation. They were higher among younger blacks, among those who identified a problem affecting blacks, among those who are Democrats, and among those with more views on issues. Note that particularly with party identification and naming a group problem, causality may well run in either direction, or both. Persons may believe their group has a problem *because* they have been exposed to prejudice. The only claim being made for this estimation is that these factors are related to the perception of prejudice.

A rather different model holds for Mexicans and Asians. As among blacks, persons who identify a group specific problem are also more likely to perceive prejudice. However, in both of these groups, age, party identification, and issue attentiveness have no effect. Perceived prejudice is associated with generation and education, although in somewhat different fashions. Perceived prejudice is positively associated with education among Asians—the best educated perceive the most. Second generation Asians perceive more than either the foreign born or those in the third generation—there is a curvilinear relationship with time in the country. Among Mexicans, foreign-born noncitizens are the least likely to perceive prejudice. Naturalized citizens and those born in this country, whether or not of U.S. born parents, are all more likely, and by indistinguishable amounts, to perceive more. Education has a nonmonotonic relationship to these perceptions. Those who had at most a few years of high school, or who finished high school but had only a few years of college, are less likely to perceive prejudice than those who completed high school or who completed college. Altogether, despite the differences, these patterns for Mexicans and Asians suggest the "glass ceiling": perceptions of prejudice increase as persons should expect to be doing better. For all *three* groups, perceived prejudice is clearly associated with the awareness of a problem linked to ethnicity or race.

PERCEPTIONS OF STRUCTURAL INEQUITY

As noted previously, the perception of prejudice is not identical with the perception of inegalitarian life chances. These structural perceptions are especially important in providing a basis for cooperation or competition.

---

[3]The coefficients and significance of the remaining variables is virtually identical whether or not the insignificant ones are included, but it is far easier to read the tables in the simplified versions reported here.

Table 5: *Factors Influencing Overall Amount of Prejudice; Regression of Combined Scale, Separately by Racial/Ethnic Group*

	Blacks	Mexicans	Asians
Names group problem	.36[a]	.36	.46
	(3.53)[b]	(4.61)	(3.93)
Age	-.010		
	(-3.76)		
Party (Dem. positive)	.21		
	(2.38)		
Has issue opinions	.05		
	(1.74)		
Foreign-born citizen		.33	
		(2.43)	
Second generation		.25	.53
		(2.39)	(3.87)
Third generation	.59	.27	.05
	(2.50)	(2.62)	(0.33)
Education (in years)			.05
			(1.88)
High school graduate		.27	
		(3.27)	
College graduate		.24	
		(1.69)	
Constant	1.10	.98	.44
	(3.69)	(11.2)	(1.17)
R^2	.13	.09	.12
Adj. R^2	.11	.08	.10
N	315	492	284

[a]Unstandardized regression coefficient
[b]t-statistic

Respondents' views of the opportunity structure in the United States were assessed directly, using the following parallel batteries of questions:

Do you think there are any groups of people in the United States today who get *fewer* opportunities than they deserve? . . . Any other groups?

Do you think there are any groups of people in the United States today who get *more* opportunities than they deserve? . . . Any other groups?

To mitigate any reluctance by respondents to express perceptions of prejudice, the interviewers solicited up to four responses to each question. Table 6 displays the responses to these items. Note that the entries in each cell of the tables are not mutually exclusive. The same respondent, for example, could state that blacks, Latinos, and Asian Americans are disadvantaged, and all three responses would be registered.

Several things are readily apparent from these figures. First, it is clear that blacks are far more likely than Mexicans to perceive that people of their race/ethnicity are disadvantaged; 42 percent of black respondents stated that blacks received fewer opportunities than deserved, while only 24 percent of the Mexicans said that Latinos were deprived of deserved opportunity. Although they were given up to four chances to say so, only 9 percent of the Asians in our sample reported that being Asian limited their opportunities. Reports that whites lacked opportunities were virtually nonexistent and for that reason are not reported.

Reports that whites were unfairly advantaged, however, were fairly widespread. Consistent with the pattern of perceived disadvantage, blacks were more likely than members of other racial/ethnic groups to report the belief that whites received more opportunities than they deserved; one out of four blacks said so, compared with 15 percent each of the Asians and Mexicans and only 6 percent of the Anglos. Besides whites, no other group was perceived to be unfairly advantaged by more than a small number of respondents, regardless of their race/ethnicity. There is a glimmer of black and Mexican resentment of Asians, in that 8 percent of the blacks and 7 percent of the Mexicans reported that Asian Americans were unfairly advantaged. This is tempered, however, by the fact that 4 percent of the blacks and Mexicans believed that Asian Americans were unfairly disadvantaged. There is also an interesting asymmetry across the board, in that respondents, whatever their race/ethnicity, were considerably more likely to perceive a particular group or groups as unfairly disadvantaged than to assert that some group received more opportunities than they deserved. The prospects for a coalition across racial and ethnic lines seem enhanced by this apparent greater sympathy for the underdog than resentment against the privileged.

Although there were substantial differences in the perceived situation of members *of* different racial/ethnic groups, there was substantial agreement

Table 6: *Perceptions That Racial/Ethnic Groups Receive Fewer or More Opportunities Than They Deserve*

	Race/Ethnicity of Respondent			
	Anglo	Black	Mexican	Asian
Fewer Opportunities Than Deserved Received By:				
Blacks	20%	42%	20%	19%
Latinos	13	21	24	14
Asians	4	4	4	9
More Opportunities Than Deserved Received By:				
Whites	6%	25%	15%	15%
Blacks	5	0	3	4
Latinos	4	2	2	2
Asians	1	8	7	2

by respondents *from* different groups as to the structure of opportunities in American society. As indicated earlier, when asked which groups in the country today received fewer opportunities than they deserved, blacks referred to blacks more frequently than to any other group. But so did Anglos and Asians; 20 percent and 19 percent, respectively, of respondents in these categories reported that blacks did not receive the opportunities they deserved. For Asians this figure was far higher than the number who mentioned Asian Americans. Blacks, similarly, were almost as likely to report that Latinos were disadvantaged (21 percent said so) as were Mexicans (24 percent). Finally, only a handful of respondents, regardless of whether they were Anglo or not, reported that any minority group received more opportunities than warranted, or stated that whites received too few opportunities. Education had little effect upon the perceptions of Mexicans or Asians. Blacks who had attended college were, however, much more likely than other blacks to see whites as advantaged, although only slightly more likely to see blacks and Latinos as disadvantaged. Education has a large impact upon Anglo perceptions; the better-educated are substantially more likely to believe that blacks and Latinos receive fewer opportunities than they deserve and that whites receive more. Overall, then, the perceptions of other groups' structural position appear consistent with the formation of alliances.

Perhaps the most crucial question to answer in order to assess alliance possibilities is what perceptions are held by persons who believe their own group to be disadvantaged. Do they see their group as somehow singled out, so that other minority groups would be at best irrelevant and at worst hostile to joint action? Or do they see structural disadvantage as something that extends beyond their own race or ethnicity? Similarly, do persons who perceive their group as having ethnically or racially specific problems become more willing to see others as disadvantaged, or does the awareness of their own problems make them more focused upon the conditions of their own group? Table 7 presents some data bearing on these points. It divides respondents in each ethnic/racial group by whether they named a group-specific problem and by whether they identified their own group as receiving fewer opportunities. Within each cell are reported the percentages of respondents with the cell characteristics who said that fewer opportunities are received by members of the other groups.

Clearly, persons who see their own group as structurally disadvantaged are also more inclined to see other groups as disadvantaged as well. This is especially true for perceptions of black and Latino opportunities by persons from other groups, including Asians. It appears to hold for perceptions of Asians, but very few people from any group see Asians as disadvantaged. Thus, a view of structural disadvantage tends to extend across groups. Perception of a group-specific problem has differing effects in different groups. Blacks who identify a problem are more likely to see others as disadvantaged. Mexicans who identify a problem *and* believe that Latinos face fewer opportunities are more likely to see blacks as disadvantaged. Otherwise, perception of a group problem has little effect, or a slightly negative one, on beliefs about other groups' chances. For Asians, perception of a group problem also has little, or possibly negative, effect, with one clear exception. Those Asians who believe they themselves are disadvantaged are more likely to see blacks as sharing that situation if they do *not* identify a group-specific problem. Thus, perception of one's own opportunities as diminished is associated with coalition-furthering perceptions of other groups. Perception of a group-specific problem may further black-Mexican coalition building but have asymmetric effects on coalitions with Asians.

As with the perceptions of prejudice, it is possible to assess the impact of various factors upon the perception that the respondent's own group or other groups suffer from structural inequity. A series of probit models were estimated for persons from each racial/ethnic group.[4] The dependent variables were dichotomous measures of whether or not some particular group was perceived as having fewer opportunities. The independent variables include those discussed before in the estimations of prejudice, plus perceived prejudice, two measures of income (home ownership and un-

---

[4]Use of ordinary linear regression would lead to incorrect estimation of the standard errors, since the dependent variable is truncated. STATA was used for estimating the probit models.

Table 7: *Perceptions That Fewer Opportunities are Received By Members of Other Groups*

	Percentage of Respondents Who See Specified Other Group as Disadvantaged		
	Respondents Who See No Problem Specific to Own Group	Respondents Who See Problem Specific to Own Group	N
Black Respondents			
Blacks not disadvantaged	Latinos Disadv. 2% Asians Disadv. 2%	Latinos Disadv. 5% Asians Disadv. 3%	196
Blacks disadvantaged	Latinos Disadv. 39% Asians Disadv. 3%	Latinos Disadv. 47% Asians Disadv. 8%	139
N	119	216	
Mexican Respondents			
Mexicans not disadvantaged	Blacks Disadv. 10% Asians Disadv. 2%	Blacks Disadv. 7% Asians Disadv. 3%	392
Mexicans disadvantaged	Blacks Disadv. 45% Asians Disadv. 11%	Blacks Disadv. 65% Asians Disadv. 10%	121
N	227	236	
Asian Respondents			
Asians not disadvantaged	Blacks Disadv. 14% Latinos Disadv. 11%	Blacks Disadv. 12% Latinos Disadv. 7%	283
Asians disadvantaged	Blacks Disadv. 83% Latinos Disadv. 58%	Blacks Disadv. 69% Latinos Disadv. 62%	25
N	195	113	

employment of the head of household),[5] two additional immigration-related variables (other-than-English as primary language and foreign born). Table 8 reports the results of these estimations for black respondents, Table 9 for Mexicans, and Table 10 for Asians.

For all three groups, the propensity to see one's own group as lacking in opportunities is higher among group members who have experienced prejudice. The key component of prejudice among Mexicans and Asians for this perception is the belief that Americans are prejudiced against their group. Among Asians and Mexicans, those who do not primarily use English are also more likely to see disadvantage. For blacks, age has no effect upon perception of opportunity. Otherwise, all of the factors that were associated with heightened perceived prejudice are associated with perceived structural inequity—identifying a group problem, being a Democrat, having opinions on issues, and being of third or later generation. In addition, those blacks living in households with an unemployed head also perceived reduced opportunities. Mexicans, too, are more likely to report diminished opportunities if they cite a group problem, are issue attentive, or have less wealth (as indicated by being renters instead of homeowners). In addition, second-generation Mexicans are somewhat more likely than the foreign born, and clearly more likely than the third generation, to name reduced opportunities.

When it comes to perceptions of other groups, the single most powerful factor in predicting respondents' views are their opinions about their own group's opportunities. Thus, estimations were made of the perceptions of other groups both including and excluding the respondent's own-group belief. Blacks who believe blacks have fewer opportunities are more likely to see Asians and Latinos each as also having fewer opportunities. Controlling for self-perception, older blacks are more sympathetic to the other groups. Excluding self-perception, the only factor related to black perceptions of Asians' chances is age; older blacks are more likely to see Asians as disadvantaged. Again, excluding self-perception, older blacks are also more sympathetic than younger blacks to Latinos. In addition, blacks are more likely to see Latinos as disadvantaged if they themselves experience prejudice, identify a group problem, or are issue attentive.

With own group's opportunities out of the estimation, the factors associated with Mexican perception of black opportunities are very similar to those associated with own group opportunities. Mexicans who experience prejudice towards their group, who identify a group problem, and who are issue attentive are more likely to see blacks as structurally disadvantaged. Language use and homeownership are irrelevant, however. The second

---

[5]Although the survey included an item asking respondents about their income, the large amount of missing data, due to refusals, makes it inadvisable to use that variable.

Table 8: *Factors Related to Perceptions by Blacks That They and Other Groups Have Fewer Opportunities*

	Blacks Fewer	Latinos Fewer	Latinos Fewer	Asians Fewer	Asians Fewer
Combined prejudice	.27[a] (3.02)[b]	.27 (.006)			
Names group problem	.56 (3.30)	.36 (1.97)			
Age		-.008 (-1.79)	-.009 (-1.92)	-.017 (-2.29)	-.016 (-2.11)
Has issue opinions	.08 (1.86)	.100 (2.10)			
Third generation	1.00 (2.22)				
Party (Dem. positive)	.30 (2.05)				
Head of household unemployed	.48 (2.36)				
Says blacks have fewer opportunites			1.61 (8.24)		.44 (1.73)
Constant	-2.77 (-4.96)	-1.73 (-4.38)	-1.32 (-4.99)	-.99 (-3.20)	-1.27 (-3.58)
LL at Convergence	-193	-158	-127	-58	-57
Prob > Chi 2	.0000	.0000	.0000	.015	.011
N	315	335	335	335	335

[a]Coefficient in probit estimation
[b]t-statistic

generation was most likely to see own-group disadvantage; all citizens, whether native born or naturalized, are more likely than the noncitizens to see blacks as disadvantaged. With own-group perception included, and strongly positively related to perception of black disadvantage, only generation in the country has additional impact. The longer the respondent's

Table 9: *Factors Related to Perceptions By Mexicans That They and Other Groups Have Fewer Opportunities*

	Latinos Fewer	Blacks Fewer	Blacks Fewer	Asians Fewer	Asians Fewer
Prejudice towards group	.39[a] (2.81)[b]	.24 (1.71)			-.42 (-1.85)
Names group problem	.24 (1.84)	.22 (1.67)			
Has issue opinions	.06 (1.70)	.08 (2.17)			
Foreign-born citizen	.35 (1.58)	.50 (2.02)	.43 (1.54)	.72 (1.92)	.75 (1.87)
Second generation	.63 (3.47)	.77 (4.00)	.64 (2.97)	.75 (2.38)	.73 (2.14)
Third generation	.18 (.88)	.61 (3.21)	.81 (3.78)	.34 (.99)	.40 (1.10)
English not primary language	.33 (2.19)				
Homeowner	-.25 (-1.89)	-.19 (-1.42)			
Says Latinos have fewer opportunities			1.56 (10.06)		.81 (3.62)
Constant	-1.77 (-6.01)	-1.95 (-6.83)	-1.89 (-10.03)	-2.18 (-7.89)	-2.27 (-7.14)
LL at Convergence	-250	-233	-185	-86	-78
Prob > Chi 2	.0000	.0001	.0000	.043	.0004
N	492	492	492	492	492

[a]Coefficient in probit estimation
[b]t-statistic

Table 10: *Factors Related to Perceptions by Asians That They and Other Groups Have Fewer Opportunities*

	Asians Fewer	Blacks Fewer	Blacks Fewer	Latinos Fewer	Latinos Fewer	Latinos Fewer
Prejudice towards group	.60[a] (2.62)[b]	.29 (1.67)				
English not primary language	.37 (1.68)					
Foreign born		-.44 (-2.48)	-.57 (-3.04)	-.32 (-1.69)	-.43 (-2.17)	-.09 (-.41)
Says Asians have fewer opportunities			1.83 (6.22)		1.54 (5.43)	
Says Blacks have fewer opportunities						1.86 (8.21)
Constant	-1.96 (-8.51)	-.77 (-4.83)	-.76 (-5.58)	-.88 (-6.21)	-1.02 (-6.84)	-1.65 (-8.08)
LL at Convergence	-82	-136	-115	-116	-101	-79
Prob > Chi 2	.0055	.015	.0000	.09	.0000	.0000
N	308	285	285	285	285	285

[a]Coefficient in probit estimation
[b]t-statistic

family has been in the U.S., the more the respondent sees blacks as having fewer opportunities. Conversely, Mexicans are more likely to see Asians as disadvantaged if they are immigrants or second generation rather than third generation, as long as they are citizens. Immigrants who do not have the security of citizenship are no more, and probably less, sympathetic than third-generation Mexicans. These generational effects, which are suggestive of a coalition of secure immigrants, hold even with the introduction of Mexicans' views of their own position. Once that is controlled for, however, those Mexicans who believe that Americans discriminate against their group are *less* likely to say that Asians suffer structural disadvantages.

Asians who believe Americans are prejudiced against their group are more likely to see blacks as structurally disadvantaged. Asians who are foreign born are less likely to see either blacks or Latinos as suffering from fewer opportunities. The story is the same with introduction of Asians' views of their own chances; those who believe themselves disadvantaged also see blacks and Latinos as disadvantaged, but the foreign born are less likely to report disadvantage for the other groups. Interestingly, the *best* predictor of Asian beliefs about Latinos' opportunities is Asian beliefs about black opportunities.

Thus, on the whole, older persons and those whose families have been in the U.S. longer are more willing to say that minorities face fewer opportunities. Economic and related "objective" factors seem to have very little influence upon this process. Prospects for a coalition of minorities are furthered by the fact that those who are aware of problems specific to their racial or ethnic group, and those who believe that their own group is structurally disadvantaged, are more inclined to view other minorities as also disadvantaged. Any coalition may be more supportive of blacks and Latinos than of Asians. Persons who believe that Americans are prejudiced towards their own group are more likely not only to see their group as having fewer opportunities but also to see blacks and Latinos as structurally disadvantaged. However, blacks who perceive prejudice are no more likely than other blacks to see Asians as disadvantaged, and Mexicans who believe there is prejudice towards their group are less inclined to believe that Asians have fewer opportunities. Nonetheless, on net, the evidence seems more consistent with an atmosphere conducive to coalition building than one rife with conflict.

ISSUE POSITIONS

The question remains as to whether there are specific issues that these groups might coalesce around. Answers to the issue questions posed in this study may be suggestive, but the caution raised in the introduction needs to be repeated with emphasis. Issues change over time. The public's perception of issues changes over time, and various political leaders have large stakes in influencing the change. Moreover, a single or a few highly salient issues can suffice to cement a coalition, even if there is great internal disagreement over a wide range of other issues. However, with these caveats in mind, the distribution of responses to the specific issues included in this instrument may be suggestive.

The issue items included several related to immigration and language issues salient in 1984 (amnesty for illegal immigrants, employer sanctions for hiring illegal immigrants, bilingual education, bilingual ballots), one each on classic guns and "butter" (increased funding for welfare, increased spending for defense), and a number of "social" issues (support for the ERA, tax support for parochial schools, prayer in schools, banning federal funding for abortions, gun control, supporting the death penalty, restrict abortions or permit choice). Table 11 reports the percentage of respondents in each racial/ethnic group, including Anglos, in favor of each issue, after excluding those respondents who had no opinion. Anglos are included for comparison. Because four of the issues are aimed at immigration, Mexican and Asian respondents are divided into the foreign born and the native born. The percentage of Democrats, Republicans, and Independents are also included for each group.

Compared with the other ethnic/racial groups, blacks tend to be Democrats who favor spending on welfare and oppose further spending on defense. Along with foreign-born Mexicans, they oppose the death penalty. Foreign-born Asians want to spend more on defense. Foreign-born Mexicans favor amnesty and oppose employer sanctions. Anglos and native-born Asians oppose bilingual education, bilingual ballots, and prayer in school and are prochoice. Native-born Asians also oppose banning federal funding of abortions, and foreign born Asians are the group most favorably inclined towards gun control.

Persons who perceive structural disadvantage for minorities may well have different views on the issues. Thus, similar percentages were derived for respondents from each group who say blacks face fewer opportunities and for those who say Latinos face fewer opportunities. The results are more or less as one might expect. Anglos who see either blacks or Latinos as disadvantaged take more "liberal" views on the issues, and are more likely to be Democrats, than other Anglos. Blacks who perceive structural inequities have very similar issue views to those who do not. They are, however, even more likely to be Democrats and far less likely to decline to state partisanship. Those who see Latinos as disadvantaged are more supportive of bilingual ballots and less supportive of banning abortion funding. Blacks who see disadvantage for either group are less supportive of gun control.

Native-born Mexicans are more supportive of amnesty, bilingual education, bilingual ballots, and gun control if they see Latinos as disadvantaged. The views of foreign-born Mexicans change little, except that they are more likely to be Democrats if they report either group gets fewer oppor-

Table 11: Issue Preference by Ethnicity/Race; Number in Favor as Percentage of Those Who Have An Opinion

	Anglo	Black	U.S.-Born Mexican	Foreign-Born Mexican	U.S.-Born Asian	Foreign-Born Asian
Increase Defense $	36	26	36	38	36	55
Increase Welfare $	67	93	79	86	75	71
Amnesty	53	54	66	86	55	57
Employer Sanctions	70	62	55	41	74	51
Bilingual Education	46	71	73	79	49	61
Bilingual Ballots	30	56	63	71	38	52
Support ERA	78	93	86	93	84	84
Private School Tax Credit	55	53	50	55	45	56
Prayer in Schools	55	74	62	76	51	62
Ban Abortion Funding	42	47	40	42	27	48
Gun Control	51	50	55	54	54	69
Death Penalty	83	61	78	64	89	81
Pro-choice	61	47	44	34	63	47
Democrat	42	82	61	44	43	30
Republican	37	5	18	26	37	42
Independent	7	5	8	8	10	7

tunities than deserved. Foreign-born Asians who perceive black and Latino disadvantage have more liberal views than other foreign-born Asians across many of these issues, and are more likely to be Democrats. The views of U.S.-born Asians shift little; those who see blacks as disadvantaged are more in favor of employer sanctions, while those who perceive Latino disadvantage are more opposed. Surprisingly, native-born Asians who see either black or Latino structural disadvantage are more likely to be Republican.

To assess the prospects for coalition formation, the real question is how the position on the issues of each member of each of the minority groups compares with those of the others. Therefore, for each issue, probit estimations (not shown here) were run to assess whether there were significant differences of position between blacks, Asians, and Mexicans. The dependent variables were the percentages of respondents in favor on each issue, after excluding those with no opinion. Blacks were taken as the reference group. Thus, significant coefficients indicated that the corresponding group has substantially different views on the issue than do blacks. Separate dummy variables allowed comparison of blacks with noncitizen Mexicans, noncitizen Asians, naturalized Mexicans, naturalized Asians, U.S.-born Mexicans, and U.S.-born Asians.

A mixed pattern of opinion emerges. All Mexicans and Asians are more in favor of defense, and less supportive of "butter" (welfare spending), than are blacks. On a number of the social issues, there are no or few significant differences among the groups (tax credits for private schools, prochoice, banning abortion funding—though U.S.-born Asians are opposed to the last one). Foreign-born Asians are more supportive of gun control than anyone else. Everyone except noncitizen Mexicans are more supportive of the death penalty than blacks; everyone except foreign-born Mexicans are less in favor of prayer in school. Blacks, noncitizens, and naturalized Mexicans support the ERA more than the other Mexicans and Asians. Although the defense and welfare issues suggest differences in liberalism, the positions on the social issues do not line up according to any simple scale.

Immigration issues are mixed in a way that represents different group situations. Mexicans favor amnesty far more than either blacks or Asians. Noncitizens are opposed to employer sanctions more than anyone else while U.S.-born Asians favor them; the others, including blacks, are in between. Bilingual education is supported by Mexican noncitizens and *opposed* by Asian citizens; blacks and other Mexicans and Asians are in between again. Bilingual ballots are favored by noncitizens and opposed by Asian citizens; blacks and Mexican citizens hold equivalent views. Thus, opinions on these issues are mixed, partly reflecting differences in immigration status, but with substantial black support for the positions of many Mexicans and Asians.

The differences in position reported above correspond to how results of a referendum on each issue, were it conducted at the time of the survey, would split by ethnicity. However, a number of the significant differences in overall group opinion across race and ethnicity may reflect other factors, such as education or age, which happen to be correlated with race and ethnicity. Moreover, variations in the experience of prejudice or in judgments of the opportunity structure may be partially responsible for differences in issue positions. One would like to compare people in each ethnic/racial group to those in others who share similar characteristics. Thus, a second series of probit models estimated issue positions on not only the dummies reflecting ethnicity and citizenship/immigration but also on control variables for these other factors. The control variables include language, party identification, and a number of demographic variables (religion, sex, homeownership, education, age). In addition, as the effects of perceived prejudice and perception of groups as having fewer opportunities are of particular interest, the measures tapping these variables were included. The results of these estimations, purged of insignificant variables as before, are reported in Table 12.

Some of the differences between the racial/ethnic groups diminish, reflecting the impact of these other variables. After introduction of the controls, defense spending is now favored more than by blacks only by foreign-born Asians. Those who see Latinos as having fewer opportunities want to spend more on defense. Those who have experienced more prejudice or who see blacks as having fewer opportunities want to spend less. Even with the controls, Mexicans and Asians still want to spend less on welfare than blacks, but the difference is now insignificant for the noncitizens.

The patterns of support across the groups for the ERA, tax credits for private schools, abortion funding, and gun control change little, although both the tax credits and gun control are opposed more by blacks who think blacks have fewer opportunities than by other blacks. Introduction of controls for age and being an Evangelical Protestant leaves only one significant difference among the groups with regard to school prayer; noncitizen Mexicans favor it more than non-Evangelical blacks or anyone else. After allowing for the fact that Catholics, men, and homeowners support the death penalty, Asian citizens still favor the death penalty more than blacks and the views of Mexican citizens are indistinguishable from those of blacks. Mexican noncitizens and non-Latinos who believe Latinos are disadvantaged are more opposed to the death penalty than blacks. The controls for religion, education, and age leave Asian noncitizens opposed to choice and naturalized Mexicans in favor.

The pattern of support for amnesty does not change at all with the introduction of other variables; in fact, none has any significant effect. The impact of ethnicity on the other immigration items, however, does shift. The borderline significant greater opposition of Mexican citizens to employer sanctions goes away; persons who do not speak English as a primary language are substantially more opposed to the sanctions than others.

Mexican citizens are opposed to bilingual education, as are people who have experienced prejudice, while noncitizens are now no more supportive than blacks. Mexicans who think Latinos have fewer opportunities favor bilingual education and bilingual ballots. Non-English speakers also favor bilingual ballots. With these controls, noncitizens are no more in favor of bilingual ballots than blacks or other Mexicans.

Thus, some of the differences in issue preferences across groups reflect differences in language status, in perception of opportunities, in prejudice, and in demographics (especially religion for the social issues). As to future coalitions, the data are sufficiently mixed that they can support either a "half-empty" or "half-full" interpretation. Perhaps the most systematic difference is that none of the other minorities, in any generation, are as supportive of welfare and other social program spending as are blacks. On the "gun" side, the preferences of all the groups are very similar, with the notable exception of the more hawkish stance of foreign-born Asians. On the immigration related issues, ethnicity and generation matter. Asian and blacks hold similar positions on amnesty, while Mexicans are very much more in favor of it. Blacks support the position of Mexicans on bilingual ballots, while Asian citizens are opposed to them. Blacks, Mexican citizens, and Asian citizens are all more in favor of employer sanctions than are noncitizens. And blacks support noncitizen preferences for bilingual education, while Mexican and Asian citizens are less in favor of the idea. On the social issues, there were fairly small differences across the groups. Asians are more in favor of the death penalty, and U.S.-born Asians tend to take a more secular view on the religion-related items, while Mexicans and foreign-born Asian citizens are less supportive of the ERA than blacks.

CONCLUSION

In both their perceptions of opportunity structures and in their personal experiences, blacks are more likely than either Mexicans or Asians to believe that their race/ethnicity has hindered them, especially with respect to their pursuit of material well-being. They also appear somewhat more likely than these others to believe that other minority groups have been hindered as well. Minority group status is far more salient to blacks than to either Asians or Mexicans. Blacks are far more likely than members of the other minority groups to feel that as a group they do not get the opportunities they deserve, that whites get more opportunities than they deserve, that they have personally experienced discrimination, and that many Americans are prejudiced against them. For the most part, they seem to be sympathetic to the lot of other minority groups.

Although Mexicans and Asians are not substantially more likely than Anglos to perceive that blacks are unfairly disadvantaged, those who see themselves as disadvantaged extend the perception of structural inequality

Table 12:   Issue Preferences of Minorities By Ethnicity, Citizenship, and Immigration, Controlling for Political and Demographic Factors[a]

	Increase Arms $	Increase Welfare $	Amnesty	Employer Sanctions	Bilingual Education	Bilingual Ballots
Noncitizen Mexican	-.17[b] (-.92)[c]	-.29 (-1.48)	1.18 (6.68)	-.33 (-1.18)	-.19 (-1.08)	-.08 (-.42)
Noncitizen Asian	.41 (2.03)	-.43 (-1.90)	.21 (1.18)	-.44 (-2.12)	-.15 (-.75)	.05 (.23)
Foreign-born citizen Mexican	.07 (.31)	-.51 (-2.06)	.64 (2.83)	-.06 (-.26)	-.47 (-2.15)	-.24 (-1.05)
Foreign-born citizen Asian	.53 (2.70)	-.99 (-5.04)	-.04 (-.21)	.05 (.25)	-.72 (-4.28)	-.71 (-3.94)
U.S.-born Mexican	.04 (.30)	-.64 (-4.21)	.31 (2.67)	-.08 (-.67)	-.32 (-2.45)	-.19 (-1.47)
U.S.-born Asian	.05 (.29)	-.63 (-3.34)	.03 (.18)	.30 (1.86)	-.64 (-4.05)	-.56 (-3.64)
Blacks have fewer opp.	-.37 (-2.91)					
Black x blacks fewer opp.						
Latinos have fewer opp.	.34 (2.59)					
Mex x Latino fewer opp.					.53 (3.06)	.40 (2.58)

	(1)	(2)	(3)	(4)	(5)	(6)
NonMex x Latino fewer opp.						
Prejudice experience	-.12 (-2.29)					
English not language				-.24 (-2.00)	-.12 (-2.35)	.22 (1.83)
Catholic						
Evang. Protestant						
Male	.16 (1.67)					
Homeowner		-.29 (-2.70)			-.21 (-2.19)	
Education (years)	-.06 (-2.76)			.05 (2.92)	-.06 (-3.23)	-.04 (-2.31)
Age					-.02 (-5.76)	-.016 (-5.77)
Party (Dem. Positive)	-.23 (-3.79)	.30 (4.74)	.09 (1.11)			
Constant	.55 (1.77)	1.53 (10.39)		-.41 (-1.59)	2.54 (7.41)	1.45 (4.66)
LL at Convergence	-496	-394	-516	-580	-545	-603
Prob > Chi 2	.0000	.0000	.0000	.0000	.0000	.0000
N	812	965	837	885	974	962

[a] Estimation excludes Anglos, so ethnic coefficients give effects relative to Blacks.
[b] Probit coefficient
[c] t-statistic

Table 12: Issue Preferences of Minorities by Ethnicity, Citizenship, and Immigration, Controlling for Political and Demographic Factors[a] (continued)

	Support ERA	Tax Credit for Private Schools	Prayer in School	Ben Abortion Funding	Gun Control	Death Penalty	Pro-choice
Noncitizen Mexican	-.17[b] (-.69)[c]	-.13 (-.69)	.53 (2.97)	.15 (.86)	-.13 (-.70)	-.37 (-2.07)	.02 (.14)
Noncitizen Asian	-.01 (-.04)	.22 (1.06)	.11 (.59)	.22 (1.04)	.49 (2.20)	.20 (1.06)	-.40 (-2.24)
Foreign-born citizen Mexican	-.51 (-1.75)	.20 (.84)	.30 (1.33)	.25 (1.12)	-.10 (-.46)	.27 (1.06)	.33 (1.56)
Foreign-born citizen Asian	-.50 (-2.33)	-.23 (-1.23)	-.02 (-.09)	.13 (.71)	.22 (1.09)	.75 (3.74)	-.18 (-1.10)
U.S.-born Mexican	-.61 (-3.46)	-.19 (-1.19)	.05 (.36)	.09 (.62)	-.04 (-.31)	.22 (1.47)	.00 (.04)
U.S.-born Asian	-.32 (-1.54)	-.29 (-1.62)	-.30 (-1.70)	-.43 (-2.34)	.12 (.66)	.89 (4.60)	.02 (.15)
Blacks have fewer opp.							
Blacks x blacks fewer opp.		-.30 (-1.83)			-.34 (-2.09)		
Latinos have fewer opp.				-.23 (-2.07)			
Mex x Latino fewer opp.							.17 (1.87)

	(1)	(2)	(3)	(4)	(5)	(6)	(7)
NonMex x Latino fewer opp.							-.36 (-2.33)
Prejudice experience					.27 (2.36)		
English not language							
Catholic	.40 (2.85)	.20 (1.81)				.29 (2.39)	-.34 (3.23)
Evang. Protestant			.59 (4.17)	.30 (2.23)			-.25 (-1.98)
Male					-.42 (-4.83)	.26 (2.70)	
Homeowner		-.17 (-1.77)				.18 (1.81)	
Education (years)	-.05 (-1.84)	.04 (2.16)		.05 (2.30)			.07 (4.13)
Age		.013 (4.33)	.012 (4.17)	.009 (3.20)			-.007 (-2.83)
Party (Dem. Positive)	.18 (2.59)				.10 (1.72)		
Constant	1.92 (5.27)	-.88 (-2.54)	-.19 (-1.17)	-1.20 (-3.48)	.23 (1.88)	.12 (.97)	-.35 (-1.16)
LL at Convergence	-305	-556	-518	-540	-601	-468	-696
Prob > Chi 2	.0000	.0001	.0000	.0001	.0000	.0000	.0000
N	917	830	864	820	916	870	1055

[a] Estimation excludes Anglos, so ethnic coefficients give effects relative to Blacks.
[b] Probit coefficient
[c] t-statistic

to blacks as well.   The experience of prejudice tends to increase the perception of structural inequity, but this extends to other groups as well. There is little evidence here for interethnic competition.

Positions on specific issues vary, with a mixed pattern of agreement and disagreement across groups.   On some issues ethnicity matters; on others, immigration generation and citizenship make the difference; on still others, none of these play much of a role.   Overall, the conditions seem to point to the feasibility, but hardly the inevitability, of coalition building among these groups.   As coalitions develop, they are likely to arise first among sub-groups—such as recent immigrants—rather than across grand categories.   A coalition could build upon the willingness to see shared conditions of disadvantage.   However, translation into broad support for specific issues will require skillful leadership.

REFERENCES

Browning, Rufus P., Dale Rogers Marshall, and David H. Tabb. *Protest is Not Enough*. Berkeley and Los Angeles: University of California Press, 1984.

Cain, Bruce E., D. Roderick Kiewiet, and Carole J. Uhlaner. "The Acquisition of Partisanship by Latinos and Asian-Americans." *American Journal of Political Science* 35 (May 1991): 390-422.

Daniels, Roger, and Harry H. L. Kitano. *American Racism: Exploration of the Nature of Prejudice*. Prentice-Hall: Englewood Cliffs, New Jersey, 1970.

Gurin, Patricia, and E. G. Epps. *Black Consciousness, Identity, and Achievement*. New York: John Wiley and Sons, 1975.

Gurin, Patricia, Shirley Hatchett, and James S. Jackson. *Hope and Independence: Blacks' Response to Electoral and Party Politics*. New York: Russell Sage Foundation, 1989.

Gurin, Patricia, Arthur H. Miller, and Gerald Gurin. "Stratum Identification and Consciousness." *Social Psychology Quarterly*, vol. 43, no.1 (1980): 30-47.

Jackson, Byran O., Elisabeth Gerber, and Bruce E. Cain. "Perceptions of Group Affect and Political Strategies in the Black Community." Unpublished manuscript, 1991.

Keefe, Susan E., and Amado M. Padilla. *Chicano Ethnicity*. Albuquerque: University of New Mexico Press, 1987.

Miller, Arthur H., Patricia Gurin, Gerald Gurin, and Oksana Malanchuk. "Group Consciousness and Political Participation." *American Journal of Political Science* 25 (August 1981): 494-511.

Pitkin, Hanna Fenichel. *The Concept of Representation*. Berkeley and Los Angeles: University of California Press, 1967.

Portes, Alejandro, and Robert L. Bach. *Latin Journey: Cuban and Mexican Immigrants in the United States*. Berkeley: University of California Press, 1985.

Shastri, Amita. "Social Welfare and Social Service Recipients in California by Ethnic Origin." Prepared for Seaver Project on "Minorities in California," Division of Humanities and Social Sciences, CalTech. Mimeo, 1986.

Uhlaner, Carole Jean, Bruce E. Cain, and D. Roderick Kiewiet. "Political Participation of Ethnic Minorities in the 1980s." *Political Behavior* 11 (September 1989): 195-231.

CHAPTER 15

JAMES REGALADO
California State University—Los Angeles

Conflicts Over Redistricting in Los Angeles County: Who Wins? Who Loses?

INTRODUCTION

California is the most populous state in the union, and its largest county, Los Angeles, is the most populous and culturally diverse in the nation. Like the state, L. A. County contains the largest concentration of Latinos and Asians in the nation. Both also have significant African-American populations. By the turn of the century, the state will become what Los Angeles County already is, a majority populated by racial and ethnic "minorities."

Most cities and counties in California having significant Latino and African-American populations have been very slow in creating conditions for the "political integration" of these populations into their respective political systems. While California is viewed as having a "progressive" legacy, it has been much slower in dealing with the issue of political integration. However, none of the state's 58 counties has been more resistant to minority political integration and none slower to provide for political change from its archaic past than Los Angeles County's Board of Supervisors. This historically exclusive, all-white, male "club" has been called one of the most powerful and secretive political bodies in the nation (Jeffe 1990, M5). In this century, not a single minority group member or woman has been elected to the county board, which by the year 2000 will govern over 10 million county residents.

This chapter will explore a formidable structural explanation, largely through examination of recent voting rights lawsuits against the county, as to why the county's largest minority group—Latinos—are neither formally represented in nor incorporated into the political system of the county's primary decision-making body. It is my contention that the Los Angeles County Board, through both its past and current members, has effectively interfered with the political incorporation of Latinos in Los Angeles County largely through its reapportioning of supervisorial districts.

BACKGROUND

Racial gerrymandering of minority communities constitutes a common practice on the part of many political jurisdictions having significant numbers of minority residents. Drawing legislative district lines in such fashion that the larger minority community is divided and carved into relatively powerless fragments among a variety of districts constitutes a dilution of the electoral strength of that community. The end result is that a full and meaningful participation of that community in the political process is either abridged or denied.

In California, use of the racial gerrymander has been broadly used during decennial state reapportionments (Navarro 1981; Project Participar 1984) and in a variety of cities within the state (Regalado 1988; Avila 1989). At both levels, Latino mobilization and protest against this vote dilution practice took place although formal challenges occurred only at the municipal level. However, it is at the county level in California where government remains most hidden, secretive, and illusive. Perhaps for these reasons, formidable minority mobilizations against and challenges to the structure of county governance and county board practices of diluting minority voting strength through the redistricting process were largely absent until the 1980s. Latino mobilization against the county board in Los Angeles in the early 1980s and the federal suits filed in the late 1980s "broke the ice." We might very well see more frequent minority challenges of county board redistrictings throughout the state in the 1990s following the example of the case in Los Angeles.

The type of racial/ethnic and class gerrymander emanating from L. A. County's redistricting plans of 1971 and 1981 so divided, fractured, and diluted Latino communities that fair and equal chances to participate in the electoral process and be represented by someone of their choosing on the county board were effectively denied.

There is a broad and growing body of literature on minority political representation and somewhat less on minority political empowerment, both beginning primarily in the late 1960s and early 1970s. Most of the earlier works dealt primarily with political struggles of African Americans for political empowerment and representation from their own ranks. There are fewer works on Latino political representation and Latino political empowerment although these are also areas of recent growth.

There is also a significant body of research that has grown immensely in the 1980s on forms of minority vote dilution and the interplay between such dilution and the political underrepresentation of minorities. Edited works by Davidson (1984) and Foster (1985) involved careful discussions and assessments of the Voting Rights Act of 1965 and its 1982 amendments in terms of both past and continuing practices of diluting minority electoral strength, including the use of the racial gerrymander. These works focused primarily on African-American communities but works by Cotrell and Stevens (1978), MacManus (1978), Tabel (1978), Cotrell (1986), Garcia (1986), de la Garza (1986), Cotrell and Polinard (1986), and Polinard and Wrinkle (1988) began a shift of some scholarly attention to Latino communities of the Southwest. Navarro (1981) focuses on California state redistricting and its effect on representation in Latino communities of Los Angeles County. Avila (1989) looks at litigation involving racial gerrymandering and use of at-large election systems to fragment or dilute Latino voting strength in California and the Southwest. Santillan (1983) and Regalado (1988; 1989) have focused their attention more specifically on racial gerrymandering of Latino communities in the city and county of Los Angeles. Finally, a forthcoming volume of work edited by Santillan (1991) will focus on reapportionment and Latino communities at the local level in different parts of the United States.

All too frequently the two areas of research (minority political incorporation/empowerment and minority vote dilution practices) mentioned in this section have been treated separately by scholars. This chapter may be seen as attempting to bridge that separation in a case study involving interplay between racial gerrymandering and denial of Latino political empowerment.

THE LAW: THE VOTING RIGHTS ACT OF 1965

The Mexican-American Legal Defense and Education Fund (MALDEF) and the ACLU of southern California, in August 1988, and the Department of Justice, in September 1988, filed voting rights lawsuits against the county of Los Angeles. In charging the Board of Supervisors with violating the voting rights of Latino citizens in the county, the suits alleged that the board's secretive 1981 reapportioning of its five supervisorial districts purposefully fractured Latino voting strength by dividing their contiguous communities among three supervisorial districts (*U.S. v. County of Los Angeles*, 88-05143 Kn [EX]). The suits, in other words, charged that minority vote dilution had taken place through the use of the racial gerrymander. Through this practice, the county board sufficiently diluted the electoral strength of the Latino community so as to deny that community equal political participation in the county's political system. Therefore, the county allegedly violated the Voting Rights Act of 1965.

In order to better understand Latino and federal legal actions in challenging L. A. County's redistricting plan of 1981, a brief overview of the Voting Rights Act and pertinent court cases will ensue.

The Voting Rights Act of 1965 (Pub. L. 47-205) was a milestone achieved in the struggle for the voting rights of African Americans, primarily in the South. Prior to the passage of the act, African Americans were largely denied the suffrage owing to the imposition of various state and local laws and devices used to deny voter registration and voting rights to most African Americans. The primary purpose of the act was to enforce the 15th Amendment to the Constitution by prohibiting the tactics and methods used by many southern jurisdictions to restrict or deny African Americans the right to vote.

There are 19 sections in the act, but those that have become most important are Sections 5 and 2. Section 5 mandates that all units of government having been judged to be discriminatory, must submit any and all changes in election procedures, laws, practices, and district boundaries, to either the Department of Justice (DOJ) or a federal district court for preclearance before the changes may be carried out. Section 2 prohibits racial discrimination in voting and contains a general prohibition against the denial or abridgement of the right to vote on account of race (U.S. Commission on Civil Rights 1965). Most reapportionment challenges have charged Section 2 violations, and it formed the legal basis for the combined suits against Los Angeles County.

The extensions of and amendments to the original act in 1970 and 1975 had the primary impact of (1) spreading coverage of the act more broadly across the nation and (2) including a broader number of (language) minority groups under the protective coverage of the act (including Latinos as a "Spanish-language" group). In its 1982 amending of Section 2, Congress overturned an "intents" standard to be used to establish a voting rights violation as decided by the Supreme Court in *Mobile v. Bolden* (446 U.S. 55 1980). The amended Section 2 reaffirmed the "results" or "totality of circumstances" standard first established by the Court in *White v. Regester* (412 U.S. 755 1973). Section 2 now reads:

> no voting qualification or prerequisite to voting or stan-
> dard, practice, or procedure shall be imposed or applied by
> any state or political subdivision in a manner which *results*
> [emphasis mine] in a denial or abridgement of the right of
> any citizen of the United States to vote on account of race
> or color . . . (42 U.S.C. 1973 [Supp 1982]).

Furthermore, its states:

> (a) violation . . . is established if, based on the *totality of
> circumstances* [emphasis mine], it is shown that the political
> processes leading to nomination or election in the state or
> political subdivision are not equally open to participation
> by members of a class of citizens protected . . . in that its
> members have less opportunity than other members of the
> electorate to participate in the political process and to elect
> representatives of their choice (*Ibid.*).

It was the 1982 Section 2 amendments that provided the conditions for racial and ethnic minorities to challenge the legality of vote dilution resulting from racially gerrymandered legislative districts and at-large election systems. They did this largely through reestablishing the results standard and setting criteria to be used in court.

The criteria set by congressional 1982 Section 2 action include the following:
- evidence of racially polarized voting,
- evidence of racist campaigning and electoral appeals,
- absence of minority elected officials,
- low numbers of minority candidates,
- losing ratios of minority candidates,
- evidence of past discrimination,
- lack of minority access to the policymaking process, and
- lack of responsiveness to minority concerns by elected officials.

It was the intention of Congress that any one, or combination thereof, of the above criteria may assist minority plaintiffs challenging electoral dilution practices, although Congress also left it up to the plaintiffs, defendants, and judges to define and interpret the criteria and standards it created (see Edwards 1986; MacManus 1985).

The voting rights amendments of 1982 required the courts to examine three general tests in determining whether a legislative body diluted the voting power of a minority group. It is up to the courts to determine if the aggrieved group is (1) geographically concentrated, (2) politically cohesive, and (3) large enough to constitute a majority in a political district.

Congressional action in 1982 became most definitively interpreted by the courts in *Thornburg v. Gingles* (106 S. Ct. 2752 [1986]). In that decision, the Supreme Court set forth a detailed legal standard for adjudicating Section 2 claims. The premise used by the Court in its ruling on a North Carolina redistricting plan was that minorities challenging an apportionment plan must prove that such plan "operates to minimize or cancel out their ability to elect their preferred candidates" (106 S. Ct. @ 2765). Under this standard, two factors became of primary importance. First, a court must determine whether minority group members had in fact experienced "substantial difficulty electing representatives of their choice" (*Ibid.*, @ 2766 n. 15). Second, a court must determine whether "significant" racial bloc voting existed. Thus, the key questions, according to the court, are whether (1) minority candidates usually lost and (2) racial bloc voting usually occurred (106 S. Ct. @ 2770).

L. A. COUNTY: APPLICATION OF THE LAW

Los Angeles County was incorporated in 1852. Early on it had a five-member board of supervisors, which governed over a population of 3,350 residents. One-hundred and thirty-eight years later, the board still has five members who now govern the county's almost nine million residents, approximately 1.8 million per supervisor and more than three times the constituency of a congressional representative. This small and powerful body of white males also controls an annual budget of approximately 10 billion dollars, larger than the budget of 43 states and with a GNP surpassing all but 13 nations around the world (Jeffe 1990, M5).

By state law, the county must provide services of public health, disease control, welfare, and elections, among others, for all county residents. For residents of the unincorporated areas of the county, which are disproportionately populated by Latinos and African Americans, the county must additionally provide law enforcement, fire protection, libraries, parks, and recreational areas. It is the board that determines specifics in terms of dollar amounts, categorical preferences, and the communities, groups, and individuals to which it will best serve and allocate funding.

As implied from the above, it is easy to understand why the county's poor and working class, which are disproportionately membered by Latinos and African Americans, are most (1) dependant upon county services and allocations and (2) directly affected by decisions made by the county board of supervisors. Although in the true incumbent fashion of looking out for one's political survival first and foremost, none of the past or current board members wanted a significant increase of Latinos in their districts. The domination of the board by a three-to-two conservative majority since 1980 has revealed an especially distant and unrepresentative body to and of the county's resident Latinos. Ideologically inspired three-to-two board votes have consistently carried the day in siding with wealthy real estate and financial interests, with those interests who are in rapidly developing lands under county control, and in contracting out-of-county services to private profit-making firms. Those same three-to-two margins have carried the day in cutting back on expenditures for health care clinics, mental health facilities, welfare services, and community AIDS education (Simon 1990, B1). A clear ideological, class, and racial/ethnic bias is determined.

Incumbent 1st District Supervisor Pete Schabarum, long-time major spokesman for the board's conservative majority, has argued that Latinos should make it on their own and not rely on the county for help. However, *Los Angeles Times* Metro Editorial Chief Bill Boyarsky counters that Schabarum, whose district was approximately 44 percent Latino by the late 1980s,

> knew nothing—and had no interest in learning—of the
> problems in large areas of his district where some of the
> county's poorest Latinos live. Conditions there are so bad
> that few can make it on their own (Boyarsky 1/12/1990, B2).

We can speculate that if this was the case of a supervisor with a large Latino population in his district, the board's two other conservative members (4th District Supervisor Deane Dana and 5th District Supervisor

Michael Antonovich), each with less than a 20 percent Latino population margin, have at least equally indifferent outlooks.

Boyarsky contends that what Latinos in the county most need is "representation at the highest levels of government so they can get a fairer share of . . . [the] public pie" (*Ibid.*, B2).

The Voting Rights Act prohibits any practice or procedure that has the effect of, or that results in, denying or abridging the right to vote. Racial gerrymandering is one such practice. In the allied MALDEF/ACLU and DOJ lawsuit against the county of Los Angeles, the plaintiffs attempted to prove that the threshold items mentioned in the previous section exist in the county and that the county board violated Latino voting rights. According to lead MALDEF case attorney Richard Fajardo,

> First, we . . . (had) to show that the Latino community is geographically compact, that is, it is concentrated in such a way that you can create a district with more than a fifty percent Latino residency base in it. (Note: This would satisfy both compactness as well as sufficient number thresholds.) If the Latino community, for example, was spread all over the county so that there was no real district that you could draw, it would not matter how you drew the lines. However, that is not the case. . . . [T]here is a geo-graphically concentrated and identifiable community of Latinos. They live primarily in East Los Angeles and go all the way through the San Gabriel Valley.
>
> The second criteria is that the minority community has to be politically cohesive. We alleged that the Latino community is politically cohesive and they tend to vote for certain kinds of candidates. We found that to be the case in the 1st District election of Gloria Molina (to the Los Angeles City Council in 1987) . . . and we expect to find it throughout the county where there have been Latino candidates.
>
> The third threshold item is racial bloc voting (estab-lished in Gingles). Latinos tend to vote for Latino candidates. The same can be stated of Whites. The White community usually also votes as a bloc . . . to block the choice of the Latino community. . . . In essence, what I am referring to is racially polarized voting. That is, Whites tend to vote for Whites and Latinos and other minorities tend to vote for a minority candidate (Fajardo 1989, 7-8).

Attorneys for the plaintiffs argued what Latino activists have argued for years, namely that Latinos, for the most part, live in communities that are geographically compact and contiguous in an identifiable area spreading from East Los Angeles through the San Gabriel Valley. That large community has been divided approximately in half with almost equal Latino populations being placed in the 3d (42 percent) and 1st (35 percent) Districts in the 1981 redistricting plan. A smaller, although significant, percentage of Latinos (24 percent) was included in the 2d District (*Ibid.*, 8-9).

Latino activists have also long argued that where Latino candidates are seen to have a competitive chance to win, more Latino candidacies will be declared, and more interest in the election will be generated in the Latino communities as measured by heightened community political activity and political discussion, voter registration increases, and voter turnout increases. This is supported by Molina's special L. A. City Council's 1st District election victory (Santillan 1988), in Roybal's 1958 candidacy for the 3d county board seat (Roybal 1988), more recently in 1990 San Gabriel Valley municipal elections (Ward 1990), and in the Democratic primary campaign for the county's 59th (vacant) Assembly District (Gladstone 1990). However, at the county board level, that competitive chance has been absent. Since the turn of the century, 13 identifiable Latinos have been involved in a total of 18 candidacies for county board seats, only one with a "name." Only Roybal (the "name") was competitive, although he, like all the others, lost (Los Angeles County Registrar of Voters 1988).

The discussion above points to a rigid and easily identifiable racial as well as class gerrymander going back at least until 1959. Although socio-economic class gerrymandering had not been declared to be illegal by the courts, a Voting Rights Act standard of maintaining communities of interest argues against the breaking up of communities that share many common characteristics inclusive of income, cultural composition, and neighborhood quality. The courts have ruled that racial gerrymandering is illegal (*Gomillion v. Lightfoot* [1960]; *Rogers v. Lodge* [1982]).

In 1958, then Los Angeles City Councilman Edward R. Roybal lost a runoff election for the 3d District County Board seat to winner Ernest Debs. The winning margin was thin, and Roybal (a Latino) and his supporters to this day argue that the four electoral recounts and the lost precinct votes from East Los Angeles robbed him of victory (Roybal 1988). The county board under Debs' direction then proceeded to reduce the "Latino threat" (East Los Angeles) in his district by broadening its class, racial, and geographic base. First, Debs had the board move the western boundary of his district to include upper-class white westside communities, all formerly part of an otherwise affluent white-dominant coastal 4th District. The next major boundary shift occurred along the 3d District's northwest border. White-dominant, middle-class San Fernando Valley communities were now included. Thus, "[t]he 3rd District, which almost elected a Latino in 1958 . . . had become a constituency where Latinos had dwindled" (Boyarsky 3/7/1990, B2).

During this same period (1959-1969), decisions were also being made on dividing the fast-growing Latino population in the San Gabriel Valley so that by the 1971 board redistricting, that population would be politically cut off from its brethren in East Los Angeles. The 1971 plan laid the social and geographic groundwork for the 1981 plan in terms of politically diffusing Latinos in the county. However, the 1975 inclusion of Latinos as a protected group under the Voting Rights Act and the 1982 Section 2 amendments made the 1981 plan challengeable whereas the 1971 plan was not.

Both the incorporated and unincorporated communities of East Los Angeles are largely contained in the 3d Supervisorial District, which included a 41.8 percent Latino resident population in the 1981 plan. However, through the mapping of both the 1971 and 1981 plans, the primarily working-class Latino communities of greater East Los Angeles were combined with white-dominant middle-class communities of the San Fernando Valley such as Panorama City, Van Nuys, Sherman Oaks, and Studio City and the white-dominant upper-class and upper middle-class communities of the county's westside such as Beverly Hills, Bel-Air, and Westwood. This is a curious and suspicious class and racial/ethnic mixture that conflicts with both contiguous communities and communities of interest voting rights standards.

By 1980 census standards, Latinos made up 36.2 percent of the population of the 1st Supervisorial District, which contains much of the San Gabriel Valley end of the "Latino corridor." Here again we get a picture of curious and suspicious class and racial/ethnic mixtures. Heavily working-class Latino-populated communities of Lynwood, South Gate, Pico Rivera, El Monte, and La Puente are included with and diluted by the more conservative white-dominant working-class communities of Paramount, Bellflower and La Mirada; the white-dominant middle and upper middle-class communities of Whittier, La Habra Heights, Walnut, and Temple City; and the white-dominant upscale communities, in the northeastern ends of the district, of San Dimas, La Verne, Claremont, Glendora, Monrovia, and Bradbury. Communities of interest and, to a lesser extent, contiguous communities standards have been disregarded and violated.

The 2d Supervisorial District, seen by most as the "African-American district," contained a 26.5 percent Latino and a 42.9 percent African-American residency base in the 1981 plan. It includes most of the county's southside, which contains most of the communities in the county having African American-dominant resident populations. Curiously, Compton, which is a primarily working-class and poor African American and Latino populated city, was included in an otherwise white-dominant and affluent coastal 4th District. It is a notable exception. The 2d District's class and racial/ethnic character is not as varied as Districts One and Three.

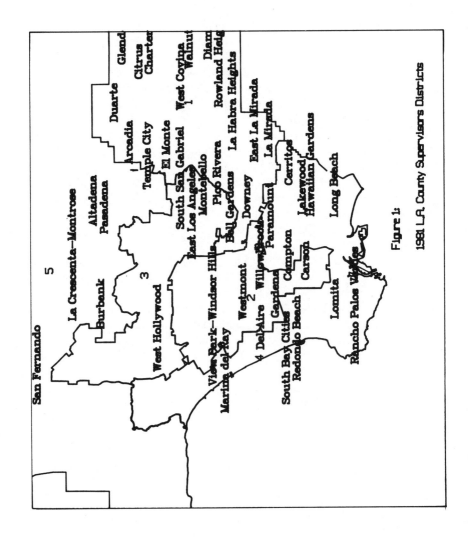

Figure 1:

1981 L.A. County Supervisors Districts

However, the exclusion of Compton and the inclusion of white-dominant middle- to lower-middle class communities such as Culver City, Hawthorne, and Lawndale into a, for the most part, class and racially consistent (primarily working-class African American) district, dilutes African-American electoral strength. Prior to and during the voting rights trial, discussions between MALDEF and the NAACP Legal Defense Fund (a case intervenor) jointly focused on strengthening the African-American base of the district by moving Compton into it as part of an alternative redistricting plan.

The 4th and 5th Supervisorial Districts were those most limited in Latino (16.5 percent and 16.9 percent) and Afro-American (9.7 percent and 5.0 percent) residency. They include much of the white-dominant wealthy communities of the county, excluding Westside communities contained in the 3d District and northeastern San Gabriel Valley communities contained in the 1st District. Where the 4th District is preeminently composed of coastal communities, the 5th District is comprised primarily of San Fernando Valley communities, northern rural communities, and some communities in the northern fringe of the San Gabriel Valley. These are the most class and racially homogeneous of the five districts and therefore least likely to change significantly through a court-ordered redistricting and/or through the normal redistricting process of 1991. The most formidable changes will come in Districts 1 and 3 where the dense cluster of Latino communities is located.

Perhaps most importantly, what the combined lawsuits centered on was the question of:

> Who gets to choose? If the Latino community had a full and fair participation opportunity to select someone they want, that satisfies the Voting Rights Act. However, if their communities are chopped up into pieces so that they cannot exercise their will, their desire as a community . . . , then there is a violation (Fajardo 1989, 10).

According to the MALDEF suit, the board of supervisors

> was aware that the plan would fragment the Hispanic community and result in the Hispanic community not having an equal opportunity to participate in the political process and to elect representatives of their choice (*Garza v. County of Los Angeles* 88-05143 kn [Ex]).

The lawsuits also argue that the plan was adopted and maintained,

> for the discriminatory purpose of diluting, minimizing, and canceling out Hispanic voting strength and violates both the 14th and 15th Amendments to the U.S. Constitution as well as the Voting Rights Act (*Ibid.*, 9).

The combined suits specifically asked the court to (1) void current district boundaries and prevent the county from holding any elections under the current plan, (2) require the board to develop and implement a new redistricting plan that would include at least one majority Latino district, and (3) order an expansion of the board from the current five seats to an unspecified number (*Garza v. County of Los Angeles*, cited). The sheer size of the districts mandates that competitive candidates have widespread name recognition, an ample campaign treasury, and broad appeal among white voters. All are problematic, at the very least, for Latino candidates (see Regalado 1988). After the Roybal case in 1958, no "name" Latino has since entered a candidacy for a county board seat. According to Professor Richard Santillan, the expectation of losing has kept more prominent Latinos away. After a while it became clear that "our communities did not need any more political martyrs" being led to the slaughter (Santillan 1988; Simon and Muir 3/10/1990). County board incumbent reelection margins run above 90 percent (Los Angeles County Registrar of Voters 1988). Building a necessary political base with white voters would de difficult enough even for a Latino candidate with broad Latino popular appeal. To add monetary requirements in the thousands and thousands of dollars merely adds to a near-impossible scenario.

Before the case went to trial in January 1990, the county board began settlement discussions with the DOJ and MALDEF. This was surprising in that the three majority conservative members of the board had resisted negotiations from the very beginning in true "hardball" fashion. The new wrinkle appeared to be that survival instincts among three of the board's members became paramount to ideological compatibility for a brief moment. Deane Dana became the architect of a plan that would ensure district safety nets for four of five incumbents by targeting a major Latino population increase for Pete Schabarum's 1st District. Schabarum, who long had personality conflicts with all other board members, appeared to be a sacrificial lamb to moot out the lawsuits.

However, when MALDEF and the DOJ were presented with the board's alternative plan, MALDEF countered with its own, which the board rejected. The MALDEF/DOJ objection to the board's alternative plan had everything to do with numbers of the new Latino district. MALDEF felt that the approximately 60 percent Latino population of the board's new district was too low in that it translated into a Latino voter registration margin of approximately 35 percent. MALDEF's plan contained a district with a 75 percent Latino resident population, which translated into a Latino voter registration margin of approximately 45 percent. This was unacceptable to Republican Dana, already under fire from conservative Republicans for targeting Schabarum. Dana became the deciding vote against MALDEF's plan and, thus, any settlement.

The trial concluded on April 10, 1990. The county's defense throughout hinged on three contentions: (1) there was never any intent or purpose to discriminate against Latino voters in the county in its 1981 plan or prior plans; (2) the 1981 plan was not in fact discriminatory to the county's

Latinos; and (3) drawing a district with a majority of eligible Latino voters was impossible then as well as now for two reasons. First, the noncitizen and youthful age of the Latino community made the pool of Latinos eligible to vote dramatically smaller. Second, the suburbanization spread of most eligible Latino voters in the county vastly reduces the number of those eligible in the central and central east portions of the county (that is, in the 1st and 3d Districts) (Simon 4/7/1990, B3).

MALDEF and the DOJ decried the county's last contention especially as a "red herring" attempt to shift the argument and focus away from a discriminatory intent and result. The board sought to (1) shield incumbents in the 1st and 3d Districts and (2) preserve conservative dominance in the process by protecting the board from Latino population growth and political accountability for that population. Additionally, the county's focus exclusively on Latinos "eligible" to vote constitutes an intentional misreading and misrepresentation of both the law and reality. All Latinos, according to the plaintiffs, are entitled to be counted in redistrictings and politically represented.

Federal District Court Judge David V. Kenyon ruled on June 4, 1990, that the Los Angeles County Board of Supervisors intentionally discriminated against Latinos in its 1981 redistricting plan. Finding the county to be in violation of the Voting Rights Act, he ordered the board to draft a new redistricting plan reflecting a Latino population-dominant district. According to Judge Kenyon:

> [t]he Hispanic community has sadly been denied an equal opportunity to participate in the political process and to elect candidates of their choice to the Board of Supervisors.
>
> During the 1981 redistricting process, the supervisors' primary objective was to protect their incumbencies and that of their allies. This objective, however, was inescapably linked to the continued fragmentation of the Hispanic population core (Simon and Muir 6/5/90).

The revised county plan was presented to the court on June 28. Kenyon rejected this alternative plan as a "nonsensical distortion" of boundary lines that were insensitive to African Americans as well as Latinos. As such, it made a mockery of the Voting Rights Act.

Kenyon approved a new redistricting plan for the county on August 3. It was a plan initially submitted by MALDEF and the ACLU. The newly approved map not only created a dramatically new Latino-dominant district, but it also threatened the decade-long conservative dominance of the board. Alongside this action, Judge Kenyon also set aside the results of the June 5, 1990, supervisorial elections in the 1st and 3d Districts. In the 1st District, retiring Supervisor Schabarum's field aside, the fellow conservative Republican Sarah Flores, was the top vote getter. Kenyon canceled the

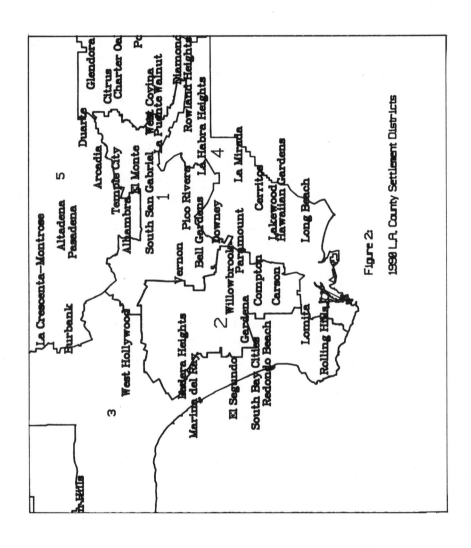

Figure 2:

1990 L.A. County Settlement Districts

November runoff for this district seat. Incumbent Ed Edelman easily won reelection in the 1st District.

The new court-ordered plan, which became delayed when the county appealed the court's decision to the 9th Circuit Court of Appeals in early August (that court placed the remedy on indefinite delay), carved the new Latino population-dominant district out of the pre-existing portions of the 1st and 3d Districts. It will be given the designation of the 1st District. It incorporates working-class Latino communities running from downtown Los Angeles through similar eastside working-class communities including El Sereno and Lincoln Heights in an easterly direction through Latino working-class communities of the San Gabriel Valley including Irwindale, La Puente, and Sante Fe Springs. The new 1st District plan increases the Latino population base from 49 percent to 71 percent (including 51 percent of the district's registered voters). It would also become more starkly partisan democratic (from 50 percent to 66.5 percent). Although Kenyon ordered a November 6 election for the redrawn district, that action and a proposed filing deadline of August 15 were made moot by the decision of the appeals court to delay a remedy.

Should the new plan stand the test of appeals, additional neighborhood class shifts will occur. Current 3d District incumbent Edelman would lose Latino working-class East Los Angeles but shore up his affluent liberal westside base by picking up Malibu and Santa Monica. Fourth District Supervisor Dana would lose these liberal beachfront communities but pick up middle-class and wealthy conservative support in the San Fernando and San Gabriel Valleys. Fifth District incumbent Antonovich would lose conservative middle-class portions of the San Gabriel Valley, formerly part of the 1st District. The 2d District of Hahn would change marginally, picking up Compton from the 4th District.

Kenyon decided against taking actions on plaintiff requests to (1) enlarge the existing number of districts from the current five and (2) require the board to submit any changes in district boundaries either to Kenyon or to the attorney general for the next 15 years. It appears that the county has won a couple of late battles but will inevitably lose the larger war. However, through the appeals action, the board majority clearly demonstrated its intent to continue to (1) deny a demographic and, ultimately, political reality taking place in the county, (2) incur additional millions of dollars in legal costs to taxpayers in battling this reality in the wake of cutting social service spending, and (3) maintain havens for conservative board incumbents.

IMPLICATIONS

The Latino-inspired lawsuits against Los Angeles County represent the largest unit of government ever to be charged with violating the Voting Rights Act of 1965. As such, this action apparently signals a major resolve on the part of communities of color to commit to battle against political jurisdictions at all levels seen to be in violation of their chances for equal participation and representation. It is widely expected that the apparently successful lawsuits against the county will have a bearing on a number of voting rights cases both at local and state levels (it is being widely anticipated that it will have a ripple effect on the California state reapportionment of 1991).

However, there is considerable apprehension in Latino, African-American, and Asian-Pacific communities that the dramatic changes being pressed on the voting rights front in L. A. County, Watsonville, and elsewhere in California will soon run up against an increasingly conservative federal court system, which through recent decisions has whittled away at civil rights gains made over the past quarter century (Fertig 1990). Can decisions weakening voting and representation rights be far behind? It is not yet clear where or if the county case might be placed in the unfolding scenario. However, what does appear to be clear is that the near exclusive reliance of voting rights communities on the courts as the most progressive wing of federal government is over. It is perhaps equally clear that Congress will be the key player for the voting rights community, as it was in its 1982 action of amending and extending the Voting Rights Act into the 21st century and as it has more recently been in the battles over the Civil Rights Act of 1990.

There does not appear to be a significant way in which Latinos can lose their case against the county. Paralleling the lyrics of a 1965 Bob Dylan song, "if you ain't got nothing, you've got nothing to lose" (from "Like a Rolling Stone"), it appears that Latinos will obtain a "stepping stone" toward a more "integrated" political environment. Indeed, major Latino "name" politicians are lining up for the eventual 1st District opening. The list includes Congressmen Ed Roybal and Esteban Torres, State Senator Art Torres, and L. A. City Council members Gloria Molina and Richard Alatorre. From this batch, efforts to eventually produce a "unity candidate" will mostly likely fail, given the stakes of this office. These Latino officials generally remained on the sidelines in collective protest of the June 5 primary, which contained the gerrymandered lines. Now, with fairer district lines, a superstar lineup of candidates, and more significant population and voter registration numbers of Latinos in the newly created district, the election of a Latino to the board is widely expected. However, without a significant expansion of the board beyond five seats, even with such representation, in a county approximating 3.5 million Latinos, political empowerment is still years away.

While many of the city councils and school boards in the municipalities of the San Gabriel Valley have become more broadly integrated with Latino representation over the past five years (NALEO 1988; Ward 1990), such integration of the power bastions at the county board level will continue to remain more elusive. Only through board expansion and minority political coalition mobilization will such changes occur more rapidly. According to a significant model of minority political incorporation (Browning 1984), incorporation demands, at the very least, community mobilization and biracial or multiracial coalition. However, structural conditions of minority fragmentation, division, and dilution long utilized to maintain white wealthy status quos have led many to applaud the legal actions against the Los Angeles County Board while still worrying about future empowerment steps.

REFERENCES

Acuna, Rodolfo. *Occupied America: A History of Chicanos*. New York: Harper & Row, Inc., 1972, 1988.

Avila, Joaquin. *Latino Political Empowerment: A Perspective*. Fremont, CA: Winchester Press, 1989.

Boyarsky, Bill. "A Good Case for Voting Rights Act." *Los Angeles Times*, January 12, 1990, B2.

_____. "Farewells Begin for the Bully." *Los Angeles Times*, March 14, 1990, B3.

_____. "Lost Drama in Voting Rights Suit." *Los Angeles Times*, March 7, 1990, B2.

Browning, Rufus P., Dale Rogers Marshall and David Tabb. *Protest Is Not Enough: The Struggle of Blacks and Hispanics for Equality in Urban Politics*. Berkeley: University of California Press, 1984.

_____. *Racial Politics in American Cities*. New York: Longman Press, 1990.

Bucy, Erik. "Lawsuits Threaten L.A. Supervisor's Fiefdoms." *California Journal* (February 1989): 41-43.

Castenada, Ruben. "Hispanic Bias Suit Hits Supervisors." *Los Angeles Herald Examiner*, August 25, 1988, A-1, 14.

City of Mobile v. Bolden, 446 U.S. 55 (1980).

Commission on Human Relations, Los Angeles County. "Population, Major Racial and Ethnic Groups, 1920-1970." Los Angeles County, 1974.

Cotrell, Charles L., ed. *Publius* (Fall 1986).

Cotrell, Charles L., and Jerry Polinard. "Effects of the VRA in Texas: Perceptions of County Elections Administrators." *Publius* (Fall 1986): 67-80.

Cotrell, Charles L., and R. Michael Stevens. "The 1975 Voting Rights Act and San Antonio, Texas: Toward a Federal Guarantee of a Republican Form of Local Government." *Publius* (1978): 336-38.

County of Los Angeles. Defendants Answer to Complaint (Case #88-05143 Kn [Ex]), September 22, 1988.

Davidson, Chandler, ed. *Minority Vote Dilution*. Washington, D.C.: Howard University Press, 1984.

Decker, Cathleen. "Latino Leaders Consider Candidacy." *Los Angeles Times*, March 10, 1990, A 24.

de la Garza, Rodolfo O., and Janet Weaver. "New Participants, Old Issues: Mexican-American Urban Policy Priorities." In *The Egalitarian City*, edited by Janet Boles, 75-90. New York: Praeger Special Studies, 1986.

Department of Regional Planning, Los Angeles County. Data Book, 1987.

Diaz, Marshall. Personal Interview. Los Angeles. Califorinos for Fair Representation, 1988.

Editorial. "In the Land of Hubris." *Los Angeles Times*, March 16, 1990, B 3.

Edwards, Don. "The Voting Rights Act as Amended." In *The Voting Rights Act: Consequences and Implications,* edited by Lorn S. Foster, 3-12. New York: Praeger Publishers, 1985.

Fajardo, Richard. In *Political Battles Over L.A. County Board Seats: A Minority Perspective,* edited by James A. Regalado. Los Angeles: Edmund G. "Pat" Brown Institute, Inc., 1989.

Fertig, Ralph D. H. "Human Rights Abuses by United States." PROTO-COL (February 1990).

Foster, Lorn S., ed. *The Voting Rights Act: Consequences and Implications.* New York: Praeger Publishers, 1985.

Fulwood, Sam III. "Employer Sanctions Issue Straining Rights Coalition." *Los Angeles Times*, May 3, 1990, A-1, 20.

Garza, et al. v. County of Los Angeles, (88-05143 Kn [Ex]).

Garcia, F. Chris, ed. *Latinos and the Political System.* Notre Dame: University of Notre Dame Press, 1990.

Garcia, John A. "The Voting Rights Act and Hispanic Political Representation in the Southwest." *Publius* (Fall 1986): 49-66.

Gladstone, Mark. "Contest on Eastside Shapes Up as Test of Latino Political Clout." *Los Angeles Times*, May 3, 1990, B-1, 8.

Gomez v. City of Watsonville, 863 F. 2d 1407 (9th Cir. 1988).

Henry, Charles P., and Carlos Muñoz, Jr. "Rainbow Coalitions in Four Big Cities: San Antonio, Denver, Chicago, and Philadelphia." *PS* (Summer 1986): 598-609.

Hurley, Timothy, and Steve Tamaya. "San Gabriel County?" *San Gabriel Valley Daily Tribune*, February 20, 1990, A-1,5.

Jackson, Byran O. "Ethnic Cleavages and Voting Patterns in U.S. Cities. An Analysis of the Asian, Black, and Hispanic Communities of Los Angeles." A paper presented at the Conference on Comparative Ethnicity, UCLA, June 1-3, 1988.

Jeffe, Sherry Bebitch. "Supervisors: Our Powerful Little Kings." *Los Angeles Times*, April 8, 1990, M-1, 5.

Kwoh, Stewart. In *Political Battles Over L. A. County Board Seats: A Minority Perspective,* edited by James A. Regalado. Los Angeles: Edmund G. "Pat" Brown Institute, 1989.

MacManus, Susan A. "City Council Election Procedures and Minority Representation." *Social Science Quarterly* 59 (1978): 153-61.

_____. "Racial Representation Issues: The Role of Experts in Determining Dilution of Minority Influence." *PS* (Fall 1985): 759-68.

Merina, Victor. "Latinos Sue, Charge Bias in Districting by Supervisors." *Los Angeles Times*, August 25, 1988, II, 1, 8.

Merina, Victor, and Ronald J. Ostrow. "U.S. Sues to Get New Supervisor Districts Drawn." *Los Angeles Times*, September 9, 1988, I, 1, 28.

Mollenkoph, John. "New York: The Great Anomoly." In *Racial Politics in American Cities*, edited by Rufus P. Browning, et al., 75-87. New York: Longman Press, 1990.

Muir, Frederick M., and Richard Simon. "Latinos Urge Board to Settle Remap Suit With New District." *Los Angeles Times*, March 14, 1990, B-1, 8.

Muñoz, Carlos, Jr., and Charles P. Henry. "Coalition Politics in San Antonio and Denver." In *Racial Politics in American Cities*, edited by Rufus P. Browning, et al., 179-90. New York: Longman Press, 1990.

Murray, Marjorie. "U.S. Presses for Delay of L. A. County Election." *City and State* (April 9-22, 1990): 1, 47.

NALEO. *The Latino Vote in 1988: NALEO Background* Paper #7. Washington, D.C: NALEO Educational Foundation, 1988.

Navarro, Carlos. "A Report on California Redistricting and Representation for the L.A. Chicano Community." *California Reapportionment and the Chicano Community*. Claremont, CA: Rose Institute of State and Local Government, 1981.

Navarro, Carlos. "Latinos Locked Out of County Power Too Long." *Los Angeles Herald Examiner*, July 31, 1988, F-1, 4.

Polinard, Jerry L., and Robert D. Wrinkle. "The Impact of District Elections on the Mexican American Community: The Electoral Perspective." A paper presented at the Midwest Political Science Association Annual Meeting. Chicago, 1988.

Project Participar. *The California Latino Position on a State Reapportionment Commission*. San Francisco, 1984.

Regalado, James A. "Latino Representation in Los Angeles." In *Latino Empowerment: Progress, Problems, and Prospects*, edited by Roberto E. Villarreal, et al., 91-104. New York: Greenwood Press, 1988.

Regalado, James A., ed. *Political Battles Over L.A. County Board Seats: A Minority Perspective*. Los Angeles: Edmund G. "Pat" Brown Institute of Public Affairs, 1989.

Regalado, James A., and Gloria Martinez. "The Politics of Reapportionment and Coalition: A Case Study of Latino Empowerment Barrier's in Los Angeles County." In Villarreal, et al. New York: Greenwood Press, forthcoming.

Ridley-Thomas, Mark, Manuel Pastor, and Stewart Kwoh. "The 'New Majority' Want Its Share." *Los Angeles Times*, October 12, 1989, B-7.

Roybal, Edward R. Personal Interview. Federal Building. Los Angeles, 1988.

Santillan, Richard. Personal Interview. Pomona, California, 1988.

_____. "The Chicano Community and the Redistricting of the Los Angeles City Council, 1971-1973." *Chicano Law Review* 6 (1983).

Shaw, Theodore. In *Political Battles Over L.A. County Board Seats: A Minority Perspective*, edited by James A. Regalado. Los Angeles: Edmund G. "Pat" Brown Institute, 1989.

Simon, Richard. "A Latino District Is Not Possible, County Argues." *Los Angeles Times*, April 7, 1990, B-3.

_____. "Board Had Racial Intent in Remapping, Witness Says." *Los Angeles Times*, January 12, 1990, A-35.

_____. "County Redistricting Trial Heads Toward Conclusion." *Los Angeles Times*, April 5, 1990, A-23.

_____. "Trial Seeking New Voting District in County Ends." *Los Angeles Times*, April 11, 1990, B-3, 6.

Simon, Richard and Frederick Muir. "Board Votes to Shift Schabarum in Redistricting." *Los Angeles Times*, December 13, 1989, A-1.

_____. "Schabarum Won't Seek Reelection." *Los Angeles Times*, March 10, 1990, A-1, 24.

_____. "Scharbarum Decision: Job Loses Appeal." *Los Angeles Times*, March 13, 1990, B-1, 8.

_____. "County Board Ideology Yields to Politics." *Los Angeles Times*, March 18, 1990, B-1, 3.

_____. "Schabarum Snubs Aide and Backs Judge As Successor." *Los Angeles Times*, March 15, 1990, B-3.

_____. "10 Jump Into Board Race to Succeed Schabarum." *Los Angeles Times*, March 15, 1990, B-1, 4.

Sonenshein, Raphael J. "Biracial Coalition Politics in Los Angeles." *PS* (Summer 1986): 582-90.

_____. "The Dynamics of Biracial Coalitions: Crossover Politics in Los Angeles." *Western Political Quarterly* (June 1989): 333-53.

Starks, Robert T., and Michael Preston. "Harold Washington and the Politics of Reform in Chicago: 1983-1987." In *Racial Politics in American Cities*, edited by Rufus P. Browning, et al., 88-107. New York: Longman Press, 1990.

Tabel, Delbert. "Minority Representation on City Councils: The Impact of Structure on Hispanics and Blacks." *Social Science Quarterly* 59 (1978): 142-52.

TELACU. *Barrio Housing Plan*. Los Angeles: The East Los Angeles Community Union, 1971.

Thornburg v. Gingles, 106 S. Ct. 2752 (1986).

U.S. Commission on Civil Rights. *The Voting Rights Act of 1965*. Washington, D.C.: U.S. Government Printing Office, 1965.

U.S. Commission on Civil Rights. *Using the Voting Rights Act*. Washington, D.C.: U.S. Government Printing Office, 1976.

U.S. v. City of Los Angeles, 85-7739 JMI MRX.

Villarreal, Roberto E., Norma G. Hernandez, and Howard D. Neighbor. *Latino Empowerment: Progress, Problems, and Prospects.* New York: Greenwood Press, 1988.

_____. *Political Coalitions: The Road to Latino Empowerment.* New York: Greenwood Press, forthcoming.

Ward, Mike. "Incumbents Take Beating at the Polls." *Los Angeles Times*, April 12, 1990, J-1, 6.

White v. Regester 412 U.S. 755 1973.

VII. CONCLUSION

The Future of Ethnic Politics in California

California is undergoing rapid and dramatic change. It's population in 1990 is estimated to be about 30 million. California's population is as diverse as any nation in the world. Indeed, if an artist were to draw a portrait of California's population, it would be more reflective of the world than of any one continent. California has two world cities, Los Angeles and San Francisco; they are to Asian and Latin-American immigrants as New York was to Europeans. This new wave of immigrants is bringing about changes in the social, cultural, and political landscape of the state. The challenge to California and the nation will be its ability to deal with the dilemmas of a multiracial society.

The new mosaic evolving in California is a testament to changes in immigration. For example, in the Los Angeles metropolitan area there are a multitude of groups from all over Asia and Latin America: Cambodians, Thais, Filipinos, Koreans, Japanese, Indians, Vietnamese, Chinese from Taiwan and Southeast Asia. Koreatown in Los Angeles is experiencing very rapid growth. There are over 300,000 Koreans in Los Angeles, and the number is expected to increase. Monterey Park, just a few miles east of Los Angeles, is one of the first predominantly Asian suburbs. It has a population of over 60,000, and over half are Chinese. In the cities of Garden Grove and Westminster, there is on one avenue over 800 Vietnamese shops, which cater to over 80,000 Vietnamese. San Francisco is still the heart of Chinese migration.

There are also close to seven million Hispanics in California. Most are from Mexico, but a growing number are from Central America. African Americans make up less than two million California residents while whites make up about 17 million. The number for each group is projected to increase except for blacks and whites. As demographics change one would expect to see changes in the political environment.

The findings or conclusions of the authors of this volume are not meant to be exclusive but rather to analyze past, current, and future trends that are likely to take shape in the '90s and into the 21st century. One interesting finding is that Asians, while unlike other racial groups in their search for empowerment, may well become in the 21st century the new swing vote, and its value to both political parties is likely to increase as they learn to become more aggressive in the political arena. Indeed, Nakanishi argues that Asians may become a new political force like Jews and their vote may help swing elections in states like California, Texas, and New York. He also argues that both parties are keenly aware of the group's potential to provide campaign funds based on the 10 million dollars they gave to both Bush and Dukakis in the 1988 election. What is clear, however, is that their electoral potential has not yet been realized and will depend on future development.

Sonenshein finds that Jews have been very successful in California politics in recent years because of four factors: their support of progressive causes, their high voter registration and turnout, their ability to donate to political campaigns and candidates, and their activism in politics. He also argues that Jews have been incorrectly evaluated because most of the comparisons have to do with how Jewish behavior differs from that of blacks. He believes that a more appropriate measure is the comparison with other whites on the same issues. He finds that Jews are much more liberal on most issues than most whites. He also points out that the old alliance between blacks and Jews is in for some refinement and that Jews and Hispanics will have to come to grips with what their relationship will be in the future.

Hispanic influence is starting to grow according to Guerra and Santillan. While their influence before the late 1960s was low, the '70s and '80s have seen a growth of their influence. They are becoming more aggressive, and as their numbers increase so will their political influence. Guerra points out that vacancies, recruitment networks, redistricting, and Democratic support have been the leading causes of Hispanic political growth. Santillan finds that both the Democratic and Republican parties are actively courting the Hispanic vote. And while Hispanics have been relatively supportive of Republican presidential candidates, they remain mostly democrats—the exceptions being Cubans and some businessmen as well as growing numbers of professionals. How well each party relates to the Hispanics' political agenda will dictate these allegiances in the 21st century.

African Americans are the smallest of the minority groups but have been the most aggressive and better organized. Yet their growth has slowed as Hispanic influence has grown. The key issues in the future for African Americans will be their ability to form coalitions with new immigrant groups and to maintain alliances with progressive whites. The key here will be how black political leaders respond to the new challenges. Henry and Muñoz do not believe that coalitions are possible given the obstacles in the path of these groups. On the other hand Uhlaner believes it is possible but not probable. DeLeon and Jackson's work shows that it is possible to find common ground. In Los Angeles, Hispanics supported Bradley, and blacks and Hispanics agree on some issues but not others. In San Francisco, Mayor Agnos has managed to hold together a progressive coalition of blacks, Hispanics, Asians, and progressive whites. And while conflicts are apparent, he has managed to date to reconcile some and delay others. The success of Agnos may well tell us much about how groups with different interests can coalesce without giving up all of their individual interests.

Finally, we should note that an increase in numbers does not necessarily translate into political power. People must register and vote. In the case of Asians and Hispanics, both their registration and turnout are low. Blacks do better but also fall below their potential. Thus, while these groups may have increased numbers, whites are likely to control the political system well into the 21st century. The simple reason is that even though their numbers will decline, they will be offset by their high voter turnout and ability to raise the requisite campaign funds. In addition, as suburbs continue to grow their influence in the political system will grow as well; this is likely to lead to policies good for suburban interest, but not necessarily good for the city. If this occurs, we are likely to see policies being made for the few and not the many. The implications of this in the long-run are not pleasant to contemplate. One thing is clear, political leadership in a multiracial society will have to learn to cope with these changes or watch the political system being pulled apart at the center by various factions. How well they meet this challenge may tell us much about America in the 21st century.

ABOUT THE AUTHORS

Susan Anderson is a writer and public interest media specialist whose articles have appeared in *The Nation,* the *Los Angeles Herald Examiner, California Tomorrow, LA Weekly, In These Times,* and *New Politics,* among other publications. She is a fourth generation Californian whose family settled in the San Francisco Bay Area in the early part of the century. She lives and works in Los Angeles.

Larry L. Berg is Professor of Political Science and Director of the Jesse M. Unruh Institute of Politics at the University of Southern California. He currently represents the Speaker of the California Assembly on the South Coast Air Quality Management District Board of Directors. His more recent articles and books include: "The Initiative Process and Its Declining Agenda-Setting Value," (co-authored with C. B. Holman), *Law and Policy* (1989); and "Losing the Initiative," *California Politics* (1988). Berg received his B.A. and M.A. from the University of Iowa and his Ph.D. in political science from the University of California at Santa Barbara.

Bruce Cain is Professor of Political Science and Associate Director of the Institute of Governmental Studies at the University of California at Berkeley. He is a graduate of Bowdoin College and went on to Trinity College Oxford as a Rhodes Scholar. His Ph.D. in political science is from Harvard University. Cain has written extensively and taught in the fields of California politics, political theory, and comparative government. He is the author of *The Reapportionment Puzzle* and *The Personal Vote* (with John Ferejohn and Morris Fiorina).

Richard E. DeLeon is Professor of Political Science and Urban Studies at San Francisco State University. He has published a number of articles and reports on state and local politics, housing and community development policies, and growth control issues. He is currently writing a book on San Francisco politics.

Fernando J. Guerra is Associate Professor of Political Science and Chair of the Chicano Studies Department at Loyola Marymount University. He received his Ph.D. and M.A. in political science from the University of Michigan and his B.A. in political science and a University Certificate in Latin American Studies from the University of Southern California. His areas of research and teaching are state and local politics and urban and ethnic politics.

Charles P. Henry holds a Ph.D. in political science from the University of Chicago. His research interests include all aspects of black politics. His two most recent books are *Culture and African American Politics* and *Jesse Jackson: The Search for Common Ground.* He is currently working on a critical biography of Nobel Laureate Ralph Bunche. Henry is Associate Professor of Afro-American Studies at the University of California at Berkeley.

C. B. Holman is Senior Researcher for the California Commission on Campaign Financing. Prior to his current position, he served as Senior Researcher for the Jesse Unruh Institute of Politics at the University of Southern California. Holman is a doctoral candidate at USC who has written about the Democratic party and the development of politics in California. Recent articles include "Go West Young Democrat," *Polity* (1989); "The Initiative Process and Its Declining Agenda-Setting Value," (co-authored with Larry Berg), *Law and Policy* (1989); and "Farmers and Their Partisan Affiliations," *Rural Sociology* (1989).

Byran O. Jackson is Associate Professor of Political Science at California State University, Los Angeles. He received his Ph.D. in political science from the University of Michigan in 1982. He worked as a social science research analyst for the Department of Housing and Urban Development and as Assistant Professor of Political Science and Adjunct Professor of Urban Studies at Washington University, St. Louis. Jackson has major publications in the areas of U.S. Housing Policy and Ethnic Politics in U.S. cities. His work on ethnic politics has research support from the Rockefeller, Ford, and National Science Foundations. He was a Ford Foundation Post Doctoral Fellow at the Institute of Governmental Studies at UC Berkeley in 1989-90.

Dwaine Marvick is Professor of Political Science at the University of California at Los Angeles. His research and teaching interests are party politics, legislative politics, political recruitment processes, and elite analysis. Publications include *Political Decision-Makers* and *Harold D. Lasswell on Political Sociology.*

William J. Middleton, an attorney with a Juris Doctor degree from Columbia University, is a Ph.D. candidate at the University of California at Berkeley. He is a part-time lecturer in political science at California State University, Los Angeles.

Carlos Muñoz, Jr., is Associate Professor of Ethnic Studies, University of California at Berkeley. He holds a Ph.D. in government from the Claremont

Graduate School and is the author of *Youth, Identity, Power: The Chicano Movement* (Verso Press, 1989). He is currently at work on his next book, a biography of the late scholar and activist, Dr. Ernesto Galarza. Muñoz served as the Latino Issues Coordinator for the 1988 Jesse Jackson presidential campaign.

Don Toshiaki Nakanishi is Director of the UCLA Asian American Studies and Associate Professor at the UCLA Graduate School of Education. A Harvard-trained political scientist, he has written over 40 articles and books on the political participation of Asian Americans, the international dimensions of minority politics, and major Asian American educational policy issues. He is currently writing a book on the access, representation, and influence of Asian Pacific Americans in major American educational, social, and political institutions.

Harry P. Pachon, holder of the Keenan Chair of Politics for the Claremont Colleges, received his undergraduate and master's degrees from California State University at Los Angeles. He received his Ph.D. from the Claremont Graduate School. Pachon served as a policy analyst for the U.S. Department of Health, Education, and Welfare and as an associate staff member of the House Appropriations Committee. He has numerous publications in professional journals and has co-authored the books *Mexican Americans* and *Hispanics in the United States.* As Executive Director of the National Association of Latino Elected and Appointed Officials (NALEO), Pachon initiated a national U.S. citizenship project, the annual *Roster of Hispanic Elected Officials*, and an annual audit of federal procurements with Hispanic businesses.

Michael B. Preston is Professor of Political Science and department chair at the University of Southern California. He received his Ph.D. in political science from the University of California at Berkeley. His research interests focus on urban politics, urban problems, and black political participation in the American political system. Recent publications include *The New Black Politics, The Politics of Bureaucratic Reform,* and "The Politics of Economic Redistribution in Chicago: Is Balanced Growth Possible?" in *Regenerating the Cities,* edited by Michael Parkinson and Bernard Foley.

James A. Regalado is Associate Professor of Political Science at California State University at Los Angeles. Regalado teaches courses in urban politics, state and local politics, and political communication. He has published in the areas of city and county redistricting, minority political representation, and health care politics, among others. Regalado was the executive director of a labor-community education center in Los Angeles from the late 1970s to the mid-1980s and is currently involved in research on the politics of organized labor.

Richard Santillan is the chair of the Ethnic and Women's Studies Department at California State Polytechnic University in Pomona. He has written and edited several articles and books on Latino politics in the United States. Santillan is currently finishing a book on Latino politics in the Midwest. His latest article is entitled "Rosita the Riveter: Midwest Mexican American Women in Defense Work, 1941-1945." Santillan is a senior consultant with the Rose Institute of State and Local Government at the Claremont Colleges.

Raphael J. Sonenshein is Associate Professor of Political Science at California State University, Fullerton. He received his Ph.D. from Yale University. Active in Los Angeles politics since 1974, he has worked in the mayor's office, on a city councilman's staff, and in political campaigns. Sonenshein's research on interracial politics has appeared in *PS*, the *Western Political Quarterly*, the *Political Science Quarterly*, the *Los Angeles Times*, and as book chapters in several edited volumes. He is currently completing a book on biracial coalition politics in Los Angeles. His teaching interests include minority politics, mass media, and political campaigns.

Federico A. Subervi-Vélez (Ph.D., University of Wisconsin-Madison, 1984) is Assistant Professor of Communication at the Department of Radio-Television-Film, University of Texas at Austin. He was Fulbright Researcher in Brazil in 1988 and 1989 and has written about the mass media system of Puerto Rico—his native country. His current research activities focus on the political content of the Spanish-language media in the United States, the political use of these media during campaigns by the Democratic and Republican parties, and theoretical aspects of the role of the mass media in Hispanics' assimilation and pluralism. He has published in *Journalism Quarterly, Social Science Quarterly, Communication Research,* and the *Howard Journal of Communications* for which he also serves as a member of the editorial board.

Carole Jean Uhlaner is Associate Professor of Political Science at the University of California at Irvine. She received her A.B. from Radcliffe in applied mathematics, an M.S. from Stanford in engineering, and her Ph.D. in government from Harvard University. Her research lies in the general area of comparative political behavior; she is especially interested in the study of political participation. She has published on political participation, ethnic politics, public choice, and women and politics. Her other articles include "Rational Turnout: The Neglected Role of Groups," *American*

Journal of Political Science; "Relational Goods and Participation," *Public Choice*; "Political Participation of Ethnic Minorities in the 1980s," *Political Behavior*; and "Candidate Gender and Campaign Finance," *Journal of Politics*.